WHAT THEY'LL NEVER TELL YOU ABOUT THE MUSIC BUSINESS

The Myths, the Secrets, the Lies (& a Few Truths)

PETER M. THALL

Watson-Guptill Publications / New York

Senior editor: Robert Nirkind
Production manager: Ellen Greene
Designer: Leah Lococo

First Published in 2002 by Watson-Guptill Publications,
a division of VNU Business Media, Inc., 770 Broadway, New York, N.Y. 10003
www.watsonguptill.com

Library of Congress Cataloging-in-Publication Data
Library of Congress Control Number: 2002103627
Thall, Peter M
What they'll never tell you about the music business: the myths, the secrets, the lies,
(& a few truths) / Peter M. Thall
1st ed.
New York, NY: Watson-Guptill Publications, 2002
p.cm.
ISBN: 0-8230-8439-6

Printed in the United States
First printing, 2002
3 4 5 6 7 8 9 / 10 09 08 07 06 05 04

TABLE OF CONTENTS

We are the music makers
And we are the dreamers of dreams,
Wandering by lone sea-breakers,
And sitting by desolate streams,
World-losers and world-forsakers,
On whom the pale moon gleams:
Yet we are the movers and shakers
Of the world forever, it seems
　　　　　—Arthur O'Shaughnessy

There are enough agents, accountants, attorneys, managers, and music publishers, not to mention friends and family, who are more than willing—for love or money—to advise young artists (musicians, singers, and songwriters) in the pursuit of their careers.

Most of this advice is well-intentioned—and it may even be timely and helpful. However, it may also be irrelevant to a particular individual's circumstances. The reasons for this are manifold. Not the least of the problems in offering advice to young artists is the fact that they customarily have limited knowledge of the music industry. Unlike participants in other industries, the major players in industries in the area of intellectual property (music, theater, film, and television) often enter the business with neither a clear understanding of its workings or history nor means to obtain the information which would convey such knowledge to them.

According to recent statistics the intellectual property enterprises in the United States contribute more to the gross national product than the airplane industry, more than the automobile industry and, yes, even more than the agriculture industry. Yet the very people who comprise the heart and soul of these companies do not usually know a break-even point from a producer point, a royalty from a Prince, or a mechanical license from a synchronization license—in short, they don't know their business. In the course of writing this book, I have discussed various chapters with senior executives in different departments of major music business companies. At the end of the discussion, all of them told me, in so many words, "You know, I learned a thing or two today." This is not to criticize them. As an attorney who has practiced in the music industry for more than 30 years, I learned long ago that it is the rare manager or music industry executive who has the requisite background to function in the industry at an optimal level, unlike, say, their peers who chose to work in the financial or real estate worlds, who *are* highly trained in their fields. Yet it is these managers and excutives who are ultimately responsible for making the decisions that will make or break their businesses.

The music industry executive's strength is enhanced only when the company he or she joins has an established and tested management training program. Although the institutions that form the music publishing and recording industry today are very well set up for precisely this kind of training, it is unlikely that these companies will also give the fledgling executive the information which I am seeking to impart in this book. For the personal manager and business manager in whose hands the artist *and* the record and publishing companies place their trust, this book is intended to provide not just informational data, but also a perspective that will help them to become more aware of the parts of the business which no one will teach them, but which they must nonetheless understand if they are to perform their functions effectively.

Ironically, when it comes to artists, it is widely accepted that really creative people will *not* know their business. After all, aren't they living in the realm of the idea—the *eigenvelt*—the world that is interesting precisely because it is not the *mitvelt*—the shared world, the concrete, tangible world that can be objectively evaluated? The late Northrup Frye, one of the twentieth century's pre-eminent English scholars and literary critics, and a noted commentator on Canadian society and culture, gave an acclaimed series of lectures at the University of Toronto several decades ago. In these lectures, published as *The Educated Imagination,* Frye spoke of the uniqueness of creative people—how creative people see things that "aren't there." What more appropriate an image for artists? What more dangerous a situation for the creative forces of the music business? Just as the script is the "currency" of the motion picture business, the creator—the writer, artist, producer, mixer—is the currency of the music business. And how can this creator—a living, breathing human being from whom the art emanates—function effectively in the world? Those who live in the imagination cannot be expected to have either the patience or the time to attain the knowledge and experience to rule their own destiny. We are all familiar with the saying "the lawyer who represents himself has a fool for a client." How much more troublesome is the vision of artists who drift through life without an understanding of their business—the customs, traditions, contractual norms, and laws of the very industry which would not even exist but for them and their artistic contributions?

Remarkably, we are talking not just about fledgling musicians, singers, and songwriters. Many of those who have topped the charts for a generation are no more sophisticated than the novice when it comes to the business intricacies that will, when all is said and done, determine their financial outcomes. Equally remarkable is the fact that their representatives—the executives at their record labels and publishing companies; personal and business managers charged with fiduciary responsibilities toward their clients; attorneys in whose trust they place their careers; investors and others from the financial arena who follow the industry from Wall Street to the Times building—are often just as unsophisticated and unaware.

Ultimately, all of the creative people who form the heart of the music industry must depend on a network of advisors in whom they need to place their trust. Nothing could possibly constitute more of a gift to artists than a competent, hard-working, intelligent, aware, trustworthy representative. And, despite the fact that too many artists' advisers are ill-informed, others—managers, attorneys, accountants, and agents—have dedicated their lives to further the artistic careers of their clients. Attorneys and accountants customarily work for agreed-upon fees. Managers and agents work for a percentage of the artists' income; in essence, they work for nothing until the day comes—if is ever does come—when the economic potential of the people they represent is realized. At their best, these people can make a difference profound enough to encourage artists and help them bring to fruition and to the world's attention the results of their creations. For many—and I include myself here—that is enough compensation for the tribulations experienced in the course of practicing our professions.

I have sought, in this book, to highlight the most treacherous pitfalls faced by both creators and their representatives and have pointed out some of the most egregious examples of the ways in which artists can be affected by customs and practices to which the industry universally adheres. It is neither my intent to alarm the artist, nor to depict the industry or its principals as selfish, overreaching ogres. On the contrary, as the music industry has become more sophisticated, it has come to terms with certain realities—financial and artistic—that have resulted in more thoughtful and fair practices than existed during the heyday of "Tin Pan Alley" more than fifty years ago. Nevertheless, I feel that the more one exposes the conundrums that face artists, the more likely it is that they will be dealt with reasonably.

The evolution of the music industry as an institution is no less a process than the evolution of any other business or political entity. In the present environment of technological advance, with the need for the artistic community to adjust to the manifold changes occurring both in the creation and the delivery of music, there is more reason than ever before to examine the underpinnings of our industry so that we can better fine-tune our business relationships to take advantage of the promises of the future.

What They'll Never Tell You is divided into twenty chapters, which identify and explore many of the most important issues that impact the musician, singer, and songwriter, and therefore the producer, the personal and business managers, the accountant and the attorney, and every level of music company executive. Some deal with fairly intricate issues; some are rather more accessible. None, to my knowledge, are addressed sufficiently in the principal books on the subject of educating the reader on the ins and outs of the music business. This book, however, takes some of the general premises of other worthwhile books about the field into a realm which is at once more practical and more vocational. I have tried to find a common ground between the academic and the elementary. Much of the methodology of the professionals in the music business, as well as of the business entities themselves, is justified (or rationalized) by years of experience, litigation, and both psychological and financial reinforcement. I have written this book on the theory that more knowledge is better than less, and a greater awareness on the part of both the representatives of talent and those who exploit it is advantageous toward promoting a successful marriage between artists and companies. I hope the information will be received as another layer of wisdom over that which already exists in significant amounts among the top professionals in the field.

Record companies, producers, or music publishers need not be concerned that all of their secrets are now out, nor should attorneys and accountants fear that their jobs will be rendered unnecessary by this book. Record company personnel may feel that I have given away too many secrets, and my peers in the legal and accounting professions may feel that I have given away for free what they charge fees for. To them I respond, like a retailer who believes the best customers are educated consumers, that educated artists, producers, personal and business managers, agents, A&R people, attorneys, and accountants will be better served and will better serve each other than the ones who have chosen, or who have been forced, to live in ignorance, or worse, in a daydream.

It is not enough to know the things you *think* you need to know about the music industry. Those who live within it—whether at the artistic or the business pole or somewhere in between—must know more. They must know what they never knew or did (and do) not even think they want to know. They must know the difference between surface and substance; between truth and lie; between reality and myth. Only then can they prosper within their industry while taking genuine pleasure in their contribution to the culture that sustains them and the rest of our world.

ACKNOWLEDGMENTS

Thanks must go to all of my own mentors over the years: in particular Bernard Korman, the former General Counsel of ASCAP, who taught me that it is okay to reexamine and rewrite what I have created; the legendary Harold Orenstein, the first true music business attorney, who taught me order and legal ethics; as well as the many people who assisted me in researching and editing this book, particularly Bob Nirkind, my editor at Watson-Guptill, and Sylvia Warren, whose knowledge of the music industry has been enormously beneficial to me and to the readers of this book.

I would also like to thank two of my former associates, Scott Francis, President of BMG Music Publishing, and Michael Simon, the innovative and imaginative Senior VP of the Harry Fox Agency, Inc.; Stewart Hescheles; Loren Chodosh and Sandor Frankel, who give attorneys back their good name; Terri Baker, the legal profession's gift to hip-hop, and her secret weapon, Cheech; David Kincaid, of *The Brandos,* who "did it himself"; the great Anna Moffo, who sang *La Traviata* 956 times and encouraged me even more often; and Ira Sallen, Senior Vice President of Human Resources, without whose wisdom I think no one would reach "yes" in their negotiations with BMG Entertainment

Thanks are also due the following people from whose insights I have benefited enormously—both in writing this book and in life: Maestro Gilbert Levine; Chris O'Malley; James Phelan; Dr. Steven Paul; Bob Epstein; Alex Murphy; Paul Adler; Errol Wander, CPA; Nat Farnham; Judy Corcoran; Kathleen Marsh; Cary Cohen, CPA; Martin Josman; Gilbert Hetherwick, former General Manager of Angel Records; Joseph Dash, former head of Columbia Masterworks; the incomparable pianist and music historian Steven Blier; and, of course, my own extraordinary staff—Jackie Kim, the new generation of music attorney, and Carol Gigante, my secretary and assistant for fifteen years. I also owe heartfelt thanks to my daughters Sophie and Emily, and my stepson Vincent, both for their support and for their frequent admonishment on reading a portion of the manuscript: "Are you sure you want to say that?"

1   INTRODUCTION

It is a sobering thought that when Mozart was my age he had been dead for two years.

—Tom Lehrer

Everyone has an idea; everyone has talent; everyone thinks that they can write or play or sing a song better than much of what they hear on the radio. There are 100 songs on the charts. Why can't theirs be one of them?

Perhaps it can. But I am fairly certain it won't.

There is an apocryphal story about David Merrick, the legendary Broadway producer. An agent said to him that his artist was talented and deserved a chance at appearing in one of Merrick's shows. Merrick went over to the window (his office, like mine, was on Broadway), opened it (you could in those days), and yelled at the top of his lungs: "TALENT!!!!" He then turned to the agent and said, "If I want talent, I can get it by the thousands. They're all out there just waiting for me to open the door. Finding talent is not my problem."

In fact, although unique talent is rare, all of us have talent to one degree or another. But what we do with our talent is the ultimate issue. And the key to opportunity. I say opportunity, not success, because all one can hope for in the music business is opportunity. *Success* depends on many factors: the ability and inclination to roll up one's sleeves and work at the craft of creation so as to actually improve and fine-tune one's skills; the ability to earn money and to provide oneself with food and shelter during the process, which can and will take many years; understanding one's limitations; and identifying an attainable goal and keeping it in mind over the years, amid innumerable distractions. It also depends on one factor over which even the most talented individual has no control: luck—ever-changing radio formats; the attention—or inattention—of an artist's representatives at important moments; timing (e.g., the release of a key single on the same day the label is shut down and its artists moved to a sister label).

I have long been sure that most of the talented people who pursue their craft diligently and over a long period of time—those who "stay in the ring"—do realize their potential. The truth of this has been proved time after time. What I am less sure about is what advice to give to the young artists who have talent but who may not have the personal or financial resources to pursue a career in the arts. One thing is for sure: these artists will not lack for advice. There is no limit to the number of people, including top professionals in the music business, who think they know it all. Sometimes advice givers are being practical; sometimes they are simply jaded; sometimes they are dead wrong—and some are greedy and will say anything to get up-front money. So, how can the artist seriously pursuing a career in the music industry maximize the chances of getting *good* advice? As I emphasize throughout the book, the best approach is to assemble a team consisting of an attorney, a personal manager, a booking agent (personal managers, who are not licensed by the states, are not allowed to seek or obtain employment for their clients), and an accountant.

SELECTING THE RIGHT ATTORNEY

There is plenty of justification for seeking out a good attorney from the outset, not least because attorneys have become an important source of business to the record and music publishing companies. Record companies know that if they maintain a cordial relationship with us, they may eventually be at the top of our shopping lists when an artist of significance comes into the picture. Attorneys are also safe—in the sense that the presentation of an artist to a record or publishing company by an attorney diminishes the possibility that the artist will create problems for the company in the future. The *triage*—the checking-out—of the artist, and of his or her bona fides, will have already been done by someone whose telephone number will be the same in the near future when a problem might arise! In addition, attorneys are licensed by state authorities and have state as well as national ethical rules that guide and bind them.

People in the entertainment industry in the United States have learned something that many in other industries—and countries—have not: the selection of an attorney should be made earlier, not later, so he or she can help you in structuring your deals and relationships in ways that can avoid problems. But, although choosing the right legal representation is one of the most important decisions that creative people make, there is no simple formula for making the right selection. Attorneys come with offices, secretaries, and occasionally ties and jackets. They come in every possible stripe and from every possible background, and it is difficult to evaluate them objectively. Attorneys with all of the trimmings appear to be more stable—more dependable—than those without. But appearances can be deceptive, and there is no substitute for extensive experience in the music industry.

It is not difficult to begin your search. Numerous websites and bar association assistance lines, as well as books and magazines, identify attorneys whose practice areas include the music business. (Three sites to start with are www.attorneylocate.com; www.vlany.org; and www.libertynet.org/pvla (New York's and Philadelphia's Volunteer Lawyers for the Arts organizations). Most attorneys, or their assistants and secretaries, are helpful and clear with callers and are happy to guide potential clients to the appropriate firm or institution for assistance. In addition, most attorneys will provide brief consultation time, at no charge, to potential clients.

Once you are in the process of narrowing down your shortlist of potential attorneys, however, things become more complicated. You will need to personally interview each attorney, and at some point all of the following questions must be answered to your satisfaction:

- Has the attorney had experience with your kind of music?
- Which record companies does the firm have the best relationships with?
- Which record companies have most recently signed the firm's other clients?
- What is the firm's policy with respect to introducing new clients to other clients like producers, managers, songwriters, production companies, etc.?
- How does the firm resolve the issue of conflict of interest in the event that it sets up relationships with other clients in your area?
- How does the firm charge for services, and what are the rates (1) of the partners and (2) of lower-level associates and paralegals?

- When rates are about to change, does the firm advise the client?
- Does the firm request a retainer (an advance against fees), and how is it calculated (e.g., does it reflect hourly rates times an estimated number of hours that will be invested before the retainer will have to be "refilled")?
- What are the firm's, and the artist's, short-term and long-term goals?
- If the agreed-upon goals are not fulfilled, or are not fulfilled in a timely fashion, is the unused balance of the retainer returned?
- How are nitty-gritty details handled? (For example, when the firm "shops" a demo, does it copy the artist on the correspondence? If contacts are made via e-mail or telephone, is it the firm's policy to provide updates on each contact, or periodically on a quantity of contacts?)

Although it may appear so, I am actually not suggesting that as a potential client you interrogate potential legal representation with a machine-gun barrage of questions. Needless to say, no one wants to be subjected to this kind of questioning. And you are still the "seller," not the "buyer," so you will have to be somewhat more circumspect in your approach. Nevertheless, these are all questions that need to be explored and eventually answered.

PERSONAL REPRESENTATION
Chapters 5 and 6 cover many of the issues to be considered in selecting both personal and business managers. Though personal managers are not subject to the same rigorous licensing procedures that attorneys must pass through, a good personal manager is more likely to be a ticket to a deal than virtually any other type of professional in the entertainment business. But, as you read on, remember that your attorney of choice can be changed easily and often. In contrast, artist–personal manager relationships are usually sealed by long-term written agreements.

Written agreements between attorneys and the artists they represent are rare. Even when an attorney agrees to work for contingent percentage income, the percentage is traditionally considerably lower than that sought by managers, and often covers a specific transaction rather than a career. In contrast, most personal managers feel it is foolish to invest their time and facilities, not to say money, in assisting an artist in career development without some contractual commitment.

Finding a Personal Manager
In 1997, Barry Bergman, the founder and president of the Music Managers Forum— United States (www.mmf-us.org) was quoted as follows:

> Occasionally, someone will ask me if I'm in charge of our country's financial assets [MMF was formerly IMF International]. I often look at them and in a very serious tone respond by saying "yes." After all, what greater assets do we have in our industry other than our artists, writers, producers, and musicians? We must never forget that without the musical creators there would be no artist managers, no record retailers, no record manufacturers, no record distributors, no industry . . . no kidding.

Now *that* is the kind of manager you want!

Unfortunately, finding a good personal manager is not as easy as finding a good attorney. Law firms can—and do—"manage" hundreds of clients. But personal managers traditionally manage one to three clients who pay the bills; they have very little time to explore the possibilities of exploiting the potential career of a start-up client. Most often, artists take a chance on managers just as managers take a chance on artists. The most useful advice I can offer is that you not entangle yourself too quickly or for too long a period, and that anything you sign, or agree to, be reviewed by an attorney familiar with the entertainment industry.

You can start your search on the Internet, with the Music Managers Forum (MMF) site mentioned earlier, which can provide you with a real head start on management opportunities and possibilities in many American cities and several foreign countries.

DEAL MAKERS: WHY YOU NEED THEM

There is something to be said for the fact that both attorneys and managers customarily socialize with executives and A&R (artists and repertoire) people at record companies (as well as with the business affairs staff with whom they may eventually be negotiating the record deal). The value of the "lunch deal," which is characteristic of virtually all businesses, is particularly consequential in the entertainment business, where ideas, not products, are the coin of the realm. A film script, badly presented, may never be taken seriously by the film company. A demo tape or CD, presented by anybody other than someone credible to the record company, may never even get a listen. But when the material is presented by a credible and powerful representative—whether attorney, manager, agent, or other professional—in a way that the representative knows will be well received and reviewed, an artist or a songwriter with promise has a chance. Perception may not be everything. But don't underestimate it. In a world of images, artful and effective presentation is compelling.

Don't Worry, Be Wary

In a classic "lunch deal," an agent approached one of his clients, a film actor whose last film (for which he was paid minimum scale) was a big success, to recommend an offer. A film company executive had told the agent (at lunch) that he was interested in optioning the actor for three more films—at $100,000 each. This sounded fabulous. However, the actor's attorney determined that the "three picture" deal was really a "no picture" deal. The film company did not have to make the films if it did not come up with an acceptable script, budget, costar, etc. In the meantime, the actor would be tied up. The actor declined the deal, and lo and behold, a few months later, with his tail between his legs, the agent called to tell the actor that the film company wanted to do a sequel to the actor's first film (which you will recall was a big success) and it needed the actor in order to produce the sequel. The fee that was ultimately negotiated? One million dollars and a percentage of the profits.

Now, of course, this benefited the agent as well as the actor. Why then, would the agent have recommended the "three [no] picture" deal? There are plenty of reasons, not the least of which is that a deal in hand—even a "no picture" deal—is sometimes perceived to be worth more than no deal at all. One of the reasons agents are so valuable (and so valued) is their relationships with the buyers of talent. Of course, having such relationships is a perquisite of being a successful agent, but it can also be an affliction for the actor or artist to endure. This is all the more reason to have an attorney who is independent of the agent and who can operate as a check and balance for the client.

Similarly, in the music business, who will provide this kind of protection if the artist has only an attorney, but no personal manager? Managers are not so quick to jump on an artist's bandwagon when the band's wagon consists only of a motley crew (pardon the pun) of guitarists and drummers without a tape or even a touring van. So the novice artist may have only one person guiding him or her. And that person is often an attorney. The healthiest situation is for a sufficient number of professionals to be engaged to guide an artist so that they each serve to keep an eye on the others. Checks and balances. Each advisor provides this service and the artist is the better for it.

However you look at it, when you put all of your eggs in one basket—*any* one basket—the eggs may come out scrambled. Behind all successful artists is a team that works more or less in synchronization to assist them in identifying and in reaching their goals. You have heard the Academy Award winners, the Emmy Award winners, and the Grammy Award winners thank these people, but now perhaps you can better understand why these faceless individuals garner so many thank-yous at awards ceremonies. Building a working team is a daunting challenge, second only to the act of creation itself in importance, but one that must be met.

DEAL BLOCKERS: HOW TO GET PAST THEM

There is no sure way to get a deal in any business. This section is not directed at artists who are creating a sensation in their home region and are attracting broad interest from various industry personnel around the country. Most artists who call upon the assistance of attorneys and managers to "shop" them—that is, to bring them, in an effective manner, to the attention of a record or music publishing company—have no such advantage. If you are a novice in the music business, three things work against you in your pursuit of a deal: insufficient time to develop your material, insufficient representative material, and insufficient attention by your representative.

Making Time

As I indicated earlier, it is also necessary for you to stay in the ring as long as possible to work on your art. Unreasonable and artificial time limits will work against you. Naturally, you have to eat; yet any day or night job will interfere with the time that needs to be spent on your efforts to manifest your talent in concrete form—songs, tapes, or performances. Therefore, the squeeze is on. You must find a way to block out hours each day, seven days per week. You have to sacrifice everything that distracts from your goal. In addition, you must have a sense of your direction.

Everyone wastes time. The secret is to know how to manage it—setting priorities, putting first things first, and other rules of life you first heard (learned?) from, of all people, your parents. Perhaps it is enough simply to have this issue identified, because once the words "time flies" are posted on the mirror, the avoidance of waste becomes possible. However, although none of us experiences time in precisely the same way, most of us have jobs, salaries, projects to complete, etc. We do not have to self-start. We have a place to go at 9:00 in the morning, lunches and dinners to eat (and meet at), meetings and conferences to attend. Not so with artists, who must learn to be proficient at managing time—whether "down" time or "up" time. They must understand, experience, and manage time in ways that the rest of us would never comprehend. Artists' comprehension of time is directly related to their ability to achieve their goals.

Building Your Material
Never think that whatever stock of creative materials you have on hand at any given moment will be sufficient to interest a company. You must continue to write, to perform—in a word, to develop your craft. Nothing disappoints an A&R person more than to hear a band months after its initial presentation and realize that there are no new songs, or that the arrangements have not evolved.

The more you perform, the more you improve your art. Why? For one thing, the mere process of playing in front of an audience constitutes a self-criticism that cannot be accomplished any other way. Self-congratulatory artists who decide that their creation is sacrosanct—locked in concrete—will not appeal to a record company, or, in the long run, to the public.

Monitoring Your Representative
Once a representative has agreed to work with you, it should not take six months to structure an approach to record and music publishing companies, to follow through on the approach, and to draw conclusions from the effort. Remember, though, the shopping function is both a privilege and a burden. Time passes; holidays intervene; people who work with a volume of beginning artists have to figure out how to organize approaches to the record and music publishing companies and then to coordinate them with the companies' responses, if any. When a representative is truly snowed under by other work, especially for "paying" clients, no amount of frustrated calls, e-mails, faxes, chocolates, or cajoling on behalf of an artist will be effective in getting the representative's attention. The truth is that you must set your own time limits and, if necessary, switch representatives regularly. You are, after all, number one on your own priority list and you must act accordingly.

STAYING THE COURSE OR CALLING IT QUITS
And now to the ultimate decision. When to give up! For every 100 records on the charts, there are tens of thousands of demos filling our trash dumps. As well they should. Why? Because they are not good enough. Now, there is no universal standard for determining what *is* good enough or what ought to be a hit. But, by definition, if your record does not take off, it isn't good enough. This is, of course, a psychological truth, not a real truth. Your recording may be perfect, but if it is not a hit, it is not good enough. Good enough means successful. If it is not successful, it is not good enough. This does not mean that

the "essence" of the recording is not fabulous. It only means that the recording, taken together with the efforts and talent of the record company, the manager, the attorney, the publicity firm, the radio promotion people, etc., has no potency.

I was standing in the back of a theater a few years ago with the writer of the "book" and lyrics of the musical comedy *Annie.* The writer had an enormous reputation as a comedy writer for television, magazines, etc. If anyone knew what constituted a joke, he did. We were watching a preview of the musical a few days before the official Broadway opening. The actor on stage spoke a particular line which was supposed to be funny, and no one laughed. In fact, they had *never* laughed at this line. Having represented the "orphans" for more than a year, I had seen the show in its developing stages at the Goodspeed Opera House in East Haddam, Connecticut, and then at the Kennedy Center in Washington. This would have been my twentieth time hearing the same line *that received no laughs.* The book writer mumbled something which I could not make out. I asked him, "What did you say?" He said, "I guess it's not a joke." I said, "I guess not." The writer was not worried. He had a suitcase of lines that were jokes, so he never looked back from his Tony award and he continued his illustrious career.

At any rate, the writer left the line in, and certainly it did not keep the play from becoming a big success, with a five-year run followed by a film. This does not change the fact that the line read like a joke and sounded like one. But it wasn't. You might think back to this story when you are hanging on tightly to a song or a recording which you "know" is a hit but which is going nowhere. Maybe it's not a hit.

Like our writer, you may have a "trunk" of songs. You may even have had a brief run on the charts with a song or two. But sooner or later, you have to confront reality and decide whether what you have accomplished is good enough.

A final point. A hit is a hit only after it has become a hit and after the artists have been paid, have deposited the checks, and the checks have cleared the bank. This confluence of events may not occur until years after the climb up the Everest that is the *Billboard* 100. Or, as we will see, it may be a longer wait than that.

You have to determine for yourself when enough is enough, when it is time to quit the ring. The art may be there, but the execution may have failed. The art may be there, but the money may have run out. The art may be there, but the patience may have expired. My best advice to artists who are contemplating quitting is to seek counsel from friends and, in particular, friends intimately involved in their profession—band mates, agency and record company personnel, even club owners who originally supported them. Record and publishing companies are populated by artists who quit pursuing their own careers. They have found a way to express their artistic ideas in a different arena. And no one need stop creating just because they have determined that a full-time career as a creator is not in the offing. The world of music is filled with stories of composers and performers who blossomed late in life. Perhaps a heavy metal career for a 40-year-old is not in the cards, but there are certainly other possibilities.

2 INVESTORS: The High Costs of Low Finance

It is extremely difficult for struggling artists to be heard by the powers that be. Just as a song needs to be played on the radio in order to sell records, artists need to be seen, heard, auditioned, or played on a cassette or CD player in order to sell themselves. This costs money, and there are individuals and companies willing to lend artists money or facilities in order to assist them in positioning themselves so they can be effectively auditioned by the ultimate buyers of talent: the record companies.

THE COSTS OF BEING HEARD

Fledgling artists need to be seen as well as heard. Record companies need to know that the sound and emotion they hear on a demo can be reproduced with sufficient virtuosity live (1) to electrify an audience when on tour and (2) to convince the public that the artistry on the record has not been faked (remember Milli Vanilli?). It is neither cheap, nor easy, to gather together musicians for a showcase at a live club or in a rehearsal hall. An already organized band has it hard enough; it is even more difficult and expensive for a solo singer to replicate what can be manufactured on a CD with sophisticated recording techniques.

Prior to the technological revolution spurred on by My MP3 and other delivery systems, showcasing one's music was achieved only via a live performance or a demo, and these traditional forms remain the predominant way an artist can spread the word. Computers have not done away with those who have to input information, as green-peaked accountants did for the past several hundred years, and the Internet has not done away with the need to create an effective product constituting the musical performance.

In the past, a home-made piano and vocal tape could serve as a "hard copy" of an artist's music. Times have changed. Over the last decade, it has become a necessity for artists to demo their songs for the record labels in such a highly sophisticated way that a normal person would be hard-pressed to distinguish the result from a full-priced Electric Lady master with all the trimmings. Musicians are able to make such demos because incredible innovations in recording equipment now allow them to build extremely effective home recording studios. This equipment, plus CD burners and MP3 file transfers via websites, is helping artists to find new and better ways to present themselves and to make access to their music more manageable. But the costs remain. These extend well beyond the cost of demos. They include all of the costs of beginning a career: from performing live, with the attendant costs of equipment, transportation, and mailings, to the cost of attending music conventions which cater to young artists, to the cost of legal and financial services, including the cost of creating the business entities that are necessary in order to function without unwanted liability to third parties, and, finally, to the cost of liv-ing—food and shelter for one's very survival. And these costs are greater than ever before.

OF INVESTORS AND INVESTMENT AGREEMENTS

Enter the investor. There are as many variations of investors as there are forms of investor agreements. I am not talking about money lenders who lend funds either in a lump sum or as needed up to a maximum amount—all in return for a promise to pay back the loan within a specific period of time, often in specific balanced installments, and always with an interest factor. Banks will usually lend money only to someone who has established good credit and has assets which can be designated as security to the bank in the event of default. A mortgage on a piece of real estate is the most common example of this model.

Artists are not usually in a position to borrow from banks, not the least of the rea-sons being they cannot fulfill either of the requirements noted above. This does not mean that finding someone willing to invest in an artist's career or demo recording is an impos-sible goal. Many people—often those with no music industry background—are willing to assist an artist in achieving the wherewithal to be seen and heard by a record company. Family members, friends, and strangers often combine to finance the artist's needs. Like anyone seeking financial aid, artists must go through the process of developing a busi-ness plan. However, one of the most important parts of plans developed by entrepre-neurs hoping to start up a small business, the forecast of earnings, is impossible to draft in an artist's plan. The highly speculative nature of all music industry endeavors reduces the artist's plan to a fairly simple agreement, one which states

- The amount of the investment
- The purpose for which it will be used
- Some kind of time frame in which the investment will be applied to the mutual goals of the artist and the investor—or returned
- Terms affecting the manner in which the investment will be repaid (or not repaid)

The most common forms of artist-investor agreements are partnerships, including the joint venture, where the partners are active participants in the venture covered by the agreement, and the various forms of incorporated businesses, including the S corpora-tion, the C corporation, and the LLC (limited liability company) (see Chapter 6, pages 74 to 78, for a brief discussion of these types).

Finding the Money

It has not gone unnoticed by many fledgling artists, or their fairly sophisticated friends and relatives, that there is a widely held perception—much of it justified—that successes in the music business can make lots of money. Therefore, those with money are suscep-tible of being convinced to throw some of it into a pot to help an artist, or, more frequent-ly, a record production company or label, or even a management company, break into the business. Artists or their representatives trying to raise money for demos and tours (or careers) through one of the corporate forms—by selling financial interests to nonparticipating investors in their future profits—need to be aware that raising money this way is no different from selling securities. If they seek to raise money from passive investors (that is, those who are not active participants in the project being financed), they must comply with securities laws.

Raising money is a difficult—and sometimes risky—enterprise. This goes not only for you, but for your representative—no matter how well-intentioned he or she may be. Just as you must exercise care in determining how best to raise money and on what terms you can pay it back, you must make yourself aware of how those who "believe" in you are seeking to raise the money as well, and if they intend to raise these funds from passive investors, then either they, or their lawyers, need to have a solid knowledge of securities law as well.

BLUE SKY LAWS

In 1911, Kansas passed the first set of comprehensive laws in the United States designed to prevent the sale of interests in fraudulent schemes or schemes whose likelihood of success was highly speculative, the so-called Blue Sky laws. It was said that the only thing that backed the securities sold in various fly-by-night enterprises being hawked to gullible Kansans was "so much blue sky." One judge referred to "vision" when describing the character of a particularly questionable venture. He wasn't talking about creative vision; he was talking about fantasy, and "fantasy" ventures are what the state regulatory agencies in the United States under the umbrella of the U.S. Securities and Exchange Commission (SEC) seek to prevent by requiring those selling securities to comply with a complex set of filing regulations.

Suppose, for example, that someone who believes in your talent decides to raise money from others in return for a promise to them to pay a percentage of profits at such time as the investment in you returns a profit. Say the original investor has contracted with you to provide $100,000, and subsequently decides to raise the entire amount or a portion of it from others. (In securities law lingo, he is said to be "offering" a piece of what he gets from you in return for a piece of the money he has promised to you.) That investor is, in effect, selling securities, and hence must comply with the securities laws of the states in which the various potential investors live—and possibly the securities laws of the United States as well. Note that whoever is making the offering must file—according to the specific state rules and regulations—in each state in which the investment is being *solicited,* even if the potential investor eventually declines the offer. And although many state registration requirements are relatively straightforward, there are nevertheless fees that must be paid to the agencies. And don't forget the legal fees.

The good news is that when relatively insignificant amounts of investment capital are sought by the person offering the "securities," both the federal securities act and the Blue Sky laws of each state offer a multitude of exemptions, thereby relieving the investor of most, but not all, of the costly and time-consuming filing and documentation procedures that would ordinarily be required for a larger investment. The bad news is that state regulations vary, and only someone thoroughly acquainted with securities law is in a position to sort them out. If an offering is made only in one state (i.e., the offer would only be made to investors located in the same state as the person seeking the investment), the offering is not occurring "in interstate commerce" and therefore federal law does not apply. However, if an offering is made to potential investors located in more than one state, the offering becomes subject to both federal and state securities laws. There are generally two types of offerings: public and private. Due to the cost of registration and preparation for a public offering, most small entertainment projects obtain financing through a private offering, which is exempt from the most burdensome requirements. Both the U.S. Federal Securities Act of 1933 and all of the various states' laws provide for private offerings.

If a person seeking investment makes an offering in interstate commerce, the most commonly used federal law is the private placement exemption offered under Regulation D of the 1933 Act. However, although the offering is exempt, there are nevertheless specific rules, requirements, and filings which must be followed. The person seeking investment does, of course, need to comply with each individual state security law as well. By filing a simple form—Form D—with the federal SEC, a small company (Friends of and Investors in Superartist?) can sell up to $1 million of equity in a 12-month period.*

There is also an exemption within Regulation D that permits offerings without regard to dollar amount provided that there are no more than, or the offering party believes that there are no more than, 35 purchasers of securities from the offering party. Rule 506 makes it clear, however, that one does not have to count among the 35 those people who are considered under the law to be "accredited" investors—that is, essentially that they are either experts in the securities field or well off financially. A definition of such investors supplied by the SEC in Rule 501 can be found at www.sec.gov/divisions/corpfin/forms/regd.htm.

Typically, Regulation D requires that a Notice of Sales on Form D must be filed with the SEC; there may be no advertising or general solicitation of investors; there may be no more than 35 "nonaccredited" investors (although there may be an unlimited number of "accredited" investors); and an offering document, such as a private placement memorandum, must be prepared and given to each prospective investor prior to the investor making the investment. This document sets out the details of the investment and its potential risks.

PENALTIES FOR FAILURE TO FILE

When anyone seeking to obtain *passive* investment to finance a demo, an album, or a career fails to file the proper documents with the applicable securities agencies, any one

---

* There was a time when the federal government divided potential investors into two groups: sophisticated investors and the rest. There were no limitations on to the number of "sophisticated investors" one could solicit. As to "the rest," there were limitations. As it turned out, the "sophisticated investor exemption" was interpreted by different federal courts in different states in different ways. The result was that a person seeking investment from an array of investors would never know whether, down the road, he or she might be found to have violated the federal securities laws or not. This uncertainty resulted in an awkward and costly situation in which people raising money would set up different companies in different states to avoid running afoul of the federal laws in any state, and, ultimately, led to the creation of Regulation D. The "sophisticated investor exemption" still exists, but it is rarely used. Regulation D has effectively replaced it in practice.

or more of the following may result:

- Having to pay fines
- Having to pay punitive damages
- Facing future restrictions on seeking investment for other projects—
  up to and including being barred for life from doing so
- Having to file retroactively at considerable cost
- Having to return the investment money with interest
- Having to cite the violation in future private placement memoranda
  in which you may be seeking investments

It is likely that if the investor is a family member or a close friend, the securities agencies will never receive a complaint; if they do, they will usually drop the issue entirely. There are provisions in the securities laws in which the disclosure requirements are treated differently when investors are a small number of "friends and family." However, securities law compliance is more likely to become an issue when a disgruntled investor—not necessarily, but usually, a stranger—feels slighted (and when, of course, the investment has gone south). Did you forget to invite your investor to the CD listening party? Did you fail to return her telephone calls? Have you miscredited or failed to credit him on the CD jacket or wherever else credit was expected? Even when you have failed to follow the laws designed to protect investors, if everyone makes a profit, you are not likely to have a problem. But angry investors who have also lost money will be looking for reasons to file a complaint (the SEC provides preprinted forms for easy complaining) and they may well find them. And, once a complaint is filed by an investor who claims to have been misled by you, the securities agencies will have no choice but to investigate. Further, certain illegal actions are more visible than others, and may be noticed even when none of your investors has complained. For example, if you advertise for investors, which, as noted above, you cannot do except as part of a formal *public* offering, federal or state securities departments may, in the course of their routine watch policies, see the advertisements, at which point they may well decide to knock on your door and pursue you. Talk about a career bummer!

INTERNET-SPECIFIC OFFERINGS

It used to be difficult enough to identify the particular states in which a Blue Sky registration had to be filed. Some were easy: the state in which you lived, the state in which your potential investor lived. Some were less easy. With the advent of the Internet, offering semi-anonymity and a very broad reach, things became even more complicated—and opportunities for fraudulent investment schemes multiplied. But in this country, no technological advancement can gain a footing for long before a law or rule is adopted which will regulate it.

Organized in 1919, the North American Securities Administrators Association (NASAA) is the oldest international organization devoted to investor protection. They list an enormous number of organizations that protect the (potentially) defrauded investor on their website, www.NASAA.org. The NASAA has recognized that the Internet has become an alternative distribution channel for people who may defraud others. Reaching people via e-mail is more efficient than the old-fashioned telemarketing method, and as this new method spread around the world, both the NASAA and the SEC had to address the issue, both to protect legitimate offerings and to identify illegitimate ones. In addition, over half the states in the United States have established Internet surveillance programs that watch for fraud. Take heed. The Internet is probably so much a part of your daily life that it would seem natural to use its long reach to interest potential supporters. But enter a chat room, add an MP3 file, encourage a well-heeled "fan" to donate money, and you're on your way to potential trouble. If you mess up once, you may be looking at jail time. If your "fairy godmother" investor decides to solicit investment funds from others and *she* messes up, you can be held responsible also.

THE SAFE HARBOR DISCLAIMER

Legislation and/or policies designed to protect people from certain risks and uncertainties that they might otherwise be subject to are called "safe harbors." The NASAA has created a safe-harbor disclaimer whereby you (or your investor) can indicate either on your home page or via other methods those states to which you are directing your offer of investments, and you (or your investor) can then follow the Blue Sky rules and regulations of those states, a move which substantially insulates you from the charge that you (or your investor) have been making offerings in states in which you have failed to register or chosen not to register. Following NASAA's guidelines does not protect people seeking investments from others from charges of fraud if they violate any rules or regulations of the state or federal securities laws, but complying with these guidelines—which is evidence that you are really trying to do the right thing—can at least shift to state authorities the burden of proving violations of the law. Unfortunately, although more than half of the states have adopted this safe-harbor disclaimer exemption, some have not.

GETTING THE RIGHT ADVICE

As you have seen, this process is *very dangerous.* It's cliché time. The securities departments of the various states and the federal government were not "born yesterday." "There is nothing new under the sun." "It's all been done before," and the securities police can "see you coming." I am not suggesting that raising money by selling interests in a company is a bad idea. In fact, it can be a particularly good idea. If Microsoft can do it, why not you? If an off-Broadway show can raise a million dollars in an environment where the odds of losing it all are similar to the record business, why not *your* career, *your* record company, or *your* newly discovered artist?

There are plenty of lawyers who specialize in securities law. The problem is that most attorneys in the music industry bar do not. Some music lawyers are members of law firms that have securities divisions, but the majority of the boutique firms do not. So, before you start raising money left and right, consult with a securities lawyer. Just as the laws are there to protect the "little old ladies" who might otherwise be taken advantage of, they are structured to *assist* you in doing it right. It will be money and time well spent. And besides, perhaps the securities lawyer knows a couple of people who have money, instead of CDs, to burn.

Paying It Back

Most novice artists maintain day jobs in order to feed, clothe, and shelter themselves. But they cannot work these jobs when they are pursuing their artistic goals. Thus, in return for a budgeted amount that will serve their needs for a given period, artists will agree to pay back their investors in one of the following ways, or variations thereof.

FIRST MONIES PLUS A PERCENTAGE

The artist can agree to pay investors out of the very first cash he or she receives from a contractual relationship with a record company or a music publishing company (known as "first monies"), and, subsequently, by paying an identical amount out of, for example, 50 percent of the next monies received. Say an investor has invested $1,000. Under this payback method, the investor would receive the first $1,000 of money not otherwise committed for recording, and half of the next $2,000 of similarly designated money—not a bad return on a risky investment.

STRAIGHT PERCENTAGE

The artist can agree to pay the investors a percentage of receipts derived from all or some of a variety of music industry sources—everything from record royalties and advances to live performance fees and music publishing income. The nature of such receipts needs to be very carefully defined, and if you go this route, you need an accountant who is intimately aware of the idiosyncrasies of the music business to insure that the parties are clear as to what investors are to receive and from which monies. Similarly, there should be a cap, or limit, on the amount of money investors can receive. For example, the agreement might specify that on a $1,000 investment, the investors will receive 25 percent of all advances from the record company or publishing company up to a total payment of $2,000.

ROYALTY POINTS

An artist who has a well-negotiated record deal will generally receive (exclusive of what the producer's royalty is) from 9 to 12 *points.* If an artist has a 10-point deal (net of producer), the investor's 1 point will constitute 10 percent of that total. That must be added to the 15 or 20 percent of the total earnings that a manager receives, the 5 percent the business manager will likely claim, and legal fees, which, even if not specifically tied to a percentage of income (a practice becoming more and more popular in California), can be considerable. The cost of legal services can amount to anywhere from 3 to 10 percent of artists' gross incomes—at least at the beginning of an artist's career, when legal services are much in demand and gross income is likely to be low. Thus, ultimately, the artist may have to pay out as much as 55 percent of his or her gross income. In such cases, since any well-run "business" is likely to require as much as 50 percent of gross income, or more, to cover operation expenses, the artist will be left with nothing—and possibly even owing money. Even assuming the lower cost figures (that is, 15 percent for a personal manager, 5 percent for the business manager, and 3 percent for the attorney), the artist would end up with less than 20 percent of gross (15 plus 5 plus 3 plus the investor's 10, plus the 50 percent for operational expenses, equals 83 percent).

Therefore, when artists still choose to pay investors a "point" or two, it is logical to establish some kind of cap on the amount of money to which investors are ultimately entitled. In this way, payments to the investors will not completely consume the artist's income. Another possibility is to limit the sources of financial return. For example, if the investor's entitlement is limited to record royalties, at least other sources are exempt from the potentially devastating effect on the artist's resources that I have described above.

Overcalls and Conversions

In cases in which the initial investment proves inadequate, artists may want to seek additional money from investors. This "last" money is often the most expensive a borrower can receive. For this reason, it is extremely wise to provide in advance, in a written document, for an *overcall* right—that is, a right for artists to claim from the investors an additional sum of money without changing the basic parameters of the understanding.

Artists may also negotiate the right to convert the investment into a loan, with interest (the *conversion* right) and have the option to pay back the investment within a particular period of time at an agreed-upon rate of interest. This option is of obvious value to the artist, and may sometimes be more appealing to investors than one would initially think. This right may mature under any of the following circumstances:

- Upon the artist signing an exclusive recording or music publishing agreement within a certain period of time.
- Upon the artist paying back a percentage (e.g., one-half) of the investment within a specified period of time.
- Upon the artist reconstituting himself with another artist or artists— for example, by changing band mates and reforming as another band.
- Upon the occurrence of negative circumstances, such as the failure of the artist's first album or the failure to enter into an exclusive recording or music publishing agreement within a certain period of time. (In such cases, all or part of the investment can be converted into a loan.)

Commissions

Borrowers may have more than investors to worry about. They may also have personal managers whose contracts permit them to commission all gross receipts. Not only may the investment itself be commissionable; when artists' earnings are being directed toward paying back investors, the record sales that generate this income may be subject to commission as well.

Only one commission is considered fair. But which one? Presumably the second— that applied to actual earnings—because investment capital is hard to come by and to reduce it by 15 to 20 percent, which reflects the manager's commission, may not be the best use to which the capital can be put. On the other hand, the personal managers may be the ones who have obtained the financing. What is that worth? Or personal managers, understandably, may not want to work for free, and part of any money that comes into the coffers of the artists may logically be money that is legitimately commissionable by them.

No one approach will fit all circumstances. But the dangers described in the previous examples warrant careful consideration and discussion by all parties involved in an investment of this nature; then, once an agreement is reached and signed, no one should have reason to be angry later.

SHOULD HE WHO PAYS THE PIPER CALL THE TUNE?

Over the last decade, the music industry has begun to attract traditionally conservative Wall Street types. While on the face of it, this sounds like a good thing, it can cause problems for the group or company that obtained the investment. For example, one independent company, a clever, creative group of music industry neophytes in San Francisco, was shut down by its Silicon Valley financiers after only a few months of operation. The label had signed a number of acts, but the terms of the deals (required by the investors) were so brutal that any of the signed artists represented by reasonably competent counsel were invariably lost to another, more competitive (and more experienced) label. The labels that acquired those acts had flexible, long-term thinkers who understood the concept of compromise in their negotiations. The investors in the company, who were not music industry professionals, decided that they had no time to be flexible. They wanted it all and they knew better. The result: they ended up with nothing. All that was left was another label to add to the scrap heap of the music business and one more anecdote with human consequences. Today they are probably bad-mouthing the music industry as a lousy business and a foolish place to invest one's money. They're wrong, but probably have no clue as to why.

It can seem amusing to observe the pratfalls and arrogance of people who are the "masters of the universe" on Wall Street but who are total idiots when it comes to the valuation and exploitation of intellectual property, and there are innumerable examples of investor-caused failures in the music business beyond the one cited above. And practically every such example involves the application of rules learned in other industries, rules which have no particular relevance to the music industry.

What is happening in the music industry is replicated in the dot-com businesses as well. Financial "experts" and their technology specialists have been establishing music industry–oriented businesses for years; yet they neither understand the concepts of the industry, nor its history, nor the mistakes that have gone before them from which they might learn a thing or two. Perhaps most significantly, they do not know the people in the industry and have not gained their confidence. One particularly egregious example involves a record company that began its exploitation of music rights by appropriating digital files of sound recordings, but not the accompanying right to "reproduce" or "perform" these files. This was *not* a good idea.

It would be a mistake to suggest that the music industry is not a gold mine for intelligent investors who seek advice from those who understand the industry best. It is, and has been, and will be.

Those who are reading this book with the intention of becoming investors in the music business must realize that this industry has a long, complicated history, and that there are reasons some companies have survived and others have not. The stars of Wall Street who think the music business is not "brain surgery" are wrong. It is.

The lessons to be learned are many and take years; there is no easy entrance into this industry. The contribution of music industry professionals is as invaluable as the investment itself.

But lest we forget, whether investors or borrowers are seeking to use money to their own selfish advantage, for artistic participation and expression, or merely for the opportunity to be patrons of the arts in a time-honored tradition, their contribution is enormously valued and can mean the difference between an artist's gaining the attention of the world and struggling during yet another unsatisfying—and unfulfilled—period.

3

WHY ADVANCES SEEM A LOT LIKE LOANS (AND VICE VERSA)

Ah, take the cash,
and let the Credit go
Nor heed the rumble
of a distant Drum
—Edward Fitzgerald,
The Rubáiyát
of Omar Khayyám

The New York music business's nickname, Tin Pan Alley, hails from the early part of the twentieth century, when the music publishers were concentrated on Twenty-Eighth Street in Manhattan. As the story goes, a composer was promoting his songs on a paper-muted piano when a fellow composer told him the piano sounded like a tin pan—in fact, he said, the whole of Twenty-Eighth Street was beginning to sound like a tin pan alley.

In the early days of the music business—from the late nineteenth century to the 1950s—a music publisher would take everything from a writer, perhaps even put the publisher's president's name down as writer, and give the actual songwriter a bone (maybe a pink Cadillac, maybe something a bit shadier). Things have not changed so much. Only now instead of bones, they give writers advances. Remnants of Tin Pan Alley remain, even as the music industry itself has matured in a multitude of ways. The paper which muted the piano has been replaced with the paper constituting the contracts that too often suppress artists' ability to glean financial security from their creative efforts.

What is an advance? In a word, it is cash. In the music business, it is cash given by a record company, production company, or music publishing company to an artist. Cash which the company is entitled to have returned, however. And there's the rub.

If you look up "advance" in the dictionary, you will find it has an unusually large number of synonyms—among them debt, stampede, and loan. In the music business, the word takes on an almost metaphysical dimension. Eyes light up, those who commission earnings get all excited, and everyone tries to convince each other that they are getting something for nothing. Although the advancing party does not receive any perceived value from the receiving party at the time the advance is given (except promises), the receiving party is now about to enjoy a bottle of champagne, a new car, and the opportunity to treat many friends (probably newfound) to a night or week on the town.

What are the real characteristics of advances? Their implications? Their advantages?

The advantages? Whatever you can do with the money. Live, eat, pay rent, pay the phone bill, buy some equipment, rent a rehearsal room, outfit your band with instruments and clothes, pay your lawyer, your accountant, and your manager something "on account," provide your fans with updated website information or postcards about upcoming dates. And don't forget union dues, without which you might not be able to afford medical insurance. There are lots of reasons for artists to take advances. Without them, most artists would be unable to function, and the record companies would be the eventual losers.

The disadvantages? The entire burden of paying back cash advances is the artist's alone. And, even if they are ultimately repaid, the publisher (or record company in the case of recordings) will have acquired, *via* these advances, long-term equity in copyrights in both musical compositions and recordings, as well as the right to control and share financially in these vast income-producing assets "in perpetuity" [read "forever"]. This is because *all* monies going in the direction of the artist, or songwriter, are advances. Music publishers do not "purchase" your copyrights, or the right to control them, when they enter into a typical copublishing agreement. Rather, they "advance," to the artist or songwriter, money which must be returned—if only out of the artist's or songwriter's share of earnings.

Shocking as it may seem, artists in the music business begin their careers more in debt than doctors who have borrowed their way through eight years of college and medical school. At least doctors own a medical degree. Artists do not even own their masters; on the contrary, as we will see, they have to pay for the records they make. Songwriters have to *return* the money they receive for selling their copyrights and the worldwide administration rights, but they do not get their copyrights back. They receive equipment loans, but often have to return the equipment. They look to the record company to provide services including, obviously, the promotion of their records; yet they are charged for the tens of thousands of dollars that it costs the record company to hire independent promotion people—people who used to work for the record companies, but who are now operating under their own umbrellas so that record companies (at least three of which at one time were operating under federal license to run enormously lucrative broadcast networks) would not be tainted with the same brush that the less reputable promotion people have been scarred with. (For more about independent promotion, see Chapter 4, page 34, and Chapter 9.)

As people in general have become more aware of lifetime investment needs and opportunities, a growing segment of the music industry's lawyers and accountants are no longer inclined to encourage artists to accept substantial advances. While it is true in most instances that advances are not repayable in cash, they are *always* repayable out of earnings. That's why they are called advances. And, as we shall see, sometimes they are subject to interest charges that can inflate what seemed to be a manageable sum into a totally *un*manageable debt.

A SAD STORY AND A HAPPY STORY ABOUT ADVANCES

One day, not too many years ago, a hungry manager and a greedy lawyer decided that one of their artists needed a quick infusion of money. Whether this was because they were insecure about the artist's continuing ability to feed the family of professionals around him by writing and recording hit records or because the artist had dug a financial hole for himself is not known. But the artist was not averse to a fat deposit into his bank account. What the manager and lawyer did, however, was to have a permanent effect on the artist and his family. These "caring professionals," with the songwriter's approval of course, sought and received several million dollars from the music publishing company to whom the writer had licensed his copyrights. The documentation concerning the payment referred to it as a "loan." Of course, interest was chargeable to the songwriter at the prevailing rate for personal loans and the loan was "secured" by the artist's copyrights. The loan (together with its accumulated interest) was payable through the earnings of the songs, just as an advance would have been. However, it was not payable in the direct way that a loan ordinarily would have been. In other words, the loan did not have to be paid back—ever—out of the borrower's (the writer's) pocket. It just generated interest, and the accumulating interest, plus the unpaid balance of the loan, would simply be applied to the future earnings of the songs—songs that had been written over many years in the past as well as songs yet to be written.

Because both the lawyer and the manager needed money also (and, in their own view, deserved it because of their successful efforts in getting the money), they obtained a combined commission rate that exceeded 30 percent of royalties. That left 70 percent for the songwriter.

Along came the IRS. They said, "Wait a minute, this looks like an advance to us: the writer never has to pay it back and his representatives commissioned it, just as if it were income. This is no loan!" The writer's representatives cried foul. Loans are not income. Only advances are income. The IRS agreed, but found the payment to be an advance, not a loan, and therefore it was viewed as taxable income. The federal, state, and local taxes, interest, and penalties totaled—guess what—70 percent of the money "lent" to the artist in the first place.

Unfortunately, the artist had retained very little of the 70 percent he netted after his representatives took their commissions. (He was not to enjoy a fabulous lifestyle after all.) So the money owed the various governmental agencies began to accumulate interest and by the time the IRS asserted its claim, the money owed had doubled.

The artist not only had nothing left, but he owed the IRS an interest-accumulating amount equivalent to what he had received in the first place. Meanwhile, he owed the publishing company millions of dollars—to be recouped out of his songwriter earnings. (In the context of music industry contracts, "recoupable" means recoverable from royalties.) Cash advances are one form of recoupable expense. Recording costs are another. Payment of royalties to an artist do not begin until all recoupable expenses have been accounted for.) *This* debt was also accumulating interest charges at a rapidly accumulating rate. The publishing company could not request repayment, remember, but it could forever hold onto the income generated by the musical compositions attributable to the writer.

And now for a happy story. A publishing company liked a band and its songwriters and signed them to a typical copublishing relationship. They would receive royalties—as writers—representing 50 percent of almost every dollar earned by their songs and an additional 25 percent of the same dollar by virtue of the fact that they were copublishers and co-owners of the copyrights to their music. The idea of paying writers one-half of the publisher's share of royalties in addition to their writers' share so that they ended up with 75 percent of every dollar was one that developed as artists began to be solely responsible for recording their own songs—a responsibility that in olden days had been the music publisher's. This particular artist's advance was modest too. Four years later, the band still had not been signed, but each member worked at a day job and the writers had been able to develop and demo their songs (30 songs during this period). The band also showcased regularly and developed a fan base; in essence, they were helped financially and creatively over a four-year period to sharpen their skills and improve their craft of writing and recording.

By the time a major record company recognized their appeal and signed the band to a spectacular agreement, their *red position* (the total of all unrecouped advances) under their music publishing contract was minuscule. This happy situation could not have occurred had the music publisher been simply parsimonious. It was the result of a carefully orchestrated process by the band's proactive music publisher through which the advances they received were carefully thought through before they were paid out and they were applied to expenses only as necessary. In no other way could the music publisher have afforded to stick with the act for that long. Consequently, almost as quickly as this band's records start selling, they will have recouped their advances and start receiving additional money—money they will have earned, not money they have to pay back! The band is also in a position where they can actually revisit the publishing agreement from a position of strength and renegotiate some of the provisions that had given them pause at the beginning of their relationship. (There are *always* provisions that give one pause.)

The cautiousness with which both the band and their publishing company addressed the issue of advances and the band's responsibility toward feeding and housing themselves also had the effect of restraining the band from having to go to its record company to seek additional advances in return for which they would have had to give up even more rights and options.

A happy story.

IS ONE PERSON'S MONEY ANOTHER PERSON'S MOTIVATION?

Many of my colleagues and clients feel that if they hit up the record company or music publishing company for a lot of money by way of advances, the companies will fight harder for the artists under contract, if only to protect their own positions. On the contrary. My experience is that companies facing huge losses as a result of a contract with an artist who is not making it are more likely to write off the expense as a bad debt than to throw good money after bad.

Nowhere is this more true than when a regime changes and the expenditure was authorized by the last administration! Many lawyers and managers will seek to express their machismo and their worth by waving big bucks in front of their clients. But by the time everyone gets paid their fees, and the IRS and state tax authorities take their pounds of flesh, there often is not left enough to do a whole lot of good—certainly not enough to effect real change in the artist's life or career. And believe me, if the artist's records do not return the investment *fast,* the record or music publishing companies move quickly on to their next dream act without losing a beat. The only one who loses is the artist, who's history, even though the lawyers and managers are already moving toward big deals for the next generation of clients.

Obviously, I am not suggesting that artists should be underrepresented or represented less than aggressively in every way; but look at what happened to Derek Jeter and Alex Rodriguez after they signed their $187 million and $252 million deals with the Yankees and Rangers, respectively: the public's focus turned from their art, and their skills, to their money. (And maybe their focus changed as well.)

Commit another error or strike out too often and the money becomes the elephant in the living room that cannot be gotten rid of; the baseball player's performance on the field, previously the sole reason for the player's existence, is replaced with something totally extraneous to his function—whether or not the money that has been paid has been well spent and is being earned. This may be a mere distraction for sports stars, but in the music field it can be devastating, especially when the line between art and commercial viability is so indistinct, determined not necessarily by the artist's talent, but by that intangible called "perception" or "image"—that is, how a potential (or former) audience sees the artist.

4

SOME UNVARNISHED TRUTHS ABOUT ROYALTIES

When a little girl asked Lew Grade, founder of ATV Music, now Sony/ATV, what two and two equal, he answered: "It depends on whether you're buying or selling."

Except for a few glaring examples (for example, the creators of *Superman* were paid off with a flat sum of money and the only pleasure they received from the success of the motion pictures based on their story was the buttered popcorn they purchased at the theater), most creators of intellectual property and their eventual distributors, such as record companies, acknowledge that they cannot fix a value on the created property. The result? A stratagem whereby creators receive a share of the success of the exploitation of their property. In the record business (and in the other entertainment-related businesses), this share is called a *royalty*. A royalty is essentially a sum of money which represents a percentage of sales.

But as we shall see, the distinction between royalty and nobility has come a long way since the days of King Arthur.

The part of a recording agreement with the greatest consequence for artists is the section dealing with royalties. In contrast to salaried employees, who create a product or provide a service and receive a regular paycheck in return, artists, who produce what is known as *intellectual property,* are compensated on a totally different model—the royalty rate. But once compensation for services is calculated on the basis of a royalty, the floodgates open for every possible royalty-reduction device that can be dreamed up by the business affairs lawyers at the record labels. It is no wonder that the section in recording agreements dealing with royalties can be well over 30 pages.

Before getting into the details of the numerous charges against artist's royalties that are written into record agreements, I want to emphasize again that the cost of recording and promoting these days is astronomical. However you may feel about the propriety of record companies charging so much against artists' accounts, you cannot deny that the investment by record companies in signing new artists is phenomenal. When A&R people observe artists at club dates, they know that if they sign the acts, their companies will have to invest upwards of half a million dollars *per act* to break them. No small risk. No small risk for the A&R people either! How many acts can they sign without success before their record companies look cross-eyed at them?

It is no wonder that A&R people are extremely cautious before committing their company to a potential financial disaster. This old joke about A&R people is funny for a reason:

Question: How many A&R people does it take to screw in a light bulb?
Answer: I don't know. What do you think?

One or two misfortunes and the A&R person will be dusting off the old bass and looking for a gig. I use the word "misfortunes" rather than mistakes because the commercial acceptability of art being what it is—intangible, uncertain, and highly speculative—many brilliant and even potentially era-defining artists fail to break the commercial barrier for a long time, if ever.

By describing the various charges against artists' accounts with record companies, as with other descriptions and disclosures made in this book, I am not expressing an opinion about the correctness of the procedures. It is the job of artists and their representatives to seek a balance in the negotiations or renegotiations of their record agreements; but the information needs to be in hand so that artists and their representatives can negotiate from an informed position. Remember: Your adversaries are not going to transform themselves into teachers. Neither the lawyer in the negotiations nor the auditor who ultimately examines the royalty statements can look to the record or publishing company to walk them through the minefields and obstacle courses that have been set up specifically to divert and confuse. Therefore, as I repeatedly advise in this book, it is essential to call in an expert who has the experience, the relationships, and the drive (the need to win?) first, to ask the right questions and second, to elicit complete answers.

While this may sound obvious, young professionals who do not have these qualifications enter the music industry every year. What they may have is a new, nonjaded way of looking at a situation; they may have a hunger that older professionals may have lost years before; but they are nevertheless inexperienced. It should not be insulting to them to seek a "second opinion" or to offer to bring in a consultant to insure that the myriad of obstacles that are placed before all negotiators in the music business (no, the companies don't discriminate) will be identified and addressed. It is never too early to call in an expert.

HOW THE ROYALTY PIE IS SLICED
AND WHO GETS THE PIECES

The parameters that I have chosen for the following scenario are but one of many combinations that can describe a royalty structure. (For example, I have assumed that the producer of the record in my illustration is an independent producer and not either the artist or a producer employed on the staff of the record company.) Suppose the suggested retail selling price of a CD is $16.98, and the record company agrees by contract to pay you a royalty of 12 percent of the suggested retail selling price of the CD (12 or even 13 percent rates are the current going royalty rates for new artists). Not bad, you think. $2.04 per copy. If you sell a mere 25,000 copies ($50,940), you're on the way to financial glory. (And that doesn't even take into account the publishing royalties, the merchandising, the touring.) Right? Wrong! (As you will soon see, this royalty is more than likely to be closer to $0.80 than $2.04—partially because the independent producer's royalty must be cut out of the 12 or 13 percent, leaving the artist with only 9 or 10 percent of the total.) In fact, you won't see $50,940 for a long, long time, if ever. In the following sections, I will introduce you to the myriad items, in addition to advances, routinely deducted before an artist starts getting any royalties. Prices other than the suggested retail list price—for example, the published wholesale price or the published price to dealers (PPD), used in markets where there is neither a suggested retail price nor a wholesale price on which to base the royalty rate—can be used as the royalty base, but the examples in this chapter apply the suggested retail selling price.

None of the following is meant to suggest that all record companies are rolling in money while their artists are starving. But the universal music industry practice that artists pay recording costs out of their own royalties is unique to the music business. This does not happen in the book publishing business, where writers receive a royalty from the first book sold and production costs are not recoupable from the writer's royalties. The only monies recouped by the book publisher are the advances paid to the authors as cash or as a contribution toward publicity expenses and other promotional costs.

Recording Costs

Recording costs are recoupable against the artist's royalties as if they were paid out in cash to the artist. These costs include everything imaginable, including studio costs, engineering costs, musicians' and singers' costs (including union payments), and the cost of tapes. They also include mastering (putting the recording into a form from which copies can be made), an item once absorbed by the record company as a manufacturing cost, not a recording cost, and one which can exceed $10,000 for an album. (With vinyl LPs, the mastering process involved making an acetate disc from which a metal "mother" master was created. Duplicate masters were made from the mother master, and these were used to press the records. Mastering is now a totally digital process—it consists essentially of balancing and equalizing the recording so that the copies made from the resulting master achieve the highest possible quality of sound on playback systems—yet the record companies routinely list it as a recording cost.)

Recording costs can be staggering. In 1969, the total charges applied against Simon and Garfunkel's royalty account for recording costs for the album *Bridge Over Troubled Water* amounted to just over $30,000. Today, the recording costs for a similar album would easily exceed $350,000.

Let's go back and see how this factor affects what the artist will actually receive in royalties on the sales of our hypothetical $16.98 CD. Since the price received by the record company from the retailer is about $10.70, we'll use $10.70 as 100 percent of the record company's receipts for each CD. (All of these costs vary from record to record and from artist to artist. But the example used here is well within the norm.) Out of the $10.70, the record company must pay the costs of manufacturing physical sound carriers (about $1.00); promotional expenses incurred by the company's own staff, as opposed to hiring an independent promoter (about $1.00); the cost of distribution (also about $1.00); union pension and welfare fees (about $0.09); and the cost of mechanical royalties to the publishers of the songs contained on the record (about $0.60) Anything left over is retained by the record company. Using our hypothetical deductions, this retained amount will be about $7.00. These are the record company's gross, or retained, earnings.

Now suppose that the recording costs listed above total $100,000. Theoretically, the record company will recoup its investment once 14,268 records have been sold ($100,000 divided by $7.00). However, the record company has other costs, including general overhead, tour support, independent promotion costs incurred as a result of the company's hiring promotion companies unaffiliated with themselves, marketing, and videos. Often, the total amount of these other costs can be just as much as the actual recording costs; in our example, another $100,000. Taking into account these other costs, you might think the record company would *really* break even after selling 28,572 units, and the royalties would start flowing to you, the artist. Think again.

That isn't the way it works. Why? Because recording costs are not recouped by the record company out of its retained earnings. Yes, the entire $7.00 mentioned above is retained by the record company, but on the books of the record company, only the amount that is owed to the you, the artist's royalty, is applied against the costs of the recording project. Let's say your royalty is $0.80 per record. (Bear with me. You will soon see that a royalty of 12 percent on a $16.98 record is not $2.04, as one would presume, but about $0.80.) Given that, 125,000 records need to be sold before the $100,000 recording costs are recouped. At that point, the record company will have received $875,000 (125,000 times $7).

Unfortunately for you, your producer, who is not paid his or her share until the record company recoups all royalties owed you which are applied to recording costs, is next in line to be paid. The producer is paid on what is known as a *record one* basis (from the first record sold). At about $0.25 per record (that is, $3/12$ of your 12 percent royalty—or $1/3$ of your 9 percent net royalty), the producer's payment on the first 125,000 units amounts to $31,250, which comes out of the record company's $875,000 gross. You have still received nothing. And despite the fact that your royalties are calculated prospectively and not back to record one, it may be some time before you see any cash.

To review: At first you thought that upon the sale of 25,000 units, at $2.04 per copy, you would have been paid almost $51,000. But since you have to pay *out of your own royalties* the $100,000 cost of recording, the sale of 25,000 copies actually will net you zero. In fact, it will take a total of 125,000 records (that is, 100,000 additional copies) sold to bring your account out the red. On these 125,000 records, you will receive *no* royalty; whereas your record company will deposit into its bank account $875,000. The producer will have received $31,250—$0.25 times 125,000 units, which will be paid by the record company out of the $875,000 it will have received from its distributors. And we have not even begun to take into account other recoupable costs that the record company can (and will) charge against your royalties.

Payment on Less Than 100 Percent of Records Sold

In the old days, vinyl records (in particular 78 rpm records, which were retired as the format of choice in the late 1950s) would often break, whereupon consumers would return them to dealers and the dealers would discard them. Therefore, the record companies would promise to pay artists' royalties based on only 90 percent of sales on the (arbitrary) assumption that 10 percent of all records sold to dealers would be worthless and they would have to give dealers a credit for these shipments. This was done whether or not any of the records actually broke. Once LPs were introduced in the 1950s, there was absolutely no justification to reduce artists' royalties by 10 percent. Supposedly, this practice ended in the 1960s.

It's back.

Many record companies today pay royalties on less than 100 percent of sales. (A&M Records, the home of Carole King, Supertramp, The Police, and Peter Frampton, *never* paid royalties on more than 90 percent of records sold. Jive Records, home of Britney Spears, 'NSYNC, R Kelly, and the Backstreet Boys, also has a nostalgic tendency to play the 90 percent game.) The record companies take what they can.

Who Pays for "New" Technology?

When CDs came into the picture, many record companies wanted financial relief for what they termed the "incredible" cost of research and development. The relief they gave themselves was to pay royalties on anywhere from 85 to 90 percent of records sold to as few as 66 $2/3$ percent. Of course, most of the record companies had invested nothing in R&D, let alone incredible amounts. But, having been surprised by the advent of a new technology for which no special consideration had been made in their recording agreements, the record companies decided to include in their record agreements a catch-all royalty reduction provision covering *any* new technology. This provision serves to reduce the royalty rate by from 25 to 50 percent of the otherwise applicable royalty rate on formats such as digital compact cassettes or minidiscs, and probably also digital phonorecord deliveries (DPDs) delivered to consumers via the Internet's digital download capability. These technologies are already with us. How will the companies deal with as yet unknown future inventions? Already, we are seeing recording contracts that provide that, when new technologies are being used, the artist's royalty will be reduced to 50 percent or less of the otherwise applicable royalty rate, although 25 percent reductions are more common.

When audio tape was first introduced in the 1960s—and for years thereafter—record companies regularly reduced 8-track and cassette royalties by 50 percent. As most tapes were manufactured by licensees of the record companies, not the record companies themselves, the reduction was perhaps justified at the time; but the companies continued the practice long after they began to manufacture tapes themselves. Similarly, until CD plants became widespread, the reduction in royalties had some rational basis. But, once they did, the rationale disappeared—even as the practice continues to this day.

A common practice among more reputable, or thoughtful, record companies, when negotiating royalty rates for new technologies, has been to include clauses providing that while there will be a general reduction in the royalty rate during the early years of exploiting these technologies, once the majority of similarly situated artists on a particular label revert to a more reasonable royalty rate, or once the proportion of sales of the new technologies increases to an undeniably large figure, such as 50 percent of the total market, the reduction will be lifted and the royalty rate will return to what most of us consider to be a "full" rate. While what used to be called the "CD concession" and now is referred to as the "new technology concession" has disappeared from some companies' recording agreements, many companies still resist paying a full rate for the CD format, even though it is 20 years since the format was first introduced and is now the principal format for all records sold in the world. We can expect similar resistance to removing "concessions" for other technologies, including DPDs, for a long time to come.

There are numerous implications of the total absence of a standard with respect to how and to what extent DPDs, and electronic rights, are dealt with in recording agreements in general and in clauses pertaining to royalties in particular. Several of them are dealt with later in this chapter; see "The Myth of Royalty Escalations" (page 36), and "The Effect of Digital Downloading on Pricing and Royalties" (page 43).

Royalty Reductions for "Special" Categories

SINGLES

Record companies traditionally pay artists a lower royalty rate on singles than on album sales even though the royalty *rate,* were it to remain the same, would be applied against a significantly reduced base. The retail cost of singles is of course considerably less than that of albums, thereby insuring a lower royalty payment even if the rate remained the same. Yet artists' royalty *rates* are reduced as well. For example, if a royalty of 9 percent were paid on an album with an effective royalty base of $11.00, the royalty would be 99 cents. If the same royalty rate were applied to a single with an effective royalty base of $3.00, the royalty would be 27 cents. Sounds proportionate. But record companies do not pay 27 cents. They reduce the royalty rate by as much as half. In our example, based on the same $3.00 royalty base, the actual royalty which record companies would pay on the sale of a single would be 13.5 cents. Simple. You ask why? They answer, "Why not?" And, as if this result were not bad enough, singles royalty rates most often do not escalate based on sales achievement levels, as do album rates.

REDUCED-PRICE RECORDS

The typical reduction in the royalty rate on mid-price and budget records is 50 percent. A successful negotiation can increase this to a two-thirds rate for budget records and a three-quarters rate for mid-price records. Often, and for no apparently good reason, the royalty rate on other types of records—such as those sold through military exchange channels; soundtracks; picture discs; etc.—is also reduced. Every reduction in rate represents another few pennies lost to the artist and producer and gained by the record company. Believe me, they add up.

FOREIGN SALES

Royalty rates are also traditionally reduced for foreign sales. This is true whether or not a record company owns or controls (through subsidiaries or divisions) its own companies outside of the United States. However, in the latter case, there is room for negotiation. In such a scenario, the record companies actually do have some justification for their position. They claim that they should not be penalized for having their own divisions, since these divisions or subsidiaries have the same operating costs as those of unaffiliated companies. The U.S.-based companies claim that it is to the artist's advantage to keep their recording careers "in the family"—that is, in one company whose interests in an artist's career are global and thus broader than those of individual companies whose interests in an artist's career are necessarily more "provincial." They argue that the benefit that accrues to the artist more than justifies the foreign divisions being compensated in the same way a company that is a stranger to the artist's record label would be compensated.

RECORD CLUBS

In order to induce consumers to join, record clubs typically give away a specified number of records as well, to allow members to purchase records at a discount from what they would normally cost in a record store. The two companies that own their own record clubs (Sony, together with Warner Records, and BMG) in essence are selling records, even at the discount, at considerably higher prices than they would have to sell to a dealer who would then mark up the record for retail sale. Nevertheless, the typical deal for an artist and producer is that the company is permitted to give away royalty-free as many of the artist's records as they sell. For the records they do sell, they typically pay 50 percent of the otherwise applicable royalty rate. Wow!

Many artists feel that they are subsidizing the company's record club operations and would much prefer to take their chances that their records would be sold in the traditional market places at regular prices, thereby generating a full royalty for themselves. The problem, they say, is that only the hottest artists and hottest records are the "loss leaders" for the rest of the record club's catalogue. Who would turn down the 10 top Grammy winners' records for free in return for purchasing a few others over a period of time at less than what they would have to pay in the stores? These "free" records, in reality, have been sold to induce the record club customers to buy other artists' records!

DIABOLICAL DEDUCTION DEVICES

Do you think that the previous examples of royalty reduction methods are egregious? Perhaps. But diabolical? That adjective must surely be reserved for the following two particularly odious devices by which record companies reduce your royalties: packaging deductions and reduced mechanical royalties on controlled compositions.

Packaging Deductions

Record companies decided long ago that while they did not object to paying a royalty per record sold, they did not see why they should have to pay a royalty on the packaging. This makes some sense. When a 78 sold for $1.00 and four 78s in a box sold for $5.00, the extra dollar was obviously attributable to the cost of the package. Or was it? Perhaps the bundling of the four records constituting a concert performance or an opera simply made the entire package more valuable in the eyes of the record company and the customer. Nevertheless, it was this logic that resulted in the birth of the first packaging deduction. Clearly, the majority of the cost of a record is for the intellectual property (that is, the songs and the masters—the music) comprising it. But some of the cost is contained in the disk (or tape) itself and in the packaging surrounding it, and record companies have succeeded in persuading artists and their representatives that they should not pay a royalty on those components.

The packaging deduction is customarily worded in terms of a percentage of the record's *royalty base price*. A 25 percent packaging deduction means that for a record retailing at $16.98, $4.25 is deducted before the artist's royalty rate is applied. (The 10 percent packaging deduction is a thing of the past; the current going deduction for CDs, and other new technologies, is 25 percent.) Thus the figures used earlier in this chapter must be adjusted even farther downward to account for the packaging deduction. Let's return to our earlier example, and see exactly how I got the $0.80 per-unit royalty.

Suggested retail ($16.98 CD) x 90% (10% breakage deduction) x 75% (25 percent new technology deduction) x 75% (25% packaging deduction) x 9% royalty rate (12% less 3% for producer's royalty) = net artist's royalty per sale

$16.98 x 90% = $15.28

$15.28 x 75% = $11.46

$11.46 x 75% = $8.60

$8.60 x 9% = $0.77 (rounded up to $0.80, this is the figure cited on page 26, the net artist's royalty per sale)

And, as we have seen, the net royalty will be further reduced for singles, record club sales, mid-priced and budget records, and other ancillary sales.

Now there are always variations on the theme. The CD concession and new technology rate may be reduced from 25 percent to 20 percent, or even to 12.5 percent. If 20 percent, the resultant royalty will be $0.82 rather than $0.77. Furthermore, the royalty rate for a sought-after artist may be 15 percent rather than 12 percent. At the same time, many producers charge 4 percent rather than 3 percent, and their royalties often escalate based on sales achievements to 5 and 4 percent, respectively. Then again, you may be able to rid yourself of the initial 10 percent "breakage" reduction with most record companies. If you cannot, then the only way to ratchet up your net (that is, final) royalty is to increase the gross royalty rate from 12 percent (in this example) to 13 or 14 percent. It is all rather fungible. The bottom line is that one way or the other, when your gross royalty rate is 12 percent of retail, your ultimate (net) royalty will be somewhere around 80 cents on a $16.98 CD. Further, you will not see any royalties at all until the company has sold enough records to recoup *all* recoupable expenses, and the number of records that constitute "enough" is invariably much higher than you might imagine.

HOW *IS* A DPD PACKAGED?

Yes, there is an ultimate excess to point out to you. The record companies have decided to apply the standard packaging deduction of 25 percent to DPDs—which, in case you haven't noticed, do not even have a package! What better evidence do we need that the deduction game is just a screen for the record companies' attempts to fix a per-unit royalty to every sale—one which fits into their overall scheme, a scheme which presupposes very few hits and very many failures. I think we would all be happier if they were just a little bit more direct; it would save us the inconvenience and the cost of having to negotiate all of these intermediate provisions whose sole purpose is to get the royalty down to *X* dollars anyway.

Reducing Mechanical Royalties

Every song included on a CD, other than songs in the public domain, is subject to a *mechanical license fee:* a payment to the holder of the copyright, usually a music publisher, for the right to use the song. The amount of the fee depends on the length of the song and the current rate as established by the United States Copyright Law, the *statutory rate.* Most record company–artist agreements include a provision stating that the record company will pay the mechanical license fees up to but not exceeding three-fourths of the *minimum* statutory rate without regard to length. This discounted rate is known in the business simply as a "rate." (The "minimum" bit is important: songs whose length is greater than five minutes command a higher license fee than songs whose length is five minutes or less.) In addition, record companies usually include a provision stipulating that no matter how many compositions are on a CD, they will pay only 10 times the minimum rate. The amount in excess of three-fourths of the minimum rate is charged against the artist's royalties. This is true whether the composition in question is a *controlled composition*—a composition written by the artist or the artist's producer—or is not a controlled composition.

Let's say that you record 11 songs. Two are "outside" songs owned by other music publishers; the others are your own compositions. One of the outside songs is six minutes long. First of all, you or your producer will have the unpleasant task of requesting that both outside publishers grant a "rate" to your record company for the compositions being used, including the six-minute song, which would normally command a higher fee than the other one. Also, since the record company has agreed to pay the fees for only 10 songs, the effect is that you have to license the 9 songs you have written for a total royalty of eight times the three-fourths rate, not nine.

To the extent the owners of the two outside songs refuse to license their songs at three-fourths of the minimum rate, your mechanical royalties with respect to your nine songs will be further reduced. To the extent they demand payment at the so-called "long rate" for the six-minute song, your royalties will be even further cut. If your publisher does not care about the way your record agreement is written and insists on being paid the full rates established by the Copyright Act, the excess the record company has to pay over three-fourths of 10 times the minimum rate will be charged against your record royalties and any other monies the company may have to pay you contractually. (And if you co-wrote any of these songs with another writer—often the producer, but just as often a totally unaffiliated writer—you would have to get that other writer's permission to license the song at this reduced rate as well.)

Finally, the applicable minimum statutory rate provided for in the contract is customarily the one in effect at the time the record was supposed to have been delivered, not the one in effect when the record is released, or even recorded. Let me show you how sinister this tidbit in recording agreements can be. Recently, before an artist could complete the recording of his new album and deliver it to his record company, he died. Consequently, he could not, of course, deliver the record "when due." When his recording was finally ready for posthumous release, the record company reminded the lawyers for his estate that the mechanical rate at which all of the compositions on the album (including the now-raging publisher of the artist's song) would be licensed was the rate that had been in effect years earlier, when the rate was considerably lower than on the date the CD was actually released. So it goes.

THE BEAT GOES ON: OTHER IMPORTANT DEDUCTIONS

Just when you think you've heard enough, there's more. There are a vast number of additional charges that must be paid out of your royalties before you see a dollar. It is notable that none of these are applied against either your producer or your co-writers or their music publishers. While they enjoy the success of the effort of all involved in making the record, only you are expected to pay back these costs.

Promotional Videos

Prior to the early 1980s, there were no promotional videos to speak of. Video promotion and outlets for video broadcast—such as MTV and VH-1—were minimal. After 1983, however, things changed dramatically, and costs for promotional videos incurred by record companies increased geometrically. Video clips lasting fewer than four mintues can cost anywhere from hundreds of dollars to hundreds of thousands of. dollars: $150,000 per video is not unusual. There are two issues of importance here: Who pays for the costs of making videos (and how many should be made) and how are royalties on the eventual commercial exploitation of videos shared?

It didn't take the record companies long to figure out how to cover these costs. An answer came from on high (or at least from the chief financial officer's floor). Charge the artist! Currently, most record agreements stipulate that one-half of promotional video expenditures is borne by the record company and one half is paid out of the artist's *audio-only* record royalties. The half borne by the record company is maintained on the books, however, and is eventually repaid to the record company out of 100 percent of the artist's share of video royalties, if any, derived from the exploitation of the video itself. These royalties are calculated at substantially the same *rate* as are the artist's record royalties; however, the price on which the royalty rate is applied differs from company to company. Escalations such as apply to audio-only record royalties are rarely applied to audiovisual royalties. But many record companies are so fearful of a market with which they have little experience (and even less interest) that their contract provisions referring to audiovisual royalties try to protect themselves by establishing an arbitrary suggested retail selling price and then fiddling with it. Here's an example from a major BMG affiliate's form agreement:

> With respect to United States sales through normal retail channels at a base price which is less than a top-line price, Company shall accrue to the artist's account a royalty of ten percent of the applicable royalty base multiplied by a fraction, the numerator of which is the suggested retail list price that equates to the applicable base price and the denominator of which is $19.95.

Right.

One further observation: Record companies are so skittish about video production that they try to maintain a very tight rein on costs. After all, a fabulous video by a major pop star could cost in excess of a small movie—$1 million or more. Scary. So, the companies trump the artist one more time by providing that even if they are the ones who have mismanaged or incorrectly estimated the budget, once the budget hits a certain number (for example, $200,000), *all* of the excess over the original budget is recoupable from the artist's audio-only record royalties.

For years, it was common to make two or three videos to promote an album, but as outlets for video presentation have diminished, record companies in general have become more expensive to operate, and record returns from dealers have become more problematical due to the advent of MP3/Internet distribution, most companies will commit to no more than one video per album, if that. They would rather commit to spending an equivalent amount on other kinds of promotion, at their option, if they feel that paying for video production is of negligible value.

Tour Support

Artists who seek to reach their audience have to tour. Touring increases artist awareness among the broadcast industry and eventual consumers and fans, with the ultimate benefit of increased sales of records and increased interest in that artist and, down the road, a successful subsequent tour. But touring is enormously expensive. The cost of travel, food, and lodging alone can bankrupt any baby band. Individual artists have it much tougher, since they may not be able to function at all without hiring backup musicians. These backup musicians, or sidemen, may themselves make their living only by providing their services to other artists' recording sessions and they may be unwilling to travel without being paid an amount of money equivalent to that which they might have made had they remained in their own cities. The benefit of a band sharing various costs (for example, a van to transport the musicians and the equipment) is not available to an artist using sidemen.

The record company does not directly share in the earnings from tours (neither from concert fees nor, usually, from merchandising sales), except in the sense that celebrity and success help all involved. However, once artists are signed, the record company usually foots the bill for its artists' tours at the beginnings of their careers. As with most of the items listed in this section, the costs incurred are ultimately borne largely, if not solely, by the artists. While record companies risk the loss, 100 percent of the tour support is recouped out of the artist's royalties.

Equipment Loans

Quite simply, artists need equipment (for example, instruments, amps, speakers, tuners, computers, etc.) with which to perform. They also need equipment with which to write and demo their songs. The record company once again is the source of aid to needy artists and lends them the money they need to rent the equipment. The total cost, of course, is charged against their royalties, even though the record company may ultimately be the principal beneficiary of the expenditure. In lieu of asking for equipment advances on a per-recording basis, artists should seriously consider purchasing some of the equipment they need for preproduction or even production of their recordings (for example, for a Pro Tools kit, which is extremely expensive to rent). Many artists tell me that ownership is power. I believe it. Once you own a piece of equipment, you don't have to hit up the record company every time you want to rent a bass rig or an Adat machine.

Independent Promotion

And now, the coup de grace.

What hasn't been said about independent promotion? It has been the subject of books, exposés, television reports, and documentaries, not to mention a multitude of conversations and debates within the record industry and on Capitol Hill. An entire chapter of this book (Chapter 9) has been dedicated to marketing and promotion, including independent promotion. For purposes of this chapter, though, suffice it to say that record companies now require artists to pay for what the companies used to provide via their own personnel as an ordinary part of their overhead. They do this by stipulating that part or all of promotional expenses, including the costs of promotional TV campaigns (see below), are recoupable out of royalties. And, as with other recoupable costs, they must be repaid before the artist's royalty payments begin to kick in.

Television Campaigns

Paragraph 7.07(b) of the Universal Records standard recording artist agreement (and, regrettably, many other record companies' contracts as well) provides that if the record company spends money on a TV or radio campaign, the otherwise applicable royalty due the artist will be reduced (by as much as 50 percent) during the semiannual period when the campaign initially took place through to, and including, the semiannual period when the campaign was concluded. Upon the expiration of the latter period, the royalty due the artist is reinstated—but prospectively only. This means that not only is the artist ultimately paying much of the cost of independent promotion, as we have seen, but is also subject to having his or her royalty rate reduced for the duration of a television or radio campaign.

Provisions like this have appeared in record contracts in one form or another for some time. They made some sense when radio was so enormously important as a source of promotional advertising and when few radio stations existed except on the AM bands. It made some sense even after the FM bands were introduced almost 40 years ago. And it made sense when the only productive TV promotion required purchasing advertising time on television shows. It makes no sense today—at least in the United States. With cable television and other forms of broadcast capabilities multiplying every year (e.g., through the Internet), broadcast time for promotional purposes can be purchased for very little money—less than the cost of the T-shirts and baseball caps which are often used for the promotion of artists' records and which no one has ever suggested (up to now) should result in a reduction of artists' royalties. (There is no provision stating that if the record company makes a poster and snipes it around towns in which the artist's fans reside or which are tour stops—which can easily cost more than a typical

$200 radio buy—the artist's royalty will be reduced during the period of the "campaign.")

Things are different in Europe, and the provision may have some validity with respect to European television campaigns—but then the reduction in royalty should only apply to those territories in which the TV campaign is actually employed.

By the way, in order for the provision to take effect, there is no requirement that the record company spend a substantial amount of money on the campaign. A $200 expenditure is sufficient to set the royalty reduction clause in motion—and what a furious reduction in earnings will result! Now if it is appropriate or effective for expenditures to be incurred in furtherance of a common cause (i.e., the sale of records), fine. But arbitrarily reducing the royalty rate for whatever number of records is sold during a period of TV advertising is not susceptible of any rational defense that I think anyone on either side can justify. Furthermore, there is usually no cap on the number of records that can be affected by the royalty reduction. As we have seen, it does not take a lot of record sales to return to the record company a lot of money. At a minimum, the applicability of the reduction should be limited to a definite number of records sold during the TV campaign period.

PREPAYMENT OF ROYALTIES

In some cases, a record (or music publishing) company will voluntarily prepay royalties. A prepayment of royalties constitutes an advance, allowing a company to recoup the advance from royalties that were otherwise earned and would become payable but for the passage of time between the end of a royalty period and the date on which the royalties are due to be paid.

Let's take a common example. A company is required to pay you advances of $10,000 on the first of January of each year—and does. Meanwhile, as of December 31 of the prior year, royalties in some amount are payable, previous advances and chargeable costs having been recouped. But wait. They are not actually payable until the accounting statement is required to be prepared and sent out—as much as four months later. Do you receive the royalties along with the statement submitted on March 31? Or does the company "recoup" the recently paid January advance out of the royalties which had already been earned, but were simply not yet due? In other words, are you really being paid your advances out of your own earned royalties? In this example, if the earned royalties as of December 31 were $10,000, you could receive either $10,000 (the advance) on January 1st and no royalties come March 31, or $20,000 ($10,000 for the advance and $10,000 for the earned royalties). There's a big difference. Therefore, a provision should be negotiated by your attorney to be added to the agreement providing that royalties earned as of the *end* of an accounting period cannot be recouped out of advances paid *subsequent* to the date on which such royalties were actually earned, even though not yet payable because the accounting is not yet officially due.

Now consider the following two situations: (1) you (the artist) need money in January and ask the record company to "lend" it to you or (2) the record company decides that since earned royalties are likely to become due come March 31, it is now time to spend some of that money in a hurry so that it can be deemed an advance, recoupable out of the very royalties that are coming due. In either case, the money being spent—

advanced—is yours. Let's say that you have earned $50,000 in royalties as of the close of an accounting period (let's stick to December 31). You usually do not know how much, if anything, you will receive at the time the accounting is submitted three months later at the end of March. But the record company does. What a good time to finance another video, or album, or tour, or spend some money on the release of a new single and the independent promotion services that naturally accompany the release. By March 31, that newly charged debt vacuums up money that would otherwise have been payable to you. At this point, you may justifiably wonder how it came to pass that you have just financed your own video, album, or tour. Not only do you have to pay for these expenditures out of future royalties; now you are paying them out of past royalties.

In cases like the above, the contract language (or lack of it) either permits the chain of events or it does not, and your representatives and the record company's representatives can either address the issue or not. In either case, after the agreement is signed, it is too late to deal with the any problems that may arise.

THE MYTH OF ROYALTY ESCALATIONS

The term *royalty escalation* (or royalty acceleration) refers to the situation in which an artist's or producer's royalty rates rise incrementally from year to year, or from album to album, or from sales level to sales level, or sometimes a combination of these. For example, a royalty rate of 12 percent may rise to 12 1/2 percent on units of records in excess of 500,000 copies and to 13 percent on units of records in excess of 1 million copies. Customarily, the increase is limited to album sales in the United States through customary retail channels (excluding budget records, mid-priced records, record club sales, etc.), and so right away, the presumed escalation does not apply to anything close to the total number of albums sold.

In addition, the conditions giving rise to royalty escalations are customarily required to be met from album to album. In other words, if your first album achieves sales of 5 million copies, don't expect your next album to start at 13 percent. It won't. The whole story begins again. In fairness, there is some justification for this in that the second album may require no less a financial commitment from the record company than the first—and perhaps more. But if the prior album sells enormous quantities, the rationale is lost. And, since record companies cross-collateralize album costs and royalties back and forth among albums, it is disingenuous to argue that each album "stands on its own" when it comes to escalations. ("Cross-collateralization" refers to the record company practice of recouping expenses payable according to one agreement with an artist or producers from monies received as a result of any other agreement with that same artist or producer. It also refers to the universal practice of charging costs incurred with respect to one specific product—for example, an album—against earnings generated by another.)

In the digital age, the concept of royalty escalations has taken on a new twist. Notice that I referred above to "units" as the standard measurement against which the escalations are applied. What if there are no units? What if the sale occurs in cyberspace? Since record companies traditionally exclude any sales except those through "normal retail channels," it has already been established as routine in recording agreements drawn up since digital downloads became a reality that cybersales do not count in the calculation that triggers the royalty escalation. Obviously, as time goes on, the trend toward instant downloading of music or sharing of music tracks will become more and more commonplace and the income generated from such exploitations will increase accordingly, and the record companies will have to adjust the definition of what is and is not a "sale through normal channels."

FREE GOODS

Practically all products are discounted from time to time, except for those that are truly in demand. (You'll never see an Elsa Peretti gold pendant at Tiffany's on sale; nor does Estée Lauder allow its cosmetics and fragrance lines to be sold in stores that customarily discount products.) Yet in the record business, *all* records are discounted to retailers *all the time*. Everyone gets a break from the published wholesale price. This allows some price variations at record stores. But one way in which record companies discount—the distribution of free goods, or freebies, to avoid paying the royalty costs which accompany the *sale* of records—is unique.

Let's see how the free goods policy works.

First, free goods are not free, nor, in the case of digital downloads, are they even "goods" in the traditional sense of the word. Free goods are a fiction created by record companies in order to reduce their obligation to pay artist royalties, music publishing royalties, and union royalties.

Suppose a record company wants to discount a shipment to a retailer for any one of the following reasons:

- As a reward for a long and profitable relationship, giving the dealer a little advantage over other dealers
- So the dealer can sell the record company's record at a price which is more attractive to customers than other records
- As encouragement to purchase a sufficient number of records so that when the record receives radio play, there will be lots of inventory available to respond to consumer demand
- As a show of appreciation for the retailer's payment record

However, as we have said, discounted records are still susceptible to the record company's having to pay royalties. So, instead of selling 1,000 records at 15 percent off the wholesale price, the record company "gives away" 150 records. It can ship 1,150 records, but charge only for 1,000 records. In this way, it has eliminated the mechanical, artist, and union royalties on the 150 "free" records.

All music publishers, and in particular, their powerful and vocal agent, the Harry Fox Agency, Inc., abhor this practice and resist it. However, they often have no choice but to acquiesce because free-goods no-royalty provisions are written into most artist–record company agreements. For the same reason, unions (most often, the American Federation of Musicians and the American Federation of Television and Radio Artists) acquiesce in this practice, as publishers do with the three-fourths mechanical royalties clauses. Were the union or the music publisher to successfully object, the record companies would simply take the excess cost out of the artist's royalty, and their ability to do so is also usually provided for in the recording contract.

By the way, in the case of free goods, members of the "family" of artists on a record label are treated *less* favorably than the record label treats strangers. Record companies will typically pay royalties on free goods to outside songwriters, and often producers with negotiating leverage, whereas it is rare for record companies to pay royalties on free goods to their own artists or to music publishers which control their artists' songs.

Let us revisit our earlier example of how many records must be sold before an artist recoups a $100,000 recording cost. You will remember that at an $0.80 royalty rate, 125,000 records need to be sold to reach this level. The producer will at the moment of recoupment be due a check for $31,250 (25 cents per record) and the artist will be due zero. Now we see that even if 125,000 records are sold, only 85 percent of them really count. The remaining 15 percent were given away for free and do not bear any artist (or producer) royalty at all. So, 147,059 records will have to be sold to net 125,000 royalty-bearing records, at which point royalties will begin to accrue to the artist. Given the additional fact that all record companies establish what they call "special programs" for a limited time period (such as the period of initial release, or the release of a subsequent album in order to stimulate interest in catalogue), "special frees" have to be considered as well. Typically, these amount to yet another 5 percent of records shipped to dealers. Thus, we are not talking about a 15 percent free goods policy, but a 20 percent free goods policy during what may well be the most significant sales period in the album's history. And the effect of this on the artist? Figure it out: in order to get to 125,000 royalty-bearing records, 156,250 have to be shipped and sold. Someone is doing quite well here. Certainly not the artist (or even the producer).

LOST OR MISPLACED ROYALTIES

Every year, millions of dollars of royalty monies that might be paid to musicians and composers are never applied for, or misplaced, due to the failures of our country—or our industry's legal and financial community—to keep current both with international copyright developments which provide certain entitlements to intellectual property holders and with the advancement of technology. Even lawyers who regularly practice entertainment law find it difficult to keep current with the "initials of the day": GVL, AHRA, WIPO, GONG, GATT, and TEA, to name just a few. However, the economic health of the music industry is strongly impacted by the laws and treaties and interests represented by these letters. Here I will mention only two of them: GVL (Gesellschaft Zur Verwertung Von Leistungsschutzrechten mbH) and AHRA (the Audio Home Recording Act).

Neighboring Rights

First, an explanation of this somewhat mysterious island of intellectual property protection is in order. The concept known as *neighboring rights* applies only to performers, record companies, and record producers. Its universe encompasses only the sound recording—not the underlying musical composition. Frank Sinatra's heirs receive nothing from the multitude of "New York, New York" performances at Yankee Stadium—many of which are televised; Bing Crosby's heirs receive nothing from the incessant play of "White Christmas" during the Christmas season. Nor do Ringo Starr and Paul McCartney receive anything from the innumerable performances of the Beatles' recordings over the air. Nor do Britney Spears, 'NSYNC, or the Backstreet Boys. Nor do their record companies or producers. Why not? Because the United States has never recognized neighboring rights—rights not actually conferred by existing copyright law but, rather, rights that are "neighboring" to traditional rights conferred by copyright laws. Most other industrialized nations have.

Almost all European countries, as well as many Eastern European countries and China and Japan, have their own versions of neighboring rights laws. (In Russia and in some other countries, the performance may include a dramatic production, and need not be recorded on a "record"; if a live dramatic production is broadcast, a neighboring right has been exercised.)

The fee structures and payment processes established by the organizations set up to license neighboring rights are not dissimilar to those established by the performing rights and mechanical rights societies around the world. Customarily, fees are negotiated separately from performing rights societies' negotiations with broadcasters. Of course, all of these organizations are champing at the bit now that the term "broadcasting" has taken on new meaning because of "broadcasts" via the Internet. Some dot-coms are attempting to dismiss the expansion of neighboring rights to the Internet because there is no actual "wire transmission." Or is there? Stay tuned.

One neighboring rights law, the GVL, due to the strength of the Deutschmark during the 1990s, has become one of the more financially successful versions of income-generating laws that go beyond the traditional mechanical, performance, synchronization, and print classifications. This German law codifies compensation for neighboring rights in Germany. The GVL is not the only organization in the world that has succeeded in enforcing claims of record producers (that is, independent producers as opposed to record companies under whose auspices records are "produced"), but it has generated large sums of money for those producers who are citizens of European Union countries. The record producers' claims are based on the argument that their contributions to the creation of the ultimate master recording are as worthy of on-going fees commensurate with the success of the recording as are artists' contributions, and hence producers are just as entitled to neighboring rights income as the artists themselves.

At present, neighboring rights money comes predominantly from radio and television broadcasters that play music for profit. While these broadcasters are used to paying fees to music publishers and songwriters for performances of their music which the broadcasters facilitate, in many countries—including the United States—they have no obligation to pay record producers or artists a similar fee. These rights have been debated for years in the United States, but the forces in favor of them have never won the battle.

Resistance to the passage of broader neighboring rights laws has been generally effective in the United States. Not only are broadcasters against the expansion of their responsibilities to intellectual property holders, but performing rights societies are also resistant to this expansion because of fears that the fees applied to the neighboring rights licenses would come out of money traditionally due to them. (Times are changing a little bit, however. For example, under the Digital Performance Right in Sound Recordings Act of 1995, digital performances now constitute protected neighboring rights in the United States and the owners of digital rights in sound recordings are now permitted to license these rights for fees.)

Internationally, there is also a trend toward expanding neighboring rights protection. Canada has recently instituted a neighboring rights law that, for the first time, allows Canadian recording artists (such as Bryan Adams) to share in the broadcast success of their CDs, just as the writers and publishers of the songs do. Americans cannot benefit from this law because, as with most intellectual property laws, there must be reciprocal treatment of Canadians in the United States in order for the Canadian music industry to provide such royalties to Americans. There is no such law in place, and the result is obvious.

The lesson to be learned here is that where recording artists or record producers are citizens of countries which recognize neighboring rights, there is a substantial likelihood that they will earn these rights not only in their own country, but in all other countries of the world that recognize neighboring rights. A citizen of the United Kingdom who produces an American artist will have an opportunity to increase his or her income significantly if someone registers the records he or she produces with all of the organizations in the European Union. There are, as one would expect, international collecting federations whose strength is the identification of works around the world via sophisticated data-processing techniques. They can assist artists and record producers in asserting their claims to neighboring rights money which would otherwise simply drift away to someone else.

AHRA ROYALTIES

In 1990, Congress passed the Audio Home Recording Act (AHRA) in direct response to the concern of music rights owners that home copying of recordings was having an enormous impact on the sale of records through traditional means. The AHRA requires the manufacturers of devices whose primary purpose is to make digital music recordings for private use (e.g., audiocassettes and Minidisc and DAT recorder/players) to pay a statutory royalty on each device and piece of media sold, with the receipts to be distributed to those whose income would be directly diminished by unauthorized copying: songwriters, record companies, and musicians' unions. It also requires manufacturers to implement a serial copyright management system (SCMS) which would prevent all but first-generation copies.

But the problem with the AHRA is twofold: First, it does not cover copying via computer hard drives and CD-Rs (CD-recordable devices), the method of choice for 99 percent of today's music copiers. Second, there are numerous possibilities for technically circumventing the SCMS. How Congress could pass a law that ties itself to a particular technology, rather than the use sought to be protected against, is beyond comprehension. As with neighboring rights, the fallout reaches beyond our borders. Why should countries whose laws *do* cover AHRA-excluded copying methods pay royalty income to U.S. interests when the United States does not provide reciprocal rights to *their* copyright holders?

ACCOUNTINGS, AUDITS, AND THE STATUTE OF LIMITATIONS

More problems arise for artists out of accounting provisions in a recording artist contract than out of just about any other provision. When artists are dependent on a record company to determine the sales of a recording and the amount of royalties due them, many factors come into play and there are innumerable concerns that arise, all of which need attention.

For example, many companies provide accounting documentation (that is, royalty statements) only when there are royalties "shown to be due." If the record company shows the incorrect amount of royalties due, then according to this language, they did not err by paying you only what the accounting "shows" to be due. If they show no royalties to be due, they may not even send a statement indicating the number of records sold during the accounting period. Furthermore, as we have seen, it may be a very long time before any royalties are actually due ("shown" or otherwise), and so this may result in the artists never receiving a statement establishing the sales history of their records over the various accounting periods, including information on total sales; where and to whom records were sold, and at what price and with what tax consequences; and whether and to what extent reserves against the eventuality of returns were maintained (see below); and whether there actually *were* any returns. Similarly, information on records sold by foreign licensees or affiliates of the principal contracting record company will not be provided. Yet without this information, the sales history of a record is hazy at best and impossible to determine at worst.

There are as many variations of accounting statements are there are companies. Only highly sophisticated accountants can rummage through the plethora of information that a record company will thrust on them during an audit in order to determine the veracity of the statements. Unfortunately, the language of the contract itself often controls the options available. As a result, artists may, in the end, be denied even their agreed-upon share of royalties due simply to the manner in which accounting statements are prepared and issued. (See Chapter 12 for a more detailed discussion of royalty audits.)

Truth in Royalty Statements

As stated earlier, all recording agreements provide that the company has the right to withhold royalties on a specified percentage of records sold, in anticipation of returns. (All records are distributed on a 100 percent guaranteed return basis, resulting in the bizarre possibility that every record ever shipped to a dealer might eventually be returned for credit one day.) These provisions have potentially far-reaching implications.

Let's say that, contractually, the record company is allowed to withhold royalty payments "in reserve" on 15 percent of all records shipped. At the same time, 15 percent of the shipped records constitute "free goods." Now, if 100 records are returned, shouldn't only 85 of them be charged against the artist's account, since the artist would never have received royalties on the remaining 15—the "free" goods—anyway? Now that we have answered that question, how many of the 100 records should be subject to the 15 percent *reserve* right? All of them? Eighty-five of them? Shouldn't returns be applied against the artist's account in the same proportion as they are shipped—that is, with a 15 percent reserve?

Now, suppose that during a particular accounting period, 1 million records recorded by a particularly artist have been manufactured and 750,000 have been shipped to dealers. Presumably, 250,000 records would remain in the record company's inventory at its manufacturing facility or at its branches. What might the artist's accounting statement look like? First of all, the actual manufacturing data will probably not appear, because, contractually, the record companies do not have to provide that information. Will the number 750,000 appear? No. Because this number, as we have seen, does not really reflect the number of royalty-bearing records. Theoretically, *that* number is calculated as follows: first the 15 percent free goods deduction is taken (85 percent of 750,000 is 637,500); then the reserve clause is applied, resulting in 541,875 units (15 percent of 637,500 is 95,625). So, given that 750,000 units have been shipped, the artist should reasonably expect that royalties will be calculated on 541,875 units, as it is still too early for actual returns to occur.

But what if the accounting statement shows royalties calculated on only 250,000 units? Is there any way to know whether this reflects a true accounting of the number of records sold during the accounting period? The answer is no. Why? Because the record companies will invariably deny the artist and his or her auditor access to manufacturing data, inventory numbers will never be provided, free goods will not be separately accounted for, and an accountant would need a crystal ball to identify how many units have been held in reserve. Sorry.

Clearly, it is very important that all accounting provisions be carefully and thoroughly considered. Their language will determine whether the artist ever receives even what the royalty provision, on its face, appears to say should be due, however problematic that provision may be in the first place.

Finally, suppose that you or your accountant suspect that, due to shady or haphazard or undisclosed accounting procedures, you have not received the royalties that are due to you. What recourse do you have? Your only legal recourse is to demand that the company open its books to an audit. But artists do not get the same benefit as all other citizens when it comes to such pursuits. Remember in the film *The Sting* when the Newman/Redford operation ran out of money and could not cover Robert Shaw's bet? They shut him out. They waited until the horse race had begun and then closed the betting window. Record companies do the same thing. Just as artists begin to get a feel for the flow of royalties in relation to the success they are having, their right to audit is closed down. (See Chapter 12, the section on statues of limitation, page 180.)

The increasingly effective alliance of artists—the Recording Artists Coalition (RAC; website, www.recordingartistscoalition.com)—has begun to look into the fundamentally unfair nature of royalty statements issued by most every record company. The RAC has enlisted the aid of the Democratic Party to introduce legislation dubbed the "Artists' Bill of Rights" that addresses injustices suffered by artists. Issues of importance to RAC include what they claim are unfair accounting practices on the part of record companies and the repeal of California legislation that has allowed record companies to enforce contracts based on the number of albums delivered, thereby circumventing the 7-year limitation that applies to other personal service contracts in California.

THE EFFECTS OF DIGITAL DOWNLOADING ON PRICING AND ROYALTIES

As technology continues to outpace the law, new methods of exploiting records are being discovered on a regular basis. The widest manifestation of these is the DPD distributed via the Internet—in essence, the electronic transfer of sound (with or without video images), digitally, without an intervening sound carrier such as a CD or cassette. Methods of exploiting these DPDs are also undergoing evolutionary processes such as the advent of subscription services offering digital downloads of limited, and even unlimited, quantity and duration.

It is evident that if the original grant of rights provisions (rights granted to the record company by the artist) in a record contract include electronic rights such as are utilized in downloading digital copies of music (and it is likely that they will be interpreted to do so), it is going to take a wizard to figure out the extent to which the royalty provisions apply to such new technological advancements as digital downloads, streaming, and webcasting. Areas of particular concern include the territory of the sale, release commitments, determination of the royalty rate, licensing of these rights to third parties, their long-term availability, and their price.

Territory of Sale

Chapter 17 discusses some of the issues involved in determining exactly *where* digital downloads may be said to take place. What country is identified as the country of sale will have on impact on royalty calculations. For example, if the download occurs in a country where the record company is entitled to pay a reduced royalty, does that royalty rate apply, or is the applicable royalty rate that which is in effect in the territory in which the server is located—or where the original content provider is located?

Determining territoriality also impacts the recording agreement's provisions relating to release commitments. What if the Internet server is located within the United States and the actual physical record is never released outside of this country? If artists have the right to recapture their records in territories in which the record company fails to honor its release commitment, should they, then, have the right to claim reversion of their rights for those portions of the world in which the record was not released in hard copy form? And if they do, can they not then offer the record for sale via the Internet, which will have the effect of global availability, thereby interfering with the exclusive rights of the record company?

Determining the Royalty Rate Base in Digital Downloads

What should the royalty rate for DPDs be based on? List price? Receipts? List price with a discount? Once the volume of digital downloads reaches some kind of critical mass, record companies are going to be hard-pressed to explain why those costs traditionally accompanying the manufacture and distribution of a record should have any place at all in the scheme of calculating entitlements of the record company and the artist. (For purposes of this portion of this chapter, I am treating the interests of producers and artists as being in synch with each other, since producers' entitlements are most usually tied in to those of the artist.) For example, the cost of artwork development and production, jewel boxes, CD manufacturing facilities, and per-unit manufacturing costs as well as packaging the product, packing the product for shipment, and other shipping costs should be out the window when all the record company must do is to provide A&R and marketing services and present a digitized version of the music and lyric track to a server.

On the other hand, some costs will be specific to the sale of DPDs. The costs associated with credit card enablers; perhaps some "agent" or "dealer" fees to third-party website providers; conversion costs incurred in the course of digitizing music files; the cost of maintaining servers; and the cost of lost sales due to piracy or, conversely, the cost of preventing digital files from being pirated are all new. And, of course, record companies will remind us that the high costs of production, marketing, promotion, advertising, tour support, videos, and the like have not been discontinued once an artist's music is offered for transmission over the Internet. And they do have a point.

However we look at it, coming up with new royalty formulas on the basis of these changes will be no small task. And perhaps *no* royalty formula will be applicable.

Royalty Payments vs. Licensing Fees

The question here is, Is a digital download a sale at all? The mere concept of royalty—and many of the now-antediluvian deductions on which royalty bases are formed—may be unworkable in the context of electronic rights. What is a digital download, if not a license? In licensing situations, the traditional record contract already recognizes that receipts derived from licenses should be shared. The split is usually 50:50.

How can record companies reconcile the nature of a digital delivery of *any* kind with the application of a royalty rate based on the retail or wholesale price of hard goods—sound carriers—such as CDs? Whether a download, webcast, or delivery via streaming, if we are to ignore the record company's reminder that their regular costs of making *any* artist successful remain constant, there is very little direct cost in getting the music into consumer's hands (or at least into their computers—and soon into their televisions—whether or not on a permanent basis). Remember, consumers are not buying a bricks-and-mortar product. Most intellectual property experts feel that, at most, consumers are obtaining a license when it comes to DPD deliveries. But try to convince record companies of this. As far as they are concerned, they have sold a record and this sale is no different from the sale of a CD package at Tower Records. If a 50:50 license revenue share can be rationalized in some areas, why not all?

Electronic Rights and "The Catalogue"

Another consequence of the digitizing of music is that the recorded performance will always be available. It will never be deleted from the catalogue. Anyone who wants a copy of it can access via computer and download it. This fact will play havoc with those artist agreements that provide for reversion of rights in the event that record companies fail to keep the artist's records in inventory or in release in whatever format is provided for. Of course the record companies, even today, repackage records from other eras into mid-price and then budget formats—ever aware of the fact that somehow, somewhere, there is someone who might want to buy the record. But this possibility of permanent availability might generate whole new versions of downward pricing (and downward royalties). (See Chapter 7, page 108, for a twist on the traditional view that record companies will own these rights forever.)

The Bottom Line on Pricing

It is inevitable that the distribution of music via DPDs will change the way records are priced. Ironically, as artists begin to acquire a larger share of the receipts, they may be less inclined to want to reduce the cost to consumers. Suffice it to say that at some point, consumers are going to figure out that the cost of getting a record to market and the risk of unwieldy—and taxable—inventories and the horror of returns are less than they used to be, and in the face of this reduction in both cost and risk, they are going to want some financial consideration. Already antitrust cases are being brought against the major record labels, both in the United States and in Europe, to stop the process of price fixing and to allow the market to set a practical and appropriate price for the product, whether it is a hard product, such as a CD, or a DPD.

Ordinarily, when negotiators either compromise on a point, or decide it is not worth arguing, they understand the implications of what they are doing. In the case of negotiating the impact of DPDs, however, no one can even imagine the consequences of failing to get it right; and no one even knows what getting it right means.

In the end, artists will probably pay the price for the current lack of precision in artist-record company negotiations and for the lack of clarity in achieving an understanding as to where a digital download occurs, what release commitments mean in the digital age, what royalty rate should be applied, whether a DPD is a sale or a license and how this choice impacts royalty rates and release commitments, and whether a record that is available in the Internet can ever go "out of print." And if the artists do not pay, the consumers most definitely will.

The record companies have two rationales for keeping their royalty calculations complicated: the first, which you may not hear directly (but I have), is to confound the artist and the artist's representatives; the second is that the worldwide computer systems of the companies are set up in such a way that these systems recognize only the established (what we might refer to as the "bizarre") interrelations among the various deductions. Anything simple would be a foreign language to them.

Attorneys and managers negotiating these agreements can fight only so hard to stop the avalanche of record companies' initiatives to cut artists' royalties down to where they want them. There is going to be a point when the party without the leverage is going to have to simply give up the fight.

5 PERSONAL MANAGEMENT: The Whys, Wherefores, and Watch Outs

The man that hath not music in himself
Nor is not moved with concord of sweet sounds
Is fit for treasons, stratagems, and spoils
The motions of his spirit are dull as night
and his affections dark as Erebus
Let no such man be trusted.

—William Shakespeare,
The Merchant of Venice

OK, I am being a bit dramatic with the quotation. And actually, I disagree with the Bard—at least insofar as personal managers are concerned. It matters not how musical your personal manager might be. What matters is how dedicated, how energetic, and how imaginative he or she might be. Add ethics and a way with numbers and you're a long way toward having it all—professionalism, enthusiasm, and results.

What values should you apply to your choice of manager and to your rationale for entering into a formal agreement in the first place? Artists are principally concerned with, and principally adept at, only their own art; yet the business aspects of conveying and transmitting this art to the public must also be dealt with if they are interested in protecting their creations, earning a living, and communicating their art to others. What's the thought process that artists should conduct before entering into an agreement with a personal manager? Pertinent questions might include: Why should you even consider obtaining a manager? What would and would not be included among a personal manager's duties? How should your manager be compensated? What should be expected and what should you reasonably *not* expect of this person?

First of all, let's concern ourselves with the schooling for managers. Sorry, there is none. Well, then, what about the licensing for managers? After all, accountants have to be licensed, as do lawyers, even dogs. What agency licenses managers? Sorry again; there is none.

Let's focus on something more concrete, then: the various kinds of managers waiting to assist artists in developing their careers. As you have no doubt guessed, there are as many types of managers as there are one-hit wonders. There are educated managers and uneducated managers; experienced managers and grads who ran the live music programs in college; managers who know songs and managers who know sounds; managers who are attentive to the business of their artists and managers who are as lost in the world of business as their clients profess to be (and often are); managers who are creative geniuses and managers who are public relations disasters; managers who have never left Landsdown Street in Boston, Beale Street in Memphis, or Sixth Street in Austin and managers who understand, or at least are aware, of the world as a marketplace; managers who are happy to have the record company do its thing and managers who are hands-on and make sure the jobs expected of the record company's personnel are done efficiently and on time; in-box managers who are reactive types and handle only what comes to their attention; and managers who are proactive and initiate activities without having to be tapped on the shoulder. There are probably no managers who have either all of the negative or all of the positive attributes listed above, although most managers exhibit at least some of both.

WHAT A PERSONAL MANAGER SHOULD (AND SHOULD NOT) BE EXPECTED TO DO

Your manager is the primary contact person for all of your business affairs, and should be able to act in your place and on your behalf. In essence, your personal manager should operate as your chief of staff in reducing to their essentials all aspects of your legal, financial, and artistic career. Your manager, should:

- In consultation with a licensed booking agent, arrange your live performance bookings, including the size and nature of venues and the manner in which the live performance will be presented
- Work with your record company on everything from approvals of album artwork to coordinating the choice of producer, location of recording, establishment of recording budget, rental of equipment and lodging, travel, promotional appearances, press and publicity, and exploitation of your records
- Assist your attorney in negotiating record, publishing, and merchandise agreements
- Approve allocations of monies expended on your behalf for advertising
- Provide informed advice and counsel on all decisions regarding your ultimate choices of producer, agent, accountant, booking agent, video director, and, possibly, attorney as well.

Your manager should also work with you to establish the image that you wish to project and the manner best suited to project—and to protect—that image, and help you set goals and establish strategies to achieve them.

A personal manager's role is not to be underestimated, but it is not always what you think it is either. Unfortunately, management contracts do not usually cite the specific areas in which a manager provides services. For example, they do not usually include language about insuring that your rent is paid on time, your rehearsal hall electricity bill is paid on time, or that, when you arrive in London to record your album, you are accompanied by a work permit authorizing you to do so. Without it, you'll be on the next plane home—at your own expense. Inattention to these kinds of details can play havoc with your management relationship and your career, and if you do not articulate your expectations, preferably in writing, you are likely to be disappointed.

Before going into details on the personal manager's role in an artist's life, a few words are in order about what a manager is *not* supposed to do. Accept the fact that it is not your personal manager's job to assume your life responsibilities, or even all of your career responsibilities. Too may artists try to delegate to others all of their responsibilities and in the end regret it. Ultimately, we are all 100 percent responsible for all of the decisions affecting our lives and careers. But most of us do not have "managers" or others who tell us or, worse, allow us to believe, that they will look after us. It is all too easy for the young artist to defer to someone who wants to take charge, especially if that "some-one" is experienced, mature, and successful at selling him or herself and his or her abili-ties in a world that most have only read about. Yet artists who look to a manager to live their lives for them and managers who claim to be able to do so are both delusional. You and your manager must also separate your own respective interests from each other's. It is the rare manager who has the objectivity to do this, but it is possible if he or she is reminded occasionally by you and the other members of the team—principally the lawyer and the accountant.

When a manager and artist first meet, they are often on their best behavior, and their wish that their respective interests should dovetail can get in the way of objective thought processes. If they hit it off, and the prospective manager is adept at self-promo-tion, the artist may be so relieved, and so anxious to get the interviewing process over with, that both artist and manager rush ahead to the next step. Their "love affair" has begun. But the curse of many "love at first sight" relationships comes along with it. I often think about how marvelously some young attorneys present themselves in inter-views, only to disappoint after being asked to write their first contract. Similarly, man-agers, even those with the most magical appeal, may disappoint when they have to make their first practical decision. (Of course, sales talent is not such a bad attribute for an artist's personal manager to have.)

MANAGING THE FIVE STAGES OF AN ARTIST'S CAREER
There are five distinct stages in the career of a very successful artist:

1. The beginnings: your career is just starting to develop.
2. The marketing stage—when you are the opening act
   (i.e., your on-stage time is before 9:00 P.M.).
3. Your career is established.
4. You are a star.
5. Your career is for all intents and purposes over, but your legacy
   comprises a catalogue of albums and, possibly, musical compositions—
   some, all, or none of which you may own or control.

Of course, not all artists reach stages 3 and 4, but stage 5 is applicable to everyone who has had even the slightest degree of success.

The roles of the personal manager differ in each of these time frames; the qualifica-tions the artist looks for in a manager differ as well. Ideally, an artist would be able to hire five different managers, one for each stage. However, the financial consequences of attempting to replace a manager as the artist's career shifts from level to level would like-ly be devastating, and so the trick is to find a manager who will grow in a manner consis-tent with the artist's changing needs.

The Beginnings
During the first level of development, your personal manager needs to draw attention to you and build your team—and your chances of success. This is the period of rough

demos, amateur-night performances at local clubs, being featured in workshops sponsored by the American Society of Composers, Authors, and Publishers (ASCAP), Broadcast Music, Inc. (BMI), or the Society of European Stage Authors & Composers, Inc. (SESAC), postcard mailings, preliminary introductions to music business professionals such as A&R people, part-time jobs and, above all, listening and learning—listening to everyone around you, learning the history and the lexicon of the music industry, reading the available books on the business of music, and attending educational forums sponsored by ASCAP, BMI, and SESAC, as well as the Association of Independent Music Publishers (AIMP).

From a musical point of view, this is the time you are sharpening your image, developing your craft, discarding almost as much as you write, replacing musicians and replacing the replacements. It is also the time for concretizing your physical image so that you look the part of what you are trying to communicate. (For some, this is easy. I represented a band which merely wore jeans, and T-shirts which they would remove at some point during the show and throw into the audience. Other bands with fashion supervisors could never match the raw, natural energy and statement that this band had.) This is the time you try to impress on others that you are something new and something special. Long hair, short hair, shaved heads—whatever floats your boat. But a statement must be made or you will be forgotten and melt into the fungible band category and disappear. "Nothing jumped out at me," the professionals will say.

Marketing

This second level of development begins just before you are "discovered" and ends after you have signed a record deal and delivered several albums which have sold in sufficient quantities for the record company to justify expending more money on your career—and not just on a particular single or two. During this stage you are the opening act for a more significant or known performing artist. By this time your professional team is more or less solid, and you and they have to consolidate—and reconcile—your musical and professional (read "financial") goals. Do you begin to appear in public with other artists of the same level of success? Do you start writing songs with them? Guesting on their shows? Do you volunteer your time and services for charitable purposes and do you begin to identify those charities whose interests you feel you can advance by your involvement? Do you reconsider whether your band is ready for the big time or whether you need to replace or add one more musician?

This is the time when your record could be moving up the charts (with a "bullet" in *Billboard*) but is just as likely to fall off the charts more rapidly than it climbed them (with an anchor, in music biz vernacular). This is the time when the "spin" on who you are, what you represent, and where you are going (really far) is most appropriately promoted. Many decisions made during this period are of a one-time marketing nature, but at the same time you will be facing issues requiring decisions that you will have to live with for the rest of your career. For example, should you expand or contract your music publishing relationships? Should you expand your reach beyond the United States into other territories of the world, even as the demand for your services is gradually building in your home country? Do you need to revisit your contractual relationship with your manager and try to determine, with your manager, whether his or her expertise, vision, contacts, staff, etc., can support the next phase in your career without help or whether it is time for your manager to consider partnering up with another—perhaps other-coastal—management firm? Is it worthwhile to move to a booking agency that can couple you with their other acts that will be synergistic both from a musical and demographic level? Is it appropriate or timely to engage a full-time publicity and public-relations firm? A proper consideration of these issues requires time, money, and thought—not just thought on your and your personal manager's part, but on the part of your lawyer and business manager as well.

The Established Career

During the third level of development, your manager must juggle the various duties that are generated by the very nature of your status in the music industry. This is the time during which you are sought after around the world, and you have to make careful decisions about whether your musical style and material need to be modified or whether doing so might end up destroying a formula that works (from a business point of view). Naturally, your musical style and your songs, as well as the instrumentalism of your performing act, will tend to evolve anyway; but many artists have messed up their careers at this point by making decisions which, on their face, sounded right but which resulted in their losing the very audiences that supported them in the first place. Ian Hunter left Mott the Hoople just when the band was breaking in a huge way worldwide. Neither he nor the band ever recovered. On the other hand, Phil Collins left Genesis and Peter Gabriel left Faces to even greater stardom. The Beatles shifted gears, used cellos, then recorded *Sergeant Pepper,* creating a musical breakthrough whose effects are still being felt almost forty years later.

Stardom

It is during the fourth level of development that a manager's true capability is tested. During this period, the manager's role must be to keep the artist on top by, among other things, sifting through the offers coming in for that artist's services and by being the catalyst for other opportunities that may be more fitting and appropriate to that artist's place in the world. The legendary Colonel Parker did not hesitate to maneuver Elvis Presley's career into television and film, even as his recording and performing career was at its peak. When should an artist or group perform and when not? U-2, Madonna, and The Rolling Stones have gone years between tours but one gets the impression that their finger is not far from the pulse of their audience. At the same time, through spreading their legendary status, they welcome new and younger audiences to their shows and as purchasers of their records. Managers can help you to understand the dynamics of your audience. Some use tried-and-true marketing techniques such as focus groups and private polls.

Remakes

Some lucky artists have a chance to reinvent their recording careers; others try with disastrous results. What happens during the attempts to hit the comeback trail is sort of a hybrid between the fourth and third stages. In essence, these artists are going backward, forced to revisit many of the strategies and goals that they had successfully maneuvered years earlier. Barbra Streisand and David Bowie tend to remake themselves—successfully—each decade, reshaping a developing musical style in their own image. Others have not been so fortunate. Blood Sweat & Tears went to Eastern Europe for the State Department in the 1970s, thereby offending the entire political right side of their audience. What did they do to remedy this? They went to Las Vegas to perform at a casino, hoping to recapture it, only to lose the entire left political side of their audience. Pat Benatar recorded a gorgeous jazz-oriented album and was unable to reinvent her Queen of Rock and Roll image. Michael Bolton recorded an album of his secret favorites—classical arias—and has recently set out upon a quest to kick-start his career with a new album and a new, for him, very hip record label. Ricky Nelson's disastrous attempt at Madison Square Garden in the 1970s to modernize his image and win new fans led to his successful, if sarcastic, hit record "Garden Party."

Dealing with the Legacy

By the fifth level, the artist's development is complete. However, there remains a residue of assets, image, and art that require of the personal manager a completely different set of responsibilities, talent, experience, and imagination. It is during this stage that the artist's catalogue of albums and musical compositions need to be attended to and exploited in order to keep them vital. This stage also requires an understanding by your manager and other professionals charged with looking after your catalogue as to what level of exploitation you want—or will permit. Some artists' catalogues are available on every compilation album imaginable—and a considerable amount of money is generated from these exploitations. Some artists' catalogues are available nowhere except as originally released and twenty years later are still selling for $18.98 (for example, the Rolling Stones). Some artists' recordings are repackaged in deluxe editions, "truck-stop" editions, etc. Some are not. How the artist wants his or her catalogue dealt with after the active career is concluded can depend on the financial security of the artist or, if a group, that of the various members of the group. Uneven needs among members of the group can result in conflict. Touring is another area in which a manager can have tremendous impact. Tim Collins believed in Aerosmith after their demise in the 1980s and they returned bigger and better than ever—as a result, according to music business insiders, in large part to the vision and relentless effort of their manager. Bringing back Deep Purple after more than 20 years was a very successful move, but one requiring delicate management guidance as well.

A final note on the legacy period: Your old, dusty and yellowed contracts had better be available or you will not be able to establish ownership or royalty entitlements for such things as "previously unreleased outtakes" or "original demos."

All managers bring with them their own backgrounds, prejudices, and paradigms of what they envision their role to be in the overall context of the artist's life. And, as I have said previously, the different functions for which a manager is responsible beyond the abstract known as career planning—marketing, budgeting, scheduling, promoting, communicating, investing, and training—are all important and each requires a different degree of attention at one time or another. Yet practically, there will simply not be enough money going to the bottom line for either you or your manager to achieve perfection in all of these areas on any efficient or regular basis. This is not to say, however, that the issues should not be brought up frequently by you (or by your manager) and addressed in an ad hoc way whenever possible. A failure in any one of these areas can poison the entire financial and artistic program that has been designed so painstakingly by you and your team.

All the more reason to be careful in choosing a manager and keeping that individual's role under some contractual control. Of course, for some it will be difficult, if not impossible, to find a person who is willing to work for nothing now and a promise to pay a percentage of some unknown sum in the future. The negotiating power—that is, the power to say no—is in the hands of the manager. Nevertheless, a few points of guidance should be useful for any artist, especially a beginning artist, in order to achieve some degree of control over how the relationship acts itself out. You have two principal goals. The first is to find the most *effective* people to represent you to the world. The second is to establish a system of checks among all the members of your team, which is the best safeguard against failure. Any system of checks must be tailor-made for the particular participants, but here is a brief list of some of the ways one can establish such a system.

- A copy of every document signed on your behalf, whether by you or by your manager, under a power of attorney, should be delivered to you and to your attorney; if your accountant should have a copy, the attorney should be charged with that responsibility.
- Establish regular get-togethers among all the key professionals on your team. Set up the meetings in the same way that organizations hold board meetings: have each person review each area that person is responsible for. Introduce new business in an orderly fashion and delegate responsibilities and deadlines for accomplishing these. Have someone take notes and provide a summary of the meeting to all of the participants within a week following the meeting.
- If the workload is getting out of hand or requires the addition of other participants, appoint someone to identify them and set up a procedure and a timetable for completing the task.
- As the workload grows, consider hiring a facilitator who understands how to flesh

out a larger business; but in any event start expanding the organizational chart by setting up committees and subcommittees that can meet without the entire "board" and establish a procedure and timetable for them to meet, identify and pursue their goals, and report back to the "board."

- Set up individual meetings with specific team members as appropriate. It is not necessary or desirable that all team members be at all meetings. For confidentiality reasons, for example, you don't want your tour manager to know everything about your concerns about the financial viability of a planned tour because the information may seep down to hired staff who may make a run for it if they feel their jobs are not secure. It is perfectly appropriate for some people to be invited into a meeting and then excused after the need for their presence has ended. You should also establish regular meetings with your financial advisors starting with your business manager; have your lawyer present at these meetings because it may turn out that you need to engage an outside financial advisor in addition to your accountant to serve your needs. (For obvious reasons, your accountant might not be the first to recommend this.)

- Send your manager to business school. I'm not kidding. U-2's 2001 "Elevation" tour grossed $143 million from 113 shows in the United States and Europe. Prince Rupert Loewenstein, long-time manager of the Rolling Stones, was an investment banker. Many business schools have two-week, six-week, two-month, and longer programs specifically designed for managers of small companies and the lessons learned can be invaluable not only as your company grows, but to *insure* that your company grows.

- Try to protect yourself from all possibilities, whenever they present themselves, for conflicts of interest between you and any of your professional representatives so that you are all in the same boat and what's good for one is good for all and vice versa. As noted below, conflicts can arise when your manager, record company, pro-ducer, and music publisher, or any combination of these, is the same party. One of the successful ways to insure open and honest performance by these entities, whether or not they are aligned, is by inviting their creative and administrative heads into some of your meetings to present their views of where you are and where you (and they) are going; and at the same time, to make themselves available to scrutiny and questioning from your professional team.

CHOOSING YOUR MANAGER

How do you choose a personal manager? Slowly. Carefully. Openly. As you meet more people in the music industry—record company personnel, music publishers, agents, lawyers, other artists and musicians, recording studio personnel, etc.—you begin to devel-op a sense of proportion and perspective. You learn about historical situations concerning other artists and you learn the parameters of trust. You learn to audition those who are auditioning you, to interview those who are interviewing you. Your instincts are useful, but obtaining concrete evidence of other people's experience, willingness to help, and level of understanding of you and your music, plus cross-checking this information with others

The Question of Clout

There seems to be a syndrome characteristic of recording artists and song-writers that encourages them to blame others when things are not the way they want them to be.

Why has your five-album publishing deal not been renegotiated even though you have only recorded one album? It has been five years after all since you received your first (still unrecouped) advance! Why did your record company refuse to finance a second video? Release a second single? Invest more money in independent promotion? Finance your tour to Europe?

Call it Greed. Call it Desperation. Whatever the problem or dissatisfaction is, it could have been avoided if your manager, or accountant, or lawyer had CLOUT. Then you would not have had to deal with these issues because the clout-bearer would have just gone in and simply fixed the problems or made them disappear.

Sometimes, the idea that there *is* such a thing as clout is sold by some professionals—who of course claim to have it—to uninformed artists. It eases the artists' insecurity and relieves them of having to take responsibility for their own careers. But mostly, I hear the term "clout" bandied about by artists, not managers. The truth is that there is such a thing as clout, but that having a manager with clout is not always the road to success. In fact, clout-bearers can even have a negative effect on an artist's career by disrupting relation-ships that have been carefully built over years. On the other hand, many per-sonal managers *can* make a difference. *Their* clout works. My concern, how-ever, is not that you should ignore power, status, prestige, contacts, or proven results from so-called powerful personal managers. Obviously, sometimes, the right call to the right people *can* make a difference. My concern is that there is an overreliance of artists on others due to the fear that only through managers with clout will *the* difference in a career be achieved. I don't believe it will, and if you follow the guidelines in this and other chapters you won't either.

whom you have learned to trust, is the best way to choose an effective manager.

At the outset, you need to consider in what areas you require the services of a manag-er. If you are a musical artist who aspires to becoming an actor, you should find a profes-sional experienced in both fields—or, alternatively, two professionals, each of whom is expert in one of the fields. The contracts, contacts, relationships, and methodologies of these two fields are enormously different; yet the standard management contract typically blends them (as well as other fields) together. If you are interested in a theatrical career, once again you must consider the specific experience of the person whom you would have as your personal manager. Often, the expertise of a given music business professional does not cross over into the areas of musical theater or drama. You certainly do not want to be in the position of having to find a manager for your manager. Rex Smith, the actor, was REX, the hard rock band before his Broadway debut in *The Pirates of Penzance.*

Once you have pinpointed the kind of experience you need your manager to have, you need to consider other crucial areas:

Does the manager work for other artists, and, if so, how many and in what genre?
While you will agree to be exclusively represented by your personal manager, your manager will be free to provide similar services to other artists. (There is at least one positive aspect to the fact that your manager is working for other artists: the fact that he or she will be dealing with an array of other industry people. The broader your manager's access to these people, the greater that person's ability to utilize this network on your behalf.)

Of course, this brings us to a frequently disturbing fact: that a manager who is working for more than one artist may have a time-availability problem. Yet the one-act manager of today, partly because of his success with you, may be a multiple-act manager (with a record label) tomorrow. This is an issue not just of time availability, but also of genre of music. If you are a heavy metal artist, for example, and all your manager's other artists are cut from the same cloth, a legion of conflicts of interest can arise.

You must therefore be careful to question both the time availability of the manager and his or her career intentions with respect to other artists or other functions. You need to make sure that the managerial services reasonably expected to be provided to you will not be materially hampered by your manager's other engagements.

And what if your manager puts all of his or her efforts into your career—full-time? One of the concerns many managers have expressed to me is that if they do so, and are fired without cause, they will be worse off than they would be in a canoe without a paddle. They won't even have the canoe. The manager who has formally contracted to manage an artist should be able to have some confidence that the professional relationship with that artist is stable. This will, in turn, allow him or her to commit more and more time to the artist as the artist's career expands. Traditional contracts that provide a term of representation and a reasonable income participation are eminently enforceable, and an artist who tries to replace a manager in changing circumstances such as those noted above will be immediately reminded of this fact. That's why they call them contracts. So have discussions about your concerns with respect to your manager's availability early and often; once you sign the contract, the issue is closed.

Is the prospective manager related in any way to your publishing company or your recording company?
If so, the conflict of interest potential is fairly serious. You should be very careful to delineate the responsibilities of your manager, your record company, and your music publisher so that each separate entity (management, recording, and publishing) can function on its own, independent of anyone's interest except yours.

Does the manager understand and share your vision—short, medium, and long range?
This may be the most important criterion of all. Your manager must also bring something to the table to facilitate and implement achieving that vision—be it experience, creativity, money, or just being hungry enough.

How assertive (or aggressive) a marketer is the manager?

A good manager must have the ability to energetically and effectively market you to the public and to the music industry. He or she must take a proactive role, particularly vis-à-vis the record company, and must be tenacious. A Scorpio (stubborn—never gives up) would do just fine. A tiger is an apt animal comparison. Your manager must be able to find, facilitate, and create opportunities for you.

Are the manager's people skills good?

An effective manager has to be able to deal with all kinds of people.

How developed are the manager's organizational skills?

We have already discussed the value of organizational structure. While it is not necessary to rise to the level of Robert's Rules of Order, tight organization can be very useful not only in tactical and strategic planning, but in identifying patterns of problems, achieving easier and more effective communications, and avoiding problems before they occur. If neither your manager nor any other team member has the requisite organizational talent to achieve these ends, you and your manager will have to hire someone who does.

What kind of reputation does the prospective manager have?

He or she should have a reputation for dedication, loyalty, and brutal honesty (and *you* must be able to deal with that). You do not need any more "yes men" than will naturally gravitate around you. Keep them around if you want to, but don't pick one for your manager.

Is your manager able to take calculated risks?

A corollary to this is, Can you accept failure if the risky move doesn't pan out? In the event of failure, you must avoid responding by punishment or rejection. In such event, your manager should be open and honest enough to discuss with you the thinking behind the risk taking and how to avoid failure in the future if possible—pushing the envelope while being realistic as to the balance between risk and reward. Short of a material breach of the management agreement, there is very little that you can do to "punish" the manager anyway. Nevertheless, I have seen too many artists turn a deaf ear to the manager and disappear into the ether rather than confront the problem directly and move on from there. The "punishment" too often will end up at the artist's door if he or she has not used the negative experience to build for the future.

What abilities does the person have specific to music?

Your manager should have a musical "sensibility," meaning that he or she can guide you in building your musical team, and in achieving an effective musical entity and presenting it. This may involve auditioning and selecting sidemen for recording dates, and even adding or subtracting from your band if necessary. In addition, your manager must be able to understand the sound system that is or should be installed at your gigs, how to deal with its cost to minimize rental requirements, and how to identify those people who can help realize your sound needs and potential.

How well connected is your manager at that level of the music industry in which you find yourself?

Does your manager have the awareness and ability to make additional contacts in order to achieve the level of familiar and effective relationships that you will need at the next level?

How well-heeled is the manager, and how is the money spent?

Particularly early in your career, your manager should be able to invest money in your career to assist you in wardrobe planning and purchase, outfitting your band's instrument and sound equipment needs, moving you around from gig to gig, and helping to defray your living costs, if possible. (I knew a manager once whose philosophy was not to spend one dime on his struggling artists. One of those artists was so frustrated that he wore a sandwich-board and walked around with a monkey and a cup looking for donations. The fact that he did this most of the time in front of his manager's home office was not appreciated and the two ultimately parted ways. The manager never *did* change his style.) The manager must have enough cash to maintain an office, communications (cell phone, telephone, fax, e-mail), and minimal staff. Your manager should also have sufficient funds to travel where required on your business.

PAYING YOUR MANAGER

There are two basic ways a personal manager in the music industry can be paid: (1) on the basis of one of numerous permutations and combinations of a percentage (commission) of the artist's gross or net income and (2) by a flat fee.

Percentage of Gross Income

Most personal managers seek to be paid a 15 or 20 percent commission based on the artist's gross income, but 25 percent is not unheard of. For reasons I will never understand, rarely do managers receive commissions somewhere in between—for example: 16 percent, 18 $\frac{1}{4}$ percent, 14 percent decreasing to 11 $\frac{1}{2}$ percent after a stated amount of commissionable income has been received, etc.

Why a promised percentage? For some very good reasons. It is quite difficult for personal managers to provide management services without being paid—but that is exactly what often happens with beginning artists. As an artist's career develops, but earnings remain virtually nonexistent, managers must invest more and more of their time, money, and staff (overhead). It is easier if the artist's career starts and fails quickly. It can be a nightmare if the career builds over time (e.g., Billy Joel, Garth Brooks, Shawn Colvin, Moby). For in this scenario, few managers have the wherewithal to dig in their heels for an extended—what may seem endless—period of time. The issue is a financial one, not an emotional one, and it often doesn't matter whether or not the manager believes in the artist. Belief cannot pay the rent, or the staff, or the costs associated with managing a working band. In addition, the accumulated investment, over time, can be enormous. A management business, like any other business, cannot survive without income. Not only are most managers in this situation unable to tap into unlimited resources in order to sustain their offices, they cannot staff themselves with capable assistants who, themselves, have careers to consider. Even successful management companies will not allow a "nonprofit center" to exist for long. Without adequate recompense, good assistants will leave or—worse—be stolen by other management companies with more action—and more money to offer. The only way to compensate the manager-investor is with a percentage of income because if the artist is successful, there really is the promise of a pot of gold (or at least a paid-off mortgage) at the end of the rainbow. No pot, no manager. That's the way it is. And I, for one, cannot blame them. I know very few lawyers who will make that kind of investment in an artist's career. Sure, some will wait a while to be paid and some will shave down their fees to accommodate a fledgling artist. But it is a rare lawyer or law firm that can sustain the kinds of losses that occur when a "baby band" or a band in the second stage of development embarks on a recording and touring career. Lawyers' overhead is usually considerably higher than managers' overhead; a manager is of a different mind-set than a lawyer and is willing to do the things that managers do well and lawyers either do not know how to do or do not want to do (e.g., play emergency doctor 24/7). And lawyers are not inclined to invest substantially all of their time chasing a career of one or two clients for percentages which are traditionally out of whack with those that lawyers, even those working for a percentage, charge in this country. Sure, a personal injury lawyer will take on a case for one-third of the recovery of a case even if the case may take five years to resolve; but John Travolta and *Civil Action* aside, such a lawyer must take on hundreds of such cases in order to sustain a law practice. Lawyers who charge a percentage for their services customarily charge between 5 and 10 percent of their clients' income; but they also are quite careful to accept clients who actually have income and not just the promise of income. They also operate out of offices with associates and assistants. It is the rare manager who does not leave the office, or the city, for that matter, for hours and days—and even weeks—on end. This routine will simply not work for a lawyer who desires to establish a stable law practice.

How does one determine what is a fair percentage of income to pay a manager? Is it a percentage of gross income, net income, or something in between? And should there be a cap, or limit, on the amount of money that will ultimately be paid in the event the artist is really successful? We are entering the smoky and mirrored house of the Manager's Piece of the Action!

On the face of it, an 85/15 split between artist and manager sounds quite—for want of a better word—manageable. Unfortunately for the artist, the manager's 15 percent is almost invariably taken out of the artist's *gross* income. For example, if your live gig brings in $1,000, the manager receives $150.00. Let's say that the costs for the particular gig (hall, transportation, equipment rental, invitation cards, flyers, postage) are $500 and there are four people in the band. Your agent gets 10 percent, or $100. After the manager is paid $150, there is $250 for you to split four ways ($62.50 each). Now suppose that the date is so badly planned (managed?) that the costs rise to $750. Unless you have another understanding with your manager, he or she will receive $150 and you will receive—0!

Of course, this scenario deals with what I described earlier in this chapter as the first distinctive time period of an artist's career—the development level. At that level, most managers either postpone payment of their commission until you are a bit more flush, or forego it entirely. But what happens when things are rolling (the end of the first and the beginning of the second level) and the single gig is expanded to 40 dates, generating performance fees of $25,000 each? The gross is $1 million. Your manager will receive $150,000 (15 percent of gross) and your agent will receive $100,000 (10 percent of gross). If the costs are $500,000 (costs of operation of one-half of the gross is usual), you will receive one-fourth of $250,000 (still assuming that your four-person band splits the money evenly).

So how does the 85/15 ratio which the management agreement allegedly established *really* turn out for the artist? You may have to get out your calculators to see that of the $400,000 paid to the manager and artist combination—the net profits—your manager receives 37 1/2 percent and your band receives 62 1/2 percent. Of the "gross" income, the relationship between you and your personal manager is 25 percent for you and your band mates ($250,000) and 15 percent for your manager ($150,000). Remember the 85/15 ratio? It's long gone. (It never really existed!) Now it's 25/15—quite a difference. As the costs increase, whether (or not) the fault of inefficient management or the inefficient work of other professionals, such as accountants and lawyers, the ratio decreases. If a snowstorm cuts into the number of performances, the costs of the touring ensemble (staff, trucks, truck drivers, lodging, travel, food, etc.) remain the same. This affects your net income more than it affects your manager's percentage of the gross. If the costs rise to $750,000? Well, you know the answer. The manager receives $150,000, the agent receives $100,000, and you receive—0.

Is this exact scenario likely? Probably not. Has it happened? Yes. Has something in between 85/15 and 0/15 happened? Often. Is it ever 85/15? No.

Let's look into how the artist/manager split is handled when you and your manager's representatives are using their heads.

NET VERSUS GROSS

One way to avoid the kind of disparity noted above is to deal with net touring income rather than gross touring income. In this way, your manager has an inherent interest in keeping the costs under control because the manager's percentage will be worth more and more only insofar as your net is more and more. Legend has it that Patti Page (from the 1950s—*Doggie in the Window, Mockin' Bird Hill, Old Cape Cod, Tennessee Waltz*) had a unique arrangement with her manager, Jack Rael, with whom she agreed to split every profit dollar down the middle. What was good for her was good for him and vice versa. If a tour made no money, neither of them did either. (I understand that they parted ways in the late 1990s after more than 45 years—time for a change, I guess.)

You and your potential manager and your respective legal representatives will no doubt spar intensely over whether this approach is as fair as the percentage of gross structure mentioned earlier. You will both try to determine whether it is fairer to *both* parties or only to *one* party to calculate management commissions on the net rather than on the gross. Remember, managers and their staffs invest a considerable amount of their resources and living time to set up an effective tour—even an unprofitable one. And it is not always your manager's fault that the tour does not work. Is it just *possible* that you are a lousy performer? Or a brilliant performer in progress? Why should you appear full-blown as if Athena out of the head of Zeus? The rest of us had to develop on some kind of timeline. You will most certainly have to as well. On the other hand, you are investing a considerable amount of your own resources and living time to write, prepare, rehearse, and perform tours—time that puts into jeopardy family relationships and puts a strain on both yourself and your financial resources. Why should you *not* enjoy the benefits of a net calculation?

In reality, very few managers will agree to a split based on net. Why? Probably because the cash flow to keep a management office running must be maintained on some functional level or the whole house of cards may come crashing down. Eventually, it is in your interest to have a financially viable management, and if that means that a hunk of the gross must go toward financing it, there are many in my profession who will give that arrangement their blessing.

This does not mean, however, that there exist no alternative ways to bring the ratio into some semblance of balance in the event that the financial facts are similar to those in my examples. Here are three.

THE FLOOR

Some artists and managers create an agreement which stipulates that no matter what the profitability of a tour (or lack thereof), the artist, or the manager, or both, are guaranteed a minimum income by tour's end. In this situation, to the extent there are any profits at the end of a tour, the artist receives a minimum amount before the manager, or the manager receives a minimum amount before the artist, or both are guaranteed a minimum amount.

After all, if your manager does not receive a share of the income during the actual course of the tour, he or she may not be able to finance the operation, pay staff—in short, do a good job. Big-time management companies do not have the same cash-flow pressures as fledgling management companies do, but big-time management companies are often too busy, too "above it all," or simply not available to bother with a fledgling act. Similarly, if the artist receives nothing, there is no incentive to continue to tour, thus impacting not only the artist, but his or her manager as well.

When a floor is established, you can provide for a reconciliation to be made semi-annually or annually by your business manager so that the actual contractual ratio (for example, 85/15 of gross income) is reestablished down the road.

THE CEILING

Whereas most people work for a fixed income (often with a contingent or even guaranteed bonus), personal managers work on the basis of financial hopes and dreams. As mentioned at the start of this chapter, they are not paid for their services other than a share of the artist's earned income. They often work for nothing until there is something to share.

But what happens when your manager's income from your career is as good as guaranteed? You, who are creating the income by your writing, recording, and performing, often feel that a cap—a ceiling—should be placed on the income of those who originally provided their services in return for a commission—a percentage of the profits. This is true of booking agents and accountants as well as managers. It is occasionally true of attorneys as well when the attorney is compensated by being paid a percentage of your income.

While "commission" professionals, at the beginning of an artist's career, are risking time, money, and their own careers providing services to artists on contingency basis, there often comes a time when the risk is gone and the compensation is truly out of proportion to the current services they are providing. Who is to say if the cap is fair, or when, if at all, it should be imposed? (For that matter, who is to say when the artist's income is out of proportion to the value of the manager's services? After all, $1 million for two hours of singing, like $10,000 per at-bat for a baseball player, is beyond anyone's ability to reasonably gauge proportion.) Even when your manager's commission is not guaranteed, there are times when artists and managers should revisit the concept of an unlimited commission and resolve to cap the manager's income at some point below which no one could reasonably argue that this individual is being underpaid.

Some artists feel that a manager's job is simply that: to manage. The manager is not expected to "create" and his or her creative and artistic advice is not sought—or deemed to be necessary. For artists who think this way, a cap may be most appropriate. However, in situations in which artists obviously require (and receive) an enormous amount of creative guidance, it is not as reasonable or as compelling to talk in terms of a cap.

Of course, I am assuming that the parties are both able to realistically assess their respective contributions—something that is, regrettably, not often the case.

THE HYBRID

Let's say your manager's commission rate is ordinarily 15 percent. A tour grosses $100,000 and the expenses, including agent, are $70,000. Your manager would ordinarily receive $15,000 and you would receive $15,000. But if the expenses are, say, $90,000, your manager's commission would totally absorb the $10,000 profit and there would be nothing left for you. Some music professionals might say that poor management may have led to this problem in the first place, so why pay the manager the full commission (in this example $10,000 and another $5,000 due later)? In anticipation of this situation, the agreement between artist and manager might provide that no matter what the net is, the artist (that is, the individual or the entire band) will not receive less than the manager. In our example, they would split the $10,000 profit into two equal parts.

As noted earlier in the section on the floor, you can provide for a reconciliation to be made semiannually or annually by your business manager whereby the actual contractual ratio will be reestablished.

The Flat Fee

This variation on the theme occurs mostly when you are an established act and it is possible to quantify objectively the value you seek to achieve from your manager. Much of what management responsibilities entail is quantifiable. Anyone can do it if they are well staffed and half-way organized and funded. Of course, much of what management brings to the table cannot be quantified, and this is where the conflict arises when the flat-fee approach is under consideration. Superstars are not usually any more willing to part with large sums of money than fledgling ones. If they are, their business managers and attorneys will often step in and protect them from the excesses of their own desires (or insecurities). But sometimes they are better off paying flat fees because, as we have seen, percentages have a sinister way of throwing off budget projections. Simple gross percentage commissions can be larger, or smaller, in relation to your net receipts, depending on things often out of your control. With flat fees, the artist has a much better handle on the bottom line.

Of course, even here, hybrids flower abundantly. No successful manager wants to do his or her magic for a fixed amount of money. Thus, thresholds are often established whereby flat fees are payable for a predictable result and a job well done and percentages or bonuses are payable according to targeted levels of success. (Note that "targeted" does not mean "guaranteed.") On some level, all stages of development have certain predictable plateaus of success, but this compensation method is most effective at the superstar level. With luck, the flat-fee scenario will be a subject of interest for you some day.

THE TERM OF THE AGREEMENT

In management agreements, the word "term" can mean many things, depending on the context. For example, the *basic term* is for the period of exclusivity—typically up to five years. However, managers will usually continue to commission, for many years to come, those products (such as records recorded or songs written) during the term of exclusivity. (These commissions are often reduced over a number of years following the end of the exclusive period of the management term.) More troublesome is the provision that after the exclusive period of the term has expired, the manager can commission deals entered into, or substantially negotiated, during the term. If, during the term of a management agreement, an artist enters into what can extend into a 10-year recording artist agreement, and the management agreement ends during this period, under the customary "form" contract, the manager may be entitled to a full commission on every record recorded for the record company pursuant to the long-term record deal. What about the impact of such a provision on an artist who signs a long-term booking agency agreement to book the artist's tours? Is the manager entitled to commission all of the tour dates booked pursuant to such a contract long after the exclusive management agreement has expired? What a disaster that would be. Yet many agreements are susceptible of such a reading, which is all the more reason to question nomenclature and make sure it means not what it says, but what you want it to say.

EXTENDING OR TERMINATING
AN ARTIST-MANAGER RELATIONSHIP

The decision as to whether or not to extend an artist-manager contract past the initial term of the agreement (which may be specified in terms of years, number of album cycles—that is, the period ending a number of months after the release of an album and its attendant tour—or both) often depends on financial criteria, for example, whether the artist grossed *X* dollars during a specified time period. But what do we mean by "grossed"? Let's say that your manager, through cleverness, persuasiveness, reputation, experience, or simply stubborn ability has convinced third parties (record companies, investors, music publishers, etc.) to advance money to you to help keep your career alive in an ever more difficult market? Let's say further that these third parties have been convinced to invest $1 million in your career—such as by advancing recording costs, paying for equipment and costumes, tour support, independent promotion, and general cash advances to keep the band going. Hasn't this manager done a great job? None of this money is commissionable, except for the cash advances. Should you discount the valuable service of a manager, who, through the sheer force of personality, has obtained significant investment so that you can stay in the ring?

Stipulating that such monies are commissionable, noncommissionable, or commissionable in part is the responsibility of the artist's attorney. (The *manager's* attorney should have only one role—to negotiate the management agreement with the artist. Ethical considerations come into play when the manager's attorney acts on behalf of the artist, simply because the manager is comfortable with him or her, or knows he will be protected by him or her, or doesn't trust the artist's attorney.) Suffice it to say that the amount of gross commissionable earnings alone does not tell the whole story of a manager's successful contribution to the artist's career. Yet, some management agreements require that for purposes of a conditional opportunity to terminate the relationship, the amount of money obtained during the specified period of the manager must be commissionable income—that is, only actual earnings—not tour support, for example—to count. Just actual earnings. This amount would necessarily be less than the number established were it to include all of the noncommissionable items.

Another factor to consider is that an artist's perspective at the time of signing with a manager is likely to be different from his or her perspective five years later when the precondition comes into play. For example, suppose the precondition to extend the term of a manager-artist agreement from a two-album cycle to a four-album cycle (or from three years to five years) is the receipt by the artist of gross commissionable income of $250,000 during the first period of the term (or the expenditure by a record company of $1 million of combined commissionable and noncommissionable income to promote the artist's career). Those numbers may look awfully large on day one of the relationship and awfully small at the end of the time the condition permitting or prohibiting termination matures. Yet for a new artist who has never grossed a nickel to receive $250,000 in three years (or to have a record company spend $1 million on promoting his or her record and career during the same period) sounds to me like a pretty successful expenditure of time and talent. But, human nature being what it is, artists do not always concur with this point of view.

Finally, you should be aware of the ramifications of terminating an artist-manager agreement *without cause.* These can extend well beyond the contractual provisions that specify actual sums of money. For example, managers may claim that their relationship is so unique that a replacement manager could cause irreparable damage to the strategic plan the manager and artist devised during happier times. So the manager will seek to enjoin, or stop, the artist from pursuing career decisions within the area of the manager's exclusivity. If your manager is also your producer, and you decide to contest such a claim, you are asking for a complicated legal battle and your career could very well be placed on hold for a significant period of time. This happened to Bruce Springsteen. His manager-producer succeeded in enjoining him from recording for more than a year, claiming that anyone else who acted as manager or producer would necessarily produce a product inferior to what he would have produced. Remember, he was asserting in his role as manager that only he, in his role as producer, should produce Springsteen's records. As exclusive manager, his advice was not being heeded. The inherent conflict of interest was not decisive. There are innumerable examples of people filling the combined roles—I would even say it occurs in the majority of cases in certain genres of music. The consequences are quite serious if the manager can find a court, as Springsteen's manager did, which is sympathetic. The consequences can also be devastating if the artist does not have the resources to bring legal action to right the wrong. The disastrous effects of enjoining a career for a year or more speak for themselves. Springsteen survived the interruption of his career, at some cost; others would surely not have.

Termination

What happens when the criteria established for extension—or termination—of the term of the agreement are not met—or when you and your manager simply no longer get along? Even if your career has developed to an outstandingly successful level, you may not necessarily be able to relate personally with your manager over a tedious and frequently tense period of time, a time during which interests and needs change and goals often diverge. Even the two Sirs (Elton John and John Reid) have broken up their long-term relationship. Contractual issues relating to the termination of the relationship between artist and manager are extremely important, because the relationship may be, for all intents and purposes, in effect for the entire period during which the artist has a viable career potential. And, even when the formal relationship is no longer in effect, a personal manager's financial entitlements will often last long after artist and manager have parted company—on a friendly basis or otherwise.

A word about written contracts. In most states, a contractual agreement of the length and consequence of an exclusive management agreement must be in writing to be enforced. Without a piece of paper that documents the intention of the parties, the parties will not be able to prove to anyone's satisfaction—not even each other's—what precisely constituted their "meeting of the minds." The details of their deal, and even the material elements of their deal, will be totally uncertain. As a result, both parties may suffer the consequences if they have to litigate their respective claims, and time and money—sometimes huge amounts of both—will be spent that should have been invested more constructively.

NEGOTIATED SETTLEMENTS

Obviously, the best course for all parties involved in an artist-manager dispute involving termination of an agreement is to try to settle the dispute quickly. Litigations are costly and time-consuming. And, whatever one may say about the justice system's effectiveness in assisting litigating parties to reach a considered and correct conclusion, you never know how a litigation will end up. My clients have won cases they should not have won, and they have lost cases they should not have lost. Even when they have won, they have lost time, opportunities, and lots of money. I am not suggesting that litigation is *always* an inappropriate route through which one can seek a remedy. Sometimes it is the only one. But negotiated settlements are the preferred route for most people—no matter what side of the table they are on. Even disputes arising absent a breach of contract have breach of contract characteristics. If an artist just doesn't like the manager any more or wants one with more "clout," and if he or she is willing to take the risk, the artist will seek to terminate the agreement and list an array of things that, taken together, he or she might be able to blend into a definition of a breach of one provision or another of the agreement. The point is that when one party wants out of a contractual relationship, a dispute exists by definition, and the parties are thrust into either a litigation or settlement mode.

If the "breach" is immaterial or unprovable, the consequences to the artist are much more serious. The artist may be forced into a settlement that impacts on his or her ability to pay a new manager; the outgoing manager may stonewall the artist, blocking his or her ability to sign with a new manager unwilling to be sued for intentional interference with a contractual arrangement; and the potential new manager may see how the artist has dealt with the old and say, "this one's not for me."

The following guidelines for achieving an equitable negotiated settlement by paying the manager an agreed-upon recompense assume that no provable breach of contract (see Box, page 66) is involved.

METHODS OF PAYMENT

The two most common ways to pay a manager in the event of termination are through a one-time payment of an agreed-upon sum of money, in which case the manager will be out of your life forever, or on a percentage basis. There are a number of ways to pay a manager on a percentage basis.

- You can pay according to a *sliding scale,* whereby you pay a full commission on product (songs and recordings) recorded and released prior to termination; a lesser commission on product recorded, but not released, prior to termination; and an even lesser commission on product recorded and released following termination up to the end of the term of the original recording agreement. Even these already reduced commissions can be further reduced, ultimately to zero, over a number of years following termination. The number of years will vary, depending on the negotiators' respective strengths. A new artist will have to bear a longer phase-out of commissions, if indeed any at all; an established artist will have a shorter period during which to pay commissions on deals entered into during the term of the agreement or records recorded or songs written (and/or recorded) during the term. In the former situation, six years is not unusual, with rates reducing gradually every two years; in the latter, two to three years seems to be the standard. (In my experience, managers will never agree that their right to commissions will end *absolutely* upon the expiration of the term of their agreement with the artist, however long it may last.) But everything is subject to the impact of other provisions in the agreement. For example, if a manager agrees to be employed for only one or two album cycles, he or she probably has enough confidence to believe that if *he* (or she) wants the agreement to extend beyond those cycles, the artist will be pleased to do so. But in return for agreeing not to require a longer term, the manager may demand, and receive, a provision that pays him or her a full commission forever on records recorded or songs written during the term.

- You can pay your manager sliding-scale commissions, as indicated above, but they

Breach of Contract in Artist-Manager Agreements

There are number of ways in which a contract between an artist and manager can be breached. Managers are in breach of contract if they:

- Steal the artist's funds
- Mix funds among the manager's and the artist's bank accounts and, perhaps, with those of other artists as well, making them hard to trace
- Make themselves totally unavailable during key moments in the artist's career development
- Participate in activities that are clearly conflicts of interest
- Are so totally inept as to render the ability to perform the functions outlined in the standard management agreement impossible

An artist is in breach of contract if he or she:

- Refuses to take the manager's reasonable guidance in such a pervasive manner as to be "unmanageable"
- Violates the exclusivity clause by utilizing others to provide the services for which the manager is exclusively selected to perform
- Fails to pay the manager commissions or expenses when due and to account to the manager in accordance with the accounting provisions (in cases in which the artist controls the receipt and disbursement of his or her earnings)
- Violates the "morals" clauses of the contract (see Chapter 7, page 98)
- Chooses to leave the band (when the agreement is between an agent and a group) and pursue a career outside of the parameters of the manager's right to expand the management role from the band to the individuals within the band, including the artist

can be calculated differently from those provided in your agreement with your manager. For example, your manager may have agreed to "stand behind" your recording costs up to a certain amount, but not more; you can modify the base on which the commission is being applied by doing away with the cap (see page 60).

- You can pay your manager according to a revised version of what constitutes "commissionable contracts" as defined in your management agreement. For example, your agreement may provide that your manager be entitled to commission all record contracts entered into during the term of the manager-artist agreement *plus* all modifications, extensions, and *renewals* of such contracts. The word "renewals" is extremely dangerous and will drag along your former manager's entitlements well into what are actually new deals that you and future managers may make. For example, let's say you had a record agreement that expired after the delivery of six albums. Your original manager would have been entitled, by contract, to commission all six of them. Now that you have terminated your agreement with the manager (after, say, two albums), and have been able, through negotiation, to substantially reduce the original manager's commission on the four remaining albums to be delivered after termination, what happens if you subsequently renegotiate and extend the original record agreement? Let's say there are four more album delivery requirements added by the amendment, for a total of eight. The original manager may be entitled to a commission on the additional albums. Even if you terminate the original record agreement, or it expires on its own terms after you have recorded the originally required six albums, if you subsequently renew it, the renewal may be commissionable as well. When negotiating termination settlements, it is important for you and your attorney to catch and change those things which you may not have had the leverage to change during the initial negotiation of the agreement.

Variations on Standard Settlements

When contemplating what an artist can achieve in a negotiated settlement with a manager, there are other things that an artist's attorney can pursue beyond just seeking a reduction or termination of commissions. In situations in which the artist's manager is also his or her production company, the artist can seek to acquire control over the master recordings produced during the period of the agreement, agreeing to pay over to the production company a larger share of income derived from the exploitation of these master recordings. The value of doing this is immense, because you then have the opportunity to keep your catalogue in one place and to utilize the early master recordings for Greatest Hits recordings.

Even if you are not able to acquire control over your master recordings, you may be able to eliminate or shorten the period during which you would traditionally be prohibited from re-recording songs contained on those master recordings. As noted earlier, this re-recording restriction is universal in production and recording agreements, but if you are able to reduce or eliminate it, you will be freer to plan your future—in particular, even if a Greatest Hits album is not a viable option, you will now be able to record a "live" album containing the songs embodied on your earlier master recordings—or re-record a song for a film or TV commercial and keep all of the money generated from it.

In negotiating a settlement with a terminated manager, you can agree to pay the manager in a way that permits you to continue your career or in a way that jeopardizes your career. Don't be precipitous and seek to rid yourself of old problems just to strap yourself with new ones. Fortunately, your manager's interests and yours, perhaps for the first time, coincide, at least in the sense that what is good for you (an ability to pay a new manager without bankrupting yourself) is good for the former manager as well. (A percentage of something is better than a percentage of nothing.) Any commission you still owe your former manager will be meaningless unless you have a career that generates income, so the best thing your now-terminated manager can do is to facilitate the transition to a new manager.

6 MANAGING YOUR BUSINESS— AND YOUR FINANCIAL FUTURE

Charles Robertson is an accountant. If they come any greyer than that they're squirrels.

—Nancy Banks-Smith

Money is better than poverty, if only for financial reasons.

—Woody Allen

How nice it would be to sit back and have one completely trusted person take care of everything but writing the songs or playing the music—maybe not grapes and champagne by the poolside, but a slew of far less appealing challenges and obligations that come up at various stages of an artist's career (like deciding what form of business organization is best, paying taxes, paying bills, auditing royalty statements, etc.). Finding a personal manager who has everything you are looking for is difficult enough. Finding one person who can handle all aspects of an artist's business is not only practically impossible, but, as we shall see, possibly not even desirable. Financial planning is incredibly important, perhaps the most important time spent by artists, songwriters, and record producers other than their creative time. There is nothing wrong with accumulating well-earned wealth and I do not know any of these professionals who are reticent to claim the rewards of their artistic efforts, yet poor advice can easily rob them of their just rewards.

This chapter will describe the choices, risks, consequences, and rewards derived from the multiple ways in which you—the creative one—may partner with others as you begin to develop a business and find the means to manage it. Whom do you look to for the kinds of services that you cannot expect from your personal manager or lawyer? The financial advisor. A financial advisor can have any one of a number of different titles: accountant, business manager, retirement counselor, etc. But before you start planning your retirement, you are first going to need a person—or more than one person—to assist you in taking charge of the myriad business and financial responsibilities you will need to face throughout your career. The accountant's role is more limited than that of a business manager. The designation "business manager" incorporates many functions, including those of tax preparers, personal assistants, accountants, and auditors. Business managers are not engaged to perform these functions as distinct jobs, with separate fees negotiated for each one as would be the case with an accountant. Their very reason for being is to assume responsibility for *all* of these functions *all* of the time. Most artists tend toward selecting a business manager as their financial advisor of choice. Here I explore the reasons why and the things you should look out for in choosing your business manager.

WHAT A BUSINESS MANAGER DOES

Tax preparers, as their name suggests, prepare tax returns. They do *not* help you manage your finances or keep records for you. Personal accountants are of course able to

Certified Public Accountants

Under most state laws, one can hang out a shingle as a "tax preparer" or "accountant" without any particular education, degree, or certification. This is not true of certified public accountants (CPAs), who are highly trained professionals. No one lucks into being a CPA. They have to have a background of business law, financial courses, tax courses, auditing courses, and government theory courses, followed by several years of apprenticeship under other CPAs. Sounds like an old movie? It is. Everything but the green eye shade.

Although one can be a CPA without being a member of the American Institute of Certified Public Accountants (the AICPA), practically speaking, almost all CPAs are also AICPA members. CPA requirements vary from state to state, but most states now require 150 hours of undergraduate education in the accounting field or 60 hours of graduate education. In addition, most states, and the AICPA, have strict continuing education requirements. To remain a member in good standing of the AICPA, accountants must, during each three-year reporting period, complete 120 hours in the accounting field.

The AICPA has recently authorized their licensed professionals to receive fees and commissions from the sale of various financial products, including insurance, which means that a CPA who is also a member of the AICPA now legally can receive a percentage of the investments that he or she suggests that a client make. This is not necessarily a bad thing, but it is something that has in some cases caused clients to experience a "weakness in the force" of protection they had been used to receiving. (See page 82, "Investing: Is Anyone in Charge Here?")

prepare tax returns, but they can also provide assistance on day-to-day financial matters, help you maintain the records you need to best deal with the IRS, and, depending on their training (see Box, Certified Public Accountants) perform audits. The business manager's role is something else entirely. Business managers can often provide the same services as a personal accountant, but they are also charged with responsibilities that touch every aspect of your business and life—for example, setting up the best form of business organization for you, obtaining and negotiating mortgages for your homes, protecting your profits through various savings techniques, paying your personal and business bills, and even working through the multitude of problems arising as a result of a divorce.

It is essential that your business manager be one who can and will agree to coordinate with the other professionals in your life: in particular, your personal manager and attorney. It should not be surprising that there is some overlap in the various responsibilities of all of the professionals counseling the artist. For example, lawyers often look to the business manager of their joint client for estate planning advice and vice versa. It is, however, necessary that the various advisors maintain some consistency. And, although it is healthy to have, and even to foster, some cross-checking among professionals, it is neither useful nor cost-effective to have professionals in one's life who are truly adversarial. When this dynamic occurs, you must confront the issue directly and promptly so that your interests (which, after all are the only interests allegedly under consideration) are well served (as opposed to the interests of the respective professionals whose own jealousies and competitive needs are totally irrelevant to the artist).

Finding the Right Person

Often, an artist finds a business manager, personal manager, or lawyer on the recommendation of a team member who is already on board. While this is a practical and often necessary fact of life, artists should be cautious about the choice of professionals who are recommended by other professionals in their lives. That said, I want to emphasize that lawyers and business managers who are also CPAs are all licensed by state agencies and are very careful not to do anything or even appear to do anything that could jeopardize their licenses to practice. Personal managers are not licensed unless they double as booking agents, nor are business managers who are not also CPAs, and one can be an accountant without being a CPA (see Box, page 69).

Because non-CPA business managers are not licensed, artists must go beyond the title of "business manager" and explore the background of the people they interview. Certainly, one need not be a CPA in order to be a competent business manager, and many business managers who are not licensed have licensed CPAs working for them. They can also outsource work that requires a kind of expertise they do not have themselves, for example, audits.

Audits

An *audit* is an examination of a person's or company's books and records. When a royalty statement is received by an artist's business manager or accountant (or lawyer, particularly if the lawyer administers the artist's copyrights), it is customary for the recipient, or a accountant hired by the business manager, to perform what is known as a *desk audit*. Desk audits are distinct from formal, or certified audits, which can only be performed by CPAs. Anyone who is responsible for collecting the artist's (or writer's) money should take the responsibility for knowing what the artist has done—songs written, albums recorded, synchronization licenses authorized, etc.—so that when a statement comes in, a quick glance can determine whether the statement is relatively accurate. Formal audits can come later, if necessary, but in many cases an error uncovered by a desk audit can be corrected immediately, often avoiding future duplications of the error. In addition, years later, the irregularity will not be subject to the settlement (read: compromise) process that is how most formal audits conclude.

Keeping Track

In most instances, your business manager will be working for other clients, and his or her staff, not the person you so carefully investigated and ultimately engaged, will handle the day-to-activities of your "account." It is crucial to have first-hand knowledge of these staff members, who can range from capable to disastrously incompetent. Unfortunately, you have no choice but to depend on other people to do for you what you would do for yourself if you had the time or the training. Therefore, it is essential that you, or your lawyer or manager, review your financial status regularly—preferably together—to keep a close eye on things.

Many business managers provide to artists on a monthly basis a computer printout of monies received and deposited into their accounts, and monies spent, which also identifies the source of the receipts and the destination of the outgoing monies. Absent is any regular tax planning or budgeting, and the client has no real awareness of the bottom line insofar as assets and liabilities are concerned or any true sense of the total financial picture. On the other hand, many other business managers *do* provide more—specifically: budgeting, profit-and-loss statements, and a monthly analysis of investment positions. The "norm" may be, in part, a function of the ability of the average client to pay fees, since all work costs time and money; but an artist who is generating fairly substantial sums of money, and is otherwise profitable for the accountant or business manager, is not only entitled to this level of service, but probably needs it. But even those who are not as profitable deserve to be advised. Otherwise, they are being short-changed with respect to the services they may think they are getting.

Some business managers (I would like to say all, but this is just not the case in the real world) meet with their clients and spouses regularly—at least twice each year and sometimes four times each year. These meetings should be inviolable. Only an emergency should keep them from taking place. For a touring artist, they can be held on the road. The artist's lawyer, and sometimes the manager, should be at these meetings. Then no one can claim to have been left out of the loop.

Having meetings on a regular basis will accomplish many things. First, it will educate the artist and his or her advisors so that after a reasonable period, they will all be able to comprehend the financial realities of the artist's situation. It will speak loudly, and in no uncertain terms, as to the reality of the artist's financial life. Can the artist afford a new house? Another child? A break from touring? A customized bus on the road? A divorce? Second, it will highlight where the artist needs to focus—on increasing income, decreasing expenses, or even redistributing income or expenses.

In fact, not all clients really *want* to know the truth about their financial health. They prefer to be "in denial," despite the fact that avoiding financial reality can put them into the very position they were fearing: total collapse of security and a loss of everything they have built up over the years. So in whose hands is the responsibility for the psychological cure going to be placed? The business manager's. This may sound like a deferral of responsibility from self to others, but the truth is that we have advisors and pay advisors precisely for this reason: to do their job. Ironically, the manager and the lawyer who do not point out to the client perceived inadequacies in the performance of the business manager's services are not doing *their* jobs. Of course, the information and the expertise are not always available to the other professionals and this is another reason to have periodic meetings among all of them. In such circumstances, no one can later plead ignorance, and in the best scenario information will be exchanged that will benefit the client by allowing reality to sink in. Decisions based on reality will obviously be more sound than those based on ignorance or—worse—fantasy.

Speaking of reality, here is an example in which an artist can be jolted into the truth. A good business manager will always give you the bad news as well as the good. When the IRS or state department of taxation examines a taxpayer's books and records, if a deficiency is found, not only does it have to be paid; the final audit report is supposed to be signed by the taxpayer. If your business manager is not straightforward with you because the deficiency (plus interest and penalties, of course) is due to the business manager's failings, he or she might sign the document on your behalf. The business manager will already have your power of attorney in order to sign checks, open bank accounts, etc. Who could anticipate that this fairly routine power might be abused? In such a case, you wouldn't suspect anything was wrong unless you were diligently observing the ins and outs of your bank account. On the other hand, the reality of this situation would sink in fast if everyone bit the bullet and you were handed the audit report for signature. From a business manager's point of view, there is value in the sign-off, as it gets the manager off the hook because it is a formal declaration that the client has examined and understood the result of the audit.

AUDITING THE AUDITOR

If you suspect your business manager (or accountant) of shady practices, or of not following generally accepted accounting procedures, you are perfectly within your rights to institute an audit of that person's books. The value of such a process is variable and depends on a number of factors, including how large your business is and how likely you think it is that the proper procedures are not being followed. Of course, the auditor an artist chooses to examine a business manager's books and records must not be the same person who prepared the artist's tax returns. Sometimes such audits will turn up illegal practices (one famous artist's accountant who ultimately went off to jail actually paid his own taxes with his clients' money, audited his own books—with predictable results—and charged the artist with the costs of the audit!). Most often they will not.

The likelihood is that when you secure the services of an independent CPA to audit your business manager's books and records, the report that is issued will affirm that the business manager is (1) not stealing; (2) not doing things that are ridiculous (e.g., putting all of your assets into a checking account earning 2 percent interest); (3) complying with federal and state tax laws; and (4) maintaining orderly and complete files in anticipation of a future IRS audit.

WHAT KIND OF BUSINESS IS BEING MANAGED?

If you are a sole proprietorship and rent a van to go to a gig or if you are a corporation and rent a van to go to a gig, which rental car expense is more likely to be deductible as a business expense? Trick question. The answer is, both. Many people going into business for themselves—and artists are no exception—are motivated to incorporate simply because they believe that unless you have a corporation, you cannot deduct certain business expenses. This is a myth. If you spend money for business purposes, it is

Should You "Do Business As . . ." or Form a Partnership?

A dba is a totally legitimate form of business. But while it cloaks you as a business (banks love them), it does not provide the shelter from liability that a corporation does. Investors do not find the dba an appealing business structure either. From an estate planning point of view, a dba can also complicate your life because there is no differentiation between you and your business. Let me put it another way. The risks and financial liabilities that characterize your dba are absorbed into your own personal identity—and this can have an extremely negative impact on tax planning for yourself and for your family.

If there are other people who make contributions to your business and share in the profits (and losses), depending on what kind of contributions they make, you might want to form a partnership, where each partner has an interest in the earnings and a responsibility for the losses consistent with such person's partnership interest. If three partners are all equal, they share these equally. Any variation is possible. But partnerships are not usually favored among individual creative people and investors, because the artistic contributions are customarily provided by only one partner and there is no rationale for a partnership structure.

deductible. Period. You do not need a corporation to do this. The Internal Revenue Code does not distinguish between business expense deductions listed on a 1040 (Schedule C) and those listed on a corporate tax return. Despite this, many accountants will suggest that deductions taken by corporations are more likely to survive an auditor's sharp eye, or that the IRS regards a corporation as somehow more "legitimate" than a sole proprietorship (a so-called dba, which stands for "doing business as") or a partnership.

Performing rights societies do not require a music publishing affiliate or member to be a corporation. John Jones Music (a dba, with a tax identifying number which is the same as John Jones' own social security number) is just as viable an entity as a corporation called John Jones Music, Inc.—and a whole lot cheaper to form and to maintain.

One reason often given for forming a corporation is that with sole proprietorships and certain kinds of partnerships, the individual (or, in the case of general partners, the partners) is personally liable for the debts of the business. In contrast, the risk of loss for one who has incorporated is generally limited to the value of the corporation, hence the term *limited liability*.

Another is that incorporating gives you—and your manager—more control over your finances. To some extent that is true. If your business is a corporation, you are paid a salary, and within a few days, withholding tax is sent to the government. Unincorporated businesses are required to file—and pay—estimated taxes four times a year (April 15,

June 15, September 15, and January 15), which takes far more planning and more careful money management. Note two things about these dates: first, the April 15 date coincides with the date on which the personal tax return for the prior calendar year must be filed. A double whammy. Second, there are no estimated taxes due during the summer or the Christmas holidays—times when most people incur out-of-the-ordinary expenses for vacations, gifts, etc.—yet overspending during these periods may result in difficulty meeting the September and January payments, respectively. If you are incorporated, you do not have to plan for those dates; otherwise, you and your business manager must burn them into the calendars of your minds.

Despite the latter advantages, I am not a big fan of establishing a corporation unless it is absolutely appropriate—and timely. First, although I hate to say it, many lawyers and business managers set up corporations for profit-making reasons. The out-of-pocket cost to establish a corporation is in the $500 to $600 range, and the fee for doing the paperwork is about the same. So the total cost is something in excess of $1,000. Set up 100 a year and you're talking $50,000 in fees. Easy money.

In addition, the costs associated with incorporating are not limited to the initial set-up costs and fees. There is an annual franchise fee for the privilege of having a corporation, and you must file two sets of tax returns: your personal tax return and the corporation's returns.

And then there is the little discussed, and less understood, provision of the Internal Revenue Code establishing the personal holding tax. This is a tax that the U.S. government has established to penalize persons who set up corporations solely to *appear* to be a functioning corporation, whereas the real reason for setting up the entity is to avoid ordinary taxes. After all, the sole shareholder usually takes out 100 percent of the earnings, after expenses, as salary, which is no different from what that person would have done had the business been a sole proprietorship. Because of this long-standing provision of the tax code, an artist who creates his or her own income (i.e., as a producer, artist, or songwriter as opposed to a company that makes records created by others or publishes songs created by others) runs the risk annually that his or her corporation may be designated a personal holding company. In fact, the tax preparer is *obligated* to check off a box on the corporation tax return specifying that such a company is in fact a personal holding company. Who needs this? The personal holding company tax is significant. I have been told by a highly regarded tax attorney that it can actually amount to as much as 100 percent *or more* of the gross income of the corporation once all the applicable taxes have been taken out and interest and penalties assessed. Hard to believe, but apparently true.

However, while the IRS may not "like" a sole shareholder taking 100 percent of the income of the corporation (after expenses) as salary, audits are not automatic and I understand that there is a high rate of success in winning these audits, so one should act accordingly. It is one of those provisions in the law that judges do not value as much as the enforcers do. For more about the personal holding company, see page 78.

Forming a Corporation

There are several types of corporations that you can establish: a traditional C corporation; an S corporation, and an LLC (limited liability corporation). Which one you establish may depend on whether you are a songwriter, producer, or recording artist—or some combination of both—and whether you are an individual or a group.

An *S corporation* is a corporation that has been "branded" special by the stockholder(s) because its purpose is really to protect against liability and would probably not exist but for that benefit; the IRS has determined that this kind of corporation should not subject the shareholder(s) to the same kinds of rigid standards that normal C corporations are subjected to and should allow the shareholder(s) essentially to deal with their corporation as if it were a sole proprietorship; thus if there is a loss in any given year, the loss can actually be taken by the individual shareholder(s) rather than be retained in the corporation. If an S corporation has one shareholder, it is taxed as a sole proprietorship; if it has more than one shareholder, it is taxed like a partnership. In either case, there is no possibility of being taxed twice on the same income.

The S corporation, which is not subject to a personal holding tax, is not for all people. For example, a foreign citizen (one without an alien resident green card) cannot be a shareholder in an S corporation. Sometimes, a new business manager will notice that a client's corporation is a traditional C corporation, denying the shareholders the benefits of an S corporation. There are ways to convert a C corporation into an S corporation, but there are also risks. Because of the importance of the personal holding company status of a C corporation, the IRS may not want to lose its edge, which it may do when a C corporation is converted into the S structure. Therefore, in such a situation, there is a risk that the corporation, with its new shiny S designation, can be taxed on what the IRS deems to be "excess passive income" (e.g., royalty income derived from song or record earnings). An S corporation that was once a C corporation can have its S status revoked if 25 percent of its income is passive for three years. Once you take out a salary in excess of $400,000 or $500,000, you are beginning to push the envelope and you may draw the attention of an IRS auditor.

S corporations operate on a calendar year basis rather than on a fiscal year basis. In the latter situation, one can legally manipulate the tax "year" in which the income is received. Nevertheless, S corporations still have to file tax returns (1120S). Whereas, for the most part, they do not pay federal corporate taxes, there may be no way to avoid state or city corporate taxes. For example, New York City does not recognize S corporations. The state and city tax can exceed 8 percent and you cannot reduce profits to zero (thereby absolving your corporation any obligation to pay corporate taxes) simply by paying out high salaries. In New York City, there is an alternative tax which is charged without regard to whether or not your corporation even *had* a profit.

Let's explore how these two structures handle profits in the situation in which a company grosses $100,000 and has $20,000 in expenses.

If your company is a traditional C corporation, there will be $80,000 left. If $50,000 is paid out to yourself or to your band members, federal corporate taxes will be payable on approximately $30,000. There are two sets of tax returns to be prepared and filed: the corporation's and yours or those of your band members. If the corporation purchases capital equipment, only a certain percentage of the cost of that equipment can be expensed in the year it is purchased; taxes must be paid on the remainder. So, for example, if the corporation purchases a Pro-Tools rig for $25,000, it may be allowed to deduct $2,500 as expenses in the year it is purchased, leaving $22,500 spent, but not deductible. (This is called depreciation of a capital asset.) There will be federal and state corporate taxes payable that year not only on the $30,000 referred to above, but also on the $22,500 as if it were income—which of course, as a practical matter, it is not. There may not be money left in the coffers of the corporation to pay the taxes on the $52,500. Indeed, if the $30,000 is also paid out as salary to you or your band member, there won't. This reality must be taken into account each time the corporation purchases something of lasting value, such as a guitar or a van, or even if it makes capital improvements to a rehearsal hall.

If your company is an S corporation, the $80,000 in our example will constitute income and will be divided among your band mates. Each band member will be taxed whether or not they take the money. This means that if some of the money is left in the corporation for contingencies or future expenses, the shareholders will nevertheless be taxed as if they had taken the money themselves. Each shareholder files his or her own tax return. There is no corporate tax return to be prepared or filed. Each of the band members can deal with his or her share of the $80,000 in whatever creative tax-planning manner they see fit [e.g., paying some money into an IRA or 401(k)] and the ultimate aggregate tax paid may be well under the tax that the C Corporation would have to pay. The capital equipment purchases, unfortunately, are dealt with in the same way as with the C corporation, but this time each individual shareholder has to bear his or her share of the portion that the government does not allow to be deducted as an expense (in my earlier example, 90 percent of $25,000, or $22,500). Medical insurance expenses are taxed in a similar manner. At the end of the year, the band members are faced with the fact that what went to the insurance company is taxed *as income*. Those band members with extra money can bear this burden more easily; those with less money obviously cannot. Those who earn extra money through songwriting income will be better off than those who do not; those who are married presumably will be less well off than those who are not if their incomes have to be shared among their family members. In fact, the economic disparity among band members may be even more glaring after a year of S corporation activity than it would have been after a year of C corporation activity.

I am beginning to sound like Tevya in *Fiddler on the Roof,* who was fond of saying "On the one hand . . . ; on the other hand . . . ; on the other hand . . . ; etc." But here it is: The C corporation may in fact be more advantageous to you in this situation than the S corporation. For example, you can move money around more easily within the corporation, and you can establish a *fiscal* tax year, which does not have to run from January 1st to December 31st. You can have your corporate tax year begin in September and end at the end of August. Thus, if the corporation expects to receive a lot of money in December, instead of having to pay taxes on this by April 15 at the latest, the taxes can be delayed until, let's say, October 15, or even later. The S corporation, on the other hand, has to maintain a traditional calendar year tax period. In addition, if you are thinking of having investors in your business, they would be far more comfortable with a C corporation or an LLC than with an S corporation structure, which is more suitable when there are a tiny number of shareholders. Even though you are permitted up to 75 shareholders in an S corporation, 1 to 5 is the norm among entertainers.

A partnership does not pay salaries to partners. Their share of profits is paid out as a profit participation, and a K-1, rather than a W-2, is issued by the partnership. An S corporation, being essentially a partnership, may elect not to pay salaries, but it is usually good business practice to pay out something in the form of salaries so that the self-employment tax (social security and Medicare combined) is paid first by the corporation and, subsequently, by the employee/shareholder as well. Under current rules, the first $76,200 of one's salary is subject to the social security tax of 6.2 percent and the Medicare tax of 1.45 percent. If your S corporation pays you a salary of $76,200, the government will be pleased because you will have caused the social security contribution to be made both by your corporation and by yourself, rather than just by yourself, which would be the case if your entire "salary" had been distributed to you as a share of profits. The social security system will have been enhanced accordingly by your "employment." A problem arises, however, with regard to the Medicare portion of the self-employment tax. This portion does not have a cap of $76,200 or, for that matter, any cap. Therefore, if you limit the portion of your profit distribution to $76,200, you will be depriving the government of the employer's portion of the Medicare tax on any excess. Many accountants will therefore recommend that you take out a salary in excess of $76,200—a good faith attempt to take care of your federal responsibilities, even though you are probably not required to do so.

The *limited liability corporation (LLC)* provides for profit-sharing arrangements that used to be available only in limited partnerships, but it also provides the limited liability that used to be available only in corporations. It is a hybrid and one that has proved extremely popular for small businesses and newly formed companies such as are the norm in the entertainment business. The LLC form is uniquely beneficial to artists who want to raise money from investors either for general career purposes or to pay for recording a master or demo.

In the past, the only protection afforded investors in a partnership was for the limited partners; the general partners were personally responsible for the debts of the partnership. Under the LLC, the general partner's equivalent, usually called the *managing member,* has the same unlimited personal liability protection afforded to those investors who are the equivalent of the limited partners in a traditional partnership.

Functionally, unlike a C or S corporation, which must adhere to by-laws strictly regulated by state law, the LLC is governed by an operating agreement, which (unless what you are doing is illegal) can be drafted in pretty much any manner you want. For example, if you want to put together a film, it is relatively easy to form an LLC that has an investor member and a managing member. To do this in a C or S corporation, you would have to have a shareholders' agreement, an annual board of directors meeting, an annual election of the officers, etc. In an LLC, you can have meetings and elections as often or as infrequently as you like. With an LLC, you can also provide that the first monies received from a project, after expenses, will be paid to the investors and all of the remaining monies, the profits, will be split as and when they are received.

It is relatively easy to switch from a partnership structure, which until recently was the preferred structure for bands, to an LLC. You can take the partnership agreement, retitle it, and that document becomes an operating agreement. You have traded a general partnership with no liability protection for an LLC with absolute liability protection. In some states you do not even need to prepare and sign an operating agreement establishing how the company is to be operated. (Of course, having one is appropriate if there is more than one shareholder.)

There has been some resistance in the bigger money markets to public offerings by LLCs. Financiers who are comfortable with the old system tend to resist new structures. The LLC is less of a structure and more of a conduit. Its house is not built of brick and mortar. It does not yell out solidity, thrift, durability. It is worth noting that although technically, no corporate book, no seal, and no stock certificates are required, corporate stationery companies are not going bankrupt; They still create a virtual "corporate kit"—replete with a sample operating agreement and a seal. Although not necessary, it works for organizational purposes and makes people feel comfortable. Now, I am told, even Certificates of Membership Interest (shades of stock certificates) are provided in the "LLC kit," and the managing member will often call him- or herself "president" rather than explain why there isn't any. These are all vestigial remains of the old days.

Despite the resistance to the LLC structure in some quarters, the LLC is beginning to replace the traditional C or S corporation as the vehicle used for furnishing services of artists, producers, and other creative talent.

Enter the IRS

When recommendations are made by business managers and attorneys as to the form one's business entity should take—whether sole proprietorship, partnership, or some kind of corporation—the deciding factor is not only what structure works best from an efficiency and cost point of view, or even what structure works best in view of the possibility of enticing investors to come into the company. What gives these professionals the most pause is what structure permits flexibility within the tax laws without drawing unwanted special attention of the IRS. For example, corporations are often established to provide the services of a creative person to a user of talent. These "loan-out" or "furnishing" companies raise certain issues that might not be present were the client to have simply provided his or her services personally. And then, we are reminded of the personal holding company problems touched on earlier, where I pointed out that there may be reasons to hesitate before even establishing a corporation in the first place.

Having a corporation "furnish the services" of an artist, or having it own and administer one's copyrights, involves establishing, somewhat arbitrarily, a salary for the artist whose artistic creations or compensation rights are integrated into the corporation. Suppose a corporation is set up to furnish a record producer's services and to collect his advances and royalties, and after a year or so, the advances and royalties amount to $400,000. The costs of operating the corporation are minimal—perhaps some equipment, legal and accountancy fees, and maybe some incidental expenses such as unreimbursed travel and accommodation costs incurred while seeking new business. Let's say these total $50,000. The balance remaining in the corporation's coffers at the end of the year will be $350,000.

Now, the business manager decides to pay out to the producer the entire $350,000 as a salary, and the producer pays taxes on this as an individual. But the IRS comes in and says, "You know, that's an awful lot of money for you to earn as a salary; we think your two months in the studio should be worth about $150,000 and that's a wonderful annual salary for an executive of this tiny corporation." Where is your employment contract, they might ask? How can you possibly justify a $350,000 salary for such a wimpy contribution of time and effort—on a Caribbean Island no less (like the legendary Nassau studio of Island Records, Compass Sound). Put simply, the IRS does not like an individual owner of a corporation taking 100 percent of the money out of it for "salary."

So the corporation agrees that the producer's salary should be $150,000. What happens to the remaining $200,000? Why, it is put back into the corporation . . . except for one problem. You can't put back what you have taken out. The corporation winds up with a profit that year of $200,000, which is subject to a tax of more than 50 percent. And, once you take out of the corporation that which is not yours, it constitutes a dividend; this is further taxed so that in the end you have your $150,000 (salary), which is subject to ordinary income tax, and $200,000, which is absolutely decimated. OK, suppose the IRS only disallows 10 percent of your salary, rather than the 57 percent disallowed in the above example. Whatever is disallowed—and 10 percent of, say, $1 million is a lot of money—will be subject to both a corporate tax and a dividend tax as well.

Beyond this, there is the reality that by the time the IRS gets around to informing you that it has disallowed a portion of your salary, you will have incurred incredible amounts of interest and penalties. And that's just the federal tax. Now the state steps in and charges even more taxes, interest, and penalties, and for entertainers who work in many states, there can be multiple state taxes due as a result of an unfavorable ruling by the IRS. There may be city taxes as well (as is the case in New York City).

Worse still, your behavior may trigger a general audit, not only for the year in question but for years down the road. The IRS can go back only three years (unless fraud is involved, in which case it can go back much longer), but it can continue to knock on your door forever. It is not unusual for the IRS to audit taxpayers for as many as five consecutive years once they get started.

The accounting services alone can be enormously expensive pursuing the long, lengthy fight that may be in your future if you play this game. And who receives the money for the defense of your position? Your business manager and your lawyer, that's who.

What were the individual's options in the first place? Of course, to have avoided a corporation. Once formed, and once used to funnel services income, the potential of steep taxation exists.

Another invitation to the IRS ball comes from setting up a corporation that fulfills the preconditions of a personal holding company, essentially one whose income is entirely, or almost entirely, due to the creative activity of its principal shareholder(s). Since the personal holding company is subject to a "gross income" test (that is, the government looks at the gross income of the corporation before it sets out on its rampage to penalize the person who created it [no, not the business manager—you]), one of the things that can be done to reduce the impending disaster is to move as much money as possible out of the corporation's gross income. However, as noted earlier, it is difficult, if not impossible, to get the income-producing asset out of the corporation without creating what is known as a corporate dividend, and the IRS just *loves* to tax corporate dividends.

How does one divert some gross income from the corporation without running afoul of the tax laws? It is not easy, and I refer you to your friendly CPA to advise you on this.

Here, however, is one approach that has worked in the past: Since songwriters are historically entitled to 50 percent of the income from the exploitation of their songs, the IRS would be hard-pressed to deny that this 50 percent can be paid by the exploiting party directly to the writer—not through the writer's corporation. Suddenly, 50 percent of the gross income from the songs no longer flows through the corporation and any penalties that might ensue from the government's determining personal holding company status will necessarily be considerably less than they would have been. Also, the "salary" paid to the writer after the corporation pays its ordinary expenses will be considerably smaller and therefore more likely to pass the "excess salary" test. Using the $400,000 gross income figure from the above example, once the 50 percent writer's share has been diverted (paid directly to the writer) only $200,000 will have been paid to the corporation. After deducting $50,000 in expenses, the $150,000 salary will constitute 100 percent of the money left in the corporation—exactly what the IRS suggested was a fair salary for two months' work. Note that this solution will not work for the recording artist or record producer because there is no similar division of their income into two distinct parts, earned for two distinct functions.

Another possible approach is to actually keep the "asset" out of the corporation and leave only the publisher's net share of income in it. Accordingly, the copyright itself will be retained in the name of the writer and the taxpayer will have the additional argument that the salary is for services rendered and that the corporation is not a sham. Keeping the copyright in the name of the writer has an ancillary value: there will never be a problem removing the copyright from the corporation because it will not be there. If, as part of tax planning, a writer's advisors feel that the writer can begin to "gift" the assets to his or her children (let's say by creating a trust) and perhaps live on the income from the songs/copyrights until death, the writer can simply place the copyright into the trust created for this purpose. Once a copyright has become part of a corporation's assets, however, it is extremely difficult to take it out and move it into another's hands—even your own—because every movement of a corporate asset has tax consequences.

Given all of the potential problems associated with incorporating—no matter what kind of corporate structure you choose—it remains beyond my comprehension why so many people in the music industry want to create a new taxable entity when there is no compelling reason to do so. I don't mean to suggest that there are *never* times and reasons to form one. For example, it may be good business and legal management to form a corporation for touring purposes, to limit liability if someone is hurt at a show. But suffice it to say that walking away from your business manager's office on the first day carrying a corporate "set" of books and seals (not the animal kind) might not turn out to be exactly the thrill you thought it would be. And I suggest that musicians, songwriters, and producers should be highly suspicious of any business manager whose *specialty* is creating corporations.

As I have said, conducting a business through a corporate structure does not legitimize it. Doing so can *add* to your problems, rather than solve them. It creates new burdens, and at the same time may not relieve you of old ones. It creates new work that was not there before. It is not only costly, but, potentially, *devastatingly* expensive. The decision as to whether to incorporate or form an LLC is a decision that should be made by your entire professional team, including your attorney and your business manager.

I think I have made my point.

MONEY MEANS OPTIONS:
RESISTING THE "KEEP 'EM POOR" PHILOSOPHY

When others are handling your money, anything is possible, and everything under the sun has happened to someone you know or have read about. Therefore, I feel it is necessary to describe a particular horrifying scenario. As you read on, keep in mind that if you choose your advisors wisely, and pay attention to what they are doing, it can't happen to you.

There is an old music business theory: keep them poor. Why? Because then they have to work. And if they work, they earn gross income. And if they earn gross income, the manager and business manager (and more and more frequently the lawyer) will commission it.

A client who is content, satisfied, and financially comfortable is not as likely to go back to the drudgery of "the road." The last thing commissioning professionals want is for their clients to retire.

Business managers (as well as managers and lawyers who commission artists' earnings) commission only what artists earn, not what their investments generate, and therein lies a potential for abuse. Even if the client is in debt, the "gross" commissioning professional cannot lose—and therein lies another potential for abuse.

A client wants a new car. He has one by noon the same day. A client wants a new house. He has his mortgage in 24 hours. The business manager has done magic for him. But weren't we all taught there is no such thing as magic? (There isn't.) There is a cost for this convenience and the cost is spread across all of the business manager's clients. The richer ones pay for the poorer ones and the poorer ones are not so well served either because they think they are in one position when in fact they may well be in another. They may receive their mortgage approval in 24 hours; but they may not be able to handle the carrying charges. Most banks will reject a mortgage application if various factors add up to too much risk. You may think there is something inconsistent with keeping the client in debt even as the rich clients pay for the poor ones. But there isn't. Ideally, the poor ones become the profitable ones for the business manager and the cycle begins again.

Interestingly, some clients believe that if they have *some* money, they can do most anything; if they have a *lot* of money they can do everything. This is categorically untrue. And although a fledgling artist may qualify for a car or house loan on paper, once the mortgage has been approved, the artist may end up with unmanageable cash-flow problems. The more you have, the more you can squander. If you had to be careful *before* you achieved your first successful financial goal, you will have to be even more careful afterward.

MANAGING YOUR MONEY

Everyone has trends. Expense trends and income trends. Among the most important functions of a business manager is to identify these trends and to guide the client's expenditures and investment opportunities accordingly. Predicting trends on the basis of data gathered over a reasonably long period is relatively easy. This is especially true with respect to artists whose biggest income-producing years are behind them but who are continuing to receive significant income from catalogue sales. It is less easy—but none the less important—to predict trends for artists who are in the beginning—more erratic—stages of their careers.

Investing: Is Anyone in Charge Here?

Many business managers, like many attorneys, work under such pressure and have so many clients that they cannot possibly give personal attention to each client in a way that the client desires or needs. When this affects your financial health, this state of affairs is truly worrisome. Let's say that you have $1 million in an IRA. How is it invested? Who is paying attention? Is it invested in a money market fund at 4 1/2 percent? Is it deposited into one, undiversified, mutual fund with the business manager's favorite broker in charge of it?

Are your investments, though sound or even shrewd, consistent with your own value system and principals? Is a portion of your portfolio invested in Philip Morris? Is this something you, who have proselytized about the dangers of smoking or alcohol, want disclosed in a tabloid or industry rag? Maybe Ford Motor Company? How about Firestone? Enron, anyone?

It will not surprise you that there is no sure-fire investment strategy that works for everyone. But there are guidelines that you and your representatives can follow and options to consider no matter what stage of your career you are in.

The danger young artists face is to be so tunnel-visioned that they focus only on their music or their fans or their live performances, while all the people around them—their lawyers and business and personal managers—are so buried in the day-to-day effort to make all of these things work in tandem that no one is paying attention to either the economic or the tax consequences of what they are doing.

Although the following information on investments is applicable to anyone, I have included it in this book because many artists, record producers, and even managers, especially those who are beginning their careers, make unwise investment decisions (or no investment decisions at all) or have unwise investment decisions made for them by incompetent—or even shady—business managers, or perhaps business managers who are just too busy to pay attention. If your business manager is unwilling or unable to help you plan your investments, or to help you find someone who can, perhaps you should find another business manager. Forewarned is forearmed.

Types of Investments

Let's say you have a $10,000 surplus in your bank account. Do you want to invest it? Keep it under the mattress? And if you choose to invest it, what do you want to get out of it? The safety of knowing that the entire $10,000 will still be there when you need it? Growth? Super-growth? And what are the down-the-road tax consequences of decisions you make today? How does the rate of inflation affect investments? These are things that you need to determine, with the informed help of your advisors.

FIXED-INTEREST VEHICLES

Certificates of deposit (CDs) are time deposits issued by a bank at a fixed interest rate for a period of time—three months, one year, five years—whatever is offered. When considering investing in CDs, you need to consider what can be serious tax consequences. If you buy a one-year CD with your $10,000 at a 5 percent interest rate (I'll use 5 percent to simplify the math), your return will be $500. At the end of the year, you will also get a Form 1099, a copy of which has been filed with the IRS, stating what you have earned in interest. (The same thing happens if you hold mutual funds in a taxable, versus a retirement, account.) If you are in a 50 percent tax bracket, you will owe the government $250, and your bottom-line return on your investment is not 5 percent, but 2 ½ percent. (One rule of thumb about investment growth is called the 70-year rule: Divide 70 by the current interest rate, and the result is the number of years it will take you to double your money. In our example, taking into account taxes, it would take 28 years. A long time. That $250 you paid in taxes could have been used for further investment or purchase of growth assets—or it could have been applied toward your winter vacation. But it is lost forever once the tax is incurred. Then again, the CD is safe and federally insured. The growth fund is not. They call it risk and reward—this time, little risk, little reward. Even worse, if you retain the CD or its term extends for more than one year, you will not be able to pull the $250 out of it in order to pay your income taxes. The income from a CD is the same as ordinary income. You have to make $500 to keep $250. But in the case of CDs, you will have to find the $250 somewhere. And, since you are in a high tax bracket, you will have to have earned $500 more dollars in order to keep $250 long enough to send it to the IRS to pay the taxes due on the gain in the CD.

Let's talk about some "real" money. Say you earn $240,000 in interest and have to pay $120,000 in taxes. This $120,000 is gone forever. In order to understand the significant impact of this in terms of a life of struggle vs. a life of leisure, consider the following: If the $240,000 were allowed to grow at 10 percent a year (on average, about what the stock market has historically done), it would be worth $264,000 at the end of one year, $290,400 at the end of two years, $319,440 at the end of three years, $351,384 after four years and $386,522 after five years. In order for the $120,000 to build up to essentially the same level, you would need to achieve growth of more than 25 percent for each of those five years—a growth rate that has never happened. Then again, the stock fund is not insured. Risk and reward again.

INDIVIDUAL RETIREMENT ACCOUNTS

The returns you get on the money you have invested in an individual retirement account (IRA) or 401(k) retirement account are not taxed until you pull the money out of them. (Since annual investment into an IRA is currently limited to $2,500, this is not necessarily the best vehicle for you to build a retirement fund; but it is nevertheless a useful one for building a bit of a nest egg—as long as you, or your business manager, keep an eye on it.) Individual retirement accounts are tax-deferred, not tax-free, vehicles. If you take money out of your retirement fund before you are 59 1/2 years old, you are taxed according to whatever tax bracket you are in, plus 10 percent. After age 59 1/2, you are taxed according to your income bracket. But consider this. Not only are IRAs *not* tax-free, they are not even safe havens. On the first April following one year after 70 1/2th birthday, you *must* start taking the money out, according to an actuarial schedule that takes into account how long the government thinks you will have left to live. The trick is to live precisely as long as the government expects you to. If you disappoint them and die later, while you may not have any money left to pull out, they will not have the chance to penalize you for failing to take out all of it before you die. Because when you die, if you still have money in your retirement fund, it will be taxed in the same way as income is taxed, according to what is known as "income in respect of decedent." There are possible estate taxes as well that may be assessed.

STOCKS AND BONDS

A *stock* is an ownership interest—a share—in a company. Stock is issued by the company to raise money that the company does not have to guarantee to pay back at any particular price. By owning stock in a company, you actually have a claim on the company's assets. These are sometimes paid out in regular dividends. Some companies do not pay dividends and your only gain comes when the stock value increases (appreciates) and you sell it. You lose when the stock value decreases (depreciates) and you sell it. Stock prices go up when the company's profits go up or there is a generally accepted expectation that they will. And vice versa. You can own stock directly in a company or through a *mutual fund,* which itself holds an array of stocks from different companies, and/or various types of bonds. Some brokers specialize in studying stocks, researching the companies issuing them, and charging a hefty commission for buying *or* selling them on your behalf. Others—discount brokers—discount the commission, but they expect you to do your own research.

A *bond* is what you receive after you have lent a corporation, a municipality, or the U.S. government money in return for a promise to pay back the loan at a certain date in the future. In the interim, the party issuing the bond and receiving your money agrees to pay you a fixed rate of interest at regular intervals, usually semiannually. Most often, you never see your bonds; they are maintained by your broker or are accumulated in mutual funds. As market forces change, the value of bonds changes.

The ins and outs of stock and bond purchasing and trading are complex, and rather than become an expert in yet another field outside of your own, you may want to select a broker, a licensed professional, to serve this function for you. One more to add to the team. But how do you know if the securities recommended by a particular broker are really the best ones for you, your income, your cash flow, and your tax situation? You don't. The market is a casino. When you hire an investment professional to make the decisions for you, your business manager and attorney had better be in on the process because they know your tax situation and your ability to dig deep and pay taxes on the dividend income you may not be able to detach from the investment.

Let's say you buy a fund that specializes in the blue chips. All of these generate dividends which themselves may reflect a decent percentage, such as 3 to 4 percent of the value of the stocks. But you don't see the dividends. They are reinvested in the fund and contribute to its appearance of growth. Then you get a 1099. This represents the dividends—the long- and short-term capital gains. If your fund has gone up, you will say, "Hey, I'm paying taxes because my fund went up. So what?" And your broker is making fees on the maintenance of the fund and your portfolio? Same thing. What do you care? Your fund went up. You ignore these two costs because everything that is presented to you shows that you are *making* money. If your mutual fund is up 30 percent, you are not going to be annoyed by the fees or the taxes. If you don't have the cash the pay the taxes, you can sell some of your shares in the mutual fund (at a profit, remember). No problem!

Then comes a year like the year 2000. In 2000, some things remained the same. Mutual fund companies still had a lot of trading activity; blue chips in the fund still yielded a dividend, and investors still received 1099s. But there was a difference that year. The value of mutual funds went down! And even as investors were looking at the sad state of their portfolios at the end of the year, they received 1099s showing what the IRS calls "gain." Taxable gain. They had to find the money to pay the tax on the gain even if their money was still tied up in the mutual funds and they didn't have the cash to pay the tax out of their other resources.

When you look at a mutual fund prospectus, it will show you a chart. Had you invested $10,000 in 1972, it would have grown to x by now. All the mutual funds have nice charts. Lots of dot matrixes. They show that during the oil embargo, in 1964, the value would have been y; when Reagan was President, it would have been z. But they never show you that each year you get a 1099. Therefore the growth only was one-half of what it appears. Figure it out.

Referring to the first example in this chapter—remember the $500 generated by the $10,000 CD—if you did not have to pay the tax, you would have had the $500 back in your pocket as well as all of the options that you no longer have because the $500 that was generated will be subject to federal income tax and, depending on what state and city you live in, state and city income tax as well. You might be surprised at how easy it is to get into the 50 percent tax bracket, which here would amount to $250.

Losses are nothing less than catastrophic when the opportunity to earn the kind of money that some artists earn in a relatively brief career disappears. And I am talking *brief!* Some of our most legendary artists recorded surprisingly few albums in their exalted careers. Simon and Garfunkel, for example, recorded only six albums from 1965 to 1969. (A subsequent live album—the Central Park album—did not come until years later). People rarely factor in the potential for loss. Dreamers never do. Many wealthy investors allocated their assets so poorly in the late 1990s that when the NASDAQ dropped, they lost everything. (The investment advisors blamed the investors for not being sufficiently conservative in their investments.) Why should artists be expected to act any less carelessly than some of the big shakers and movers who got wiped out in 1929 or 2000 or 2001 as a result of the careless allocation of their assets?

This brings us back to sound advice and counsel from your—the artist's—business managers. They will tell you that markets do not rise in a straight line—nor do they usually fall in a straight line. A 10 percent average over five years may have been achieved by one year of 15 percent growth, one at minus 3 percent, one at 0 percent, two at 6 percent, and one at 26 percent. Markets don't move in consistent ways. They do not perform at 10 percent, 10 percent, 10 percent, 10 percent, and 10 percent. They never will.

People will tell you that except for income-producing real estate there is no return like the stock market over time. This seems to be true. But, as we have seen, *average* return and *actual* return are not the same. Furthermore, losses count more than gains and if you lose money and have a bad experience you may be scared off the market forever and that is a loss that you cannot calculate. What if you dealt with a broker who was unethical, or chose unsuitable investments, and then the market crashed. Not only do you have a mess on your hands; you also might decide to transfer your upset with the broker to a hatred of the market itself.

But even if your broker has been honorable and you lost money simply because the economy went south for a while, or you had a personal need for emergency money and you could not get it out of the market without taking a horrible loss, you might tire very quickly of the market as a resource for your financial well-being. This could be a very bad result indeed.

You may be thinking, "Well, I am very computer savvy and I am becoming fairly expert at dealing with e-trade. Why can't I do it myself?" Outside of the fact that you should be doing what you do best—writing, performing, managing, producing, whatever—why do you think that you can possibly do as well as a professional? Handicapping stocks is a complex process. Sure, when the market is going up at the rate of 30 percent a year, which it did in the late 1990s, you don't have to be a genius to increase your portfolio. But I suggest that as with any advice, it is worth it to spend enough money to get good advice on your investments. And what better advice to get than that of a team of people, all of whom are watching each other on your behalf: your attorney, your accountant, your investment/financial advisor, and yes, even your manager. The chances are that the synthesis of the team effort will result in everyone doing the right and the best thing for the artist's financial life and family. Enough said.

Making It and Saving It

Beware of Greeks bearing gifts. Remember the Trojan horse? How about those millionaire lottery winners? Once you start making money that you do not need for your living expenses, there are going to be a million people wanting to latch onto you.

Just as in all businesses, there are good guys and bad guys. Hundreds of thousands of people have passed the securities exam. But what is their motivation? Are they interested in you as a person, a husband, a father, a breadwinner—a rock star? Or are they dancing to your music as they charge you fees retail? You have to use all of your talents of perception to consider the motivation of your representatives. There are those who will tell you that stockbrokers merely sell the flavor of the day—that if they were really that good, they would be traders—or analysts. This is obviously an oversimplification. But whenever you put your money into the hands of someone who can control its activity, you are taking a risk. Not necessarily an unreasonable one, but a risk nonetheless. And you had better be sure about the person you hope will steer you around or through that risk.

Consider the fees and expenses of maintaining your portfolio. Brokers don't make money for people; they generate activity in accounts. I am not saying that they "churn" the accounts, but they themselves do not make any money unless they are buying and selling, that is, unless your assets move in your account. They get a percentage of every purchase and every sale. At their worst, they meet in the morning and say this is what we're going to sell today. They often do not do adequate research and you are as anonymous as the rest of their clients. One thing is certain: In essence, they are salespeople. Often they are under pressure from their superiors to sell products which offer higher commission payouts. A friend of mine who moves in the investment world says brokers are in the moving business, not the storage business.

Am I suggesting that you revert to the mattress method of savings? No, of course not. But I would be remiss if I did not point out the dangers that should, at the minimum, be investigated and addressed before you risk your hard-earned capital.

Deferred Payments vs. Cash on the Barrelhead

Successful young artists who suddenly come into more money than they have ever had in their lives are likely to blow most or all of it on cars, companions, or even a home recording studio that may be a luxury in view of their particular circumstances. So a business manager might consider: "How can my client *not* take so much now and get used to having less money so later on there will be some left—especially if things do not work out as hoped careerwise?"

One answer is to defer payments. Like anything else, there are pros and cons to deferring payments. No taxes are payable on deferred payments. Then again, you have lost the opportunity to build the money into a larger sum. So an alternative route would be to take the money when offered, provided that you are disciplined enough not to spend all of it. A good business manager will encourage you to have some kind of savings plan from day one. Combine this with the overwhelming odds that you are likely to fail *despite* how talented you may be and you can begin to see why it would be smart to follow Grandmother's advice to put away some money for a rainy day.

One of the psychologically enticing aspects of having lots of money in your pocket when you are young is that it makes you feel as if you are on top of the world. One of the possibly devastating aspects of having a lot of money "burning a hole in your pocket" is that you are likely to spend it all on things that are not enduring—that is, *not* on real estate or sound investments. Of course your business manager will encourage you to save some percentage of the money, but your instinct is to laugh because you know you are going to make it big time.

Or you may think that the advisors are telling you this because they do not believe in you. This is simply not true. They are telling you this because they care about you and know the reality of the situation. They are looking at things with a less romanticized vision than you are—which is not only sensible, but it is what you want in a financial advisor. A business manager who says "Let's put away some money" is saying it because he or she has seen people less (and more) talented than you and less (and more) lucky than you *not* succeed. Your manager wants to *insure* that you are covered in any event.

Insurance

In all likelihood, insurance protection is something that your business manager will be responsible for. As noted earlier, the business manager's aura of protection goes beyond your work—into your life. Of course, you can select an insurance agent yourself, but by doing so you will have added a new—unnecessary—layer to your team which you might want to avoid if you are ever going to write that next song or record that next track.

In the past, business managers worked closely with one or more insurance agents to identify and secure the best insurance for their clients at the lowest cost: homeowners' (covering risk of theft, loss due to fire, etc.); automobile; an umbrella policy giving you an added layer of protection; and life insurance. They were not meant to profit from the choice or amount of insurance obtained, but sometimes they did, and no one—certainly not the client—was the wiser. Recently, the American Institute of CPAs changed the rules which had prohibited CPAs who are AICPA-certified from being agents for insurance companies. Now it is permitted and the client is suddenly faced with a potential conflict of interest. If the business manager benefits from the policies he or she secures for the client, how does the client know that the advice being given is valid?

The good news is that whereas in the past clients would never know for certain that they had all of the requisite insurance to protect their assets and their heirs, now, most certainly, they will. Obtaining appropriate insurance will not easily fall through the cracks any longer. The days when a comfortable retirement with grandchildren at the door might have been replaced with an IRS agent at the door may well be over now that business managers who are also CPAs can truly have their hands directly on insuring their clients' assets, life, and retirement.

And for the first time, fees are split with your financial advisors, and this practice, and its cost, is right up there in plain sight—on the balance sheets proffered by your business manager. He or she is being paid. So what. Everyone else who provides a service is getting paid.

LIFE INSURANCE

There are many books and Internet articles out there that cover the subject of insurance. I bring it up here, in the chapter on managing your business, because the entertainment industry in general and the music industry in particular is a high-risk arena: there is a high risk of failure, of early burnout, and, sadly, of early death. Musicians are always under pressure to write more music, more hits; they have to tour and tour and tour. Drug abuse has been an occupational hazard for over a century. Even the average artist is put into the equivalent of the Final Four before learning how to dribble. Once the lawyer and the manager have finished their jobs and a contract is signed; once the A&R people and the record company have established a plan with the promotion, marketing, publicity and sales team, the ball is handed to the artist, who is asked—no, expected—to sink (sing?) a three-pointer immediately. Without intending to be morbid, my point is that some artists become uninsurable at a relatively young age.

The lesson here is that any artist, songwriter, record producer, or manager who secures life insurance early has successfully "buried" a sum of money, that is, put the money away into a protected place, where it will be available no matter what happens down the road. That person will not have to pay taxes on the cash value of the policy as it grows. And, in many states, the value of a life insurance policy is protected from creditors in bankruptcy proceedings. Life insurance, then, can be regarded as one kind of investment vehicle, and should be considered by the artist and the artist's representatives so that an informed decision can be made.

As many of you know, there are essentially two kinds of life insurance: term and whole life. Term insurance is what it sounds like: insurance against an early demise which expires at some specific point in the future. If you die within that time, fine. If you die after that time, you're not only dead, but your estate or beneficiary does not receive the insurance. The appealing thing about term insurance is that it appears to be cheap. But once the term ends, it is over and there is no residual value remaining. Whole life insurance appears to be expensive, but it actually works as an investment vehicle in that its cash value grows over a period of years. You can cash in your whole life insurance policy at any time, or borrow against it. Once fully paid, the policy remains in effect until you die, at which point the insurance company will pay your beneficiary the face value of the policy. What does all this have to do with you?

Consider the following scenario. A young artist wants some of the advance monies from his or her record contract to be used to purchase life insurance. The recording relationship lasts for three or four years, then the artist is dropped from the label. If the artist has purchased whole life insurance, the payments will be very expensive; if for term, they will not be. Thus we see some justification in favor of term insurance, at least at the beginning of an artist's career. Artists who subsequently make it big can convert the term policies into whole life and build equity; if they fail, the policy will end or they can keep it going for far less money than a whole life policy would have cost.

On the other hand, let us imagine that the record company can buy a whole life, cash value, life insurance policy. The company fronts enough money in the first year or two of the recording agreement so that the policy is fully funded, and does not require any further premiums for it to remain in force—the "cash value" can be borrowed against. The artist can now continue making payments, or, if the relationship with the record company continues, the record company can. Theoretically, this policy can be paid off quickly and it will last for the artist's lifetime. Now that's planning.

Note that up-front payments of a life insurance policy's premiums may have unfavorable tax consequences. However, if the recording company is willing to make those up-front payments over two years, it should have no problem spreading them out over several (five to six) years, thereby avoiding a tax problem for you.

Let's say a recording artist has succeeded over the years and makes a bundle of money year after year after year on his or her catalogue of records and/or songs. The artist's business manager wants to invest prudently. But maybe having an IRA is *not* prudent. Is an IRA creating wealth for the artist or is it just sitting there, not doing anything except grow at a snail's pace? Maybe this particular artist does not need an IRA at all. Recall that at 71 $\frac{1}{2}$, the artist must start withdrawing the money, or be taxed on it anyway.

Suppose, instead of putting money in an IRA, the artist purchases a $5 million life insurance policy. By the time he or she reaches 70 years, this policy can be worth $10 million dollars! At that point, the artist can live high on the hog because the policy, at his or her death, will be worth so much. Without such a policy, the artist must be careful not to spend too much, so that enough will be left for his or her heirs. Putting it simply, the policy makes the artist richer.

There is another advantage to choosing this option as well. If the artist's advisors gamble wrong and royalties stop, the policy still has value and the artist can borrow against it or cash it in. (There are ways to withdraw money out of a life insurance policy without paying tax on the withdrawals.)

AFTER YOU'VE PEAKED: CATALOGUE MANAGEMENT

It is very difficult to maintain communication and democracy among band members during their prime; it is nearly impossible afterward. The musicians go their merry way; some prosper, others do not; some marry, others divorce; some die and their estates are ruled by their ex's, their executors, or their children's guardians. Their contracts are over, their high-powered personal managers and lawyers and business managers are long gone (remember a percentage of no earnings equals zero), and their catalogues—their legacies—are slowly but surely degrading. Yet an artist's or band's catalogue is most definitely an asset, one that needs coordinating—in a word, managing.

Regrettably, you cannot usually rely on your (former) record company or music publisher to exploit your catalogues of songs and master recordings—especially if you don't own or control them. The only way you can rejuvenate your catalogue is by being proactive, and designating capable people—whether your attorney, or some combination of your attorney and the multitude of music supervisors and clearance houses that can be appointed—to take charge. In addition, there should always be a savvy accountant involved. But I have rarely known of an artist appointing anyone to take responsibility for managing a catalogue of music. Most artists think that their catalogues will be nurtured automatically. More magic thinking.

Sure, the legacies of the great composers of old—Cole Porter, the Gershwins, Irving Berlin, even Leonard Bernstein—are all handled by "executors" who are charged with maximizing the "estate" and "protecting" the artists' images. But this section is meant for live artists, or, if the artists are deceased, their live heirs. Some attorneys or business managers are uniquely positioned to coordinate the exploitation of both song and record catalogues—even if the artist owns neither the song copyrights nor the masters. If you can find someone to do this, even someone who is new to your life, you will be well served, as catalogue exploitation is a business in itself.

As noted, there are a variety of people who can take a song and get it revived, whether by re-recording it or coupling recordings of it on compilation records, or by taking a master and finding a place for it in a film, a commercial, or on a variety of compilation records. (The Buddy Holly catalogue was lying fallow until Linda Ronstadt recorded two of his songs. This was followed by the film *The Buddy Holly Story* and the musical *Buddy,* which remains a staple of the stock and amateur circuit and has had a 10-year run in London. And don't forget *Mamma Mia!,* the "tribute" to ABBA. Or *Smokey Joe's Café,* which gave new life to the songs of Leiber and Stoller.)

Although there is no single person who can "wake up" a catalogue, your attorney, or someone operating under the attorney's guidance, can play a kind of "central command" role. This person, working with an accountant, can also monitor the master recording licenses that will inevitably be authorized by the record company (which, through multiple sales and mergers, is most likely a successor to the artist's original company). The income from these licenses should tie in exactly with the mechanical licenses issued by the music publishing company (which, like the record company, is most likely a successor to the artist's original publishing company). Where they do not tie in, someone has either cheated or made a mistake—and the result is usually not to the artist's advantage. This comparative analysis is best handled by a person who has the time and ability to scrutinize royalty statements as they come in (or track them when they do not come in).

There is no reason why an artist or writer cannot seek permission to "work" a catalogue that he or she does not actually own or control; believe me, the record company and publishing company are likely to be thrilled, especially since in many cases, they have long ago forgotten that they even own these works. Any number of deals can be worked out with them so that any income that is received can be shared with the artist and writer on the one hand and their "agent" for exploitation on the other, all the while providing unexpected new income for the record and publishing companies.

But someone has to initiate it.

As always, the best way to achieve a particular goal, in this case the optimal exploitation of one's catalogues, is to assemble a competent team of persons expert in the music field and charge them with coming up with a strategic plan for accomplishing the goal. After all, there is money to be made.

WHEN YOUR JOB IS MORE THAN A GIG

For most of us, inherited wealth is not the way we will end up providing for ourselves, our families, and our progeny. This will come only through our own hard work and income. Therefore, if one is fortunate enough to be offered an important, well-paying position at a company in one's field of choice, there is no legal document in one's work life more important than the employment agreement. Being offered an employment contract and signing one (or more) are seminal events in an executive's life. Many provisions in employment agreements are standard, no matter what industry the company is in, and to provide a context for employment contract provisions that are of special concern to the music industry professional, I first review many of the customary provisions in standard employment agreements. As some of these can mean financial success or failure for the employee signing the contract, it is crucial for the employee—and his or her advisors—to pay careful attention to all of them, including so-called boilerplate provisions.

TERM OF EMPLOYMENT

Assuming an employee is confident of his or her abilities, obviously, if that employee can keep the term shorter, rather than longer, his or her options will be increased many times over. In employment agreements, the word "options" is usually used to describe the right of the employer to determine whether to extend the term of the agreement. Surprisingly, even some of those whom one might consider the more savvy first-time contracting executives do not initially understand this. The right of the employer to control the length of the term of the agreement is a very powerful tool used by employers to wield power over their employees.

Of course, some executives may, for security or other reasons, prefer that the term be longer rather than shorter. Given the mercurial nature of some industries—including the music industry—even if an executive is confident in his or her ability, three to five years of guaranteed salary and bonuses does not look so bad. An additional reason some employees prefer to contract for a longer term is that a longer term will affect the magnitude of the payout in the event of early termination.

DUTIES

While the title of the person who is being hired is usually set forth in the agreement, it is not always clear what that person's responsibilities are, what the reporting lines are, and, ironically, what kind of flexibility the employee has to actually fulfill his or her responsibilities and even go beyond them in exceeding the expectations of the employer. It is important for the employee, and the person he or she is to report to, to talk through these issues and to find a way to clarify any ambiguities and to incorporate their understandings and expectations into the written document.

Here is an excerpt from a typical—and typically ambiguous—employment contract:

> *Employee shall have all the authority and responsibility customarily associated with such position in a company of the size and nature of the Employer.*
>
> *During the term, Executive shall devote substantially all of his business time and his efforts, business judgment, skill and knowledge exclusively to the advancement of the business and interests of the Company and to the discharge of his duties and responsibilities hereunder.*

Clear? Clear as mud. And the consequences—in terms of the provisions in the termination section of the contract, which doesn't come up until pages and pages later in the document—can be serious, as one of the bases for termination for cause is the "repeated failure or refusal to materially perform one's duties and responsibilities as set forth 'in this agreement.'" There are two things you or your representative need to consider here: securing what are called "notice and cure" provisions, which require the company to tell you of a problem and then give you the opportunity to explain or fix it, and/or articulating with precision what the employee's actual duties are supposed to be. If you do neither, you will have to live with the ambiguity of the "duties" provision and you will be relegated to a negotiation, upon termination, consisting of arguing "on the one hand, on the other hand" with the company's legal department.

REPORTING LINES

One area of concern at the time of the initial negotiation is to insure that the employee has the right to report to a particular position in the company, for example, the president or the CEO. Prospective employees are not usually allowed to attach the name of a particular person to that position (so-called key man clauses, which provide for this, are anathema to most corporations), but they can try to insure that no other person will come between them and their functions *vis-à-vis* "the president" (or CEO, or VP of operations, etc.). Being specific about the position to which the employee is to report protects against the employee's being marginalized or layered by virtue of the placement of another position between the employee and the person to whom he or she was expected to report. The employee may even have aspirations for the higher job—or perhaps was even promised that such advancement was in the cards—but if the employee no longer reports to the person he or she was supposed to report to, the chances of moving up are naturally reduced at best and eliminated at worst.

If the contract specifically addresses this issue and the company doesn't live up to the provisions, a variety of remedies are possible. Some of these will come out of existing applicable law; others may actually be inserted into the contract: for example, the employee will have the option to terminate the agreement—possibly with a penalty assessed against the company. Damages might include the immediate vesting of stock options, a flat fee payout, the continuation of health-related benefits, a reduction of the ordinary mitigation responsibilities of the employee, or relief from certain post-term responsibilities, and perhaps a re-relocation provision that expired after a year of employment can be revived afterwards if the termination is due to this kind of event.

CONFIDENTIALITY AND COMPETITION

When an employee's skills, experience, and relationships are specialized within any particular industry, the most egregious limitation that can be placed on that person is a prohibition against competing, at a future date, with the company with whom he or she is entering into an agreement.

Anticompetition provisions take several forms and are designed to protect against different outcomes. One such provision seeks to protect against the disclosure, or use for the benefit of others, of any information regarding the activities of his or her employer which is of a secret or confidential nature. This information can take the form of financial information, contracts, contacts, contract proposals and negotiations, plans developments, administrative procedures, and dealings with a party with whom the employer has entered into contracts. Obviously, in every field, and in particular in an industry whose "architecture" is essentially closed—such as the music industry—even so-called "private" information is hard to protect. Gossip runs rampant; publications (such as *Hits* magazine) and Internet sites (such as The Velvet Rope) are successful in large part because of their very active rumor mill. Anyone in the music industry, and his or her attorney, must be clear with each other as to the parameters within which they are expected—and willing—to keep a closed mouth. A music industry employee's very strengths may be as a person who knows "everything and everybody," and zipping such a person's mouth may be impossible or counterproductive.

Another aspect of anticompetition provisions applicable upon departure deals with restrictions on the part of the employee to solicit other employees or contracting parties and bring them to the employee's new company (whether a third-party company or the employee's own entrepreneurial venture). There exist many state, federal, and even constitutional provisions that can reduce the impact of such provisions, but a litigation may ensue which can be very expensive in terms of time, money, and the stress it brings to the litigant. It is not a bad idea to exclude from such prohibition the employee's personal assistant or secretary.

Finally, an employee may comfortably (or not) agree to refrain from soliciting former colleagues but should not be precluded from hiring them should the colleagues themselves seek such employment on their own volition. I have always been reticent to "steal" a lawyer (or secretary, or paralegal assistant for that matter) from another firm with whom I do business, but once the person announces that he or she is leaving and is going to knock on yet another competitor's door or on mine, I feel no such reluctance. This is a fine point, but it can free up the employee a bit and creates more room for discussion before a real legal claim for violation is brought. It is easy to prove that a former employee violated a "Thou shalt not hire" clause, but it is much harder if the clause is limited to "Thou shalt not solicit."

STOCK OPTIONS

The coming (and going) of the age of the dot-coms has universalized this subject beyond the bounds of the traditional corporate boardroom. In order to value the offer or in order to even know what to ask, a great deal of information is necessary and it is useful to have a business manager familiar with such issues assist your attorney in counseling you as a prospective employee.

Of course, some companies (e.g., Bertelsmann AG; Peermusic) are not publicly held companies and stock options are simply not available to their employees. But there are many ways to "equalize" an offer from a public company with that from a privately held one. The principal way is to seek to insure that the executive's compensation is commensurate with that of other people at that level. Participation in compensation programs can take many shapes, and stock options are not necessarily the most advantageous to the employee. Some benefits are far more immediately vesting than stock options can be, especially in cases of termination with—or without—cause.

Following are a few recommendations to those who may be receiving stock options pursuant to an employment contract.

- You may secure acceleration of vesting in the event of a termination other than for cause or in the event of death, disability, or departure for so-called "good reason."
- You can secure accelerated vesting based upon the financial performance of the company (i.e., a profit metric or some aggregated stock price appreciation) or the employee's (your) performance or on other specific criteria.
- You should be sure to determine whether the options are qualified under the tax code (i.e., they are capable of producing taxable value for you, the employee, at the capital gains rate) or nonqualified (i.e., the proceeds will be taxed at ordinary income tax rates).
- Find out the exercise or "strike" price—the price you have to pay for each share of stock when you exercise the option. This price is usually the market price of the stock on the day you received the option. The difference between the strike price and the current market price on the day you exercise (buy) your stock is taxable in the year the event takes place. This tax will be a problem if the stock you buy is illiquid (does not trade on a public stock exchange). Remember, just as if you are holding real estate, you are holding stock, not cash. You may have to sell it to get enough cash to pay the tax, and in closely held, nonpublic companies, it is often difficult, if not impossible, to sell your shares until the company goes public or is bought out.
- Check the vesting schedule to make sure that you are receiving the best possible vesting rate (or "most favored nation" status vis-à-vis similarly situated personnel).
- Read your stock option plan and make sure your postdeparture option exercise rights are acceptable. Do unvested options lapse? Under what circumstances will you be able to exercise vested options after your departure and for how long postdeparture will this right last? Do you have to exercise the options—that is, buy the stock—on or before your departure or do you have some time after you leave? Suppose, for example, you are forced to exercise the options within, say, 30 days of leaving or lose them. Remember, you will have no job and maybe no cash. If there are

taxes due (see the fourth bulleted item above), and you don't have the cash to pay the taxes, you will not be able to afford to exercise the options. Does the plan allow for "cashless" exercises, namely, the right to exercise an option and simultaneously sell the underlying security, thereby enabling you to cover the exercise price out of the sale proceeds? Or must you write a check and fork it over to the company?

PERKS

Some perks are based on profitability; some are not. In some areas, parking space counts big time; in others, not at all. In some cities, the lease of cars (especially diesels during gas shortages) matters more to the employee than most any other term of the employment agreement! Other perks include the reimbursement or assumption of attorneys' fees if the employee sues on the contract (and wins); reimbursement for attorneys' fees expended simply to negotiate the employment agreement in the first place; graduate schooling (e.g., special weeks' or months' programs at universities for management training; MBA programs; other programs for executives offered by various business schools [sometimes with a cap of X dollars per year]; the cost of a home office [e.g., the cost of an up-to-date laptop, cell phone, DSL line]; special medical plans, etc.)

There are often formulas established for bonuses based on earnings; the assumption of country or university club dues (which are otherwise not deductible by the employee); daily car service and preferred class of air travel and hotel accommodation. Sometimes the perks can be as simple (and as useful) as a budget to hire a staff assistant who will make the life of the executive easier and more productive. School fees for children's education is a popular perquisite which is nothing less than a necessity in certain cities. While the schools in Geneva or Paris or London are ostensibly better, on average, than those in American cities, the employee who is based outside of the United States may wish his or her child to obtain an "American" education nevertheless; and the cost for this is substantial, as is the cost of SAT preparation, which is practically essential for an American child brought up in a foreign country. This can amount to many thousands of dollars in the child's junior or senior year in high school.

TERMINATION

Temination as used here means the ending of the contract other than by its natural expiration. Two main categories of termination are termination *without* cause and termination *with* cause, and their consequences differ. If the termination is with cause, there may be no more payment of the contractual salary, or other compensation, such as perks, as of the date of termination, and the employer may even claim damages from the employee. (For example, the employer may require that the employee return money previously paid by the company.) Prospective employees should check the language of for-cause termination clauses carefully. Some companies, for example, are including inappropriate electronic communications (e.g., offensive postings to message boards and chatrooms) as causes for termination.

Termination "without cause" is more difficult to define. It occurs when, for example, the employer decides that the employee's job definition is not correct or not being filled as well by employee *A* as it might be by employee *B,* or simply because the budget for the division has been reduced, leaving the employer with no alternative but to cut staff. In this situation, the contractual provision usually requires payout for the entire term of the agreement, *with mitigation.* This means that the employee must seek, in good faith, another job equivalent to the one that he or she had with the employer. During the job search, the employee's contractual salary will be paid out, for the term of the original agreement, until such time as the employee finds another job. [It is possible to negotiate provisions that state that in the case of termination without cause or termination for good reason (see below), the employer must make available out-placement services to assist the employee to find another equivalent job.]

It should be noted that in the event of termination without cause, even when the employer is paying out compensation as required by the agreement for the remainder of its term, the employer is not usually required to continue offering other benefits (e.g., car allowance, health insurance, etc.). Under COBRA rules, an employee is entitled to retain medical insurance for eighteen months after leaving the employment. In most cases, the employee has to pay for this continuation, although I know some cases in which attorneys have succeeded in arranging for the employer to pay the COBRA amount for the duration of the unexpired term if the employee does not secure other employment. (Note that this sum might constitute taxable income to the employee, and only the tax accountant will know for sure.)

The negotiating strategy of an employee who might one day expect to be terminated without cause is to provide in the original contract the right to be paid out the entire balance of his or her salary *regardless of mitigation.* This is difficult to get.

In cases where the employer wants to limit the payout term, it is possible to agree that "with cause" results in no payment and "without cause" results in a payment equal to the lesser of base compensation for three to six months or base compensation for the then remaining natural term of the agreement.

Change of Control

In some cases, the employee may wish to end the contractual relationship if a change of control in the company occurs. This can be negotiated in the contract to constitute a termination without cause, but the consequences may be different than other kinds of termination without cause. The company which takes over control of the employer company will be responsible for the consequences of such a provision, not the contracting employer, so it is sometimes fairly easy to obtain a provision that in the event of a change in control, the employee will have the right, for example, to terminate the agreement and be paid out the balance of the contract in a lump sum without mitigation.

One complex issue connected with changes in control is the following. According to Section 280G of the Internal Revenue Code of 1986, an employee who receives more than 2.99 times his or her base compensation as a parachute payment in the event of termination without cause triggered by a change of control is susceptible of having to pay an additional excise tax, imposed by Section 4999 of the code, of 20 percent on the entire payout *in addition to all other compensation-related taxes.* (The base compensation is averaged, based on whichever is shorter, the preceding five years or the duration of employment with that particular employer.) Big-gun employees will ask for (and occasionally obtain) a provision that authorizes the company to "gross up" a payout to compensate the employees for the cost of the excise tax in the event the payout is likely to constitute an "excess parachute payment." One way or another, they will get what they want.

If you are new to a company or are starting at a lower salary and working your way up, the five-year averaging will mean that you face the risk of receiving an excess parachute payment in the event of a payout on change of control. If you are at risk of being slapped with the tax, your counsel should attempt to get the company to agree to the gross-up mechanism. And the companies, for their part, should resist this strenuously as the formula used to calculate the gross makes the payout, which includes the expected contractual amount plus the tax factor, really expensive.

Termination by the Employee for "Good Reason"

There is a developing concept that employees have the right to terminate their own employment when there is "good reason" to do so. As noted in the "duties" section, above, specificity or ambiguity regarding duties is a double-edged sword. If these provisions are ambiguous, it will be difficult for the employer to point to a specific requirement and allege failure giving rise (barring cure) to the right to terminate with cause. At the same time, it will be harder for the employee to claim termination for good reason. A decent middle ground for the employee is to have the general duties described in ambiguous terms and, then, in the "good reason" section, enumerate very specific good reasons, such as:

- Any reduction in the executive's minimum annual compensation, target percentage of executive's annual bonus, or any other material employee benefit or perquisite enjoyed by the executive other than as part of an overall reduction in such benefits or perquisites applying to the company's senior executives generally
- Any failure to continue the executive as [insert title]
- Any material diminution in executive's duties or the assignment to executive of duties that are materially inconsistent with executive's then current duties
- Any other material breach by the company of any of the provisions described in the agreement
- The occurrence of a change in control (provided that the executive remains employed with the company for six months thereafter)
- The failure to obtain the assumption of the executive's employment agreement by any successor to all or substantially all of the business or assets of the company

Morals Clauses

Most talent contracts include provisions that protect the employer from having to retain the employment of an employee whose moral character is embarrassing to the employer. Ordinarily, these provisions speak in terms of being convicted of a felony or some similar criminal act. Some companies, however, have experienced considerable embarrassment by virtue of their employees' behavior which, although not rising to the level of criminal, is nevertheless abhorrent to whatever the company stands for or claims it stands for.

Thus arises the general "moral clause," which one should be particularly cautious to negotiate carefully. Most people will sign an agreement that permits termination with cause if the employee commits a felony. However, the language of many contracts is so general as to give the employer a right to terminate with cause a contract that otherwise would be solid and free from attack. For example, one of the television networks provides that behavior *inimical* to the employer may permit the termination of the contract for cause. During negotiation, the network in question offered the following definition of "inimical" when pressed:

> *Those actions that are harmful to their reputation and/or business inter-*
> *ests as determined by the employer.*

So much for the negotiation "victory" of establishing a definition.

A cause for termination that frequently finds its way into boilerplate morals clauses is the word "insubordination." What on earth does *that* mean?

When faced with such provisions, the only thing that one can request is an additional provision establishing a right on the part of the employee to have an opportunity to correct any deficiencies based on the severity of the claimed offense. Never was an "opportunity to cure" more desired, or more warranted.

Clearly, from the employee's perspective, to have to suffer these provisions is a horrendous burden. But provision or no provision, someone who publicly embarrasses his or her employer and, by his or her conduct, jeopardizes the business relationships and business reputation of the employer will be fired. Should the employer pay lots of money to make the miscreant leave if the contract does not provide for a breach of morals to entitle the company to fire the employee "with cause"?

One way to deal with this eventuality may be to provide a substantial reduction of the "without cause" payout amount in the event of the violation of the morals clause. A hybrid termination—for example, "with cause when the cause is a breach of the morals clause short of a criminal act"—could trigger a situation in which *some* money can be paid, although less than that paid out "without cause."

RELOCATION AND RE-RELOCATION

Remarkably, relocation provisions are often ignored by employees leaving one venue and traveling to another. In initial negotiations, the company's thoughts are, quite naturally, focused only on the future placement of the employee, as are the employee's, the employee's family, and regrettably, often the employee's attorney's as well. No one thinks of the end; they are all focused on the beginning.

A favorable provision will provide that, whether the contract is terminated for cause or without cause, the employer must return the employee and the employee's family and belongings to the place of origin. Sometimes, the provision returns the employee only to the place of origin if the contract ends in the first year; thereafter, the employee must pay. Sometimes the provision stipulates that the employer must return the employee to wherever he or she wants to go in the world, provided the contract runs out its entire term.

Relocation and re-relocation expenses should specifically cover a trip or trips to the new location of employment for the employee and perhaps his or her spouse so that they can establish schooling arrangements for their children and select a home prior to the official commencement of employment.

In addition to moving and relocation expenses, there are many costs involved which the employee may have to assume if the employer is not asked to assume them. For example, if the employee has committed to rent a summer house or paid a deposit on private school fees prior to the time he or she was asked to relocate, the company should be expected to reimburse the employee for such costs. These costs may be incurred at either end of an employment and therefore reimbursement provisions should apply both to relocations and re-relocations. Similarly, there will likely be storage fees that must be assumed, costs of selling one's home (realtor's commission, attorneys' fees, document preparation, recording fees and inspections), whether for relocation or re-relocation. There are additional expenses such as property taxes, interest on one's mortgage, improvements to make one's home (at the new or old site) ready for sale, and concessions that are made to sell the home (at the new or old site) to a new buyer.

VISAS

Special issues arise if an employee whom a company wishes to hire is resident in the United States via a special visa (rather than, say, a green card). Sometimes these visas are obtained by employees' own service corporations and they need to maintain the status they have acquired while they pursue their application for a green card. If a new employer requires that the employee terminate his or her application and re-apply with the new employer as the sponsor for the visa, even if the employer is prepared to pay for the costs of the switch, do not forget that once the employment ends (on the contract's own terms, or with or without cause), the employee will be in serious jeopardy of having to return to his or her own country *unless the company assumes the responsibility of reinstating the employee's status once the employment is ended.*

DISABILITY AND DEATH

The problem with the term "disability" is that it requires an objective standard, and a contract that ignores establishing such an objective standard is susceptible of interpretation that can be devastating to an employee who suffers an injury which *he or she* believes to be a disabling injury but which the company does not. Most companies will agree that if a competent medical authority certifies disability, then they will respect the diagnosis. The contract should provide this.

Disabilities can be either short-term or long-term, and it is a good idea to have these terms defined contractually, so their different consequences can be evaluated by the employee and negotiated if they are not to his or her advantage.

Death, of course, requires no objective standard, but some consideration should be given to the need for life insurance, and the cost of such insurance. The prospective employee should discuss with his or her financial planner how much life insurance he or she would require at different points during the term (especially during extension terms, where the needs might be less, but the costs considerably more). Some planners suggest that the life insurance payout approximate two to three times the employee's base salary with additional insurance added during the term by one times salary for each new child born during the term. This can be a "perk" that is life-saving for the surviving spouse and children and should be considered carefully.

PROVISIONS THAT SURVIVE TERMINATION

Provisions that survive the end of the agreement should be carefully considered because they may have an impact on future employment. For example, there may be promises made regarding company policies (e.g., secrecy; see the section on confidentiality, page 94) that the employee will have to adhere to even long after the contract expires. For the most part, termination will have a deleterious effect on unvested stock options. Unvested options customarily expire on termination except for the most senior executives with some leverage. Companies are loath to extend or alter the terms of options—and it is not due to malice that they behave like this. There are considerable negative accounting consequences for a company that varies the terms of options for employees, especially if the modifications are unevenly exercised.

If termination occurs without cause, or in the ordinary course of the expiration of the term of the agreement, it is possible to negotiate an immediate vesting.

The employee may incur accounting fees in the event of future audits by state or federal authorities covering the tax years constituting the contract term. Under certain circumstances these should not have to be borne by the employee.

Employees who share in profits or have the right to receive royalties may find that their own right to audit the company expires upon termination even though they have not yet received accountings reflecting monies earned during the term. And in some cases, monies are earned and payable after the term, even as the audit clause that would have been the basis of verifying the accountings may have been negated by the effect of termination. Similarly, profit shares and royalties may be payable only through the end of the contract term, and the language providing for this result may be so obscure as to be easily missed by someone reviewing the contract. (See below, under "A&R Incentive Plans.")

VACATIONS

Sometimes, or for some people, it is awkward to highlight vacation issues when negotiating an employment agreement. Work, compensation for work, and productivity are considered to be the real focus of the contract, and nonwork and holiday issues are not. Nevertheless, everyone (including the person you are negotiating with) considers this to be a legitimate area to discuss and the specific needs of each employee should be addressed. If one is uncomfortable allocating a block of valuable negotiating time to nonwork issues, the negotiating position can easily be presented in writing (and in detail, with recommended contract language) by the employee's attorney.

One area of concern is vacation accumulated by employees who don't take their vacation time—either because they are the most dedicated or the most neurotic employees the company has. Many companies have rules that require that vacation time must be taken during the year in which the vacation time accrues. The more structured the corporation, the more likely it is that it will have rules that affect everyone's options—no matter how highly placed the employee.

There are many and varied solutions to the problem. One that is becoming popular is the right to be permitted to take time off equivalent to two years' vacation allowances. In other words, the vacation time accumulated over two years can be joined into one long holiday, which practically amounts to a sabbatical and can be very appealing.

Another solution is simply to allow the employee to take the vacation time in cash. However, while this relieves the corporation from having to replace the employee for the period of the vacation, the result may be an exhausted employee, which could threaten productivity, so many companies have a policy against that option.

One final vacation hint: Depending on how the unused vacation time can be rolled over from year to year, some senior executives use the vacation provision as an uncategorized slush fund that will be paid out on termination without (or even with) cause. Senior executives may not use the four or five weeks allotted to them, and an employee who accumulates unused weeks (e.g., two weeks a year for four years), will have additional severance on termination commensurate with the unused vacation weeks. Companies do not like this, but if the rollover practice of the company permits it, why not try for it?

EMPLOYMENT ISSUES SPECIFIC TO THE MUSIC INDUSTRY

Most industries do not face the same kinds of issues present when a music business executive is in the negotiating stage of an employment agreement. First and foremost is the issue of how to calculate compensation payable to those who sign artists or writers to the companies that employ them. (The issue of incentive is generally applicable to all industries, but provisions dealing with incentives for A&R executives are peculiar to the music industry.) Second, music industry companies have historically not been as "corporate"—as structured and as rule-driven—as other, more traditional companies. Third, there is often an urgency in placing an executive in a position quickly lest the chance to present him or her at a high-profile industry event passes while the lawyers and human resources personnel are haggling over details. Also, many executive employees in the music industry are not your usual three-piece-suit types; their *raisons d'être* are creative, and they themselves are likely to chafe at the stratified regulations that bind employees in companies in other industries. Indeed, more and more often, former high-profile celebrities are being hired by record and music publishing companies, giving rise to the same kind of problems that a television network has in dealing with its talent: other commitments. Finally, the nature of their work requires that provisions be included—for example, those pertaining to "fan mail"—that are not at issue in other types of companies.

A&R Incentive Plans

There are a variety of ways—or incentive plans—to calculate compensation payable to those who sign artists or writers to the companies which employ them. Most companies have their own "incentive" plans, and most of these have their own peculiar provisions affecting the termination of benefits. Suffice to say that the best result one can obtain in an A&R incentive plan is that the financial interest that the employee may acquire in a given artist's recordings or songs continues *after* the termination of employment. This result is rarely obtained. But as with many other positions taken by employers, there are many variations on the theme, and an employer who wants to accommodate the employee may be receptive to one or more of these.

Before addressing the *amount* of compensation traditionally offered to A&R executives, I want to first point out that it is important to be specific in identifying the particular artists and sound carriers (e.g., records, DVDs, etc.) as to which said compensation is *payable*. For example, if an A&R executive is the first to notice an artist, goes to a number of that artist's showcases, participates over a period of time in discussions of material, instrumentation, selection of a manager, strategies to interest the senior record company executives, etc., and ultimately is responsible for persuading the senior executives to sign the artist, that exec is likely to be considered qualified for the A&R incentive plan.

But what if the artist already has a record released in Europe (think: Macarena, *Chant*)? Even if the A&R person "discovers" the record, identifies the artist, takes the steps necessary for the U.S. record company affiliate to sign the artist, or merely to release the record, and works the record and the artist in the United States as if he or she had gone through all of the other processes described above, that person still may not qualify for the A&R incentive plan unless the language of the plan is flexible enough to include this variation on the theme. The same concern is present when an A&R executive is successful in persuading an artist who has been previously "discovered" by another label to come aboard the executive's own company. Many plans exempt from coverage any artist who appeared on another label, or any artist whose records have sold 250,000 or more copies on another label. (One might call this provision a *dis*incentive.)

Unfortunately, many of these plans are written in stone and are not negotiable. The person negotiating for the record company will usually say that the A&R person has to trust that his or her superiors will "do the right thing" in situations other than the standard ones. So much for creative lawyering. I do not know whether this attitude is a function of orders from on high or merely of laziness on the part of the company's staff assigned to draft modifications in language, but it is prevalent, certainly among the majors.

The A&R exec—or representative—trying to establish whether he or she is entitled to an incentive royalty on a particular artist or record is usually left only with the language of the incentive plan to resolve any questions, and I heartily recommend that every A&R person, before signing the agreement, read it *very* carefully, keeping in mind any "fluke" situations from his or her personal past—or even the historical past. For example, ABBA was the direct outgrowth of the two B's (Bjorn and Benny), whose single "Ring, Ring the Telephone" was going nowhere on a now-defunct label, Playboy Records. If the inducement plan for the A&R person at Atlantic who convinced the label to sign an agreement under which they would spend their entire careers included language requiring that he or she had to have "discovered" the artist, the A&R person would not be entitled to any participation in the group's success. Another remarkable turn of events (positive for the new label and pathetic for the old) occurred when Elton John's first single was similarly going nowhere on Bell Records, the predecessor in interest to Arista Records. A few entreaties and a few more dollars and one of the largest-selling artists of the twentieth century switched to UNI (MCA, now Universal) and the rest is history. As in the ABBA example, under similar language John's A&R person at UNI would not qualify for compensation. Now isn't that ridiculous?

Sometimes the preamble of the incentive plan itself gives some hint as to how a conflict about identifying artists or records that qualify for a royalty can be resolved. Following is an excerpt from the BMG A&R incentive plan.

> *This plan is designed to meet the following objectives all of which are intended to support eligible A&R positions:*
>
> ■ *To reward eligible A&R employees for their contributions in maximizing roster development, recording and sales of BMG Classics' product.*
> ■ *To assist in attracting and retaining qualified A&R employees.*

While this language may be in conflict with the exact language of the royalty provision, which most likely speaks in terms of acts "first signed or discovered" by the A&R person, a court could easily fit a Macarena, a *Chant,* an ABBA, or an Elton John into the definition if sufficient ambiguity were present to allow it to do so.

VARIATIONS OF ROYALTY CALCULATIONS

The royalty payable to the A&R person (often referred to as an "override") is customarily established at one rate for the United States and one-half of that for the rest of the world. A 1 to 1 $\frac{1}{2}$ percent royalty rate is fairly standard. This is usually calculated on the same basis as is that of the applicable artist signed by or served by the A&R person, and customarily amounts to from 9 to 12 cents. Here are some other variations.

- Sometimes the royalty is attributable only to recordings sold in the United States or in a territory somewhat less than the entire world.
- Sometimes the royalty will be capped at a certain amount of money (e.g., an amount equivalent to the A&R person's salary).
- Sometimes the royalty is payable from record one after recoupment of the recording costs at the artist's net (i.e., lower) rate.
- Sometimes the royalty is payable from record one after recoupment of the recording costs at the combined artist and producer rate (a faster rate of recoupment).
- Sometimes the royalty is payable prospectively from the point that the company has recouped the recording costs at the artist's net royalty rate.
- Sometimes the royalty is payable prospectively from the point that the company has recouped the recording costs at the combined artist and producer's rate.
- Sometimes the royalty is payable in the manner described in the four bulleted paragraphs immediately preceding this one, but instead of recouping only the recording costs, *all* (or many) costs attributable to a particular album (including video, marketing, promotion, touring, and other costs) are recouped at one rate or another as noted above.
- Sometimes the royalty is payable after a portion of the A&R person's salary

is recouped—i.e., as if a portion of the A&R person's salary is an "advance."

- Most often, the royalty is payable only until the expiration of the term of the A&R person's employment agreement or, alternatively, the royalty is payable (sometimes in a diminishing amount) over a period of years (one, two, or three) after expiration of the term of the A&R person's employment.

- Sometimes, though rarely, the royalty is payable after the expiration of the term (at least for a while) of the A&R person's employment agreement, if the employment expires on its own terms or is terminated "without cause." Sometimes, also rarely, the royalty is payable after the expiration of the term (at least for a while) of the A&R person's employment agreement, if the A&R person terminates the agreement "for good reason." The clauses pertaining to collection of royalties after termination can be extremely important, and the A&R person, and his or her representative, must review all such provisions carefully.

- Sometimes the royalty is payable with respect to all of the recordings made by the artist whom the A&R person signed or serviced.

- Sometimes the royalty is payable with respect to all of the recordings made by the artist whom the A&R person signed or serviced, with the exception of recordings made pursuant to a renegotiation.

- Sometimes the royalty is payable with respect to all of the recordings made by the artist whom the A&R person signed or serviced, with the exception of recordings made pursuant to an extension agreement.

- Sometimes the royalty is no longer payable if the A&R person dies or is disabled during the term. Sometimes it is.

- Sometimes the A&R person's contract requires that special credit provisions be provided on records (i.e., "A&R'd" by that person) and the royalty is payable only on records containing this credit.

- Most often, the royalty is payable only on USNRC albums (United States net sales through normal retail channels). Thus the royalty is not paid on singles, mid-priced records, budget records, records sold through record clubs, records sold via armed forces PXs, premium sales, educational and institutional means, licensed uses, governmental distribution and mail order; and tracks derived from full-length CDs sold as part of compilations. (Note that sometimes a reduced royalty will be paid for records sold in some, but not all, of these categories.)

- Sometimes the royalty is paid not only on USNRC, but on sales outside of the United States as well, excluding ancillary sales. Sometimes the royalty is paid not only on USNRC, but on all sales outside of the United States as well, including ancillary sales.

- Sometimes the royalty is paid at the same rates as the artist's royalties are calculated; sometimes it is paid at an arbitrary "half rate."

- Sometimes, the royalty is paid only while the artist is in the "black." This has the effect of the A&R person's royalties being retained by the record company once the artist has commenced recording of a subsequent record and has placed his royalty account "in the red" all over again.

- Sometimes royalties payable with respect to one artist whose recording costs are recouped are withheld by the record company because another artist or artists as to whose records the A&R person is entitled to receive royalties is in an unrecouped status. In other words, the accounts are cross-collateralized. This is of course a disaster in most situations for the A&R person.

- Sometimes (this is an especially hard one to take) the A&R person is a producer of the artist's recordings as well and the contract reduces the producer's royalty by the amount that the A&R person would have received pursuant to the A&R royalty provisions.

The above list is a partial one only. The possible variations are endless. Clearly, any A&R person considering employment must read and understand the consequences of the standard provisions and, hopefully, be able to negotiate changes peculiar to the employee's own situation and needs.

If the foregoing is not enough to depress the A&R person, there is another truth to deal with in this area: the royalty payable to the A&R person is almost always subject to most, if not all, of the same reductions and limitations as the artist's royalty is based: for example, allowance for reserves; packaging deductions; a reduction for digital mediums such as DVD, CD, DAI, and Internet downloads; and reductions commensurate with what the artist's royalties are reduced by (e.g., if the artist is paid on 85 or 90 percent of records sold, the A&R person's royalties will be reduced accordingly).

Finally, it is not unusual for a record company to refuse to allow the A&R person (who is an employee of the company, after all) to audit the books and records of the record company with respect to his or her A&R royalty. The argument given for this is that the auditor would discover information whose confidentiality is of such consequence that the management of the record company's business would be compromised were the information to be disclosed to the A&R person. Similarly, record companies often resist attorneys' efforts to obtain for their clients the right to an upward royalty adjustment if the *artist's* audit claim results in a settlement with positive implications for the A&R person. For example, if the artist, producer, and A&R person are all accounted to for 400,000 records sold in Australia and it turns out that the record company mysteriously, and erroneously, forgot to account for an additional 200,000 records, while the artist's royalty account will be adjusted upward, and most likely the producer's will as well, the A&R person's account will not be, and there is no way for the A&R person to even know that such an adjustment has taken place.

Even when the A&R person is permitted to examine the books *while* he or she is employed, upon termination of employment, the right to audit may also be terminated, making it difficult if not impossible to verify the amounts owed—that is, amounts earned and payable during the term of employment. Sometimes, profit shares and royalties may be payable only through the end of the contract term, and the language providing for this result may be so obscure as to be easily missed by someone reviewing the contract. However, as noted in the list above, payment responsibilities insofar as A&R royalties and the like are concerned may be able to be extended if the contract has been terminated by the employer without cause or by the employee "for good reason."

Employment Agreements with Celebrities and Others Otherwise Engaged

When negotiating A&R agreements for a person who is also a talent in his or her own right, the attorney representing that person needs to consider carefully what is singular about the person, and whatever exceptions are appropriate to that person should be sought during the employment contract negotiation. It is surprising how many requests for exceptions are likely to be granted—even when the eventual employee's leverage is not so great. Currently there is a trend, which began, albeit slowly, a few decades ago, toward hiring celebrities for A&R positions. For example, Mitch Miller, head of A&R at Columbia in the 1950s and 1960s, also had his enormously popular television show. And, although Clive Davis has not been seen waving a baton at a chorus lately, few record executives can boast his extraordinary visibility. Today, L. A. Reid (Arista), Quincy Jones (Quest), and other well-known music industry personages are heading up some of the industries' most visible record labels, or providing consulting services, and also appearing on television and at high-profile parties.

Such employees, and others like them, while exclusive for a category of services—e.g., A&R person—may wish to pursue other interests, from endorsements to broadcast commercials, to maintaining their own websites and offering merchandise, to recording or writing for others outside of the exclusive relationship. An employee who is also a songwriter may want to pursue a separate career as a theatrical show writer, or to continue writing for motion picture or television soundtracks.

An employee who has had a prior career as a producer's manager or an artist's manager may want to continue to pursue these interests during the term of his or her employment or at least during a phase-out period during the term of his employment. That person may wish to continue to receive financial compensation arising from a prior manager's agreement with an artist or producer. If so, he or she will have to provide for this in the employment contract to avoid a conflict of interest and a breach resulting from nondisclosure.

A record company A&R person with a public persona may wish to appear on *Hollywood Squares* or similar programs; to appear as a guest on talk programs and even prime-time situation comedies or specials; even to be, say, the "music minute" reporter on *The Today Show.* A&R execs who are also performers may wish to continue to appear in front of live audiences.

Mail

In certain talent contracts (for example, video jockeys on cable channels or on Internet "radio" stations), the issue of fan mail arises. This is a real concern to people who receive it and to the companies whose employees receive it. Certainly, it should be collected and forwarded to the employee. But should it be read? The employer will often claim the right to open it, read it, and even answer it; sometimes the employer will agree to keep it private when it is marked "private" or "personal" and deliver it to the employee directly.

There are copyright issues to be considered as well. Who owns the letter? Who—the employer or the employee—can benefit from ideas expressed or suggestions offered in the letters? Obviously, fan mail can be very useful to both the employer and employee. The manner in which it is collected, read, categorized, registered in databases, etc., is of real concern to both and the way in which this is handled can and should be specifically provided for in the employment agreement.

There are cyberspace issues here, as well. What about e-mail? Most cases dealing with this issue have held that the employers own the e-mail of all employees. They not only have the right to access the employees' e-mail files (including the "mailing list"), but they can snoop on employees' exchanges. What about e-mails from fans to the employer's website? To the employee's website? To the employee's website which is managed (and owned?) by the employer? The law in such cases is fast evolving, but it will apply only to those situations where the employer and employee *have not themselves dealt with the issue in their written contracts.*

The Ownership of Ideas

It is not unusual for employers to attempt to treat all intellectual property created by an employee during the term of the employment as the property of the company. As such, the company will seek not only to own the results of the employee's creative thinking— that person's intellectual property—but also to bind the employee to nondisclosure of such intellectual property.

As noted in the opening sections of this chapter, uniquely in the music industry many of the very people whose professional services are sought to *foster* creative development in others are themselves creators. It is anathema to them to be asked to sign an agreement which assigns to the employer all the results of their creative services— including, by definition, their "ideas" and the expression of such ideas (such as songs, artistic approaches to production, arrangements, etc.). While the provision against disclosure or use of information may be said to have a generally rational purpose, it may be abusive and overreaching under certain circumstances, and for certain people.

Contract language in the realm of works for hire will often specify that the employee must warrant that *all* ideas, creations, literary, musical, and artistic materials and intellectual properties created or developed by the employee *during the course of employment* will be owned by the company as works for hire. And, often, these provisions are buried in general boilerplate warranty paragraphs. Obviously those who are hired for creative purposes must be most cautious about such provisions which do not provide for compensation. An A&R person who contributes ideas as part of his or her job does not usually intend to relinquish ownership in songs written outside of the parameters of the job description—particularly for no compensation. While ideas, as such, are not susceptible of copyright protection, the *expression* of ideas is, and this fact should be considered carefully in each case before signing an employment agreement that contains language which is improvidently or heedlessly conceived. As with other provisions in these "standard" inducement plans, business affairs lawyers are reticent to make *any* changes in language, so your attorney's battle on your behalf to avoid a potentially catastrophic result, where your company owns your creations without having compensated you for them, will not be an easy one.

8 RECORD PRODUCERS:
Are They As Sharp As Their Points?

<table>
<tr><td>

The first cut

is the deepest

Baby I know

—Cat Stevens
</td><td>

In the world of recording, the media have told us more than we want to hear about artists and record companies. But one role player who has traditionally succeeded in keeping a fairly low profile is the record producer. (This is not necessarily so in urban music, where often one identifies the recording more with the producer than with
</td></tr>
</table>

the artist.) There are a number of developing trends in the world which may well have a huge financial impact on "producers" of recordings. I am of course talking about individual producers rather than record companies which "produce" recordings. Unfortunately, in many international laws and treaties (e.g., the Rome Convention), the term "producer" refers to a record company, not an individual. There is a trend, however, toward identifying individual producers as a class of people in the music industry who deserve ongoing entitlements as a result of the use or misuse of their recordings in much the same way music publishers and songwriters are compensated.

Who was the first producer? It is hard to say, but Walter Legge, formerly the chief creative person at EMI in London, claimed to be the first. (Norman Lebrecht, in his "tell all" book *Who Killed Classical Music?* refers to him as the most disagreeable personage ever to intrude upon musical performance.) It was Legge's aim to "make records that would set the standards by which public performances and the artists of the future would be judged." He tried to make records not only match live performances, but to exceed them in quality. He certainly succeeded. A huge percentage of EMI's "Recordings of the Century" bear his imprint as producer. Legge even created an orchestra, the Philharmonia of London, for recording purposes only, yet today the Philharmonia is one of the world's most respected performing orchestras as well.

The old adage about the chicken and the egg has some resonance among producers. Who is responsible for an artist's success, the artist or the producer? This is a question that will, most probably, never be answered to everyone's satisfaction. The producer shapes the recording, but depending on the nature of the artist and the artist's particular talent, the producer's role will differ dramatically from artist to artist.

HOW 25 PERCENT CAN EQUAL 100 PERCENT

In Chapter 4, I more or less glossed over the producer's cut of the artist's royalties. Let's look more closely at the financial impact of the producer's deal on the artist's ultimate take-home pay. Let's say that an artist's royalty rate from the record company is 12 percent of the suggested retail selling price of records. Not unusual. A customary producer's royalty would be approximately one-fourth of that rate, or 3 percent, leaving the artist with 9 percent. Another way to put it is that the producer receives 25 percent of the total royalties, but 33 1/3 percent of what the artist receives. So it would seem that for every $9 dollars credited to the artist's account (and notice the "credited"; the artist may never see this money) the producer gets $3.

Not so. Here's why.

First, and most significant, after recoupment of recording costs, the producer customarily gets paid from record one—the first record sold. The artist does not.

Let's say the recording costs are $100,000 and the 12 percent royalty works out to about $1.08 per record. [In this example, I am assuming that a royalty "point" is worth about 9 cents ($0.09). It can be higher.] The record company will usually recoup these recording costs (that is, pay themselves back) at the so-called "net artist rate," that is, 9 percent (12 percent less the producer's rate of 3 percent). (I am assuming, for the sake of this example, that the producer is solely responsible for producing the entire CD; it is entirely possible that the producer's share is not calculated on 100 percent of the tracks on the CD, as pointed out below under "Pro Rata Royalty Share.") At $0.09 a point, a 9 percent royalty rate works out to be about $0.80. At $0.80 per unit, it will require a sale of 125,000 records before the recording costs are recouped. At that point, the producer is entitled to be paid his or her 3 percent royalty from record one. At $0.27 per record (3 times $0.09), the producer is entitled to a check for $33,750. The artist? He's entitled to nothing at this point.

Is the producer receiving 25 percent of the total royalty paid out by the record company? No. He is receiving 100 percent! The record company receives about $7.00 per record sold through its distribution system. Thus, 125,000 in sales represents more than $875,000 in cash receipts to the company.

Let's examine what happens when the record has achieved sales of 250,000 units. The producer's royalties have now reached $67,500. The artist royalties are now in the positive column also. Once the 125,000th sale has occurred, the artist will be due royalties of $0.80 per record on all units sold after that. The differential between 250,000 and 125,000 is 125,000. Therefore, the artist will have earned a grand total of $100,000. This is beginning to look better for the artist.

The total royalties payable by the record company (which, lest we forget, has received by now $1.75 million from its distributors) have amounted only to $167,500. The producer's $67,500 share amounts to 40 percent of the total royalties paid (hardly the 25 percent the artist originally had in mind), and the artist's $100,000 share will be 60 percent of the total royalties paid. In fact, the producer's share of total royalties will *never* be 25 percent. I am not saying this is unlikely; I am saying it is impossible. Watch.

More bad news: the artist will not receive the $100,000 which he or she has earned according to the above scenario. It will take many more sales before the artist receives the first royalty check. Why? Because, as noted in Chapter 4, in the music business, not only does the artist pay out of royalties the cost of producing his or her own recordings; the artist also has to pay for tour support advances, equipment advances, independent promotion expenses (more about this later), video production expenses (or at least one-half of them), and an array of additional expenditures. So it can require 500,000 album units or more before the record company has recouped all of these advances and expenses. At that point, the producer will have received

$135,000 in royalties (3 percent, or $0.09, times 500,000 units) and the artist will still have received: *zero.*

In essence, record companies, unlike all other businesses which create and exploit intellectual property (movies, television, book publishing), get to make huge profits on products, the worldwide copyright to which they will own for upward of 95 years, without having actually paid for them. Granted, they risk losing the investment, but when a record succeeds, the only thing they have lost is the use, for a year and a half or so, of that money.

CROSS-COLLATERALIZATION:
IT DOES NOT APPLY TO THE PRODUCER

Because the cross-collateralization provisions contained in most artist-record company agreements do not apply to producers, the disparity between the relative earnings of the producer and the artist on a particular record does not stop with the calculations listed above. When the artist records a subsequent album, its costs will inevitably be charged against the prior album's royalties as well, but the producer will not have to face this additional headache. Once that 125,000th sale has occurred, the producer is home free for all time and will get his or her share of every record sold, every use on a compilation, synchronization in a film, soap opera, TV special, or commercial—even as the artist is wallowing in "debt" due to the right of the record company to recoup costs associated not just with that particular record but unrecouped costs related to both prior and subsequent records as well.

Whether this practice will continue or be modified in the future is something that will require some serious thinking on the part of artists' advisors who specialize in this field and who understand all of the ramifications of the producer receiving "a couple of points." It is endlessly surprising to me how many artists and their representatives do not understand the true significance of cross-collateralization provisions, or, more aptly, the absence of them in producer agreements. Perhaps when they do, what is sought to be a creative partnership may become a financial one as well. Meanwhile, since the industry still protects producer royalties from the application of any recording costs but those that he or she is involved in, the producer's attorney should take steps to ensure that on a particular recording project (e.g., an album), only those costs attributable to the portion of the album that that particular producer is working on will be subject to recoupment. If the producer has to wait for the artist's royalties to accumulate until the entire album's recording costs are recouped at the artist's royalty rate, and the producer has either produced less than 100 percent of the whole album, or the record company has engaged other producers or mixers to fine-tune the work of the producer, the producer will have a long time to wait before receiving royalties "from record one"—if in fact they are *ever* received.

It should now be abundantly clear that three "points," calculated as producers' royalties, is a lot more attractive are than nine points calculated as artists' royalties are. To put it another way, the work/reward ratio is a lot more favorable for the producer, whose creative input and labor end once the recording process is completed, than for the artist, who must "work" the record for months afterward, pursuing promotion, marketing, and touring efforts to bring the record to the attention of potential buyers.

SOME POINTS FOR PRODUCERS

Despite the basic disparity between the producer's share and the artist's share of royalties—which works in favor of the producer—there are a number of contractual snares and pitfalls that producers should be aware of. From the outset, the producer's representatives must obtain a copy of the artist's royalty provisions, without which they will have no basis on which to determine what the producer is supposed to receive.

Producers' Royalty Provisions: The Basics

The royalty exclusions or reductions in the producer's agreement should at least coincide with those in the artist's agreement. That is, whenever the artist is to receive royalties for particular uses, the producer should receive royalties as well. If the artist does *not* receive royalties for certain uses (e.g., special compilation CDs given away with new automobiles), the producer may have to suffer similar consequences. However, although producers customarily live with the provisions in the artist's agreement, they needn't do so if they have some leverage. Ancillary uses such as promotional giveaways are a considerable source of licensing income, and even if the record company's agreement with the artist denies the artist a share of that income, if the producer has any leverage, why be hoisted by the same petard? The artist's negotiating position might have been weak, the artist or the artist's representatives careless or not assertive, or perhaps the artist's representatives simply decided that it was not financially sound for the artist to pay the legal costs of fighting for *absolutely everything* in an 80-page agreement. That does not mean that the producer must suffer the same consequences.

It should be a given that the terms of the contract with the producer be clear to all concerned—artist, producer, producer's lawyer and manager, and so on—and that all agree on what the deal is. But you would be surprised how often this is not case. For example, did they agree to a royalty of 3 percent of retail, going to 3 ½ percent at 500,000 units and to 4 percent at 1,000,000 units? Did they agree on the correct number of tracks? Did they agree on whether the producer would do the mix? Did they agree on whether the artist/record company can reduce the royalty if they bring in another person to do the mix? The remix? Does the producer realize that all recording costs in excess of the agreed-upon budget may be directly charged to him or her? Will the producer's royalty be paid after recoupment of recording costs attributable to his or her production only, or will it be paid after recoupment of the total recording costs on the album?

Will the producer receive royalties directly from the record company, and has the record company formally agreed to this? Or has the record company simply acknowledged receipt of a letter of direction requesting that it honor the request of the producer—which has become the customary way record companies have chosen to deal with this issue.

The following sections cover some of the important contractual issues the producer and the producer's representatives must be aware of. All of these issues should be thought through, and, as with anything else, if the producer and the producer's representatives have faced them and chosen not to request changes after having been fully informed of the consequences, that's fine too.

THE PRODUCER'S SHARE OF RENEGOTIATED ROYALTIES

An artist's royalty provisions may—no, *will*—be modified upward once the record agreement is renegotiated. If the improvements are retroactive, it is important that the producer-artist agreement allow that improvements in the producer's royalty be made along with improvements in the artist's royalty—especially because the renegotiation will presumably have occurred, at least in part, because of the success of the record which the producer produced! Increased royalties may also be the order of the day upon a record's achieving certain sales levels. For example, if a record is a success, and the artist's royalty increases, from, say, 12 percent to 13 percent at 1 million units, does the producer's percentage dip from his 25 percent ratio to $3/13$ths, or 23 percent? While this is 23 percent of the total, it is only 30 percent of what the artist receives, a 10 percent decline from 33 $1/3$ percent! It might surprise you that this is exactly what happens unless specific provision to the contrary is made in the producer's agreement. Sometimes royalty modifications are applied prospectively for future records of the artist, and in that event, it is not likely that the producer's royalties can be adjusted for the existing record.

NEW TECHNOLOGY

In the area of digital or new technology, it is not unusual to see provisions establishing that a producer's share of the royalties on such uses be calculated according to a specific percentage of the total. The figure 16.67 percent is one that is often used, and it is obvious that the result will be an overall reduction from the 33 $1/3$ percent of the artist's share cited above.

This 16.67 percent (or any other number used) is totally arbitrary, and can have dramatic impact on what the producer gets from ancillary sales of records which, in the new Internet age, may actually constitute a greater percentage of total sales than those through normal retail channels. Recent producer agreements have been quite innovative in the area of determining the producer's share of income derived from digital downloads. I have seen as much as a 30 percent reduction in the producer's royalty share. Sometimes I think that the record companies, or the artists' attorneys, insert these provisions just for the hell of it. There certainly is no justification for them, and as the gross share of income derived by virtue of digital downloads is certain to increase over time, producers' attorneys should be on the lookout for such provisions. Too often, by the time the producer's attorney gets to the bottom of the royalty provisions, his or her eyesight, let alone consciousness, is blurred and these kinds of provisions slip through the cracks.

DELAYS

Sometimes the negotiations on a project go on so long that it is appropriate to ask that a "start-up" advance (customarily 50 percent of the total producer's advance against royalties) be paid to the producer even though the paperwork is not complete. One reason negotiations may be dragged out is uncertainty on the part of the artist—or record company—as to the number of tracks for which the producer may be asked to perform producer services or that he or she may be asked to mix. The producer should not be penalized for this uncertainty.

PRO RATA ROYALTY SHARE

Customarily, the producer will receive a pro rata share of the total royalty, depending on how many tracks are produced in relation to the total number of tracks on the album. Note, however, that whatever percentage is decided upon can be the subject of heated renegotiation later. For example, suppose the one track that the producer produces is the track that "makes" the record. I recall a situation when a movie soundtrack was released and the only track of any significance was the title track to the film, which was a big hit in and of itself. The record company sold millions of albums, and the artist and producer's brilliant track was dealt with as if it were merely one of a dozen of tracks on the album. There is no rule that says the track cannot bear a royalty *as if* it were five or six tracks on the album. At least this way the track will earn money for the artist and the producer commensurate with its real value. (The soundtrack to *Foul Play,* starring Goldie Hawn and Chevy Chase, contained "Ready To Take A Chance Again," which was the only important song in the film—or on the album. Barry Manilow sought—and received—royalties as if the recording represented 50 percent rather than 10 percent of the album's content.)

If the number of tracks to be produced is indefinite at the time of negotiation, the producer's agreement can take into account the uncertainty by including a series of contingency provisions, reducing the total royalty base on which the producer's royalty is calculated by, say, 5 percent for each reduction in the producer's contribution by one track. For example, if 10 or more songs produced by the producer appear on the album, the royalty will be calculated and paid on the basis of 100 percent of the base royalty (e.g., 3 percent, going to $3 \frac{1}{2}$ percent at 500,000 units and to 4 percent at 1 million units). For a nine-song contribution, the royalty would be calculated and paid on 95 percent of the base royalty; for an eight-song contribution, the royalty would be calculated and paid at 90 percent of the base royalty; and so on. This is only an example. There are innumerable permutations, and the relative strength of the producer and the artist must always be taken into account when concocting the formula to be used. The point is, producers should not be penalized and have their royalties reduced by the mere addition of "filler" tracks on the record which do not bear any qualitative comparison to the tracks they have produced.

A-SIDE PROTECTION

A producer who has not produced all the tracks on an album does not want the track or tracks he or she *has* produced to lead the sale of a single or a CD single (which might contain more than two songs) and receive merely a pro rata share of royalties based on the total number of tracks on the particular recording. Customarily, when a producer produces the great majority of tracks on an album, or when he or she is "star" producer and is brought in to produce only one or two key tracks, that producer is afforded what is known as *A-side protection.* This means that if the producer's track is on the A side, he or she will receive a full royalty without regard to whether other tracks that the producer is responsible for are incorporated onto the B side (or, in the case of CD singles, the B or C sides). Producers may even insist on language in their contracts providing that their track(s) *not* be included on the B side, in the hopes that the track(s) will be contained on the A side one day. It is important for the producer's representative to understand what is actually going on in the studio—how many tracks are being recorded, whether the artist or record company intends to bring in another producer to record additional tracks, etc.—so that he or she will be in a position to negotiate this provision effectively given the particular nature of the recordings that the client is making in relation to the album as a whole.

CREDIT PROVISIONS

There need to be provisions setting forth the credits to be accorded the producer—size and location on the CD, back cover, liner notes, etc. One thing that is often carelessly handled is the nature of the credit when the producer is providing his or her services through a service corporation. If the producer's services are being furnished by the producer's corporation, it would be inconsistent for the CD to carry a simple credit, "Produced By [Producer's Name]." If the words "For [Name of Service Corporation]" were not included, the IRS could infer that the producer's claimed tax position, that of being employed by a corporation, was not true. There can be nasty tax consequences as a result of this apparently innocent lapse. Therefore, the contract provisions relating to credit must take this into consideration. Of course, some producers, like artists, do not want to appear too "corporate" and are willing to take the risk.

Producers may also want to avoid the situation in which their names are connected to a particularly goofy corporate name in credit lines and in advertisements. Presumably, they want their work to be taken seriously. This is not as easily achieved when the credit reads, say, "Produced by [Producer's name] for "Take the Money and Run, Inc.""

Producers should make sure that provisions are included stating they will receive credit in every medium they might wish or expect and in a reasonable size and typeface. Nothing is more disconcerting than for a producer to open *Billboard* and see that no producer credit is given in the full-page advertisement celebrating the record's release—or platinum achievement. And don't neglect consumer ads. *Rolling Stone* (believe it or not, this is not considered a "trade" magazine), *People, Vanity Fair*—all are consumer publications that can reach the artist's potential audience and there is no reason to have the producer's name removed from those ads, which will most certainly be read by industry professionals. Yes, they do read things other than the "trades."

Producers might also want to consider requesting that their credits *not* appear with respect to mixes or remixes by third parties, or that their names as producers be retained but not as mixers.

AUDITS

As stated previously, the producer's royalties are dependent on the artist royalty provisions. Therefore, the producer's representatives *must* have an unredacted copy of those provisions in order to be able to determine what the producer is supposed to receive.

Other audit-related issues are the following. Are there provisions covering whether the producer is bound by the accountings to the artist and/or the audit provisions of the artist's agreement? Does the producer have the independent right to audit the record company? Can the producer "piggyback" on the artist's royalty audit and insure that his or her entitlements are covered as well as those of the artist in any eventual claim that is asserted following the conclusion of a royalty examination?

RE-RECORDING RESTRICTIONS

Customarily, producers are expected to warrant to the artist and the artist's record company that they will not for a period of from two to five years after the completion of their production services produce or co-produce a master recording for any other artist or record company which embodies any musical composition they have just produced. When the producer also writes the songs being produced, this can be an unreasonable restraint on future exploitation of the producer's own compositions. This can be even more restrictive if the producer is also an artist and might like to record his or her own versions of these compositions.

AUTHORSHIP

It has become the norm for the contract with the producer to provide that the producer must warrant that he or she has not made and shall not make any contribution to the authorship of any compositions recorded and that he or she will not claim any right, title, or interest therein. If the producer *has* made an authorship contribution and the contract is still in the draft stage, the language can be changed. But what happens when a producer has already signed a contract containing this provision and then makes a significant authorship contribution? In such a case, I usually advise my producer clients not the leave the studio until a piece of paper confirming the co-authorship, and the exact splits, is initialed by all contributing authors.

SAMPLED MATERIAL

Most producer contracts specify that *delivery* of the masters is deemed not to have occurred unless and until all written licenses and permissions from the owner(s) of sampled material have been obtained and delivered to the artist and record company. More often than not, except in the hip-hop genre, it is the artist who decides samples are necessary and who selects them, but it is the producer who is contractually responsible for obtaining the permissions, upon terms and conditions acceptable to the artist and the record company, and it is the producer who is responsible for any fee or other payment due in connection with the use of any sampled material that is not approved by the artist and the record company. That's quite a responsibility. Do all producers know that such provisions exist? Have their lawyers or managers ever told them about this particularly tricky delivery requirement? Sometimes a producer will become aware of this provision only when the back-end advance, having been used by the record company to pay for the costs of samples, does not arrive on schedule (or at all) or has been reduced. Of course, the previous example covers the situation in which the artist is signed directly to directly to the record company and the producer is separately, and independently, engaged. When the record company signs the producer who provides the services of the artist, or when the producer *is* the artist, the sanctions on producers, which I am suggesting be avoided in sampling situations, will not apply.

Another issue involving sampled material involves cases in which the record company is sued by unaffiliated artists or other record companies claiming their material has been sampled without permission. A producer who has had nothing to do with selecting samples should not indemnify the artist against losses resulting from claims by the owners of the sampled recordings. The same warning applies to the songs embodied on the recordings. The producer is in no position to warrant the originality of the musical compositions written by the artist and should not be responsible for any costs related to the fact or claim that these songs may be plagiarized by the artist.

INDEMNITIES

Producers, who by definition are supposed to be the responsible ones in charge of hundred thousand dollar budgets, are often asked to protect the record company from eventual claims arising out of a large number of potential problem areas. Producers and their representatives must be particularly careful about what the contract requires them to indemnify. For example, if the producer has nothing to do with selecting samples, he or she should not indemnify the artist or record company against losses resulting from claims by the owners of the recordings sampled. The same warning applies to the songs. For example, the producer is in no position to warrant the originality of musical compositions written by the artist and should not be responsible for any costs related to the fact or claim that these songs have been plagiarized by the artist. Finally, as with all indemnities, no one can guarantee that a claim will not be brought by a third party seeking compensation for damages. Claims themselves are very costly to defend, and the only thing that the indemnity should apply to is losses resulting from these claims—presumably confirming the veracity of the claims—not the cost of a successful defense of a claim. Claims settled without the consent of the producer should not be subject to the indemnity provision unless the producer has consented to the settlement.

UNION REQUIREMENTS

The standard contract requires that the producer adhere to all union agreements having jurisdiction over the recording, and producers and their representatives should be aware of what this entails.

Among the most tedious responsibilities are the filing of union session reports within a set number of days (usually 14) following the applicable recording session. These session reports are, in themselves, rather complicated in that the producer must accurately report the number of sessions; overtime, if any; and, in the case of the American Federation of Musicians, indicate who is the leader of the musicians. (Every union session must have a leader, who receives "double scale.") Many producers have assistants who are familiar with the rules and regulations of the two principal unions (AFM and AFTRA) involved in the making of recordings. Union regulations for theatrical productions are especially complex and costly, and some theatrical show producers are paid substantially for the services of their assistants in addition to their own fees. But any way you look at it, the record producer is charged with these responsibilities and the ramifications for failing to honor them can be serious.

PRODUCER-ENGINEERS

When a producer provides services as an engineer as well as a producer, if the fees attributable to his or her engineering services are included in the customary advance paid against producer royalties, it is appropriate to divide the advance into (1) the engineering fee, which is not recoupable against royalties, and (2) an amount recoupable against producer royalties. How the "advance" is divided can have a tremendous impact on earnings because the faster the advance is recouped (i.e., the lower the amount of what is designated as the advance), the more quickly the producer will receive royalties that, as you will recall, go back to record one. These early royalties can accumulate in substantial amounts, and if they are never "released," because the advance is never recouped by the record company, there can be significant financial consequences for the producer.

LOCATION OF RECORDING

Producers are often comfortable in their own environment. They know about the studios in their geographical area; they are aware of the availability and level of quality of techs, equipment, parts, etc. If the consensus among the record company's A&R person and the artist and the artist's representatives dictates that the recording be made, in whole or in part, outside of the producer's preferred location, two factors come into play. First, there are conceivably additional costs for transporting people and equipment (for example, the Pro-Tools engineer the producer prefers to work with), all of which will add to the production budget and delay the release of the producer's royalties after the advance has been recouped. If possible, language should be added stipulating that the producer is not responsible for such additional costs. Second, the producer's own comforts must be considered—for example, travel, accommodations, rental car, per diems, perhaps a trip "home" if the process takes more than a month or two. All will have to be dealt with, and the producer's own manager or attorney—whoever is negotiating the agreement—should be familiar with the producer's minimum requirements in this area.

COMPLIMENTARY COPIES

The producer's representatives must make sure the contract contains a provision requiring the record company to deliver to the producer, at its expense, at least twenty-five (25) copies of the CD as soon as it is released. You would be surprised how many times a record company will try to weasel out of giving producers the copies of the CD that are rightfully theirs and which they need for a variety of reasons, not the least of which is auditioning for new projects.

The Producer as Author

All record companies require that producers acknowledge that their duties are performed as employees for hire and that the products of their efforts are works for hire. Under the Copyright Law of 1976, which went into effect in 1978, there is a crucial distinction between a *work for hire* and a work created by an artist or author that is *not* a work for hire. There are two legal categories of works for hire:

- Works created by employees of a company "within the scope of his or her employment."
- Works created by independent contractors that have been specially commissioned for use (1) as a contribution to a collective work, (2) as a part of a motion picture or other audiovisual work, (3) as a translation, (4) as a supplementary work, (5) as a compilation, (6) as an instructional text, (7) as a test, (8) as answer material for a test, or (9) as an atlas, provided the contractors have signed an agreement with the commissioning company stipulating that the works they produce shall be considered works for hire.

Original works that do not fall into one of the above nine categories are not considered works for hire. In the late 1990s, an amendment was passed to the copyright law that added sound recordings to this list, but in September 2000 that amendment was repealed.

The significance for a musician or songwriter who has *not* created a "work for hire" is that even if he or she transfers, or grants, to the record company the copyright in the work, the grant can be recaptured by the artist at any time during a period of five years beginning at the end of 35 years from the date of execution of the grant. Notices of intent to terminate can be filed 10 years before that, and these notices will begin to fly into record companies' offices starting in 2003. This issue will be of particular relevance to record producers who have contributed more than traditional production services, that is, producers who have actually *created* the product no less than if they were the artists themselves. Such producers have become the norm in certain genres of music. To my mind, these producers have every right to be called "authors," and it will be interesting to see if they can garner the support for a share in the recapture wars that are certain to erupt shortly. We will begin to learn, in 2013, whether producers will be able to capture rights in their sound recordings that record companies now think they own forever.

Notwithstanding the uncertainty swirling around the work for hire issue, record companies have strengthened their resolve to lock in producers to the concept. Not only must all producer/artist agreements pursuant to which the record companies will take direction to pay producers directly include work for hire language, but record companies are now insisting that certificates of employment be signed as well—before the actual producer agreements are concluded. This insistence on producers admitting in writing that the record they are about to produce is a work for hire—*even before they receive their start-up advance*—is becoming universal in the United States. Many lawyers are up in arms about their clients signing a document that says that the record company owns the results of the producer's services even before the deal is fully negotiated, let alone reduced to a signed writing. Some lawyers withhold their objection if they have at least a brief deal memo signed between the artist and the producer. Those with no leverage will allow the certificate of employment to be signed even if the actual deal is far from concluded—just so that the producer can go into the studio and begin working. After all, they feel, sooner or later, they will be paid for their services since a record company would be hard-pressed to say that they own something when they have not actually paid for it. In any event, here is one more document which benefits the record company, may well turn out to be illegitimate, and requires expensive lawyer's services to review.

PRODUCERS AND NEIGHBORING RIGHTS

As uses of recordings multiply due to the spread of the Internet among all peoples of the world, assuming that unauthorized sharing and piracy can be controlled, income for all participants will increase as well. This section is included to alert producers and their representatives to the fact that some institutions and mechanisms exist now, and others are in the process of being established, which can be used to generate additional income for individual producers which they do not enjoy as of the date this book is being written. While the passage of truly meaningful neighboring rights legislation has been blocked for generations in the United States, there are some cracks in the wall of resistance—notably the Digital Performance Right in Sound Recordings Act (DPRSRA) of 1995, which mandated licensing fees for certain digital transmissions by subscription services.

For the first time, artists (together with their record companies and their producers) are being paid for the performance of their music. Frank Sinatra and others whose recorded performances generated fortunes for the broadcasting industry over the years, and who fought for neighboring rights legislation for decades, must be singing for joy in the other realm.

Over the last few decades, record producers have gotten into the act, claiming that radio performances of their music should generate a "residual" for them as well as for the music publishers and writers. The record producers of the current period see themselves not just as functionaries, but as intellectual property creators and contributors no less important to the ultimate product than the song. Of course, recording artists feel the same way, so there is quite a large population of people hungry for a larger piece of the pie. As the pie itself continues to grow, perhaps producers will receive a fairer hearing.

Record producers note that film companies refer to the script as the "currency" of the motion picture and music publishers refer to the song as the "currency" of the recording, and they contend that, by analogy, their contribution is the "currency" of genres like rap, hip hop, and dance music. And frankly, they are not wrong.

There are two issues here. The first is whether individual producers are "authors" in the sense of various world copyright conventions. For example, the Rome Convention, to which the United States is not a signatory, stipulates that when a work is broadcast, a fee must be paid to the producers, to the performers, or to both, of the broadcast work, or phonogram. The phrase "broadcasters of phonograms," has been the subject of intense litigation in Europe because, as I have noted earlier, individual producers are claiming that the word "producer" refers both to individual producers and corporate (record company) producers. The consensus of those who have considered this issue is that it was probably the intention of the drafters of this convention and others that the "producers" for whom the conventions have sought to provide protection are indeed the record companies and not individual producers, who are trying to slip themselves into the coverage afforded by the treaties.

The second issue is a practical one. Even if the individual producers prevail in their claim—or succeed in promoting legislation supporting their claim—is there enough support in the industry to force broadcasters to pay yet another fee for the operation of their business? It does not appear that there is. Currently, the organizations that collect neighboring rights income for artists and record companies have no direct contractual commitment to individual producers. It is probably not through the record company that the artist will be paid neighboring rights income, and therefore the traditional producer agreement and the letter of direction to the record company will not cover the issue of neighboring rights income. One of the things that the producer can do in the meantime, however, is to piggyback on the rights of artists, where they exist, and share in the same ratio as they share in other income sources via the producer agreement (e.g., foreign, club, budget, and other forms of ancillary income). This will require that the producer agreement with the artist specifically identify sources of income that may not be collected directly by the record company, with the resultant pay-through of a share to the individual producer. These new sources that are collected directly by the artist will have to be accounted for and paid separately by the artist, who is not traditionally equipped to account on a regular basis to others. Thus, the producer agreement might include a letter of direction—"To Whom It May Concern"—such that in cases in which artist income for neighboring rights is paid directly from broadcasters to artists (or to artists' agents), the paying party is directed to also pay the producer his or her contractual percentage (for example, 16.67 percent) directly.

It will probably be a long time before individual record producers will be able to claim a share of the neighboring rights income currently destined, where it is permitted, for the pockets of performing artists and record companies. They will have to overcome the economic resistance of a large number of interests as well as the perception that their creative contribution to a master recording is something less than "authorship."

GETTING YOUR RECORD HEARD: A Practical Guide to Marketing and Promotion

Half the money
I spend on adver-
tising is wasted;
the trouble is
I don't know
which half.

—Lord Leverhulme,
in David Ogilvy's
*Confessions of an
Advertising Man*

The record is written and recorded. It is manifested (finally) in a master recording from which "derivatives" will be made and shipped (or digitally transmitted) to the consumer. There are now left only two functional dominions—or realms—which affect the recording artist's eventual success or failure: the contract terms and the record company's promotional tools. The contract describes the mutual promises made between the record company and the artist; it defines and delineates the structure of their relationship and it refines how their respective rights and financial entitlements are to be governed and how they are to be achieved. The promotional tools of the record company are the hundred or so actions it can take to maximize the chances that potential buyers will hear the record and that the artist(s) will achieve the highest profile possible. Of these mechanisms, which include advertising of all kinds, videos, and public appearances, the most important is radio promotion, that is, obtaining airplay time. And whereas in the past promotional campaigns were handled and paid for by the record companies, increasingly the trend has been toward independent promotion, where, although people inside the company *manage* the promotional campaigns, people outside the company are charged with the real task and costs are borne in part or in whole by the artist.

Advertising and publicity of course continue to have their place in the overall marketing of a record. But print advertising is not particularly effective in the music business, and radio and television advertising is prohibitively expensive. Other forms of publicity—such as interviews in trade magazines, appearances on television talk shows, or articles inserted into consumer magazines—all require a "story." Beginning artists rarely have one that can be effectively publicized. Merchandising a new artist will not be very extensive—perhaps limited to delivery of posters and in-store displays to record stores, with no guarantee they will be used. Thus in most cases, radio promotion is the only viable route with which to bring an artist and the artist's recording to the attention of eventual buyers.

MARKETING TOOLS

A well-intentioned record label executive might say: Here are 100 things we can do to market you and your record. We can:

1. Arrange for in-store appearances.
2. Get you mentioned in *Hits* magazine.
3. Take ads in trade publications.
4. Get you mentioned in *Billboard.*
5. Send postcards to advise everyone of the impending release.

6. Put stickers on the record and on telephone booths in towns where you have elicited interest.

7. "Snipe" the city (put posters up on abandoned buildings).

8. Bring you to conventions to perform.

9. Utilize Broadcast Data Systems (BDS) and SoundScan.

10. Hire an independent publicist.

11. Do a video.

12. Do another video.

13. Get you on a television show.

14. Get a track of yours on a soundtrack to a cool movie.

15. Send you to Europe and other foreign countries.

16. Send you on tour in the U.S.

17. Hire independent radio promotion people in addition to those on our permanent staff.

18. Take out ads in towns where you have fans.

19. Send you on a radio promotion tour in the U.S.

20. Send you on a radio promotion tour in Europe and other foreign countries.

21. Arrange for radio interviews by satellite to foreign countries.

22. Arrange for an "event" with a flying pig balloon à la Pink Floyd.

23. Host a number of "listening" parties to introduce your album.

24. Hire ethnic-specific marketing people to reach your biggest fan base.

25. Feature your record as the "Record of the Week" on our website.

26. Co-op advertise your album (e.g., by paying for one-half of Tower Records print ads in the Sunday paper).

27. Prioritize your album by delivering it to key radio stations 120 days before the official release date so that upon release, you will have 40 parallel one-station ads (see "Airplay," page 132).

28. We can place your music on the Internet and digitally download "teases" to interest consumer in purchasing the record or listening to it via downloads or via streams.

You get the idea.

THE GOAL-ORIENTED CAMPAIGN

These "hundred tools" are on the table at all times, and the senior record executive who oversees marketing, publicity, and promotion departments, and is charged with "breaking" the act or the album, will choose among them, and others. Yet the decisions will not always be tied to an agreed-upon goal shared by the artist and the record company.

Instead of saying, "Here's our goal; let's apply the tools," record company executives often say, "Look, here are our tools, let's apply as many as we can afford and see what sticks." While everyone (including the artist and the artist's manager and lawyer) is applauding the record executive for convincing the record company to apply any given tool (like a cutting-edge video), they often lose sight of the goal—if indeed any goal has ever been articulated, let alone agreed upon. And before the coda fades to black on the

$100,000 video, an entire career may be lost. Indiscriminate application of marketing tools makes the record company no less the victim than the artist.

This is top-down management, not bottom-up management where goals are identified and money and labor are spent efficiently and effectively. To mount an effective goal-oriented marketing campaign in the music industry requires a fundamental familiarity with the practical side of the business. Yet the lawyers and business affairs executives of record companies, whose job it is to negotiate the many-faceted, intricate legal and financial relationships between the parties, are often light-years away from understanding how a record is sold—how the company can help an artist to succeed.

It is very easy to work the next Britney Spears record. It is nearly impossible to work the new "new band" record. How do you get the label to work the new band product after the first week, when it has sold only 200 units nationwide? And how in fact does the label arrive at the 200-unit number? Will it rely on SoundScan, which is merely a statistical sampling? Will it totally ignore sales at Mom and Pop stores, which is where any new band's core fan base will begin to show interest? If a record does not show a lot of sales activity in the first two weeks, not infrequently the label will give up on the record. It is on these first two weeks' activity that much, if not everything, that the artist has dreamed about for a lifetime, depends. One wrong format decision, one bad decision as to where the money is spent, and the artist is history.

Identifying the goal, keeping your eye on it amidst all adversity and turmoil, prioritizing functions, avoiding distractions, managing time, capitalizing on opportunities—all of these are characteristics of the highly successful entrepreneur. And all of these are characteristics of the highly successful artist. Yet just as every artist is different from every other artist, the goals of every artist are different from the goals of every other artist, and the means toward those goals will differ, even among artists who share similar aspirations. For example, some bands do not really want to be a band; they just want to make five records every 10 years for five decades. Others realize that their fan base is everything and that time spent in front of 200 people at a time will go much further toward achieving their goals than doing an in-store appearance or radio convention visit three thousand miles away. Some do not aspire to have trade magazine ads and stories, but rather prefer to utilize "bounce-back cards" to establish a database of like-minded fans. The business side of things is anathema to those kinds of artists. Their goal is to be like *Hootie* and *Phish*—that is, to reach their fan base because it is to them that they have something to say, not to the readers of *Time* magazine. These bands' methodologies have the intended design of making the record company irrelevant insofar as building a sales base is concerned. Michael Bolton actually held parties after his gigs, inviting fans to a hotel suite where beverages were served (nonalcoholic, I'm told). The purpose was not just to have a good time, but to use this unique opportunity to identify his true fans and to be able to contact them later—for example, on the release of an album, or when Bolton would be coming to their town or area again, maybe even a few years down the road. Then again, the methodology of a singles band may be completely different. A track on a movie soundtrack is golden to this kind of act.

All artists are special. They have different attributes, different natures, and different missions. Some of these differences are addressed in one way or another in the contract. Most are not. The *contractual domain* provides structure and rules to the artist's professional life. The *practical domain* is primarily concerned with the goal of success.

THE RECORD CONTRACT

The goal of "success" is never mentioned in the record contract itself; nor do artists' professional representatives always think through contract negotiations with success in mind. Too often, the negotiations center on what to do in the event of failure—not success. Most recording contracts specifically deny that success—constituting the sale of so many records as to make the relationship profitable in the short run and enormously so in the long run—is a function of the contractual relationship. Other than the ostensible artistic aim of using one's art to express oneself, is it not the perceived goal of every artist to become a hit artist? Why, then, is the contract never couched in these terms?

Suppose record executives and the artist's representatives *can* agree on what makes a particular artist unique and then agree on which tools should be utilized to promote that artist. Do any of the parties concerned know what the contract says on the subject? Do any of them care what the contract says? How often do the thousands of music industry people in New York or Los Angeles—let alone elsewhere around the world—make marketing decisions on the basis of the contract? I would suggest hardly ever.

Maybe they don't *want* to know what the contract says? Does the manager disclose to the record company just before a decision about tour support funding is due that a (least important) member of a band has just quit the band? The contract will require that a notice be sent within a set number of days after the occurrence, but you can be sure it will not be sent even if the manager or attorney is aware of the contractual requirement.

Do the delivery requirements under the contract jibe with the likely release date six months later? Has any record *ever* been delivered on time? Has any marketing director ever said, "Don't deliver the record now; we can't do anything with it until the second quarter of next year." On the contrary, no record company business affairs lawyer ever misses the opportunity to notify an artist (certified mail, return receipt requested, with copies all over the place) that he is 100 days late in delivering the record and therefore the contractual consequences will take effect. (For example, the mechanical royalty rate in effect when the artist "should" have delivered will apply, not the mechanical royalty rate in effect when the artist "did" deliver the record.) Ironically, when the record is actually delivered, it is often the case that the timing is perfect for the record label to release the record. In other words, the delay may have worked to the record company's advantage. Yet the contract penalizes the artist for "late delivery."

Is all of the money that is being charged to the artist being applied to the correct account? How does the actual way in which the marketing budget is structured affect the profit-and-loss statement of the record company with resultant decisions as to whether to pick up an option or to not "throw good money after bad"? What does the contract say about that? What mechanism does the contract provide to resolve the multitude of issues of this nature that arise during the course of an artist's career?

If the artist's team (manager, lawyer, business manager) believes the contract does not contain adequate provisions for promoting the record, does the team build another 30 percent "overbudget" contingency into the recording fund to insure that it can access this money when it is needed? If not disclosed, is this ethical? Is it dangerous? Is it tantamount to stealing? Do the potential disadvantages of this kind of practice—for example, setting a tone and establishing a reputation that might hurt the artist and the artist's team—outweigh the potential advantages?

The label will direct its own overworked publicity department to apply its necessarily generic styles to the artist's album (although rarely to the artist's "career"), and if the publicity department cannot generate much press, the artist is usually blamed. It is nearly impossible to restructure a label's departments, least of all the publicity department, to custom-fit a particular group. It is a rare contract (believe it or not, a few *do* exist) that will commit a record company to covering the costs of an independent publicist to market an artist's record in every important market.

Much of what *is* in the contract is never enforced. Here's just one among many possible examples. The last paragraph of section 11.03 of Sony Music's form agreement requires that an auditor hired by an artist to examine Sony's books may not be at the same time engaged in "any other examination." Paragraph 11.03.1 goes on at some length to spell out exactly what the auditor may or may not do, in what time frame, then, at the very end, says:

> *The preceding provisions of this paragraph 11.03.I will not apply if Sony elects to waive the provisions of the last sentence of paragraph 11.03 which require that your representative shall not be engaged in any Other Examination.*

Originally, these clauses were presumably inserted to frustrate the auditor who commences an audit for one client, sees an error affecting other artists, calls the other artists, and says, Hire me for a third of what I can dig up for you, and I will audit your account at the same time as I am proceeding with the audit I have just begun. And, at the request of clients' auditors, fearing the potential consequences (especially to themselves) of this provision, I have repeatedly invested hours and hours of time negotiating modifications to such clauses. The fact is, however, that the likelihood of their ever being enforced is nil, and so, practically speaking, my efforts are a waste of time and money.

For a 70-page (or more) document that costs between $15,000 and $20,000 (or more) in legal fees to negotiate, that is a sad commentary on the practicality and efficacy of the services that the label forces the artist to obtain. Too often the advance at the commencement of a contract term goes to the lawyer and the manager, and there is little left over for the artist who will have to quit his day job to devote full time to his career. And let us not forget that to the extent that the incredible amount of time the artist will have to devote to promoting the record—including all of the late-night gigs in god-forsaken locations—sells records, out of the net sales dollars most will go to the record company.

Tour Support

Having a provision in the contract committing the record company to provide deficit tour support guarantees that a band will have the chance to perform live. It means that the record company will absorb losses associated with an artist's tour; in essence, it is a subsidy. Customarily, record companies are very "hands-on" with respect to planning the tour, selecting the cities visited and the clubs played, budgeting, etc. If the budget is, say, $50,000 for a 12-city tour, yet projected gross income is only $20,000, the record company promises to bear the burden of the $30,000 balance. The provisions that establish this in a typical contract are no different from one artist agreement to another, and most stipulate that such support will be provided for a tour schedule that is approved by the record company and the artist (so-called "mutual" approval). Although such a provision may be totally satisfactory for many artists, for some it may not be. For example, the artist and the artist's manager may disagree with the record company as to what tour schedule will best achieve the aims of that particular artist and will differentiate the artist from other artists. The record company's "approval" of a tour plan is not only irrelevant in this situation, it is a waste of money—money which might more effectively be spent elsewhere, or saved until an *appropriate* tour opportunity comes along.

Here's an example, which concerns a new band that was given the opportunity to be the opening act for a well-known group. Now, it is axiomatic that any good new band will be bringing to the stage a style and an interpretation that is unknown to the public, and the more talented the new group, the more likely it is to bring an innovativeness that will take some getting used to. In fact, the better the new band, the more likely it is to be dismissed by an audience with an established taste. In this case, the new group knew that the audience would be likely to hoot them off the stage, but the record company and the agent thought that partnering with the famous band and playing in front of large audiences would be a great coup. The record company agreed (joyfully, I might add) to lend its contractually-agreed financial tour support to *that* tour and to *that* tour only. As it turned out, not only was the audience impatient to hear its favorite act, it was totally turned off by the nature of the new band's music. You can imagine the frustration of the artist and manager when a few months later the perfect tour opportunity materialized at a festival with a number of like-minded bands whose much larger audience was complementary to our—now depressed—new band. Why depressed? Because there was no money left with which to introduce the band to the very people who would have liked them and would have bought their records.

Recording Costs

What may seem to be incidental marketing costs can play havoc with both your marketing budget and your ever-growing royalty deficit. For example, is a radio edit a recording cost? If the royalty department codes a radio edit as a recording cost, the artist may have a surprise in store when the royalty statement arrives months later. Some singles have 12 different radio versions. At $5,000 per edit, that's $60,000. At $0.80 per CD (see Chapter 4, page 31, for an analysis of the artist's "rate"), an additional 75,000 albums have to be sold to pay for these costs. If you do not even know how to label a radio edit, it may cost $10,000 to do an audit before the issue is faced and, perhaps (perhaps not) resolved. And meanwhile, 75,000 albums which bear no royalty for you will have generated more than $525,000 in additional revenues for the record company, even as the artist's royalty account remains in the red.

Mutual Approval

"Mutual" is an often-used contract word. Lawyers think they have attained something when an approval right (e.g., tour support) is made "mutual" between the record company and the artist. In reality, even when a contract says that approval of certain matters shall be subject to mutual approval by the record company and the artist, the record company always has the last word. Further, many contracts provide that the artist shall not withhold approval "unreasonably," whatever that means.

Mixers

Not the college kind. The studio kind. Often, labels will force a mixer—or a producer—on an artist. The costs of hiring a fabulous mixer (and there are a few) for two weeks—which is what it might take to remix an already finished album—can equal the costs of hiring a producer for three months! And if you are an East Coast group and the mixer of the moment lives in Hawaii or Malibu, you have to add the cost of a trip to the other coast for the band (or two of its members) and perhaps the manager. Then there are the hotel rooms and per diems. And let us not forget that the mixer will only work in such and such a studio, which charges $1800 a day for 15 days. Total cost: $60,000? $70,000? $80,000? Why not? After all, it will help sell records to have Mr. X's name on the back of the disc. Or will it? Some feel that Mr. X's name will mean something only to *Billboard* addicts or other industry types. No doubt some 15- to 18-year-olds have heard of Mr. X—or can distinguish between his mix and others' mixes—but most have not. Others will tell you that the mixer is the difference. The labels will call it marketing, but your royalty account will not reflect any difference between this and other recoupable recording costs.

Maybe Mr. X *is* the only person in the world who can burnish the record to the point that it will be the hit it would otherwise never have been. I do not know if this is usually the case—or never the case. Once a record is essentially completed and the producer has mixed the record and it is ready for mastering, record company executives often lose financial and artistic perspective and bring in a famous "mixer" at enormous cost to both fine-tune the record and to lend his or her name to the project so that certain people in the industry (including the executive's boss) will think of the record as quite cool indeed. The artist and the artist's manager usually go along with this procedure largely because they themselves can't be sure that it will *not* actually make the difference between a bubbling-under rating success and a major hit and they themselves are susceptible to the "star" treatment. Who would not want Tom or Chris Lord-Alge to mix their record? But since so many factors enter into whether a record is a success, I am convinced that the added cost and time are of somewhat less value than the involved parties think they are. Whatever the reality, for the insecure artist and manager, not to mention the record company executives themselves—whose jobs are, in a way, on the line if the half million dollars invested in our proverbial baby band is not earned back—how much better to cover oneself than to hire the tried . . . and the true. After all, the cost will ultimately be charged back to the artist.

Videos

Gotta have a video? Every band wants a video. Why? Is the money allocated to the band sufficient to produce the video and also do the other things that are better directed toward the artist's goal? For example, two months on the road? Which is the more efficient way to spend the limited money? Is MTV or VH-1 going to play your video? That's a good question these days and it must be explored and answered before the artist and the artist's team agree to let the record company spend $50,000 to $100,000 on a video that might in the end be a really expensive home movie. At the beginning of the 2000s, many record deals were providing for a commitment of money to the promotion of the artist's record which may or may not take the form of video expenditures. If a record company takes the position that a video does not make sense in the context of the marketplace, the record company will often agree to invest the same amount of money in other, mutually agreed-upon, promotions. On the other hand, the company may resist spending even contractually agreed-upon money on a video when there is not any reasonable likelihood that the video may ever be seen.

When all of the money is spent (or misspent) and the record company and the artist have the tour they do not need, the mixer they do not need, and the video they cannot use, the band members may have to return to their day jobs to survive, thereby relinquishing their one golden opportunity to work the record that took 2 years to make and 20 years to prepare for. The manager, the business manager, and the lawyer will be off doing other things too since they cannot survive forever on the fumes of hope. They have overhead to pay and families to support. Their commitments can be stretched only so thin. So the implications of marketing and promotion decisions are very far-reaching indeed. The stronger the artist and the artist's representatives are, and the clearer they are as to the goals of the artist and how to reach those goals, the more likely it is they will be able to apply the artist's values to the task at hand and at the same time keep the record company in line.

RECORD COMPANIES CAN ONLY DO SO MUCH

With all due respect to music industry professionals, with the exception of some A&R executives, not many of them have a clue as to how the record business really works— i.e., how to make a hit record or a hit artist. Young (and some old) business affairs executives whose job it is to arrange the relationships among all the constituents of the record label often do not understand one iota of how their business works, nor, as often as not, do the artist's attorneys and managers. They have never made a record, delivered a record, experienced the recording of a record in a studio, or applied the principles in the contract to exploit the record. They do not understand whether a radio edit is a recording cost or a marketing expense.

I am not singling out young business affairs executives for any reason except to point out that while those in this department can—most impressively—dictate a 50-page contract off the tops of their heads, it is the rare document that serves to assist either the record company *or* the artist (and manager) in choosing among the tools traditionally sought to "break" the artist or the record once the record has been delivered.

But there is an exception. Among the most important young record company executives is the A&R man (or woman) who championed the act in the first place and was instrumental in getting the artist signed. While the A&R person's job is officially concluded when the act is signed and the record is completed, no one can prove more of an asset to the common goal of breaking the artist and the new record than this particular professional. The A&R person is the conductor of the orchestra. The A&R person has to spot signs of weakness; cajole departments to focus on the artist; siphon off money slated for a different line item or different record; lead the participants—including the manager, lawyer, and business manager—toward understanding the common goal; watch out for people and political situations at the record company that may get in the way of reaching the common goal; and persuade the record company to believe in the band as much as the A&R person does. The A&R person coordinates the record company's worldwide efforts to bring the record—and the artist—home successfully.

Conversely, the absence of an effective A&R person can have a devastating effect. The artist's representatives must be sensitive to the strengths and weaknesses of the A&R person and be ready to compensate for these weaknesses and to exploit these strengths. Failing that, the effort to make the artist and the artist's record a high priority at the record company—always an uphill battle—will be nearly impossible.

VICTIM OR VICTOR?

Most artists get one chance to make it. The days of multiple album opportunities to click with the public are over. The Billy Joels, Bruce Springsteens, and Garth Brooks might have made it anyway, given their enormous talents and energies, but the fact is that they *were* given several albums' opportunity to reach their goals. The situation an artist does not want to be in is the one the overwhelming number get into, the one where they say, "OK, we messed up . . . . We made a lot of mistakes on that first album. . . . Next time let's make sure we don't make the same mistakes." They won't likely get the chance.

We have seen some of the mistakes. Here are a few more.

If the artist and/or the artist's team do not concur with the label's marketing people, and can't find a way to diplomatically redirect the label's focus to what they believe is the correct direction, the artist can be (1) written off as difficult, (2) avoided like the plague when subsequent marketing opportunities arise or (3) called an ass (or worse). Rarely will the artist be listened to with respect in the future.

Here is a possible scenario, one that will resonate with many artists and their managers. An artist (seeking to achieve a personal goal of reaching fans through live performing and building a fan base in however many months or years it might take) is needed by the record company in Seattle. The only problem is that the artist is in South Carolina ready to perform before his fiftieth club crowd of 200 people. (That's 10,000 potential record buyers.) So she cancels the gig, loses $2,000, and flies to Seattle to make an in-store appearance and to stop by a radio station that has never heard of her and is doing a favor to the record company promotion person. But there is no direct flight from South Carolina to Seattle, so she has to fly to Atlanta and then to Denver and then to San Francisco and only then to Seattle. She arrives at 3:00 A.M. because heightened security measures have delayed departures from San Francisco and the weather in Seattle is stacking up the planes that wish to land there. She misses the radio appearance, but that's OK because the record company has another in-store scheduled for Portland, Oregon, at midnight the next night, tying in this artist's record with the crowded release event of the latest entry into the *Titanic* film video extravaganza which is sure to draw hundreds of people who will learn about the artist for the first time in a sort of captured environment (although they could care less).

Do you see how an artist can become the victim of a goal-less label? Ironically, the record company itself is no less a victim of its own indiscriminate, injudicious application of the tools that are supposed to enhance an artist's acceptability, not to destroy it.

Sound exhausting? It is. Sleep deprivation is a leading cause of craziness among recording artists. They are forced into taking stimulants in unhealthy amounts—whether coffee, cigarettes, drugs, or all three. Welcome to the ozone that surrounds too many of our young artists. Before they know it, they're on the proverbial merry-go-round on their way to rock and roll hell. Their inexperienced young managers, lawyers, and business managers often have no idea how to stop the spiral, and the rest is history.

I am not suggesting that a misguided promotional trip to Seattle (or even a wisely chosen trip to Seattle) will send the artist into drug addiction. But the insanity that surrounds the period that record industry professionals call the "album cycle" is real and is fundamentally dangerous to careers and to lives. There is a saying in the record business that today's buzz is tomorrow's hangover. Nothing could be more true.

TELEVISION CAMPAIGNS

Mostly in Europe, but also in Japan and in other countries, record companies have discovered the value of television advertising for their products. Of course television advertising campaigns are very expensive, and record companies have decided that, rather than charge artists for all or a part of the cost of this form of promotion, they should reduce artists' royalties to, say, 50 percent of the otherwise applicable royalty during the period in which the campaign is running. Now it is the artist who finds that this can be very expensive.

A few ways that artists can get some relief from this recent intrusion into the royalty calculation are the following:

- Limit the effect of the provision to "substantial" television campaigns.
- Acquire the right to exercise veto rights over either the campaigns themselves or the extent and coverage of the campaigns.
- Limit the application of this provision to the locations where television campaigns have been proved to be effective.
- Try to get some handle on the projected costs and the proportion of expense to return so that your judgment is better informed. As your career expands from using bounce-back cards to having your records featured in television advertisements, your manager will have to accumulate knowledge pretty quickly about the efficacy of such campaigns. The information is available, but much of it is overseas. The tele-

phones and e-mail servers to foreign affiliates are all operative and should be used in order for your manager to make decisions on the basis of what, for example, television advertising has done for other artists, where, and at what cost.

RADIO PROMOTION

What good is a good record if no one ever hears it? How easy it is these days to produce a wonderful recording in the confines of one's own home studio. But what to do once you have completed it? How do you get potential buyers to actually listen to it? In fact, the only way is for your record to be played on the radio. Really. I know, it sounds somewhat obvious on one level and ridiculous on another. But can you conceive of another means? Snipe (sticker) every city and small town and college in the world? Play every city and small town and college in the world? I don't think so. Just as television was the catalyst behind the success of Andrea Boccelli and The Three Tenors (and even the Irish Tenors), so radio is the only catalyst we know behind the success of recording artists. Sure, the Internet is beginning to have an impact and Ani DiFranco has figured out how to sell records out of the back of her van, but for most of us, the only way we will hear about a new act is through radio performance—and possibly summer festivals. Therein lie the opportunities—and the headaches.

Airplay

In the world of radio promotion, some stations, known in the business as "parallel one" stations, have more influence than others on *Billboard* and other chart publications. To have a record added to a playlist on, say, 40 parallel one stations in the first week of a record's release will most likely assure it a spot on the Hot 100. Therefore record labels will usually see to it that those stations receive advance album copies way in advance of the release date, usually at least four months. Radio stations know that getting the albums on the release date, or even one to three months in advance, indicates a lower priority at the label. It suggests that less money will be committed, fewer marketing tools will be used, and there will be less follow-up from the record company divisions (field sales personnel, publicists, etc.), fewer in-stores, less co-op advertising, fewer radio station personal appearances, etc.—all those things that will eventually confirm to the radio station's listeners the correctness and foresight of a particular radio station programmer or DJ for having chosen that particular record as "hit bound." The importance of a company manifesting its commitment to an artist and recording cannot be overemphasized. Radio station personnel will, at best, be cautious before "going on" a record that it is not convinced a record label is fully committed to.

Radio Promotion and Payola

A combination of FCC rules and federal statutes govern payola, which is defined as the unreported payment to, or acceptance by, employees of broadcast stations, program producers, or program suppliers of any money, service, or valuable consideration to achieve airplay. In short, payola is a bribe. One FCC rule references the applicable statute and FCC policies on payola (47 C.F.R. Section 73.4180). Simply stated, the

Federal Communications Act requires persons who have paid, accepted, or agreed to pay or accept any consideration for the broadcast of any material to report the fact to the station licensee before the material is broadcast (47USC Sec. 508). If the material broadcast is paid for, the Act further requires the station licensee to announce that fact on the air and to identify the sponsor (47USC Sec. 317). The 1988 FCC Public Notice referenced in 47 C.F.R. Sec. 73.1480 explains the FCC's payola policy. Failure to adhere to these reporting requirements can subject the violator to a fine of up to $10,000 or imprisonment in a federal penitentiary of up to one year, or both.

On February 25, 1988, four persons were indicted in U.S. District Court in Los Angeles, California, for payola violations. One of those indicted was charged with having made "undisclosed payments from 1980 to 1985 in the form of cash and cocaine" to station personnel in order to secure airplay for certain records. These four persons were later convicted.

What does this have to do with record promotion? Let's just say that in the absence of regulations like the ones cited above, there would be little chance for an artist to succeed on his or her own merits. Money talks just as loudly in the record industry as in politics. Just as an incumbent politician with millions of dollars in his coffers usually buries a newcomer, those in the record industry with easy access to the media can leave their less fortunate competitors in the proverbial dust. Remember: in the United States, and increasingly throughout the world, if you can't get played on the radio, you can't succeed. Period.

I like to believe that if a talented person stays in the game long enough, the person's creativity will win out over such adversities as better funded or more established competitors (for the airwaves), old-fashioned, though proven, musical styles, and xenophobic arbiters of taste. Unfortunately this idealistic view runs afoul of the incredible power of the broadcasting industry. I will not restate the history of payola except to say that there have been times in our history during which illicit means to attain radio play ran rampant throughout the radio industry. These included cash payments to disk jockeys and radio programmers as well as other kinds of favors, such as expensive gifts (television sets, cars, etc.), sexual favors and, of course, drugs.

The federal government has apparently done a fairly good job at terminating this practice. But the record industry could not quite give up the advantages gained during the heyday of payola. So the leopard merely changed its spots one day. The road between the record company and the radio station was irrevocably placed on permanent detour. Let me explain.

The Independent Radio Promoter

Record companies today rarely expend the lion's share of their promotion money on their promotion division staff's own efforts to promote radio play. For most of the history of the music business as we know it, one of the record companies' vaunted talents was to promote their products. They sold themselves on these strengths. Even today, they have sophisticated promotion departments. What is different?

Several years ago, in the midst of several federal investigations of the presence of payola in the record industry, the major record companies had a brilliant idea. Why should the suited executives subject themselves to these tawdry, tedious, and expensive investigations, all of which were centered around the foot soldiers of the industry? Why indeed when the risks were so great. For a CBS (which owned the CBS Radio and Television Network as well as several other stations) or an RCA (which owned the NBC Radio and Television Network, as well as several other stations), violations of federal payola regulations by their record divisions threatened the most lucrative assets the corporate giants owned, their broadcasting licenses. Simply put, broadcast licenses would not be renewed for felons.

What to do? Simple. Kill the messenger.

The record companies, as a group, fired most of their promotion department personnel. Now that the villains were no longer employed by the record companies, the broadcasting/record companies could breathe more easily. Only there was one problem. The record companies could not promote their records without promotion people. You might say that this was like cutting off your head to spite your body, but the record companies had a solution.

Enter the independent promoter. Who *was* the independent promoter? In many cases, the same person who had previously been employed by the record company. Now, instead of a W-2, the company filed a 1099 with the IRS. The independent promoter was an independent contractor and was not under the "supervision, guidance, or control" of the record company, let alone the parent company. The parent was safe. The record company was safe. Voilà! Saved from the feds. If the "independent" promotion people violated the law, there was no clear line of authority and therefore no clear culpability on the part of the record companies that could implicate their parent companies and, among other things, jeopardize their broadcast licenses.

The internal cost of a promotion department decreased enormously (the companies retained a head of promotion and a skeletal staff), and there were lots of promotion dollars available to spread among the "indies." The promotion people thus hired of course did not let a good thing go unexploited. They began to charge more and more money to the record companies for their services. But the record companies were not so dumb. They insisted that the fees they paid be tied to the success of the promotion people: How about $4,000 dollars if radio station WXXX were to "go on" the record? $10,000 if radio station KZZZ were to add it to their playlist? And so on. This was getting expensive. But for whom?

Paying the Indies

The costs of external promotion were running far higher than the costs of the now-disbanded internal staffs. But the record companies had another brilliant idea. Why pay for these "extra" services to promote the artist. Why not let the artist pay for them? After all, the philosophy in the record industry had always been that the artist should pay for recording costs (out of royalties, so ultimately out of his or her pocket). Why shouldn't the "outside" services of people engaged to help promote the records be considered recording costs and additional advances?

Certainly a record company's investment is considerable: beginning with the A&R

department that finds the artist in the first place; the business affairs and legal departments which sign the artist; the enormous investment of the actual recording costs; the art department; the manufacturing and distribution facilities; the marketing department; the publicity department; and let's not forget the dozens of executives who run the company, or the rent that must be paid for the company's marble towers. Welcoming the reduction in overhead resulting from the downsizing of their promotion departments, the record companies were reluctant to suffer the increase of costs when a generous alternative was available to them: simply make it a contractual obligation for the artist to pay for independent promotion of his or her records. If the video clip, which was intrinsically promotional in nature, was now a cost to be borne out of royalties by the artist, why not the dollars spent on independent promotion, an absolutely essential expenditure? What more useful cost than one focused solely on the most proven way of establishing the artist's success: getting airplay for the record!

And so developed the practice of charging the artist with the cost of independent promotion. It is ironic that the artist and manager must fight with the record company in order to convince it to expend monies on independent promotion only to be obliged to pay for it themselves. Even the manager loses. If the money is charged against the artist's royalties, customarily the manager will not commission the earned royalties used to recoup the costs of independent promotion—thereby forfeiting the manager's commission on every recoupable independent promotion dollar spent. Some companies hand over the promotion money to the managers for disbursement. In such cases, assuming the managers are honest and do not skim anything off the top, they get to touch, but not spend, the money that, in part, reflects what would have been their own earned commissions if the promotion efforts had been successful. Ironic.

In recent years, the record companies have settled into a kind of stand-off with the artists whereby they seek to be repaid (out of royalties) only one-half of the monies expended on independent promotion. This goes a long way toward ameliorating the damage to the artist's bank account. Two facts remain, however: one is that these are costs that the record companies traditionally bore themselves and now have found a way to charge back to the artist; the second is that the amount spent on independent promotion—and the timing of such expenditures—is totally within the control of the record company. Thus if the artist's account is otherwise in the black (or if the cost of independent promotion can be recouped against other earnings such as mechanical royalty earnings), the record company can actually use the artist's own money, otherwise payable at the end of an accounting period, for the purpose of further promoting the artist's records, avoiding all risk that would be associated with advancing its own funds for such a purpose. Hmmm.

Icons and Iconoclasts

Many books have been written about the excesses of independent promotion people and their actual or alleged associations with organized crime, drug dealers, etc. (e.g., *Hit Men; Off the Charts; Stiffed—The True Story of MCA, the Music Business and the Mafia*). These are informative, occasionally amusing, and frequently disturbing. Feel free to read them. The point I want to emphasize is that whatever incarnation of payola exists today is a direct descendent of institutions originally established by record companies' greed. I say "greed" because when they recognized the inherent willingness of a radio station programmer or DJ to compromise their ethical responsibilities, instead of changing the way they did business, they simply reestablished the promotion system. But this time they did so in a manner that had the appearance of being more "at arms length" than had previously been the case, when the promotion staff was employed and under the supervision and control of the record companies themselves.

One day, in the 1980s, Warner Bros. Records' legendary chairman Mo Ostin unilaterally terminated the use of independent promotion people because of what he perceived to be abuses which were inherent in the system and which no one, however pure his or her motives, could control. It was an enormously courageous decision. Unfortunately, Mr. Ostin's solution was short-lived, and the system continues today more or less as it has over the past twenty years.

THE SAME OLD SONG (ONLY THE CODA IS NEW)

There developed a practice in the fairly recent era of independent promotion whereby the independent promoters themselves would cross the legal line drawn by federal and state laws of bribery, and in particular, the FCC regulation cited at the beginning of this chapter. The record companies, while having insulated themselves from their own employees' actions, were nevertheless anxious about having to pay such evidently tainted sums to independent contractors in return for such specific services as getting a record played on a particular radio station and being listed as among the top 25, top 15, top 10, top 5 or number 1 songs on such station's play charts. For, as noted earlier, each successful "add" would generate another few thousand dollars to the independent promoter.

One of the ways in which the record companies have further insulated themselves from the specter of association with unethical and illegal business practices rivals their most ingenious solutions of the past. They have figured out how to pay for independent promotion on the one hand but how not to pay for it on the other. I do not mean that they have found a way to charge someone (in this case the artist) with the cost. That we have already observed. No. Now, they do not even have to suffer the indignity of writing the check! How do they achieve this, the best of all possible worlds? The answer, as I alluded to earlier, is simple: they give the *manager* the money and the manager is expected to run the radio promotion campaign.

To nobody's surprise, the independent promotion people hired by the managers at the specific behest of the record company are usually the very people that the record company designates. But the manager, who has no one to whom he or she can shift the responsibility, is the one who will be the focus of governmental interest if the issue ever comes to the forefront again (as it inevitably will). Here again there is a disparity between the experienced and the inexperienced. The independent manager who has little experience in such things, or who does not have a trusted network of (honest) promotion people who can present programmers and DJs with rationales for adding their records to playlists, is at a distinct disadvantage compared to the experienced manager who does.

And the record company's dilemma? How to obtain necessary promotional assistance with the least risk, both from a financial and from a liability point of view. Promotion is essential if those programmers who determine which records are to be played on their airwaves are to be made aware of them. Sales people in all fields—from watches to books, from fashion lines to airplanes—are the front-line soldiers of their respective industries. How to insure their effectiveness is a challenge that has to be faced constantly. Things are no different in the record industry. However, the rewards, being so enormous, and the high-profile charges over the years of payola, make the promotion people of the record industry stand out.

It is not an exaggeration to say that without promotion and promotion people, there would be few, if any, superstar recording artists. Many of the promotion people are stars in their own field and deserve the kudos they so infrequently receive. What makes music industry promotional people different from those in other fields with similar functions is that in the record industry the people engaging their services—directly or through the artist's manager—are so successful in detaching themselves from the process that sometimes all control is lost and anything goes.

Under these circumstances, the fact that the artist is expected to pay for all or a portion of promotional services is bizarre to say the least. The artist has no expertise in such matters, and probably does not even know one promotion person from another, and yet the artist's entire career can depend on the success of the promotion person's efforts.

SOME FINAL THOUGHTS

As with anything else in their lives, artists must take the ultimate responsibility for achieving their own career goals. By the time they have found out that their undying faith that their record company, manager, lawyer, business manager, and agent know what they are doing is a chimera, it may be too late to achieve those goals, which, even if not specifically articulated, reside somewhere in their subconscious.

There is no simple solution to this dilemma, but I can offer a few suggestions. I speak as much for the professionals around the artist as for the artist because, after all, their common goal is success—artistic success, financial success, or some combination of these. For a manager, lawyer, etc., who has invested months and eventually years of their lives in the belief that a particular artist has what it takes to reach the level of success that will match the artist's promise, a mismanaged album release or a failed promotional effort has an effect only slightly less painful than for the artist who has to start all over again. (Don't forget that the first album was developed over the artist's life to that point—often 20 years or more; the second album has to be conceived, written, and recorded within as little as a 9-month period.)

It can be as frustrating for the professionals surrounding an artist (including the record company executives) as for the artist to watch a dream crash. For them, with their enormously expensive overhead expenses, it can be more than frustrating; it can be devastating. I know of no law firm or accounting firm specializing in representing artists that has not had dozens of these experiences over the years. How much can one take before a decision has to be made to shift out of the "baby band" business representing talent

A Brief Look at the Promotional Picture—From the Artist's Point of View

At a standard, mainstream, record label, promotion staff is broken down according to radio station/formats (top 40, easy listening, R&B, etc.). Each format has numerous releases each week, and the promotion people responsible for those formats make appointments with radio programmers to present the records they are pushing that week. A promotion person representing a major label may get a half hour session, during which he or she will be able to play no more than 5 or 6 records out of the 15 or 20 "singles" the company wants to promote. (People not from a major label will be lucky if the pitch session lasts 10 minutes.) There is a good chance that yours will not be one of the 5 or 6 played. (Even if it is, it faces stiff competition. After all, the programmer's station may only add one or two new artist records a week—from *all* labels.)

So, you've gone through all of this effort—from putting your band together, working the clubs, finding your representatives, securing a deal, recording your record, and beginning your promotional tour—in short, climbing the rungs on the ladder that is the development stage of your career—and your record does not even get played for the radio programmers. Maybe the promotion person really likes your band or your record. So what. He can do only so much. Maybe if you're lucky, he will hand over your record to the programmer and say, "Listen to this; if you can find a spot on the overnight, I'd appreciate it. I'm not going to play this for you because you don't have the time, but I'm sure when you get a chance you'll love it." One thing the programmer may be thinking as the record is flipped into the circular file is why, if this is such a good record, was it not one of the five or six the promotion man chose to play for the station. That your record was an afterthought solves a problem for the radio programmer. It need not be considered at all.

and into real estate law representing institutions? Well, not to worry. Those professionals will always retain their love for music, their affinity for musicians and songwriters, and their willingness to negotiate the ups and downs of the music business.

As with any problem one faces in life, there are several ways to address this dilemma. Although the following suggestions have all been covered, either explicitly or implicitly, in previous chapters, they bear repeating here.

- Stay in reality.
- Ask questions, then evaluate the answers with a degree of skepticism.
- Learn from your mistakes.
- Observe others. Learn from their mistakes and from their successes.

- Keep around you a variety of professionals with information and experience different from yours and absorb as much as possible.
- Make sure your team is functioning as a real team. All team members as well as key personnel at the record company must meet regularly (once a week before and during the high-activity release period of an album cycle). Set long-term and short-term goals; assign responsibilities with time tables; establish mechanisms for communication when the parties cannot meet in person.

Finally, it is not inappropriate to suggest that all team members recommend to each other self-help and/or management books that are sold by the carload at any major bookstore.* There is, after all, something to be learned from many of the writers of these books and there is no reason why these lessons should be the private reserve of corporate America. I should also point out that many record companies are deeply invested in management training in the form of lectures, retreats, annual meetings, and even continuing education coursework. Since corporations and even our vaunted record companies care enough to provide education on management and self-fulfillment to their executives, why shouldn't the rest of us—lawyers, managers, business managers—take some courses also? After all, it is in our hands that the ultimate business responsibilities of the artist's career rests. (And it wouldn't hurt for the artist to pursue some of this knowledge as well.)

---

*Popular self-help books reduce to a small number (usually 10 or under), the methods by which people can identify their goals and best achieve them—Ten Ways to a Happier Life, Five Steps to Fame and Fortune, The Seven Habits of Highly Successful People, etc.—and the messages of these books are, at least in part, transferable to the needs and aspirations of the emerging musical artist. Some other possibly useful titles I recently observed at a local bookstore are Don't Sweat the Small Stuff—It's All Small Stuff; The Dynamic Laws of Prosperity; Profiting from Experience; A Quick and Simple Guide to Taking Charge of Your Life; 365 Daily Lessons in Self Mastery; Dare to Be Yourself; and (I liked this title): An Idiot's Guide to Managing Your Time. And let's not forget the estimable The Power of Positive Thinking.

10 TOURING CONCERNS:
Trials and Tribulations

Recordings are really for people who live in Timbuktu.

—Aaron Copland

This chapter is not meant for the faint of heart. The subject is touring: moving large numbers of people and huge amounts of equipment from place to place so that from one to ten singers and musicians can entertain even larger numbers of people. The fans do not have to find the artists; the artists will come to them . . . for a price. And that price is not just the price of the ticket; it is often the price of a career, a marriage, a life.

The secret of successful touring—club tours but especially grand tours—is in the details. A competent tour manager will know whether all the equipment and transportation chosen for a tour fit together well and what it will take to make everything work. Although it should go without saying that one should choose a competent and experienced tour manager, many artists feel secure with certain people who have been associated with them since the days they were hauling their instruments around in a borrowed van, and they like to reward these people by advancing them to higher positions in their touring lives. While this is probably how most tour managers do get their starts, it still is important to be cautious when selecting people whose competence may mean the difference between success and failure of each performance and, ultimately, of the tour itself.

THE CLUB TOUR

New artists are marketed in essentially two ways: via radio and via live performances. Any other way, Ani DiFranco excluded, does not have the same success factor. Whatever the Internet does to ease the distribution of their music, artists and their art must first come to the consumer's attention. Distribution is everything. We explored radio promotion in Chapter 9. It is time to talk about live touring.

It will come as no surprise that in order to fashion a successful endeavor, there must be an enormous amount of coordination among the artist, the record company, and the artist's lawyers, managers, business managers, and booking agents. You may say that this is beginning to sound as if it is going to cost "real money" and you are right. A young rock and roll band will need subsidies to travel from club to club and city to city. And the travel map is not haphazardly drawn; it very carefully traces the response to the record on radio and among fans.

Of course, not only does the artist not make any money from this process, his or her unrecouped red position at the record company will begin to rise astronomically.

Another characteristic of the club tour is that just as little kids do not always understand "the value of a dollar," artists at this stage of development are not expected to understand what they are supposed to be doing, and therefore the record company, which usually pays the deficits incurred by such tours, places the artists in a totally dependent mode. Like children, they are given allowances (although they are called per diems), told where they can stay, what they can afford, and what to do. They awake to different rooms and different cities on an almost daily basis. A tour during the promotion of an album can last a year or more and take the artist to 50 or more cities, often more than once, and a half-dozen countries. Their lives are no more similar to yours and mine than the lives of minor league baseball players traveling from game to game by bus.

This process can continue for years, and it is no wonder that by the time artists get to what I call the "grand tour" years, they are likely to be out of touch with what most people consider reality.

Out of the Clubs and Out of Business

Most professionals who live and breathe the world of live performing feel that club business is dead. Attendance is down across the country, and very few clubs can do anything resembling profitable business absent the implementation of other money-making methods such as merchandising, satellite radio broadcasts, and Internet distribution of the live shows (for example, via Digital Club Network). Beer deals, Web deals—you name it. Club owners, often with the help of record company subsidies, will do all they can to keep open these terribly essential venues which are vital contributors to the dissemination of music and musical ideas reflected by an evolving culture.

Nevertheless, prospects are that fewer and fewer clubs will comprise important start-up venues as part of the global concert business, where many hundreds of millions of dollars are at stake. It has become extremely difficult for record companies and promoters to focus on, and invest in, developing acts on the club circuit.

THE GRAND TOUR

Sounds like a movie and sometimes it must feel like one. *Almost Famous, The Rose, Truth or Dare, Helter Skelter*—their depictions of the "road" are not exaggerated.

Of course, now we *are* talking real money—often millions. And for artists who reach this privileged stage, the ultimate financial return for the years of effort by the artists and their representatives can be astronomical. Yet, no matter how much is made, it can be squandered as a result of any number of excesses, errors, and extravagances of the artists and their handlers.

The Tour Budget

The accompanying table is a real-life example of a touring budget for a 65-show tour—over a period of four months—for a moderately successful five-member band. Observe how many different categories of costs must be dealt with. Each category requires specific expertise, or experience, in order both to estimate potential costs and then to meet these costs on budget. For this tour, the net profit would be divided by the five memebers of the band: $3,854,000 divided by five equals $770,800 for each member of the band.

The issue often facing artists and their representatives is not so much whether costs are reasonable or should be cut, but whether there has been sufficient time and expertise invested in preparing the budget to justify getting the tour underway in the first place.

Sample Tour Budget

INCOME

Performances:

$100,000/show x 65 shows $6,500,000

Sound and lights (reimbursed by venue):

$17,500/show x 65 shows 1,137,500

Merchandising (guarantee) 1,000,000

    Total $8,637,500

EXPENSES

Commissions

    Management @15% (excluding sound and lights reimbursement)* 1,125,000

    Agency @10% (of performance fees only) 650,000

    Business management @ 5% (excluding sound and lights)† 375,000

Hard production costs (including trucking, sound, lighting, equipment rental,

    equipment supplies, set construction & design, set fee, misc.) 700,000

Pre- and post-tour expenses (such as air fares, advance, equipment purchases,

    transportation, wardrobe, immigration [i.e., cost of services to obtain

    permits or visas for countries in which performers are not citizens]) 120,000

Ancillary production and tour costs (including payroll and fees for individual

    band members; entourage, including road manager, tour accountant,

    assistant road manager, security, press, and publicity; management assistant;

    crew, including production manager, stage manager, crew chief, rigger,

    engineer, drum tech, guitar tech, guitar tech, guitar tech [at least three of

    them]; keyboard programmer; carpenter; ground man) .350,000

Per diems (individual band members, entourage, and crew) 120,000

Hotels (band, entourage, crew, and drivers) 425,000

Transportation (air fares, bus rental, bus drivers' fees,

    limousines and taxis, auto rental) 400,000

Tips and gratuities 11,500

Misc. Expenses (e.g., wardrobe maintenance and cleaning,

    shipping and postage, dues) 300,000

Insurance (nonappearance, liability and excess liability,

    equipment, Workers' Compensation) 300,000

Legal 45,000

Publicity (independent/not paid for by record company) 20,000

Rehearsal costs (rehearsal studios in home city and on the road; local labor,

    hotels and apartment rental, telephone, food and drinks, equipment rental

    and supplies, transportation, payroll and fees, per diems at

    $4,250/month for 4 mos.) 17,000

Contingency 50,000

    Total expenses $4,783,500

    Net profit on tour $3,854,000

*Note that for this tour, the manager makes 1 1/2 times as much as of any one member of the band. While the amount of the manager's commission is calculated at 15 percent of the gross, it actually works out to be 29 percent of the net. For a 20 percent manager, the numbers would be $1,500,000 to the manager. or 34 percent, with each member of the band receiving $695,800.

†For this tour, the business manager makes about 50 percent of what any member of the band makes. While 5 percent of the gross may not seem like much, that actually works out to be about 10 percent of what the entire band receives when the manager is a 15 percent manager and about 11 percent when the manager is a 20 percent manager.

Even a cursory glance at the budget numbers listed in the table reveals that it costs a lot of money to mount a major tour. When so much money is involved, and the profit margin is usually so much smaller than in my example, the difference between success and failure can be the result of fine decisions in one area or another. A small mistake in estimating personnel costs, multiplied by many persons over a long tour, can be nothing short of disastrous. Both the projected income and the projected expenses must be analyzed carefully, and the projections for both must be flexible enough to allow for all kinds of contingencies *over and beyond* such things as weather and illness and other insurable events.

Now, what if you put on a tour supposed to attract 1 million people and no one comes? What if the current single of the artist goes from a bullet on the charts to an anchor? What if the next single is a bomb? What if the entire promotion staff of the record company leaves for another company? Or the promotion staff at the record company is forced to shift its attention from the touring group's record to a different one that is exploding well ahead of and beyond expectations. I have seen these things happen time and time again. But, although there is really no way to control events, what can be controlled is the financial discipline that can avoid disaster. Timing is very important in planning a tour. And it takes time to plan a tour to promote an artist's latest release. By the time the stage is built, or the venues are booked, the record may have tanked, or the economy may have gone south, or both. In 2002 no less a star touring group than the Rolling Stones postponed a potential hundred million dollar tour because they feared that their demographic was getting too old at the same time the economy was experiencing a downturn. Seductive as it may have been to the group and their advisors, all of whom stood to make a fortune, the decision protected them from what could have been a financial, as well as a potential career-ending, debacle.

While it is customary for an artist and the artist's business manager to find a way to help out a promoter who has taken a bath at a show, this is not something that anyone wants to experience. A misjudged and poorly planned tour can easily result in one of these sad late-night negotiations where the artist has to help out the promoter by waiving fees, bearing unplanned expenses, and perhaps agreeing to terms for a future date that are less favorable than they should be.

TOUR RIDERS

Performance "riders" are the multipage addenda to the (usually) one-page employment contract that establishes the basics of a booking: the date, the location, the price, the terms of payment, the number of shows, and whether the act is headlining or not. The rider is where the fun begins. Rather than review all of the customary provisions, suffice to say that they cover everything from staging, sound, lighting, and electrical requirements to backstage food and drink (a generous serving of moo goo gai pan was my favorite—but for 65 dates?).

What is important here is, again, not so much the content of the rider, but the thought that goes into drafting it. It matters who writes it, who reads it, and who sees it. There are hidden costs included within the rider that can bankrupt a tour if the person who draws up the budget is not aware of them. While the costs of advertising (for example) and the nature, variety, and extent of the backstage food are usually borne by the promoter, what happens when the promoter suffers significant losses and looks to the artist for help? After all, in the promoter's opinion, it is the artist who failed to draw the crowd—not the inefficiencies of the record company, not the local radio promotion people who awoke too late to the fact that the artist was coming to town, and not the inept (or nonexistent) advertising by the promoter. So, the more costs the promoter incurs because of the artist's whims, or the artist's manager's misjudgment or mismanagement, the bigger the financial hit the promoter may experience later—and the less likely it is that promoter will be willing to accommodate you when you want to play that venue again.

Even in the event of a successful concert, these superfluous costs can have a considerable impact on the artist's net income derived from the date. The profits of a concert are customarily shared by the artist and the promoter on some percentage basis, with the much larger share (upwards of 80 percent) going to the artist. When the expenses incurred as a result of excesses sought in the rider are higher than they should be, the net to the artist is naturally lower than it could be. Remember, in traditional arrangements, the manager, business manager, and agent are all commissioning the gross, so they do not have the same stake as the artist does in controlling costs, which ultimately determine the net profit.

Most of the time, the artist has no clue as to the goings-on behind the scenes that cause expenditures to spiral upward, expenditures which, in a nanosecond, can exceed those imagined in the artist's wildest dreams mere months before. That is too bad, since the artist will end up paying for *all* of them.

FOUNDATIONS OF SUCCESS: TEAM PLANNING

The preparation (or lack thereof) for a grand tour can have a profound effect on an artist's future. A poorly planned tour can not only destroy the fiscal health of an artist, it can also kill a career. In no other area is it more important that planning time be spent wisely by the artist's team of advisors and nowhere is it more appropriate for all of these advisors to be in constant communication with each other. The purpose of establishing and maintaining fluid contact among advisors is not to make it impossible for any of them to claim innocence if something goes wrong—that will not help revive a bank account or a career. Rather it should be established so that the advisors will be able to truly test each other's judgment on critical decision making. In a finely tuned organization all the information gained as a result of following the guidelines in this chapter would be shared by all of the important decision makers within that organization—including, of course, the artist.

Trucking and Busing

There are a number of issues that must be explored before projecting a budget for this extremely expensive category. First and foremost, or course, is the reputation and track record of the companies you will deal with. If you have knowledge of a reputable firm, fine. If not, will you need a broker (who will add to the cost)? Following is a comprehensive list of items that need to be evaluated in the planning stages by the artist's professional representatives—and occasionally by the artist as well. (For simplicity's sake, I have used the pronoun "you" to refer to the artist and the artist's team, collectively.)

CONTINGENCY PLANNING

- How committed must you be to reserve the vehicles—for example, once the deal is agreed, what is the cancellation policy? 7 days? 14 days?
- Is everyone absolutely clear about dates, and has some flexibility been provided, in case there is a need to change start and end dates as well as venues in between; nothing can add to costs as much as inattention to such details.
- Has anyone thought of negotiating a renewal option if the tour does particularly well and the artist is in a position to extend it?
- Has anyone thought of negotiating a termination option if the tour does not do particularly well and the artist is in a position to end it? What is the "kill" price and is it reasonable?
- If there is a mechanical failure, what kind of damages can ensue and what kind of costs will the trucking company be required to bear to provide alternative transportation? In the case of buses, who decides what this alternative transportation will be to insure that the artists arrive at their destination in the same shape as they would have if there had been no mechanical failure? The same issue applies to gear in the trucks that obviously must be at the venue in time for sound check and, of course, the show itself.

INSURANCE AND LIABILITY

- What are the claims procedures?
- What kinds of insurance must be provided, how much does it cost, and how secure is it?
- Is there a way to make sure that the trucking company bears some liability in the event the drivers commit acts of negligence or incompetence due to poor training or substance abuse? Or worse?
- Who is responsible for mechanical failure and can it be insured against?
- How is third-party liability and property damage dealt with?
- Since the artist will have to reimburse the trucking company in the event the artist's guests trash the bus or cause damage, the artist (and, if a band, each member) and the entire entourage (wives and husbands included) had better be forewarned of the possible liability.
- If the vehicles are used for any illegal or unlawful purpose (such as a violation of a federal, state, or even municipal statute or law applicable to the operation of the vehicle or possession of drugs), the vehicles themselves can be subject to confiscation by the authorities. This would be a disaster! Who knows what the damages could be? At the least, the artist would be liable for the fair market value of the vehicles (as depreciated) or even the actual cost of replacing them with brand-new vehicles. The artist might also be liable for lost profits if the vehicles were scheduled to be leased to a customer following the expiration of the current contract. Even if the artist does not do anything illegal or unlawful in the bus, many of these contracts require the artist/group to agree not to permit *the vehicle to be used for such purposes. Thus an affirmative obligation is placed on the artist regarding the eventual risk of cost.*

- Even if the artist is completely insured, if a loss occurs, the insurance rates on the next tour will be even higher. It is a good idea for the attorney, or business manager, to inform the artist about this issue.
- In the event of injuries or death of the artist's personnel or passengers resulting in claims in excess of the insurance, or in the event of damage to or loss of baggage, cargo, or personal property not caused by the artist, who is responsible for the costs incurred or, for that matter, the legal fees to defend the eventual lawsuits?

THE DRIVERS

- Who is responsible for the drivers? Their accommodations? Their insurance? Their withholding taxes? Their benefits? Their Workers' Compensation fees? Their per diems?
- How do you know if the drivers have good driving records?
- How do you know if the drivers are familiar with the particular type of vehicles you are leasing or with their unique characteristics?

DAY-TO-DAY EXPENSES

- Is there a basis for comparison to determine whether the projected costs (per day/week/month) are reasonable?
- Who pays for the diesel fuel? Oil?
- Who pays for ordinary repairs?

THE VEHICLES

- Has anyone examined the licenses, permits, and certifications of the trucking company and compared them to the vehicles that are being leased? This and similar nit-picky details can be delegated by the tour manager, but *someone* needs to be responsible for them.
- Did anyone see the vehicles before they were selected for rental?
- Have the selected vehicles been inspected by someone on or hired by the artists' team? It is a good idea to have someone who knows about these things inspect the vehicles before possession is taken because, like rental cars, they will have to be returned in the same condition they were in when first handed over to the artist. Photographs or video would not be a bad idea—put an issue of that day's newspaper in front of the photographs to establish the date on which they are taken.
- Is there a list of the vehicles' serial numbers so the touring group can be sure it is getting what it paid for?
- Has there been an understanding reached about security of the vehicles? For example, where will they be parked and under what kind of protection when they are not moving? The lessee (artist) will be responsible for sabotage, vandalism, floods, etc., and will customarily be insured against these eventualities. However, if the vehicles are damaged or stolen after being left unlocked or unguarded, the insurance claim on behalf of the artist might be rejected by the insurance company asserting that negligence on the artist's part contributed to the loss.

- Is the artist responsible for the cost of moving the trucks or buses from their places of origin to the location where the equipment can be loaded (insofar as trucks are concerned) or to the location where the band and crew are to be picked up (insofar as the personnel are concerned)? Is the artist responsible for the cost of returning the trucks or buses to their places of origin?
- Are all concerned aware that the vehicles must not be altered in any way? The owners really do not like their buses and trucks repainted with advertisements screaming out how many booties the band will shake.

SECURITY DEPOSIT

- What is the security deposit and are the terms of its return clear?
- If the security deposit is to be returned "less damage," does this mean "less damage caused by the artist or the artist's entourage"?

BREACH OF CONTRACT

- What kind of cure period is available to the artist and to the trucking company? Is a one- or two-day period practical when curing the particular breach in two days can result in a cancellation of a date and the attendant loss of guarantees and the possible incurrence of additional damages due to the promoter's losses?
- If there is a breach by the artist, can the trucking company (1) terminate the lease, (2) recover the vehicle, (3) accelerate damages—such as by demanding payment of the entire remaining portion of the lease fees, (4) charge interest, and/or (5) seek reimbursement for other costs and expenses, such as attorneys' fees?

BOILERPLATE

- Finally, has everyone paid sufficient attention to the so-called boilerplate provisions (the standard language found in most contracts)? We are dealing with vehicles worth hundreds of thousands of dollars, and simple things like notice provisions—including those regarding who receives copies of notices and those relating to the choice of applicable law and location of any lawsuits—can either protect the artist or put the artist at incredible risk. In the arts world, in general, it is customary to provide that the laws of the states of New York or California or Tennessee apply to the interpretation and construction of contracts. There are three main reasons for this: (1) These states have a long precedential history of cases affecting entertainment industry contracts. (2) Their courts are familiar with the entertainment industry and will be able to comprehend factual situations that arise as entertainment industry contracts are performed (or breached); they are sympathetic to the artist's interests in such situations because the entertainment business is so important to their economic health.

Sound and Lights

It is not a stretch to say that the quality of sound and lighting at a concert is the most important production element on any tour. Achieving anything less than perfection can jeopardize the tour and a career. To assure artists that all of their art and work will not be lost in a haze, more time and energy must be invested in formulating agreements affecting sound and light facilities than in agreements involving any other elements of the tour.

DESIGN

The first contractual obligation should be with the artist's sound and lighting designers. Following that, the contract with the vendor of the sound and light equipment and operating personnel must be carefully drawn to provide that the equipment and services will be provided strictly in accordance with these designs. It is appropriate and wise to attach to the vendor's contract a paper copy of the sound designer's and lighting designer's drawings and specifications. Otherwise, there is no way to pinpoint what it is that is being contracted for.

Standard equipment and services are provided by a variety of companies. Specialty equipment and services are provided by a company such as Vari-Lite, Inc., owners of the patents to the remote-controlled "self-propelling" lights. If an artist's manager does not know whom to deal with, the artist's agent probably will (or the lawyer or business manager, if either has some experience with this aspect of a tour).

TECHS

The companies that provide sound and lighting equipment to artists on tour often provide two different levels of technology: (1) standard equipment and services pursuant to designs provided by the artist's sound designer and lighting designer and (2) specialty equipment and services provided by companies that own their own technology. Both deals are essentially the same, but because there are often two sound and two lighting companies providing the product and the services, a little coordination is needed.

PERSONNEL AND TRANSPORTATION COSTS

It is customary for the servicing companies to provide personnel familiar with the equipment. Their cost is built in to the price of the lease. When this is the case, the artist will be expected to bear not only the cost of the technicians, including their salaries, but also payroll taxes and Workers' Compensation. Most of these are not subject to negotiation; however, the following costs are usually negotiable:

- Transportation of equipment and personnel from the home base of the lighting company
- Transportation of equipment and personnel to and between all rehearsal locations and concert locations
- Transportation of equipment and personnel back to the home base of the lighting company
- Cost of accommodation for the personnel commencing on their arrival at the first rehearsal.
- Cost of per diems for each member of the technical staff

INSURANCE

As with other elements of the tour, insurance (liability, damage to equipment, equipment failure, delay in replacing or repairing equipment, etc.) is an important issue and all of the concerns applicable to the failure of the trucking and bus companies to accomplish what is expected of them apply here as well. In particular, many tours experience, and actually plan for, a "hiatus." What must the artist pay during such a break in the touring schedule? Sometimes the fee is reduced for the equipment; more often, the personnel are sent home and the equipment is moved to a secure location for the hiatus period. There may be scheduled downtime as well as unscheduled hiatuses, and the professionals negotiating these agreements must provide for these contingencies in the contract. Surprises are costly.

Air Travel

You're tired of buses. You're tired of weather and traffic delays, breakdowns, and the sheer time it takes to go from place to place. Speed is now in your vision of how you would like to conduct your tour. Time to rent an airplane and hop on.

Now that you have forsaken the bus for the airplane, and have factored in the additional costs (and savings), let's discuss the unique issues that arise from your newfound adventurousness. What is the main difference between a bus and a jet plane? No, it's not the wings. It's the availability! Whereas buses can be replaced and substituted for fairly easily, airplanes cannot. There are several important differences between these two modes of transportation:

1. Planes are inspected more regularly than buses, and if they do not pass inspection, they will be grounded. This happens far more frequently than you can imagine.
2. It is easy for a plane to fail inspection or to be grounded voluntarily because a part is needed; most airports do not keep a lot of spare parts around.
3. Air routes are much more closely monitored and controlled than ground routes.
4. Weather and traffic can wreak havoc on flight schedules; buses can more easily locate alternate routes.
5. Finally, if you think that bus drivers have to be rested periodically, imagine the rules affecting jet plane pilots!

One detail that is true of *both* buses and planes concerns location. Whether you are traveling by bus or by plane, you will have to find a way to get it from its home base to the city in which you are rehearsing and from which you will depart for your first date. And—you'd be surprised at how many people overlook this detail—you actually have to return the vehicle to its city of origin.

An attorney for one of our era's biggest touring acts told me that he actually has a solution to these problems—one that I think is more easily achievable than to open up a new air route in an otherwise overwhelmed traffic lane: he prays. Here are some other approaches.

THE BIGGER THE BROKER, THE BETTER

One of the tricks of the trade is to deal only with brokers who have access to other planes. While we in the music industry like to encourage young, small entrepreneurs in many areas of the business, here is one situation where the bigger the broker, the more likely it is that you will get what you need when you need it.

Force Majeure

All air travel is subject to the vagaries of weather and air traffic conditions. That is why it is a good idea to try to insert in touring agreements involving moving from venue to venue a little extra language in the *force majeure* clause (the clause that essentially says that if a failure to perform is the result of an "act of God"—such as hurricane, earthquake, strike, or other disaster—neither party to the agreement will be held to be at fault). The extra language would include "failure of transportation" outside of the control of the artist. This would include a failure of the aircraft to pass inspection; it would also cover a delay due simply to too much traffic. August is usually one of the busiest months for air travel and it is also one of the preferred months for large touring acts. Capacity problems at airports can wreak havoc on a tightly scheduled tour. There may be more takeoff and landing slots authorized by federal law than existed just a few years ago, but there also is a backlash by commercial travelers against private carriers. Airports have been forced to delay private planes because of pressure from commercial travelers. A big-time rock band will not engender a lot of sympathy when it is a question of their being on time for a gig versus a grandmother trying to arrive in time for her grandchild's birthday celebration. In the year 2000 alone, LaGuardia Airport experienced 2,505 delayed flights in August—about 1 in 5. One particular scheduled flight was late 30 out of the 31 days in August. A well-oiled, tightly scheduled tour can be severely disrupted if the artist's jet has to idle for three hours on the runway. According to the air traffic division manager for the FAA Eastern Division, "You don't have to be the sharpest knife in the drawer to know that I'm going to have aircrafts left over that I can't accommodate when 10 flights are scheduled to leave and 12 are scheduled to arrive within four minutes on a typical day."

VARIATIONS ON LEASES

There are actually not a lot of variations or provisions open to negotiation when it comes to airplane leases. Probably the most important one is whether the plane comes with or without fuel. This may sound like a no-brainer, but believe me, when the cost of fuel is factored in to the lease price, what appeared to be a good deal, one within one's budget, can go south in no time. Aircraft are traditionally leased in "wet" or "dry" conditions. A "dry" lease may mean not only that the aircraft comes without fuel, but that it comes without crew or maintenance also. In that case, an aircraft management agreement must also be entered into with a vendor of such services in addition to the aircraft lease agreement. Oh the legal fees!

WARRANTIES UNIQUE TO AIRCRAFT LEASES

In the ordinary course of events, you might expect to receive at least these warranties from the leasing company: that the lessor owns the aircraft and has the right to enter into the lease and that the aircraft has been maintained in compliance with applicable federal regulations and is "airworthy." But many other, similarly reasonable, warranties that one might normally expect to receive are not always available from the companies that lease jet planes. In view of the fact that many tour schedules are poorly thought through and the pressures of time and availability provide for few, if any alternatives, warranties such as "merchantability or fitness for a particular purpose" are often specifically excluded and disclaimed. There is simply nothing you can do about it if you want that plane NOW.

Similarly, leasing parties—the artists—often have to make certain warranties with respect to things they do not have knowledge of. For example, the artist may be required to affirm in the leasing contract that the artist's corporation is authorized to assume the enormous responsibility of undertaking a costly aircraft lease. This authorization may not in fact exist, as the certificates of incorporation of traditional industry corporations often do not permit such an undertaking, and a warranty made and breached can have dire consequences to the shareholders.

PAPERWORK

Don't forget to file a signed copy of the lease with the FAA, Aircraft Registry, Flight Standards Technical Division, P.O. 25724, Oklahoma City, OK 73124, within 24 hours after the execution of the lease. And, at least 48 hours before takeoff of the first flight under the lease, you need to notify the FAA Flight Standards District Office, General Aviation District Office, Air Carrier District Office, or the International Field Office nearest the airport where the first flight under the lease will originate informing them of (1) the location of the airport of departure, (2) the departure time, and (3) the registration number of the aircraft.

Are you beginning to get the idea that your life and those of your representatives (and bankers and insurance companies) may be a lot more complicated now that you have forsaken the bus for the airplane? Nevertheless, plane transportation works most of the time. As long as your cabin pressure transducer doesn't fail! And as long as the lessee's (the artist's) one hundred million dollar insurance policy is actually in force! And don't forget the "engine reserve" and "airport-related expenses"!

All of this is to emphasize that aircraft leases, like any other contract entered into on behalf of an artist in the music industry, must be considered carefully and by expert counselors. And the cost for the lease as well as for the maintenance services and the legal fees must be calculated into the total cost of the project in sufficient time for the artist to be fairly—and safely—represented. Sufficient time means time to drop the idea and find an alternative way to transport your equipment and personnel.

Pyrotechnics

Many performing artists seek to enhance their live shows with pyrotechnics, the name given to special effects displays that use explosive materials. Silver fountains, concussion effects, airburst effects, flame effects, fireworks, gerbs, waterfall gerbs, flame additives, flash powders, saxons, bullet hit simulators, fireballs, comet effects, flashpaper comets, shock tube initiator, and crossette effects have entered the lexicon of the live tour.

My favorite pyrotechnic device is the remote fire pickle, which is just a variation on a television remote—and which doesn't really look like a pickle. Luna Tech, Inc., located in Alabama (website: Pyropak.com) is probably the premier supplier of pyrotechnics for performing acts. Here are some of their instructions for use of the remote fire pickle:

> There are two buttons located on the pickle and both must be pressed simultaneously to fire. This provides an extra margin of safety, in the event the pickle is dropped or knocked out of the operator's hand. The pickle has a red LED to indicate the SAFE/ARM status of the Master. . . . It is recommended that no more than five feet of cable be used to ensure that the Master is within sight of the operator.

Sounds like fun. Anyway, here are some of the things groups need to consider when planning the pyrotechnics part of their shows.

COSTS

In addition to being hazardous, these effects are not inexpensive. A full-effects show at an arena venue can cost upwards of $5,000 per show. In addition to the equipment and personnel supplied by the pyrotechnics company, some states require a locally licensed "shooter" to be present—one more body to travel, accommodate, feed, insure, and pay.

PREMATURE FIRING

Some of the pyrotechnics-related equipment used in a performance can endanger the safety of all personnel and customers at the venue. A recent notice from the principal pyrotechnics supplier to all artist productions that use its pyrotechnics services warned that certain "IR-controlled video projectors can result in premature firing" of explosives (benignly referred to as "effects"). Testing effects ahead of time can help, but given current advances in electronics, and remote digital equipment, ranging from sound and lights to laser and pyrotechnics, it is a wonder that there has not been a major tragedy resulting from an erroneous signal initiated innocently. Talk about a show-stopper!

LOCAL LICENSES AND PERMITS

Needless to say, numerous local licenses and permits will be required, and all competent tour managers/production managers know that. (Here is another in the long line of reasons for hiring only experienced personnel—from personal manager to attorney to business manager (who, more than anyone else, will know all of the details of such regulations because the business manager is the one who writes the checks) to, of course, all touring staff members.

SAFETY ISSUES

Dealing with a reputable pyrotechnics company has obvious advantages. Among them is the likelihood that when pyrotechnics equipment is aged or stressed through use, the company providing the services will insure that either new equipment compatible with the old is provided or that the old or damaged equipment is refurbished properly, expertly, and safely. Whether you are buying or renting a car, a jet plane, or a pyrotechnics stage display, it is always wise to ask about its age, in whose hands it has been, how many "miles" it is been driven, and where it has been used. Among the pieces of equipment that your production manager should be sure to examine are the cables that connect the active parts. Most of these pyrotechnic effects come with complicated diagrams of the firing connections. A typical diagram showing how to hook up a flame projector looks like it belongs in a World War II film about blowing up a bridge. This work is, in a word, scary; and as incredible as the effects are, fortunately the steps taken, and instructions provided, to insure the safety of the personnel and the concert-goers are usually equal to the task.

For example, the PYROPAK Grid Rocket is a tube device attached to a steel cable stretched between two points designed to be fired to simulate a rocket-propelled projectile. The Grid Rocket burns approximately 3 seconds, which translates to approximately 120 feet (36.5 meters) of level "flight." This effect is so powerful, and the rocket covers so much ground, that special precautions must be taken to prevent the effect from burning the material around it. According to Luna Tech's instructions:

> A minimum vertical Safety Clearance of 20 feet (6 meters) is required between the Grid Rocket and any people or flame sensitive materials. This is, of course, subject to any applicable local regulations. As always, when using any pyrotechnic effect outdoors, be sure to calculate the possible effects of wind on your Safety Clearances. Always test-fire your system before the performance.

Most pyrotechnic effects are designed to work with certain equipment only. Start to extemporize and you're asking for trouble.

WHERE DID YOU SAY MY FIREWORKS WERE?
UPS, Fed Ex, Airborne Express, RPS, and Viking all provide Internet facilities to track the shipment of goods, and you can find out literally within seconds exactly where your shipment is. This is particularly useful when your shipment contains hazardous materials, which, if in the wrong hands, could present more than a few problems.

ELEMENTS OF TOURING AGREEMENTS: COMMONALITIES AND IDIOSYNCRASIES

All agreements written to cover elements of tours are related to each other in many ways even though the subject of one is to move equipment, another to move and accommodate people, a third to provide the equipment that is transported, etc. Some elements are common to almost all of them: the need for an equipment manifest; language stating that all technicians work at the direction of the artist's production team; language that makes it clear that payments due to the lessors of the equipment are "lease payments," or "rents," not simply "payments," which might be interpreted to connote a sale; the right to terminate the agreement on short notice. Others, such as clauses related to equipment provided to specialty vendors and clauses related to liquidated damages, are not as common.

THE EQUIPMENT MANIFEST

Neither the trucking company nor the airplane lessor will agree to transport the equipment unless and until certain information regarding the size, content, dimensions, etc., of the equipment is provided. They will need materials and parts to secure the equipment during transportation, and they want as much information and notice as possible to insure that they can transport the equipment safely and securely. Before they will transport anything, an *equipment manifest,* spelling all these things out, must be drawn up, approved by the business management, the personal manager, and the technical staff of the artist, and given to the company responsible for transporting the equipment. The sooner the equipment manifest is finalized, the better.

TERMINATION CLAUSES

The artist must have the right to terminate all or many of the touring agreements on short notice in the event the tour is not succeeding or selling tickets. There is nothing worse for an artist financially, and emotionally, than to have to cancel a tour for lack of interest and at the same time have to pay the megacosts of the tour just as if the tour had proceeded on schedule.

SPECIALITY VENDORS

Given the sensitivity of some of the equipment, some companies require a special kind of truck to transport it, for example, an "air-ride" trailer. And, believe it or not, some of these companies insist that their equipment ride "in the nose" of the trailer. This may seem a bit technical to you, and it certainly is to me, but I am mentioning it because these companies are putting incredible value into the hands of the artist and the artist's staff. Whether or not the artist's staff *in fact* has the right kind of experience to handle the specialty equipment, the leasing companies have nothing to do with the choice of the touring staff and their insistence on some kind of control over how the equipment is handled and transported should not surprise the artist's team.

LIQUIDATED DAMAGES

Liquidated damages (that is, an amount of money agreed in advance of a problem) in favor of the artist are more easily negotiated in sound and light agreements than in trucking and busing agreements. A smart vendor of equipment will negotiate a fixed sum of money to be paid if for any reason the vendor is in material breach of the agreement. This is customarily established as daily fees for each day of a scheduled performance which is missed and a similar amount for each day for which the artist must find a substitute vendor.

OWNERS AND OPERATORS: WHO NETS THE NET?

The traditional model of the concert business is the net deal. The artist receives a guarantee against a percentage of the net—typically 85 percent. Any marquee headline attraction will try to get this deal. Another common model provides the artist with a percentage of gross—typically 60 percent. Both of these structures are known as the "four-wall" model because essentially the promoters rent the venue—the four walls—empty, and take care of the rest themselves. Of course the rental cost includes the essential features of the venue such as ushers, some security, etc.

But the four-wall archetype has become archaic because so many venues—particularly amphitheaters and even some arenas—are now owner-operated. In such buildings, the standard 60 or 85 percent models can be bettered. The risk is substantially lower to owner-operators because there is a whole litany of ancillary income streams available to them such as parking fees, concession profits, a piece of the income derived from merchandise sold by the artist, and the insidious facility maintenance fee. Much of the income generated by these "add-ons" supplements the ticket price—did you wonder why they have gone so high? (One oddity of this paradigm is that the "parking" fee is collected per ticket, not per vehicle. For 20,000 tickets, at $3.00 a ticket, that's $60,000. A recent hard rock all-day festival added $13.50 to each $60 ticket. None of this went to the artist or the promoter. Talk about an add-on!)

As noted, the artist does not usually share in add-on income. Accordingly, there is an upward pressure on the owner-operators by artists and their promoters to increase the standard model percentages. Remember, the owner-operators are not paying rent. While they may be contributing their receipts to service their debt on their buildings, they are nevertheless, in essence, renting out their own homes. Further, in owner-operated venues, suites which are rented by the owner-operators at a premium to season ticket holders, sponsors—even scalpers—are not included in the calculation of the artist's share of earnings. Note that with municipal facilities such as Madison Square Garden or the Staples Center most of the money generated by a performance is still accounted for within the 60/40 gross or 85/15 net calculation. It is when so much income is "outside" of the deal that booking agents on behalf of their artist rosters try to squeeze even more out of the gross, or net, reflected by the portion of receipts which they can claim a percentage of.

As of this writing, upwards of 80 percent of the country's amphitheaters are owned and operated by a huge concert promotion organization called Clear Channel, which has absorbed most of the independent promoters in the country. The remaining 15 to 20 percent are controlled by House of Blues concerts.

One final thought about the sharing of "grand" tour money. In the merchandising area, it used to be that the venue would either simply make room at no charge for the artist's merchandise to be sold, or would provide booths and sometimes staff, in return for a small percentage of the merchandise income—routinely 3 to 10 percent. Those days are over. Now the venues charge as much as 40 percent of the merchandise income in return for permitting the merchandise to be sold in their halls. This is the main reason why the price of T-shirts has risen from $10 to $30 and why the cost of other tour merchandise has gone so high.

I was, however, approached by Chinese journalists, one of whom observed how interesting it was that I combined politics—which is practical—and music—which is fantasy. I replied that they had it the wrong way round!

—Former English Prime Minister Edward Heath

While the purpose of this book is to explore those things that "they will never tell you," it is sometimes necessary to put the previously unknown into a familiar context. So please bear with me while I provide a brief overview of merchandising.

One does not merchandise people or things; one merchandises intangible rights. In the case of the performing and recording artist these consist of:

Artists' individual name

Artists' trade names

Artists' likenesses, including photographs

Logos and artwork identified with artists

There are two principal ways in which artists exploit their merchandising rights: touring and retailing. Obviously, many of the issues discussed below will not have particular application to bands engaged in touring via small club performances or festivals, but some will.

There are a variety of companies which specialize in marketing merchandise to fans; some are actually owned by the record companies and some merchandising rights are actually granted to the record companies at the time the original record deal is entered into. This chapter contemplates a more traditional situation, one in which an artist is free to license merchandising rights to one or more independent companies. In the case of touring, the period of the license most often coincides with the length of the artist's forthcoming tour. Retail deals are traditionally for slightly longer periods.

The following sections deal both with issues that are specific to tour merchandising and with issues specific to retail merchandising.

TOUR MERCHANDISING
Delivering Heads

Touring agreements differ depending on whether or not the act is a headliner. The main characteristic of these deals is that, while the merchandise company will provide a substantial advance to the artist—an advance which will help finance the production elements of the tour—the company will insist on the artist "delivering" a certain number of audience members—affectionately called "heads"—and the failure to do that will have fairly dire consequences. It is a rare deal that does not include such a delivery commitment, so it is worth explaining how these provisions work.

Contracts are often ambiguous in terms of identifying the kinds of "heads" that are to be delivered. For example, does the artist have to be a headliner? This becomes important because when the contractual requirements to deliver heads have not been met, there arises an issue as to whether the artist, or an individual member of the artist's group, can fulfill those requirements at some future time by live performances *other* than as a headliner.

If the artist is not a headliner, the parties determine a formula in the contract by which the number of heads is "imputed." For example, the particular mix of headliner and supporting act or acts may suggest that one artist, the supporting act, is likely to draw only about one-third of the total audience. Thus, a per-head dollar figure will be negotiated and divided into 33 1/3 percent. If that dollar figure (which is the figure that the parties minimally expect the fans of the supporting act who are attending the concert will pay for merchandise) is, say, $4.00, then each person who actually shows up at the concert (this is a count that is attainable after all) will be deemed to be contributing about 8 percent toward the "imputed" total (33.33 divided by 4 equals 8.33). Thus for every 12.5 people that show up, 1 (or 8 percent) will be deemed to be attributable to the supporting act. The reason the merchandise companies do not simply divide the total attendees by 3—which would represent one-third of the audience) is that the two-thirds of the audience that is there to see the headliner is far more likely to pay money—and pay more money—for merchandise than those who are present to see the supporting act.

Suppose, for example, a merchandiser is prepared to offer $1,000,000 as an advance to a headliner, and intends to sell merchandise at its stands for the supporting act, which is expected to draw one-third of the audience. The headliner has "guaranteed" that over the course of the tour, the act will perform before 450,000 concert-goers, and in fact the number of attending concert-goers over the course of the tour does add up to 450,000. Yet of that number the 150,000 that are likely to be fans of the supporting act are only counted as 12,000 people (i.e., 8 percent). Adding the 300,000 heads imputed to the headliner to the 12,000 heads imputed for the supporting act yields 312,000 "heads," 138,000 short of the contractually promised 450,000.

No matter how cleverly one can try to calculate the value of a head, the fact is that in most situations, merchandisers would rather not impute *any* heads to an opening act. In fact, most merchandisers assume that no one is showing up at all at the gig, let alone someone to see the opening act. At the same time, they will tell you that even if some of the 19,000 people showing up at Madison Square Garden are there to see the opening act, and not the headliner, even they will probably buy the headliner's T-shirt, not that of the supporting act.

In the end, it is really an issue of how much money the artist can negotiate by way of an advance and how much has to be paid back if projections do not meet expectations.

Anyway, this is the thinking.

If the "guaranteed" number of "heads" is not "delivered" (sorry for all the quotes, but each of these terms is in the realm of fantasy anyway), the artist will "owe" (sorry again) the merchandiser either an amount of money which was advanced against the guarantee which has not been met, or (get this), the artist will owe the merchandiser an amount of heads at some future date on a tour which has not even been scheduled!

There are numerous problems with this solution. One is that for liability purposes artists customarily establish separate service corporations to present each tour and the corporation is often dissolved, or at least put into mothballs, after the tour ends. (Dissolving a corporation is an act which can expose the shareholders to liability for the corporation's actions and promises and therefore is not an action which should be taken lightly.) Merchandisers are aware of this process, and, since the promise made by the defunct corporation to "owe" future heads is of no particular value, the merchandiser does not want to hear about the artist's touring corporation: it will insist on personal guarantees and usually will get them.

Personal guarantees are also problematic because once an individual member of a band guarantees something personally, that band member is in potential danger for a long period to come—even if the member leaves the band and joins another or goes solo.

A well-known band from a British commonwealth country was on its third album and third tour. Unfortunately, the interest in this group suddenly waned and the tour failed. However, a lot of money had been paid to this group by way of an advance by a merchandising company. The money was naturally spent—mostly on preproduction expenses—building the stage, designing the lighting and sound, guarantees for trucking, buses, etc.—but the band did not perform to the required number of heads. The manager commissioned the advance, as did the business manager, for a total of 20 percent of the advance. Unfortunately, the entire advance was lost by the merchandiser, so each individual member of the band owed the merchandiser 100 percent of the money (not 80 percent) until the merchandiser was fully compensated.

Complicating this was the fact that only one member of the band had any funds set aside from previous earnings and that same member of the band was the only one who would have a career following the demise of the band itself. Thus this one member was suddenly responsible not only for the return of the money, but, alternatively, for "delivering" the undelivered "heads" at some future date. She (she was the lead singer) ultimately honored the obligation of her band, took a role in a Broadway show for four years, and paid back the merchandiser.

In negotiating the band member agreement at the inception of a group artist's career, an understanding should be reached as to what will happen in the event of a loss such as that just described. Under customary partnership law, if one band member is liable for the acts of the group, the member can cross-claim against the other band members for damages. Provisions of the band member agreement may supersede or even controvert this result.

WHOSE FAULT IS IT ANYWAY?

In the example related above, neither the manager nor the business manager returned their share of the merchandise advance—in part because they felt they had done the job they were hired for. They deserved to be paid out of the gross because, essentially, they would have worked for nothing unless and until some money found its way into the artist's coffers. Clearly, however, this was not a good result for the artist. Suppose the artist felt that the tour should not have been structured so ambitiously, that the people who planned it had not made a realistic assessment of whether the band could support such a tour financially. And to whom would the artist have looked for the proper guidance? The manager and the business manager, of course.

As with many such situations, various factors go into determining whether management has or has not been good. It is difficult for nonmanagers to put themselves in the place of managers in given circumstances and to understand the pressures these people face. On the other hand, in most other businesses (including the "businesses" of government and war), people are expected to take responsibility for their actions. Shouldn't the same rules apply to those of us in the music industry who are responsible for doing a particular job to assist the artist to achieve a full potential—record company personnel, the business management office, the tour management office, the attorneys' office, the agent's office, etc.? There may be hundreds of people involved in planning a tour, but when an artist does not deliver the sufficient number of heads, guess who pays? It is not out of the question for an artist to ask his or her professional representatives how they define their jobs and what responsibilities they believe they are undertaking. It might surprise everyone when those discussions take place.

ACCRUING INTEREST AND ACCRUAL DATE

Once a merchandise deal is breached due to the failure of the act to fulfill its promise to deliver a minimum number of heads, financial consequences begin to multiply. (Of course, the minimum number of heads might not have purchased the projected amount of merchandise anyway, but the breach is in the failure to deliver the heads, not in the failure to sell the merchandise.)

Some deals require that the unrecouped balance at the point of the failure becomes subject to interest charges (at various, not always easily discernible, rates). If the rate is a variable one, and has increased at the time or times the interest becomes chargeable, the consequences can be enormous. If the interest accumulates for however long it takes for the artist to mount the next tour, the artist can be looking at a very large debt indeed. One thing that the artist can do in advance is to limit the "debt" to an increased number of heads that he must deliver; so that, at worst, he will not owe real cash to the merchandiser. This is a better result, if not a totally satisfactory one.

In addition, there is always the question of *when* this interest begins to be charged. For example, some deals provide that it begins to be charged 60 days after the tour ends or is supposed to end. Some provide that the interest begins to accrue after the final accounting, which can occur quite soon after the end of the tour. As far as the merchandising company is concerned, it is "out" the money on the day the advance is paid, and the calculation of the number of "heads" the artist is required to deliver takes into account that the requisite number of heads (concert-goers) will be "delivered" only over a period of months *after* the money has been advanced. That is, a merchandising company will often increase the number of required "heads" proportionately to the time frame during which it expects to be recompensed for its investment. Thus, the argument goes, the failure of the band to deliver the number of heads over the anticipated period will cost the merchandiser more than simply the unrecouped balance and, once the contract is breached, the merchandiser will want the interest to accrue from the date the advance was given, not from the alternative dates mentioned above. Of course, there are ways to modify this extreme position, but it is important that the artist and the artist's team understand what the merchandiser is likely to try to do. As with any unsatisfactory provision, negotiations may result in (1) doing away with it entirely; (2) specifying another date, (3) reducing the advance, and therefore the risk, or (4) some combination of the three.

It is also possible, on occasion, to negotiate an interest "hiatus"—a period during which no interest will accrue or during which a reduced rate of interest will accrue. The hiatus might be, for example, a period not to exceed 6, 9, or 12 months between tours, the purpose being that the artist then can record a new album and carefully prepare the tour associated with the album without worrying about paying interest on an "advance" that was turned into a "loan" due to circumstances that might have been any number of peoples' fault. As with all entertainment industry deals, contract provisions will be more or less favorable, or harsh, in direct proportion to the amount of the advance. It is not always cause for celebration when the manager announces a $1 million deal. The flip side is buried within the contract language!

UNRECOUPED BALANCES

Obviously, if the artist promises to pay back the merchandiser in the event of a failure to deliver the agreed-upon number of heads, and then the tour is canceled for reasons beyond the artist's control (illness—maybe even an act of God), the artist should not have to pay back more than the unrecouped balance, at most. Merchandisers will object to this result because they want not just to receive their advance back, but to make a profit as well. Nevertheless, if the advance has been recouped because enough dollars per head were accumulated before the tour was canceled, even if the contractual number of heads were not technically delivered, the artist should be relieved of the promise.

SHARED RISK

On occasion, the merchandise company will permit the operating company of the act (which, as you will recall, is usually a corporation with limited liability) to assume *some,* if not all, of the risk and thereby get the artist off the hook on a personal level for at least that portion of potential liability.

SAYING NO

As noted earlier in this book, sometimes negotiating strength lies solely in the power to say "no." Merchandising is an option, not a necessity. To be sure, there is income to be had, but there are tremendous risks involved as well. To gamble with the future financial security of an artist by foolishly making guarantees that might bankrupt the artist, or the artist's group or any of its individual members, is not a game that I think most artists would want to play. As with everything, there has to be a balance between risk and reward. It is true that merchandising money will often assist the artist in getting the tour off the ground by providing the seed money to organize the tour in the first place. But there are other sources of money which involve far less risk, and an artist in a secure financial position will have a stronger negotiating position down the road, when it *does* makes sense to enter into a merchandising deal. However, those other sources are not commissionable by the artist's manager and business manager and not always presented as an option.

WHEN A BAND MEMBER MOVES ON

Special problems can arise when a member of a band that owes a debt to a previous merchandise advance wants to join a new band. As stated above, depending on the language of the original merchandising agreement, each band member may be responsible for that debt. For example, suppose the bass player of a now-defunct band is under an obligation to deliver the entire number of "heads" agreed upon by the previous band. If the bass player were, say, offered an opportunity to play with Garth Brooks during his upcoming world tour, he wouldn't be able to accept it because Garth Brooks would never take on a musician with such a debt. It is here that the issues of whether an act's responsibility to pay back the merchandising company only via income received as a headliner is of particular relevance. If in the original merchandise agreement, only headliners were liable for making up deficiencies in delivering "heads," or if the bass player had the option of paying back all or some of the unrecouped debt (plus interest) in money, rather than in "heads" on behalf of his or her band mates, the bass player would be free to take a job with another touring band.

The marketplace may also provide a solution for the band member who joins an existing band. The old merchandise company can make a deal with the new band's merchandiser, so that some of the merchandise of the old band member might be sold through the new band's outlets. While this is unlikely in the example noted above because of Mr. Brooks's status and power, it is an option that has been exercised in some instances.

Head-debt obligations, like others involving a situation where an advance is paid and the contractual commitment is not fulfilled (e.g., the delivery of a minimum number of songs or the recording or release of a minimum number of cuts in an exclusive songwriter's contract, among many others), can theoretically extend for a lifetime. At some point, however, such obligations become insurmountable, impossible for the artist to meet. Most states' laws will permit a party to ultimately walk away from a never-ending duty to fulfill a contractual commitment that is either out of the party's control or is virtually, or actually, impossible to fulfill. The artist's representatives should understand the state laws in this area that apply to "head" provisions in the contract so that they can determine just what the artist's true burden will be in the event promises are made and not kept. This is an example in which the boilerplate provision known as "applicable law" can have enormous negative (or positive) impact on the artist, notwithstanding many lawyers' (and clients') inattention to this provision—which, on its face, has nothing specifically to do with the deal. Here is another reason why, as indicated in the previous chapter, New York, California, or Tennessee law is often chosen by artists as the applicable law by which the provisions of an entertainment business contract are interpreted. These states courts have often considered issues raised in the context of commitments extending far into the future.

One practical way to stop the nightmare before it starts is to provide that in no event will the obligation to continue to provide "heads" last beyond the commencement of the recording of the album following the one which is the subject of the tour which failed to fulfill the merchandise contract's promises. Even if the artist ends up owing money to compensate the merchandiser, money is a finite thing, and a promise to pay money is always open to later compromise. For example, if a merchandise deal ended up unrecouped by, say, $100,000, the artist might pay the money back when he or she was able to pay, pay it off over the course of time, or work out a compromise when the artist's next tour was about to commence whereby a new deal with the original merchandise company would be negotiated, part of whose terms would be a reduction or forgiving of the old debt.

Territory

While in the United States, the United Kingdom, Australia, and Canada, it is customary to specify the number of "heads" that must be delivered, in the rest of the world, the preferred route, even for headliners, is to *impute* heads according to a predetermined formula (see above, page 157).

As with all agreements which go beyond one's own country's borders and which apply to a territory that is less than "the world," the contract must be clear as to what exactly the territory covered by the deal *is*. It is important to list each country and even each portion of certain countries (e.g., French-speaking vs. German-speaking Switzerland) separately. "Europe" may or may not include the United Kingdom. "Scandinavia" may or may not include Iceland or Greenland. The "European Community" will not include Switzerland unless specifically added. It is a good habit and a money-saving (and face-saving) step for the attorney or manager who is negotiating the contract to take the time and trouble to look at a map and list the countries making up the "territory" for which the artist is seeking to grant merchandising rights.

Hall Charges

As noted in Chapter 10, the venue itself customarily charges a significant percentage of the gross sales in return for which it allows the artist the space within which to sell merchandise to the concert-goers. These "hall charges" differ from venue to venue, and they are negotiable. Nevertheless, they can exceed 30 percent of gross sales. Madison Square Garden will seek as much as 40 percent. The buyers are in control these days. In the past, hall charges could be limited to from 3 to 10 percent, or eliminated altogether. No longer. Outside of the United States, however, many venues have not yet caught up with the sophistication of the American halls, and considerable savings can be had there. For many venues, getting the act in the first place is the primary consideration—particularly in situations where the act can just as well ignore a particular city or country in its world tour. Sometimes the hall charges are less than what is anticipated (or predicted by the merchandiser); the artist's contract with the merchandiser can specify that when this occurs, the artist will share any such savings with the merchandiser.

Partial Advances

Some merchandise companies (particularly the more established ones, which have learned from bitter experience) will spread the advance (i.e., the amount of which is "guaranteed") over the course of the tour, paying in installments so that they can protect themselves in the event that things go awry and the artist fails to deliver the requisite number of heads. Doing this makes the "advance" more of a "guarantee." The problem for the artist is, of course, that installment "advances" are not really advances at all. The "guaranteed" money, while still money, is of a different nature than advance money. First of all, the artist will be more tightly held to the head-delivery promises that have been made. In this scenario, the merchandise contract will break down the number of heads into segments of the tour—usually weeks or a number of shows, frequently eight. The head-delivery requirement will be proportioned to those segments. Thus if the number of heads guaranteed is 450,000 (as in the example above), 45,000 heads per week might be the number that has to be achieved before an "advance" is deemed recouped so that the next "advance" payment will be paid. As soon as delivery promises are not kept, the money flow will stop. Second, the amount available to the artist as seed money to set up and begin the tour before the initial flow of money from ticket sales is in hand will necessarily be significantly less than what would be available if the entire amount were advanced.

The ramifications of this dependence on "installment" advances can be enormous. One potential problem—the inability of the merchandise company to fulfill its promises to deliver the money when due—can be covered if the merchandiser's bank agrees to issue a letter of credit stipulating that if the merchandiser does not pay the promised sums when due, the bank will remit the promised sums on the merchandiser's behalf. Another, which involves the cash flow that is the currency of any well-planned tour, is not so easily solved. If a hunk of money is taken out of a tour precisely when the attendance levels of a particular leg of the tour drop, the effect on the remainder of the tour—a remainder that may include the biggest dates—can be catastrophic. After all, the costing of the entire tour—the trucks, buses, sound, lights, personnel, travel, etc.—are all prorated across the entire tour, not in equal segments per leg of the tour. These are very significant concerns to the business manager and personal manager, who are trying to plan the tour efficiencies. In this case, the tail of the dog—the merchandise agreement—may indeed wag the dog. Among the consequences of having to halt a tour due to lack of funds are, of course, the claims that will arise from promoters and venues with respect to the canceled dates and the mess that the record company will be in for having incurred promotion expenses in cities in which the artist fails to appear.

Some Practical Considerations

Music lawyers are not used to multiple agreement transactions. The record deal, the publishing deal, the producer agreement: these are agreements that are made one at a time, have only a little to do with each other, and are addressed on a per-artist basis very irregularly and over a course of years. When an artist decides to embark on a major tour—in particular a world tour—there are dozens of major agreements to be entered into over a very short period of time. Some law firms, management firms, and business management firms are not staffed to cover all the bases in such circumstances.

I can attest to the fact that when a major artist decides to mount a major tour, the lawyer's world changes very quickly. But, just because the merchandise agreement is only one of a dozen major agreements to be entered into does not mean that it deserves less attention to detail. This attention can take time and cost the client money, and the lawyer must weigh relative values of spending time and client's money against the practicalities of just how much total time and money are available. Nevertheless, if the following issues are not specifically dealt with, the agreement that is eventually signed may bear no resemblance to what the parties desire or expect out of the relationship:

- Whose personnel will be used?
- What is the itinerary of the tour and how are revisions to be dealt with?
- Who transports the merchandise and at whose cost?
- Will the merchandise be offered for sale in display cases provided by the artist?
- By the merchandiser? And who transports the display cases and at whose cost?
- If there are not display cases, should they be built? At whose cost? Who will own them after the tour is over?
- What kinds of controls are in place to insure sufficient supplies for the expected demand?
- Is the insurance adequate to cover the possible loss of merchandise?
- Is the product liability insurance adequate?
- Who is responsible for protecting the venue and the tour city against pirated merchandise?

Advertising

Imagine an artist who has made a commitment to avoid commercial advertising and the stigmas that go with it (at least in this country). The artist is backstage preparing to go on stage for a performance before 20,000 people to whom he or she will be representing the values of an "outsider"—a unique spokesperson for the "not ever to sell out" class—and that artist picks up a copy of the souvenir program for the tour and discovers pages of advertising by liquor companies, tobacco companies, and yes, even Ford Motor Company and Firestone espousing the qualities of their products and identifying with the values of the great artist who is about to perform. The job of an attorney is not just to review the written word in a contract submitted by the merchandiser; he or she must also "imagine" the things that are *not* there. This is one example. The attorney should insist on a provision that prohibits the inclusion of advertising material on, near, or in association with the artist's merchandise, unless the artist or the artist's representatives have given their approval in writing, in advance.

Even if the artist does not care about the products he or she is associated with (Lou Reed advertised Honda Motorcycles and the Rolling Stones had Budweiser ads on their tickets!), or has approved the inclusion of advertising in connection with his or her merchandise, one must be careful to insure that the money derived from the advertising is included among net receipts of the merchandiser and therefore shared with the artist.

Tour merchandise royalty structures do not usually take into account this kind of income and the issue should be dealt with directly and clearly during the initial negotiation.

Exclusivity

While the artist may be exclusive with the merchandiser, is the merchandiser exclusive with the artist? One would think it would be very disturbing—emotionally and financially—were the artist to find that among the merchandise being sold at the merchandise booth was merchandise of other acts that had performed at the venue over the past season—or even merchandise featuring the logos of the venue itself (e.g., Madison Square Garden or Radio City Music Hall). The sale of this merchandise will naturally reduce the net sales of the artist's merchandise and should be prohibited if possible. This is an example of why it is useful to work with an experienced merchandiser, who will know what can and cannot be done at various venues and the issues will be on the table from the beginning—to be resolved, if possible, in plenty of time before the date is played.

RETAIL MERCHANDISING

Most tour merchandising agreements have a retail component as well. The Internet is having a revolutionary effect on retail sales, as opposed to tour-oriented sales. Although this is not yet having a significant effect on the royalty rate structure, eventually it will have to because there will no longer be any intermediary vendors to justify the kinds of commissions retained by merchandisers. In the meantime, in negotiating a retail agreement, care must be taken to address the difference between customary store distribution and Internet distribution.

In traditional retail deals, the term of rights is quite a bit longer than for those limited to touring. The latter are based approximately on the length of an album release period (about nine months to one year). With retail deals, three years is not unusual. Some other issues that arise with regard to retail sales include the following.

The Role of the Tour Merchandiser

One of the first issues to be dealt with in retail merchandising is whether the tour merchandiser will act as a manufacturer and distributor or as an agent, licensing to third parties the manufacture and distribution of merchandise. The latter involves considerable risk to trademarks and quality control. Even though the immediate concern of the parties negotiating the tour-merchandising contract deals with the tour aspects of the relationship, the retail portion should be very carefully negotiated to protect the artist's rights. It should not be treated as an afterthought.

Cross-Collateralization

If an artist decides to place retail rights under the control of the tour merchandiser, two specific financial distinctions should be made: first, there should be a separate calculation of compensation as between the two contracting parties because the services to be rendered are totally different; and second, there should be no right on the part of the tour merchandiser to apply success from one realm against failure from another. In other words, the income from one realm should be separated from the debt from the other. Whether or not this distinction is achievable may depend both on the artist's leverage and on the amount of money at risk. As noted previously, as more money is advanced or guaranteed, fewer rights can be reserved and deal terms benefiting the licensing party (the artist) will suffer.

Exclusivity

Does the artist wish to reserve the nonexclusive rights to issue certain licenses directly or through another agent, or must the artist give exclusive retail rights to the tour merchandiser? Remember, a merchandiser may be very good at tour merchandising, but inadequate or inattentive to the tasks required of an agent. There may be opportunities brought to the artist's attention that involve areas in which the merchandiser is not actually involved or has no relationships; the contract can permit the artist to license those areas even if the deal with the tour merchandiser is otherwise substantially exclusive in nature. A problem may arise if the artist wishes to make available for retail sale through another vendor or agent some of the same merchandise that has been created by the tour merchandiser who has been eliminated from the retail side of things. This possibility must be dealt with as well.

Even when the retail rights extend beyond the term of the tour merchandise license, the artist may want to restrict the tour merchandiser from licensing the use of the tour logo, which has been designed for use with a specific tour. The first tour—and term of agreement with the tour merchandiser—may be long ended while the retail rights continue and a second or even third tour, each with its own logo, may have commenced. The artist may want to control these separately, particularly if the artist grants tour merchandising rights for tours two and three to a competitor of the first tour merchandiser.

Sample Approval

The need for the artist to have the right to approve samples of the merchandise is obvious; how to deal with the issue of the time it may take to provide those approvals is not. If the artist is responsible for approving designs and samples—as he or she should be—and the merchandiser must move so fast in manufacturing the products that the rights are not cleared properly, the merchandiser will jeopardize both the merchandising company and the artist. At the same time, if the merchandiser does *not* move quickly (and to the merchandiser, that is the name of the game), sales opportunities may be lost that will never arise again. As with a Broadway show or an airplane flight, once the curtain goes up, or the plane takes off, the empty seat—a commodity that had real value five minutes before—is worthless. Systems should be established early on to facilitate, insofar as possible, prompt submission of materials for approval and response by the artist or his or her designated representatives.

Trademarks

The laws and cases regarding trademark protection are complex. Music business lawyers usually refer trademark legal work to others who live and breathe it daily and who read up on the latest changes regularly. Of course large law firms, including large entertainment law firms, will have trademark specialists. There is a body of law in the area of trademark that establishes that a trademark owner must maintain almost absolute control of the reproduction of the owner's marks, failure of which may result in losing the federal, and possibly state, protection that has been acquired through years of use and official trademark registrations.

This issue becomes concrete when an artist sublicenses his or her name, likeness, logos, trade names, and trademarks either directly or, through a merchandise "guru," to a variety of third parties. Mere approval by the trademark owner of these licensees is not enough to establish the kind of control that the law requires. The artist, either directly, or through an agent, must have total control over the manner in which the trademark is reproduced, the quality of the reproduction, and the manner in which the trademark is used.

Once a licensee misuses an artist's trademark, if the artist does not take significant steps to cause the error to be corrected, the artist's trademark can be placed in real jeopardy. If the artist has been careless in monitoring the use of the trademark, or if he or she, or a licensee, uses it in a manner that, under trademark law, can divest the artist of his or her rights, it may not be possible to stop a third, unauthorized, party who will raise the defense that the artist has abandoned the trademark. The culprit will claim that he or she can continue selling the product and will be exempt from infringement claims and all of the attendant liabilities that infringers can suffer. An example might be when an unrelated, and unauthorized, third party manufacturers and distributes a coffee mug with a Rolling Stones "Tongue" or a Prince "No name" symbol. As with other clauses in entertainment-related contracts, merely identifying the issue and requiring control over the use of one's trademarks is not enough. Someone must be put in charge of, and be held responsible for, insuring that those steps that are necessary to protect the marks be taken, and taken consistently over the course of the term of the merchandising agreement.

In the area of trademark protection, one of the parties whom the artist should be protected against is, ironically, his or her own merchandiser. It is wise to put into the merchandise contract a provision that insures that the trademarks, trade names, copyrights, and other intellectual property rights of the artist will *not* be disputed or attacked at any time by the merchandiser *and* that by being authorized to use and to license the use of these rights, the merchandiser is affirming that the rights are indeed vested in the artist and that the merchandiser is not acquiring any of those rights.

The merchandiser should also be familiar with the rules governing the requirement that manufacturers identify the source of the product (i.e., who manufactured it and where?), and there is still some vestigial belief that proper copyright notices and trademark notices must be affixed to products to protect the intellectual property rights in the logos, trade names, etc., although such formalities are, in fact, no longer necessary. Many artists have a problem with corporate names being used to identify the owner of a trademark or copyright. "Bob Dylan, Inc." is not something that an artist who has evidenced an anti-establishment bias in his career would like to see plastered over all of his program books or T-shirts. In this scenario, the merchandiser thinks (mistakenly) that "Bob Dylan, Inc." must appear somewhere on the T-shirt, and so includes those words on the T-shirt, together with a copyright symbol (©) and a year date. But Bob Dylan is—rightfully—annoyed because of his life-long opposition to the "establishment." In fact, the merchandiser could simply have used the initials BDI, which would satisfy both Bob Dylan and the law. Your "merchandise lawyer" must be familiar with the ever-changing laws of copyright to determine if the merchandise can be distributed without this designation, or, at a minimum an abbreviation of the corporate name (in this case BDI) or some variation thereof.

Net: Gross Less Sales Tax?

Interestingly, in deals in which royalties are calculated as a percentage of net receipts, "net" is often defined as gross less sales tax. Let's see what this means. A product is sold for $10.00. Tax on this is an additional $0.825 in New York City. Thus the consumer pays $10.83. If the royalty is to be paid on "gross less sales tax," $0.83 is deducted from the $10.00, leaving $9.17 as the "net." Here is an example where imprecise language affects the artist's pocketbook. Obviously, the intention (probably of both parties) is that the royalty will be paid on $10.00, not $9.17, but when push comes to shove, it is surprising what arguments one can come up with (and then maybe settle in return for some compromise elsewhere). Therefore, the definition of net receipts should be "gross 'net of' sales tax," not "gross 'less' sales tax."

Of course, depending on the nature of the merchandise and the location of the sale, there may be other "taxes" such as import duties, value-added taxes, etc. that may be added to the suggested sale price of a particular product and these should be handled the same way. The same issue applies to shipping and handling charges, which are prevalent in Internet sales.

Boilerplate: Don't Overlook the Obvious

Many of the boilerplate provisions found in tour merchandising agreements are also applicable in the retail area—such as insurance and territory issues. Just because these are routine provisions does not mean that they do not have weight and should not be fought over vigorously. For example, in the insurance area, among the warranties an artist should require is that all of the goods and materials that are used in the merchandise are safe and fit for the purpose and use intended. One of the mechanisms utilized by artists who are subjecting themselves to potential liability by depending on the quality of products produced by third parties is to require that the third parties themselves be sufficiently insured against eventual claims by people claiming injury from the products. One way to guarantee that this is the case is to require that the third party (in this case the merchandiser) provide a certificate of insurance proving the existence of whatever amount of insurance the artist's representatives feel is sufficient to indemnify the artist in the event of adverse claims. In addition, the artist will usually want to be named as an "Additional Insured" on the merchandiser's own insurance policy. This is customarily provided when requested (if, of course, the company is in fact insured in the required amount). One thing to watch out for is the possibility that the insured amount may be used up by claims against the merchandiser from completely unrelated parties.

Therefore, the contractual clause requiring a certificate of insurance naming the artist and the artist's touring company as "Additional Insured" should also provide that the amount of insurance that is sought to be provided is isolated from claims from any other parties against the merchandiser.

SOME GENERAL CONSIDERATIONS

Many merchandising issues are applicable both to tour merchandising and retail merchandising. A primary consideration in both areas, of course, is to maintain what I refer to as "institutional memory." As time passes, and particularly when an artist has switched representation, the artist and his or her team must be very careful to be sure that there are no previous agreements or provisions of agreements that have carried over into the present (or the future).

Another key issue has to do with the request that merchandising companies are increasingly making for irrevocable letters of direction to the artist's record company, music publishing company, even performing rights society, requiring them to pay to the merchandising company, in the event the merchandising deal does not play out as expected, earnings generated by the artist and otherwise payable directly to the artist. This is a disaster for a variety of reasons—not the least of which is that although the amount of money cited in a letter of direction is by necessity a fixed number, the actual sum of money due the merchandiser at any given time is, more often than not, a matter open to considerable dispute. The "deficit" number is always changing and, in changing, becoming less and less; yet it is unlikely that the merchandiser will send follow-up letters to the artist's record company, publishing company, etc., changing the original number.

Among the other areas of general concern are confidentiality, compliance with local laws, sell-off and inventory, the disposition of artwork and photographs, audits, and life and disability insurance.

Confidentiality

For some reason, people are very nosy about the relationship between artists and their merchandisers. Perhaps it is because the deals are so straightforward (advances, royalty rates, "heads" attending concerts, etc.) that it is easier to comprehend the value of these deals than to get into comparison shopping with information about record royalties where a royalty "point" can mean anything you want it to mean. There is no reason to educate other competitors for artist's rights or merchandiser's money as to what deals can be squeezed out of the merchandisers. After all, the artist and the merchandiser pay substantial fees to professionals to work their way through the complexities of these deals and both the information about them and the process that accomplishes consensus are, in a way, proprietary. Accordingly, there should be included in these agreements a clause, with teeth, protecting their confidentiality.

Compliance with Local Laws

Nothing pleases a small-minded prosecutor more than a little publicity that can be garnered from attacking a high-profile artist for "participation" in breaking a local law. The contract with merchandisers must address the fact that the tour, and retail licensing deals as well, will involve many different states with many different laws, rules, and regulations. The merchandiser must be responsible for compliance with these and most of these agreements so provide. But the ultimate impact of any such provision will be found in the indemnity provision, which should be carefully considered when the initial contract is negotiated.

There are innumerable laws with which most of us in the music business have no contact whatsoever at any time in our professional careers; yet these laws can cross our paths in the merchandise area suddenly and with devastating result. For example, many types of products must bear posted warnings if the merchandiser and the artist are to be insulated from liability. If merchandise products with small parts are designed so they might appeal to children, specific child safety warnings often must be posted. Sleepwear for children must be fire-retardant. Claims arising out of the failure to abide by these laws may result in a court award of damages in an amount so high that no amount of insurance typically maintained by the merchandiser will be enough to offset the possible liability to the artist. There may be criminal liability as well. The artist's representatives must use all due diligence to satisfy themselves that the merchandising company knows exactly what it is doing in the area of compliance with local and federal laws—yet another reason to use a company with a proven track record.

End-of-Term Inventory and Sell-Off

Any contract that involves inventory has to come to terms with what happens when the term of the agreement is over. In the area of tour and retail merchandising, the artist and the artist's representatives have to insure that the merchandiser does not manufacture or authorize the manufacture of goods—at any time, let alone toward the end of the contract term—in excess of approximate market demand. It is customary to seek a written inventory (allowing an auditor of the artist to actually physically assist in counting the inventory) both at the end of the license term and after the sell-off period (usually six months to a year after the term expires). Believe it or not, it has happened more than once that more inventory was on hand *after* the sell-off period than at the end of the official license term.

Once the rights to sell have officially ended, the artist should have the option of either purchasing the remaining inventory in stock at cost (plus maybe 10 percent handling) *or* demanding that the remaining inventory be destroyed. In the latter event, the artist should have the right to send in an auditor to observe the destruction, and the merchandiser should have the obligation to provide an "affidavit of destruction" to put the final nail in the coffin on that deal.

In the retail arena, a problem sometimes arises when inventory somewhere out there in the marketplace is returned to the merchandiser by sublicensees long after the events described above have taken place. Under these circumstances, the merchandiser will itself have inventory on hand *after* its rights have expired. The provision in which the artist is permitted to purchase (or destroy) remaining inventory doesn't help in this situation. This kind of anomaly can be avoided if the artist has been apprised of the identity of all the merchandiser's sublicensees and their addresses. Of course, if the artist maintains control over the choice of sublicensees, as part of his or her trademark monitoring responsibilities, the artist will likely know their identities anyway. Artists who are "hands-on" in this regard are more, rather than less, likely to be able to protect themselves if merchandisers glut the market with products. And those who are not hands-on? Well, you know the answer.

Artwork and Photographs

The artwork used for tour merchandise may duplicate the artwork on the record album (which the record company owns) or it may be created by a designer or photographer hired specifically for the tour merchandise. In either case, the artist's rights to exploit this artwork beyond the tour itself may be severely restricted. Even if separate permissions for retail licenses are acquired from the record company or the designer (or photographer), the artist's attorney must make it clear whose responsibility it will be to clear these rights, and at whose cost, as well as whether the rights clearance will include providing camera-ready artwork. The costs include the costs of obtaining the rights themselves, as well as the cost of attorneys' fees for clearing the rights and negotiating and processing the contract establishing the terms of the rights clearance.

Both the artist and the merchandiser must insist that all persons who create art or text for the merchandise (e.g., in program books) sign, wherever possible, work-for-hire agreements establishing the artist or the artist's service corporation as the owner of the result created. In this regard, the representatives of the artist must be careful, in acquiring rights to artwork, designs, and photographs, to make sure that the artwork may be cropped, reshaped, edited, or even adapted in a way which might, in the creator's mind, violate the original. In many countries of the world, even if there is a total buyout of rights, the "moral" rights of the artist or photographer may be violated by such actions; and there is no concept of a work for hire outside of the United States. Using a French photographer for an album cover, and then fiddling with it in a way that transforms it into something that the photographer feels damages his or her art, and therefore his or her reputation, may be problematic. The unacceptable change can be as simple as cropping a painting or photograph to fit a CD jewel box and then cropping it again to fit a DVD and then cropping it yet again to fit a cassette J card. I have actually had to deal with a situation in which artwork for a tour was purchased and for which agreements were signed, where the artwork had to be reinstated in its original form for use outside of the United States under the threat of litigation for violating the artist's "moral rights." I am not suggesting that one never use foreign nationals to create or license artwork for a United States–based group, but I do want to alert those artists and their managers and other representatives whose artistic reach extends beyond our borders that they may be acquiring fewer rights than they think they are acquiring.

Coupling

Just as the artist may be dismayed (at the least) to discover commercial advertising attached to the souvenir program for the tour (or, heaven forbid, the T-shirts), he or she may be very confused (at the least) to discover that some of the merchandising products feature not only the artist but another artist as well. This possibility is yet another reason to be careful to approve everything that is manufactured. Nevertheless, some things slip through the approval cracks and it is important for the contract itself to forbid the coupling of other artists' names and likeness or other logos, trademarks, etc., on the subject artist's merchandise—or even on advertisements for the merchandise.

Life and Disability Insurance

Companies that are investing substantial monies in pursuit of the purchasing capabilities of fans of a particular artist are naturally concerned lest the artist die or become disabled through illness, and seeking life and disability insurance against such contingencies is neither unusual nor unreasonable. There is, however, a practical problem: The artist usually has to undergo a physical examination—one that is conducted by a doctor other than the artist's own, and not necessarily one that is conducted by someone who is bound by any privacy or confidentiality concerns beyond those of the medical profession. Add to this an artist who is prone to taking drugs of any sort—or smokes marijuana occasionally—and you are inviting a lifetime problem (for example, suppose the examining doctor denies the artist insurance, and, years later, the artist has to complete an insurance form which asked the question, Have you ever been denied insurance?) And then there is the problem of a female artist, especially a "star" who is required to submit to an examination by a male doctor (or doctors) who has not been scrutinized by her own doctors. (I have had many situations in which my female clients—and not just the supermodels—have been made to feel very uncomfortable during physical examinations by doctors who come to their homes and either behave like star-struck fans or, worse, act in ways that are, to put it euphemistically, less than "professional.") The solution, of course, is to have one's own doctor do the examining and this is something that is often permitted by the insurance company. The contract itself can prescribe this option.

Piracy

Bootlegging, or copying an artist's logo, trademarks, and trade name, and selling merchandise without authorization, is as old as show business itself. Ordinarily, merchandisers will have mechanisms (and lawyers) in place to keep piracy to a minimum—especially during tours. The days of bootleg merchandisers setting up shop in the parking lots of rock and roll arenas are pretty much over; but the days of bootleggers are not. Different genres of music invite different styles of stealing, and it is important that the merchandiser be skilled at stopping these thieves in advance if possible. In recent years, courts have become educated in the ways of this unauthorized underworld and have been willing, in many instances, to grant temporary restraining orders, in advance, against the John Does, the as-yet-unidentified thieves. Enjoining behavior before the person has his or her day in court is generally anathema to all courts (and a remarkable remedy in a democracy when you think about it), but in bootlegging cases U.S. courts have come to embrace this procedure as the only way to stop the piracy of artists' merchandise by people who would otherwise simply disappear in their vans never to be identified and never to be caught.

Of course taking any formal legal action requires a coordinated effort, and there is considerable cost involved. Who pays for this? Who is responsible for initiating actions to prevent the sale of unauthorized merchandise? Are these costs cross-collateralized against the retail side? The language in the contract should answer all of these questions.

Bootlegging will occur wherever there is a vacuum. In the retail area, bootlegged merchandise runs rampant where the subject of the piracy does not him- or herself fill up the shelves with legitimate merchandise. Doing so actually minimizes the risk that illegal products will appear. In the course of selecting a merchandiser, the artist should determine whether the merchandiser is effective in distributing product to the retail side. (If Internet sales are going to be part of the deal, is the merchandiser adept at insuring that *its* website is placed up front on a search engine?) At the time the basic merchandise agreement is being considered, artists' representatives should raise the issue of the efficacy and the reputation of the merchandiser in pursuing bootleggers and in filling up distribution channels in response to demand for the artists' products.

Audits

I would like to mention briefly the issue of audits and general examinations of the books and records of merchandisers. I cannot think of another situation in which the ability to check books and records on a regular basis is more appropriate. The fact that most dealings for merchandise on the road are in cash, the fact that the road personnel of merchandise companies are often picked up for temporary duty and are not known (or bonded), the fact that the income is derived from so many sources and in so many locations outside of the centers of the music business: all of these unique characteristics of the tour merchandise business leave open a lot of room for carelessness, let alone abuse and downright stealing. The tour accountant, who, it goes without saying, should have a familiarity with merchandising operations in general, needs access at all times to the books and records of the venue and the merchandiser so that these monies can be monitored on a daily basis. Remember, we are not just talking about the artist losing some money; we have also seen that there are considerable consequences to the artist in the event that guarantees are not met. Even when all of the provisions of an agreement have been honored, sloppy accounting can have the same effect as a material breach of the performance-guarantee provisions of the agreement.

AUDITS: Truth or Consequences

**Money doesn't
talk. It swears.**
—**Bob Dylan,**
It's Alright,
Ma (I'm Only
Bleeding)

After all the negotiating is over, the career has slowed down or stopped, and the records have run their course, when the action is all in the past, the shining knight finally appears—ready to bring sense out of chaos, truth out of lies, rationality out of illogic, money out of nowhere. Who is this hero? The accountant! This may seem an unlikely role for this often-disparaged professional whose salient personality traits are supposed to be passivity, cordiality, and conservatism. But the accountant may be the only person who has the understanding and experience to turn failure into success, to turn short-term earnings into long-term security. In football, success or failure starts with the quarterback. In the record business, success or failure at the beginning may well depend on how good the lawyer and manager are, but in the end, it surely rests with the accountant.

EXAMINING THE AUDIT

Useful and effective audits do not have to wait until the end of an artist's career to be conducted. In fact, as we saw in Chapter 4, the longer one waits, the more likely a person who wishes to audit another will be shut out. Except as otherwise indicated in this chapter, when using the term "audit," I am referring to audits of record companies by artists or producers. In brief, an audit is an examination by an expert of the financial books and records of a company which has agreed to make periodic payments—in particular royalty payments—to another person: the artist or producer, or as you will see later, the songwriter.

When most of us hear the word "audit" we think of the government breaking down the door, or a fancy accounting firm (Arthur Andersen?) certifying the financial statements of a public company. But in this chapter, I am not referring to audits that actually "certify" whether statements are correct; indeed, this will never occur because in the end compromise is the name of the game in the music business, leaving precision in the dust. In my experience, record company or music publishing statements have *never* been certified as accurate. The only purpose of an audit—an examination of books and records—is to determine if there can be raised a convincing argument on behalf of the auditor's client that there are any significant underreportings or underpayments by the party which is supposed to write the check.

The parties in whose interest an audit is customarily performed are:

- The *artist* who audits the record company.
- The *producer* who audits the record company. This audit may have to piggy-back on the artist's audit because the record company may limit the producer's access to the

record company records rather than open them up to multiple audits of essentially the same data.

- The *publisher* who audits the record company either directly or through the efforts of its agent, most often the Harry Fox Agency, Inc.
- The *writer* who audits the publishing company.
- The *writer's own publishing company* which audits the writer's administrating publishers or subpublishers.

When the Artist Audits the Record Company

After the record has been produced and released, and the costs of and returns on its active life are in, the auditor enters the game to determine if the record company has accounted for and paid the artist what the artist was entitled to pursuant to the agreement with the record company. Record company audits will examine issues such as free goods, returns, mathematical calculations of statements (do you remember *your* multiplication tables?) and cut-outs. (*Cut-outs* are records taken out of inventory because of their totally poor sales history, and, essentially, given away for a pittance and marked accordingly so that they cannot reappear as a "return" at the other end of the record company's distribution system.)

Interestingly, the accountant *within* the record company whose job it is to defend the company's interpretations of the contract and its practices does not ordinarily report to the chief financial officer of the company, but to an operations executive, or even to the head of legal of business affairs. Why is this? Because the audit is looked upon as just another deal to negotiate, to settle, to compromise. It is the end game of the process of identifying and signing the artist, selling the artist's recordings, and turning them into "catalogue." The audit is expected, it is anticipated, and in a way it is welcomed, because for the first time, the open questions—crucial questions as to accuracy in payment calculations—will be closed for all time. Closure, both for the record company and the artist—is a good thing. And when the record company has to make a settlement as a result of the audit procedure, it is not just a vindication or victory for the artist; through settlement, the record company closes a chapter in which it has often miscoded charges, miscalculated royalties, and distorted the intention of the parties as reflected in the written contract.

Some audits may result in inflated settlements, others in underpayments. In fact, record companies often view audits as a group—they review the annual audit picture and balance the costs of defending the onslaught of the artist's (or publishing company's) auditors. If an artist is important and handled by an important auditor, there may be a generous settlement. If not, not.

Further, even when the record company pays up, it may be just so the artist and the artist's auditor will go away. Rarely, if ever, will the record company provide an articulated statement as to how much they erred or in what categories. Audit settlements do not ordinarily specify the rationale behind them. Even when the particulars of a settlement are quantified by category, rarely will companies change their practices in the future, or even admit to the errors of the past. Their goal is to get the auditor out of the building and close a chapter in the life of the artist and record company. A cash settlement is a small price indeed to pay for that.

When a Publishing Company Audits the Record Company

A publishing company's audit of a record company most often is pursued by the Harry Fox Agency, Inc., which represents about 80 percent of all publishers in the United States, and, through its affiliated mechanical rights societies around the world, most publishers based outside of the United States as well. Two issues that are unique to audits initiated by publishing companies are (1) unmatched lists and (2) controlled compositions.

UNMATCHED LISTS

The term *unmatched lists* (also referred to as *suspense lists*) refers to data collected, more or less efficiently (often less), by the record company with respect to musical compositions on which mechanical royalties are payable but the party entitled to the royalties is not identified. Even if the record company knows whom to pay, it may not pay because it has no executed license agreement from the publisher or from the publisher's agent (again, usually the Harry Fox Agency, Inc.) The careless and haphazard way that unidentified compositions are listed and accounted for by record companies is legendary in the music industry, and if an auditor does not know where to look, the income will be lost for the audit period. Remember, once a period has been the subject of a resolved audit, that period is, essentially, closed for all time, and is no longer subject to question. Further, you can be sure there is nobody at the record company who is pointing the auditor in the right direction. If the auditor is not plugged into the idiosyncratic ways in which record companies hide—or misplace—royalty-generating events, and income, the audit's effectiveness will be lessened accordingly.

CONTROLLED COMPOSITIONS

Controlled compositions are dealt with at some length in the next chapter. Suffice it to say at this point that controlled composition clauses are often "custom" negotiated for each artist, and a full and complete comprehension of the particular clause at issue is essential if an auditor is to be able to verify the accuracy of accounting statements from the record company. Some countries—in particular Canada—have established certain floors on controlled compositions clauses which will have the effect of overriding some of the clauses now written into contracts. Sophisticated thinkers are at work here, and the auditor will have to muster all of his or her insights and experience just to keep up with them.

Auditing Copublishers and Subpublishers

Copublishing agreements are between two entities which agree to share ownership of the copyrights to a given body of compositions as well as the compensation due to the owners of the copyrights. The term *subpublisher* refers to a foreign publisher who represents the interests of a U.S. publisher. In either case, the companies involved are often multinational corporations.

THE FLOW OF MONEY

We will see in Chapter 13 how multinational companies or companies whose rights are themselves represented overseas by subpublishers have different views as to what "receipts" are and whether they should pay royalties on those receipts or the royalties should be paid "at source." The multinationals (and I am using this term intentionally, because these companies are not set up and have never been set up to be "global" in the sense that they create one concerted worldwide effort to exploit artists and their copyrights) move their money around so facilely that it is a wonder that even the home office knows where it is.

Sometimes, in fact, the home office doesn't. Until PolyGram Music Publishing was sold to Universal Music, it had its headquarters in Baarn, The Netherlands. Yet its home office was in London. When you made a deal with the U.S. affiliate, it was impossible to figure out who would possess the books and records of U.S. sales, or of the foreign sales. What's more, Polygram counted its money in Dutch guilders!

Money is exchanged and moved back and forth faster than at an Atlantic City poker game—and with much more success. Like good poker players, these companies keep their information "close to the vest"—so close, in fact, that it becomes prohibitive to try to follow it without the aid of the CIA (which, on occasion, has other things on its agenda).

Moving money from country to country—paying, receiving credits for, and simply getting the benefit of international tax treaties (as to which, be assured, these multinationals are expert)—will befuddle even the most astute auditors. How much more baffling the money chase became with respect to PolyGram Music statements when this company was finally absorbed into another multinational—the Universal Music Group—in 1999. And that was before Universal (owned predominantly by Seagrams of Canada, but partly by Matsushita of Japan) was sold to Vivendi (of France). See what I mean?

There is an inherent disadvantage in dealing with a multinational publishing company in that the Harry Fox Agency—although owned and run by the American National Music Publishers Association, theoretically the songwriters' last chance for an honest count—does not always audit the affiliated record companies. For example, Harry Fox does not audit the major record companies on behalf of their publishers which license their sister record companies directly, bypassing the Fox agency entirely. The publishing companies will tell you that they conduct internal audits by their own in-house people, but these are easily tinkered with so that the combined company can produce a profit-and-loss picture that says what the company wants it to say. This is an obvious impediment to achieving an accurate "count" and, more importantly, as will be seen later, it will reduce the chances that an efficient and conscientious audit will be able to correct registration errors, whose correction, ironically, would benefit both the original publisher and its administrating publisher.

This disparity among music publishers and the lack of vigor with which some pursue audit rights can be a serious handicap; and, while it should not discourage songwriters or their self-owned publishing companies from entering into administration or copublishing arrangements with a multinational, it would be appropriate to address this issue at the time the contract is negotiated rather than after earnings that might otherwise have been uncovered by a more zealous publisher have been lost forever.

ACCESS TO REGISTRATION INFORMATION

It is important for auditors to have access to copies of the foreign societies' accountings to their publisher members—whether these publishers obtain rights of representation directly, for example, in the case of music indigenous to their territory, or through a worldwide or regional administrator. No foreign society will allow a U.S. (original) publisher to audit them directly; but each country's societies operate differently and depending on the copyright owner's negotiating leverage, it is at least within the range of possibility to obtain access for the auditor to so much additional data that the success of the audit process will be geometrically more promising.

Occasionally, the impediment established by foreign societies can be overcome by the original publisher when *it* becomes a member of the foreign rights society itself or when it establishes in the foreign country an affiliate company which becomes a member of the foreign rights society. This avenue is not widely taken for a variety of good reasons—not the least of which is figuring out what to do with the foreign entity (if one is created) once it is established. For once the original publisher has created a new tax entity in a foreign country, it may find that there are tax consequences beyond the publisher's original expectations both in that country and in the United States. Even the possibility of dissolving the entity can have severe tax implications.

THE BLACK BOX OR "SOMETHING IS ABYSS HERE"

The infamous "Black Box" phenomenon is discussed in several chapters of this book. In the context of audits, let me make a few observations. The mechanical and performing rights societies of each country around the world, which are usually combined into one society per country, quite regularly realize that they cannot attribute the earnings of a particular song to a particular owner/publisher. What are they to do with this money? Customarily, they drop it into an account for later distribution. There are several kinds of income that end up in the abyss of Black Box accounts: unallocated income, unclassified income, and unidentified income. While they sound alike, they are not, and only your auditor knows for sure which is which.

In addition to the three above-mentioned typical categories, black box income will include monies which were set aside by a foreign rights society for expenses but which were not needed because the organization did not spend its full budget. There is also income representing monies reimbursed by rights societies by way of specific rebates of society commissions [such as the so-called "Restausschutung" payments by GEMA in Germany and similar payments by SDRM (the mechanical rights society in France) and STEMRA (the mechanical and performing rights society in Holland).]

Some of this income represents surplus proceeds or collections (such as the so-called "Verwertungsverfahren" proceeds in Germany), including those received by way of newly introduced types of distribution or newly introduced types of income in which monies are not separately allocated and attributed to specific musical compositions.

The sums that find their way into the Black Boxes of various countries can be enormous. For example, it is estimated that the Italian Black Box absorbs more than 30 percent of SIAE's (Societá Italiana degli Autore Editore) gross income. Indeed, entire catalogues whose income has never been allocated correctly have been "lost" into one Black Box or another. One would like to think that the inability to allocate income from musical compositions on such a scale is due to carelessness and lack of diligence. However, I would be remiss if I were not to mention that over the years, a lot of Black Box income has been found to have been accumulated because various parties, including the foreign publisher members themselves (some of which were merely subsidiaries of the original U.S. publisher in which writers placed so much trust), intentionally misallocated funds or misregistered songs.

You may ask, how in the world would an auditor get access to the information needed to verify the accuracy of royalty statements from countries in which the Black Box exists. The answer varies from country to country; but if a knowledgeable auditor can get into the books of the company which is the official member of the relevant performing rights or mechanical rights society, the information is all there.

TELEVISION CAMPAIGNS

As stated in Chapter 9, record companies often reduce the artist's royalty rate—by as much as 50 percent—during the period in which they mount a television campaign to promote a record. No record company executive dealing with an auditor will volunteer the basis for the reduced royalty arising out of such a provision. The entry on the royalty account will merely indicate the reduction and there will be a notation that the reduction in the royalties was due to promotional expenditures. It may cite the contractual provision, e.g., "Promotional expenditures pursuant to Paragraph 7.07(b)." While there is nothing the artist can do about this, it is important for the auditor to verify that the promotional expenses in question were not only incurred, but incurred in an amount justifying the royalty reduction. For example, was the expense in the nature of a one- or two-time television buy, or was it a real campaign as contemplated by the contract?

INTEREST CHARGES

It is not unusual that when one party is adjudged to owe another party money damages for breach of contract (which would include the submission of inaccurate accountings), the party claiming the deficiency will seek (and occasionally receive) interest on the monies due that were either not paid at all or not paid on time. Both the federal government and state governments charge interest when taxes due have been underreported (and will often pay interest or credits when money is due to the reporter). This would seem to be an equitable way to compensate the damaged party with the intended salutary effect of discouraging similar acts in the future.

Record and publishing companies offer no such compensation—even in egregious situations. Nevertheless, it is customary to at least *make* the interest calculation. If the deficiency is due to a misunderstanding, or to a disagreement, or to a different interpretation of a contract clause—i.e., mistakes in interpretation that do not represent a pattern of deception—the record company or publishing company can claim "innocence," which will usually frustrate a claim for interest. However, processing errors, a total lack of payments, or cataclysmic underreporting or underpayments—like tax evasion vs. tax avoidance in the IRS's world—will more likely give resonance to the claim that interest is due. Merely asserting a claim for interest may be enough to ratchet up an eventual settlement.

The methodology of settlement between artists and record companies, or publishing companies and writers, is so entrenched that interest is rarely paid; indeed, it is often not even sought in view of the remote chance of recovering it. More likely, the auditing party will receive an "interest factor" in the context of an overall settlement. It will not be designated as such, but as long as the auditing party is satisfied with the total settlement figure, why should it matter how one categorizes the elements that make it up?

STATUTES OF LIMITATIONS

Most states have statutes that limit the number of years during which a person can assert a contract claim arising from a perceived breach. These statutes customarily establish the limits at six or seven years. However, record companies and publishing companies traditionally seek to modify these statutorily granted protections by reducing—to one, two, or sometimes three—the number of years during which a person can assert such a claim Their justification is that it is too difficult and costly to maintain records back as far as six years. The fact that such records must be kept under the rules and regulations of the Internal Revenue Service is conveniently ignored.

The goal obviously is to chip away at artists' and writers' opportunities to review their careers—and their attendant income—after a reasonable time has passed. Even with today's intricate global banking network and vast communications facilities, it can take at least a year and often two or more years before income earned in various parts of the world is reported. To require that an audit be conducted within days or weeks following (or preceding!) the submission of accounting statements is to deny the artist or writer the fair opportunity underlying the logic of states' more generous statutes of limitations.

There are a couple of things that a negotiator can do to ameliorate this problem before the contract is entered into. In particular, in dealing with a multinational company, audit rights should be expanded to extend to subsidiaries and affiliates. (I have had deals fall through when such requests were refused. There is enough paranoia among artists to not add to it by refusing a reasonable request to audit wholly-owned subsidiaries.) Similarly, one can seek a provision permitting, under certain circumstances, a year-to-year extension of the period during which the right to audit remains viable if the gross sales of product reach certain levels. For example, the time period during which the artist or writer (or producer) experiences a substantial financial success is not only the time that an audit may really matter, it is also the time period in which the record company might be most receptive to the argument that a fair evaluation of one's career cannot be made with blinders on. That is, it is reasonable to stipulate that when large blocks of income are to be reported, transferred, and examined, the artificial statute of limitations sought to be established by the record company should be extended.

While long-term (more than three years) audit provisions are never specifically granted, it is not unusual for a royalty-paying entity—particularly a music publishing administrator like a Universal Music Publishing Company—to agree to audits to be performed *during* the term, or one comprehensive audit covering the entire term to be performed within one year following the end of the term. For a five-year contract, this audit would occur in the sixth year after commencement of the term. If, in a case such as this, an audit is performed and completed during the term, the period covered by the audit will usually be closed for all time once settled. The comprehensive final audit would have to pick up where the last one ended. But sometimes, audits are conducted and no formal audit report is submitted. There are two reasons for this: first, the auditors may not have found anything significant or may want to wait to see how the company deals with a future accounting period; second, the auditors may have found an error in the client's favor and are reticent to bring this to the company's attention. Hence this audit is *never* completed and the bar to return to the audited period never drops.

Mechanical Licenses and Mechanical Variances

A *mechanical license* is a license granted by the owner of a copyrighted composition giving another entity the right—for a fee—to record, manufacture, and distribute copies of the composition. Legally, however, the mechanical "license" document frequently used by music publishers is not a license agreement at all, which would be subject to the usual statute of limitations period of six or seven years, but a "variance," or modification, of a provision in the U.S. copyright law. The statute of limitations for claiming copyright infringement is three years from the date of infringement. Chapter 14, page 204, discusses mechanical variances in more detail, but let me point out several issues that are relevant to the statute of limitations on audits.

1. In a contract negotiation in which a writer or music publisher (which may be the artist's own company) is trying to retain the right to audit a record company's books and the audit right extends for, say, one year following the expiration of the deal (as mentioned previously, for a five-year deal, this would extend to as long as six total years), is it possible to include in the audit books and records relating to mechanical licenses, infringement claims as to which, according to federal law, must be brought within three years of the infringement?
2. Under U.S. copyright law, can the record company, by contract, reduce the three-year copyright infringement provision to two years? (Record companies traditionally try to place *all* rights and entitlements onto a fixed and predictable schedule, and recording agreements now customarily *include* a "license" to mechanically reproduce the musical compositions on the record rather than draw up and issue a separate license or variance document.)

CONDUCTING AUDITS IN FOREIGN COUNTRIES

Naturally, it can be very expensive to conduct an audit of a record company in the United States. Yet both the cost and the logistics of conducting audits in more than one foreign country on behalf of a small publishing company or owner to the rights of a record catalogue can be even more daunting. I have two practical suggestions in this regard:

1. The first is to audit one country at a time and to proceed to other countries only if claims are detected in the first country or countries. When auditors begin to see common errors, they can move on into other countries.
2. If possible, combine resources and audit foreign companies in tandem with others similarly situated. For example, the Association of Independent Music Publishers (AIMP), based in New York, is comprised of hundreds of small companies. Banded together, these companies can—and do—pursue audits of companies which are common to their colleagues' subpublishing schemes.

While there are very experienced music business auditors available outside of the United States (particularly in the United Kingdom), if you want to have the privilege of personally knowing your representative or using one you have successfully worked with in the United States in the past, there is no reason you should not engage that person's services for audits outside of the United States. In addition, many U.S. accounting firms have offices or correspondent firms outside the United States (again, particularly in the United Kingdom). Even if you ask your U.S. representative only to oversee or review a foreign audit, or act as a consultant, you may be better served than if you let a foreign auditor, no matter how qualified, conduct the audit alone. Your U.S. representative will know you better, know your catalogue and history better, and have a continuity with you that one-time auditors will not, by definition, have. I should also note that it is no more costly to have a U.S. auditor go to Milan (the center of the Italian music business) than for a U.K.-based auditor to go to Milan. Airfares and lodging expenses are similar, and the only issue is whether professional fees are competitive, which in large part they seem to be.

A FEW PRACTICAL SUGGESTIONS

It is not necessary for "fear" and "audit" to be spoken in the same breath. And an audit need not be expensive. In fact, it need not be formal at all. Remember, an audit is a process by which accounting statements are verified. There is often sufficient information within the recipient's control such that regular monitoring of the statements will serve essentially the same purpose as a formal audit. If a recipient, attorney, or accountant has kept track of the recipient's writing/recording activities, a fairly satisfactory job can be done on a regular basis to determine the accuracy of statements and accountings.

Here the issue is how to verify whether song and master licensing—usually done by separate parties—shows up consistently in accounting statements. Most artists can identify their discography and their music catalogue (and if they cannot, it is not such a bad idea to hire someone to organize and categorize this information so it can be used). In addition, most artists these days have the right to approve the licensing of their recordings in films, TV programs, and commercials, and on compilation or flashback-type records. Those artists who control their own publishing administration may also have the right to approve the licensing of their songs, so there is some awareness of these uses that can be documented and filed for future use in an audit. In cases in which the recording right is automatic by virtue of Section 115 of the Copyright Act (Scope of Exclusive Rights in Nondramatic Musical Works: Compulsory License for Making and

Distributing Phonorecords), they will be approached to issue mechanical licenses. All of this data is readily available, and the information can be checked against accounting statements easily, without the delay or expense occasioned by a formal audit.

Desk Audits

On receiving an accounting statement, it is advantageous and judicious to review it immediately. In doing so, the recipient should determine:

- Has the statement been received in a timely fashion?
- Does the statement cover all applicable copyrights (or masters)?
- Are the splits (for example, artist-producer, artist–record company, writer/co-writers-publisher, writer/co-writers-copublisher) correct?
- On record company statements, do all the catalogue numbers match the actual releases?
- Do the reported releases match the master-use licenses entered into by the record company? (For example, Warner Special Products is charged with licensing, for TV, films, and record compilations, master recordings owned and controlled by the Warner Music Group's record companies. Customarily, permission to issue these licenses is sought from the artist or the artist's representative, and these requests should be maintained in a separate file so that they can be compared with the actual accounting statements when they are issued, sometimes years later. A license for a "Greatest Rock Songs of the 80's" compilation record in New Zealand or some other foreign territory will not generate a royalty on an accounting statement for as long as three years after the sales occur.)

Technicalities *Do* Matter

Do any notices have to be sent to preserve rights? Most contracts require that specific objections be made within a brief time after receipt of statements or any right to raise objections during an audit will have been waived. Believe me, when it comes to these "details," the record company most certainly knows its standard contract provisions relating to audits and follows them to the letter. For this is where the money is, and *their* bottom line, like the bottom line of any business, is *the* bottom line.

Errors in Excess of 5 to 10 Percent

Artists' and writers' lawyers and accountants like to insert into contracts a provision that if an audit determines that an error of 5 or 10 percent has occurred in favor of the auditing party, the party being audited must pay for the costs of the audit. What is the value of this? Actually very little (other than the representative's bragging to a client that he or she got this into the contract). Why? Because, as indicated earlier, most audits result in settlements, and a settlement is just one way for an audited party to tell you to go away. (The settlement figure will always take into account the costs of the auditing party—even if this item is not separately articulated.) There is rarely, if ever, an admission of liability, so it is often futile to seek to particularize the audit result.

The record company does not want to be precluded, in future audits, from asserting the same defenses it has chosen to raise in a prior audit. Paradoxically, the more the deficiency, the more likely there will be a settlement and the less likely there will be a sufficient articulation of the areas being settled. The preliminary audit claim will particularize the areas in which the claims are being asserted. But in the end, a lump sum payment will probably be offered and accepted, after negotiation, rather than breaking down each articulated claim. The greater the overall deficiencies, in total, the more likely the audited party will simply offer a lump sum to resolve (get rid of?) the audit.

It should be noted that in Europe and in Australia, coincidentally, settlements are less the norm and these provisions are easier to obtain. It is therefore more viable in deals outside of the United States to seek a provision providing for this kind of relief.

THE RIGHT TO AUDIT: A CONTRACT ISSUE

In New York State, there is no inherent right on the part of a royalty participant (or a party who has received a promise to be a royalty participant) to have access to the books and records of the promising party. Record companies that do not insert audit clauses into their artist contracts or permit them in mechanical license agreements are impeding access to the very information on which *all* remuneration to the artist or publisher is necessarily based. Companies that refuse to insert such clauses after a request that they do so are acting in bad faith and should not be trusted.

In addition to insuring that a reasonably and clearly worded audit clause is included in an agreement, it is a good idea to check with a professional auditor *before* any royalty-based agreement is signed. As we have seen, even an audit clause may not be sufficient to give the royalty participant all of the rights he or she may need or think have been received. For example, if the publishing agreement between a songwriter and the songwriter's publisher (or copublisher) is in the nature of a "receipts" deal whereby the administrating publisher pays the writer based on its receipts, how is the infamous Black Box income to be treated? The receipts contract may limit the writer's income to "money allocated to specific songs." Yet Black Box income is just a pot of money that is paid to publisher members of foreign rights societies. It is not necessarily money allocated by specific title. If it were, it would have to be shared with the writers or original publishers. For example, if an original publisher-writer's (say, the Beatles) catalogue represents 10 percent of the total income of a particular German subpublisher, and the German subpublisher is rewarded by GEMA with $1 million of "unallocated" income, rebates of rights society commissions, etc., then, theoretically, 10 percent of this should be attributable to that catalogue. The way to obtain Black Box income is to provide specifically for the original publisher-writer to be paid in direct proportion to the amount that the publisher-writer's catalogue earnings bears to the amount allocated to the society member (i.e., the subpublisher) by the society. If the subpublishing deal provides that for every $1 collected by the subpublisher with respect to a specific song, 15 percent is to be retained by the subpublisher and 85 percent is to be paid to the original publisher-writer, then, in the $1 million example above, 85 percent of $100,000 (which is 10 percent of the million dollars of Black Box income received by the subpublisher) must be paid to the original publisher-writer—in this case the Beatles' publishing company.

Since upward of 30 percent of all publishing earnings in Italy (and 15 percent and more of such earnings in France and Germany) flow into the Black Box, a goodly portion of a writer's income may be unintentionally diverted right out of his or her bank account—all because of the use of a phrase ("specific songs") which appears, on its face, to be straightforward but may in fact lead to the loss of substantial monies.

Obviously, once an agreement has been signed, it is too late to remedy a situation that has become a fait accompli.

SOME FINAL WORDS

What does a formal audit—as opposed to a desk audit—accomplish for the client? A survey has suggested that a 10 to 15 percent recovery over and above the accountings presented by the record companies is not unusual. Settlements are reached in 95 percent of all audits, and only 10 percent of the remaining 5 percent end up in court. The chances are that the audit settlement will end for all time any controversy that may have arisen about the issues raised by the audit—whether these be substantive (e.g., nonreporting of income) or definitional (e.g., disputes over the meaning or contractual words or phrases). A careful choice of an auditor and cooperation among the auditor, the attorney, the manager, and the artist are essential to achieve a fair result.

13 | MUSIC PUBLISHING: THE ODYSSEY OF THE SONG

Let's talk about music publishing. It worked for Beethoven; how will it work for you?

This is the most intriguing, most complex, and surely the least understood area of the music business. Yet every budding recording artist should have a high degree of awareness and sensitivity to this stepchild of the industry. For even the novice songwriter knows that long after the records are relegated to the oldies bin and the live performances are a distant memory, music publishing income will endure. This is the annuity, the social security, of the songwriter. How an artist's songs are owned, exploited, and, most of all, protected, can determine whether or not the artist's career will, in the end, be a financial success, or whether he will have to, God forbid, get a job.

Those who are interested in music publishing are not lonely. The company enjoyed by the songwriter includes the music publisher who, in exchange for services, participates in the income and the asset accumulation as each musical composition gains value. Users of musical compositions have a distinct interest in them: record companies, film and television companies, product owners who use compositions in commercials, etc. And let's not forget website owners and Napster copycats. Everyone wants (needs?) a good song.

In most respects, music publishers' and songwriters' attitudes to and interests in musical compositions often coincide. There are areas in which their interests diverge, and these are covered later in the chapter, but predominantly they have the same goals: protecting the controlled use of the song, maximizing the eventual income from the song, and insuring that copyright protection is as broad as possible throughout the world.

Music publishing is a creation of the music business. Yet music publishers are the most significant contributors to the maintenance of copyright rights throughout the world and the most effective lobbyists for those rights. Collectively, in many ways, they are the engine that makes the entire music industry run.

WHAT IS A MUSIC PUBLISHER—
AND WHAT DOES IT PUBLISH?

There is no simple, universal definition of what a music publisher is, and the term appears in the U.S. Copyright Law only twice. Yes, there are references to copyright owners, authors, and "rightholders"; many references to "publication" (the distribution of copies or records of a work to the public by sale, rental, lease, or lending); and language about performing a work "publicly" (i.e., at a place open to the public or at any place where a substantial number of persons outside of a normal circle of a family and its social acquaintances is gathered). But the lawmakers were not the ones who had to figure out how to commercialize the concept of publication. Others did. They created the "publisher." A publisher can be as simple as a name under which the author does business (dba, or "doing business as") or as complicated as a multinational such as EMI Music Publishing Company, which looks after the rights of more than 1 million musical compositions.

This chapter will explore the changing role of the music publisher in the twenty-first century, discuss some of the traditional concerns of publishers and songwriters alike, and identify some of the ways in which music publishers' interests and methods diverge from those of the writers. Before we proceed, however, let me define briefly some of the terms that I will be using in this chapter.

- An administrating publisher is the entity responsible for the myriad tasks associated with licensing and collecting income derived from the exploitation of musical compositions. There may be one or more administrating publishers, each responsible for a portion of the song.
- A copublisher refers to a publisher that actually owns a portion of the copyright to a song, often the so-called "publisher's share." A copublisher can be an administrating publisher, but is not necessarily one. For example, an artist who writes may copublish his or her own songs, but it is usually the other copublisher—perhaps a major such as BMG Music Publishing Company—that provides the administrating—or song management—services.
- A subpublisher is the foreign equivalent of the American administrating publisher. Subpublishers are vital to domestic publishers because they belong to performing and mechanical rights societies around the world and can collect directly, and monitor accurately, the monies generated by the exploitation of musical compositions in their respective territories.

Traditionally, music publishers have had two major roles:

1. To administer, exploit, and nurture copyrights. The rights specifically granted to copyright owners of musical compositions under the U.S. Copyright Act are the right to perform, to mechanically reproduce, to synchronize, and to print. Music publishers seek to insure that federal and world copyright protection is sought and acquired, that users of their musical works throughout the world are properly licensed, and that users of the works pay the requisite fees—for mechanically recording the works on records, synchronizing them on film or video, performing them live or through broadcast, or reproducing them via visual notation. Music publishers also actively seek out potential users of their copyrights, for example, by convincing a musician to record a song or a film or television company to include the song in a film or video production. To accomplish this, music publishers may have multiple copies of the work printed or otherwise made available to potential users.
2. To provide sufficient funds (a) to help a songwriter live while he or she is writing, (b)

to cause songwriters to meet each other wherever they are in the world for the purpose of encouraging cowrites, and (c) to pay for the cost of demonstration recordings which are the means by which potential users of the works get to hear them in the first instance.

This chapter is primarily concerned with the first of these functions: administering, exploiting, and nurturing copyright.

COPYRIGHT: A BUNDLE OF INTANGIBLES

What exactly is a copyright?

The concept of *copyright,* that is, the right to reproduce an original work, has undergone an extensive evolution since the first U.S. copyright law was passed, in 1790. For example, the 1909 copyright law protected musical compositions from being mechanically reproduced, without permission, by any "parts of instruments." At the time, the "instruments" (devices) in question were player piano rolls and eventually Edison cylinders—the first record players. It was not long before circular records were being produced (from 78s to 45s to 33s), then tapes (from 8-track to cassettes), then CDs, DVDs, etc. Eventually, we began to refer to the various devices by which musical compositions are reproduced as "sound carriers" because we could no longer specify what form the "parts of instruments" might take. Now, of course, we do not even work solely with *forms.* We work in cyberspace (MP3 and other digital download formats) with DPDs. Thus over the last 90 years, the rights of copyright holders under the copyright law have been found to apply to every one of the devices used to reproduce them, even though most of these "parts of instruments" had not been invented, or even imagined, in 1909. We are introduced periodically to new technologies, such as computer programs and Internet applications, which invite expansion of what are often referred to as the "bundle of rights" subsumed under copyright legislation.

Establishing Authorship

Under United States Copyright Law, the exclusive right to own, control, and protect one's creation from unauthorized reproduction is a right granted upon the *creation* of the work. Most people do not realize this. They think they have to "copyright" the song first. Well, rest easy. Upon creation, any original work of authorship "fixed in any tangible medium of expression" has federal copyright status and protection. [Note that copyright protection does not extend to any "idea, procedure, process, system, method of operation, concept, principle, or discovery" (Section 102 of the Copyright Law), nor does it extend to any work "authored" by the U.S. government.] However, the subsequent *registration* of a claim to copyright in Washington, D.C., gives the creator some wonderful additional benefits:

- The right to sue in federal courts for specific statutory damages and to seek injunctions for unauthorized copying.
- The right to collect compulsory license royalties according to the rules established in the Copyright Act of 1976 (misnamed, because the Act didn't actually take effect

until 1978). Section 115 of that Act provides that "to be entitled to receive royalties under a compulsory license, the copyright owner must be identified in the registration or other public records of the Copyright Office. The Owner . . . is not entitled to recover for any phonorecords *previously* made and distributed."

■ Concrete and credible *evidence,* via the Certificate of Copyright Registration issued by the U.S. Copyright Office, proving that the work had indeed been created and was in existence at the time the claim to copyright was filed.

The copyright certificate rendered by the U.S. Copyright Office obviously does not prove that the person claiming authorship or ownership actually wrote or owns the work; but it does prove that the *claim* to ownership in the song was in fact filed on a certain date. It is also *prima facie* proof of the facts stated thereon. This means that if the copyright registration form says that writer A wrote the song, and writer B says that he or she actually wrote the song, the burden of proof in any legal proceedings is on writer B to prove that he or she, not writer A, wrote the song. This can be a very valuable piece of paper indeed. This does not mean that for every composition a songwriter creates, he or she must register a separate claim to copyright in Washington. The Copyright Office will accept multiple registrations (e.g., a CD or tape containing 10 songs can be the subject of one registration). Finally, if for some reason—usually financial—a songwriter cannot formally register a work or works with the Copyright Office, the writer can still mail a registered package to him or herself (or to an attorney) containing a copy of the work and leave it unopened. In any copyright infringement action, it is necessary to prove not only that the defendant had access to another person's work, but that it was substantially similar as well. But if the defendant can prove that the work existed *before* the plaintiff's work was even written, the rest doesn't matter and the artist is home free.

Digital Print Rights

This represents a new world for music publishers. Whereas for most of the twentieth century, phonograph record owners became used to the addition to their financial vocabulary of new and different means of transmitting music for home use to consumers, music publishers have long been reduced to concerning themselves with the *four* rights mentioned above: performing rights, mechanical rights, synchronization rights and print rights.

A millennium gift to the music publisher is, virtually, a fifth right: a new product which has been developed in the digital age—digital sheet music. This is an awesome addition to the arsenal of music publishers and one which has not yet been entirely recognized for what it is: a revolutionary method of distributing "sheet music" inexpensively, instantly, and with a great deal of variety and satisfaction—24/7 and forever "in print."

Digital print rights are the rights to digitize musical notation and graphs (such as guitar tablature) as well as textual information (such as lyrics) in a manner in which they may be used through all means of digital delivery, such as the Internet, on CDs, as part of DVDs, and via music scanners. As of this writing, one distributor of digital print rights, Musicnotes.com, includes digital data representing pitch and duration which can be accessed through midi (musical instrument digital interface) or by way of CDs themselves. Digital print rights are exploited the same way digital audio rights are exploited, except they can be translated into a readable visual text identical to musical notation. As with digital audio rights, they provide immediate access to content and do not require a trip to a music store or reliance on concrete media, such as a CD. Unlike audio rights owners, digital print rights owners have thus far conquered the problem of protecting their assets from unauthorized appropriation.

There are approximately 8,000 dealers of musical instruments and products in the United States. About 4,000 of them carry printed copies of music; perhaps 100 of these specialize in the print area, and it is estimated that those 100 do not provide more than 1 percent of the world's printed music to their customers, despite the fact that some do order the music for later delivery. (Note that a similar situation exists in the record industry: probably fewer than 1 percent of the sound recordings in existence are actually available from your local CD chain store.)

Thus, the vast majority of music is not available to the public. In fact, the vast majority of music never sees the light of day in the music publishers' offices either. Talk about intangible rights! The title of the song "For Your Eyes Only" is apt: No matter how hard you try, you will not be able to find, in a store, a printed sheet music copy of it to perform or record yourself. Go ahead. Try! But you *can* find more than a dozen versions on the Internet in the form of digital "sheet" music—everything from piano to solo alto saxophone.

And yet, music publishers uninitiated in the ways of the digital world carelessly "bundle" digital print rights along with traditional print rights. Whether you label it a fifth right or merely a distinct part of the fourth right (the print right), the digital right should be regarded as a different asset from the traditional print right, neither replacing nor supplanting it. Ironically, digital print may save the sheet music business because the efficiencies of print companies over the past 50 years have so steadily declined that there is a danger that the lack of profitability of this area of the music publishing business may kill off what remains of this business—from manufacturers (print companies) to dealers.

As everyone knows, finding the particular edition of sheet music that one may seek is nearly impossible. Either the work is not in print, or it is not in stock. Or it may be part of an expensive music "folio" and not be available on its own. With digital versions, there are no warehouse, inventory, selection (read: "labor"), or shipping costs. A digital version is always in stock. And it is *instantly available.*

Time was that sheet music of a hit song would sell in the 1 million copy range. From "Bicycle Built For Two" around the turn of the last century to "Over the Rainbow" in 1939, million sellers were frequent. The heyday of sheet music sales ended around the time that phonograph records took the place of piano rolls and player pianos. Singing in the living room or in the ice cream parlor had lost its flavor, and vinyl records took over from real live people who followed sheet music to create sound on a piano. Sure, "Titanic" sold a million copies in the late '90's, but this was an aberration.

Today, those involved with the digital distribution of sheet music are finding that the desire to possess the actual musical notation of a sought-after piece of music has not only not disappeared, it has probably increased! Given the huge population of music

makers in the world, the desire may have been there all along, but the potential consumers were stymied by their inability to obtain the product they wanted. Those days
appear to be over.

Finally—a perfect application for the Internet!

Enough about the bundle of rights—except to wonder, What next? It was only a few
years ago that we were talking about sound carriers embodying the intangible rights of a
song; now we are trying to comprehend intangible delivery systems sending the intangible rights into your computers, television sets, MP3 players, cell phones, and, yes, even
your watches—unless they are otherwise engaged doubling as digital cameras! Let's go
back to the real world, where songs are the motivation behind some heinous behavior
displayed by record companies toward copyright holders and to which publishers often
respond with deplorable judgment.

FINANCIAL SECRETS AND REALITIES

The fact that the majority of musical compositions are controlled by music publishers that
are themselves owned and controlled by the biggest users of music—record companies,
film companies, television production companies, and (after the AOL acquisition of
Time/Warner) Internet companies—makes for some interesting negotiations, and not a few
potential conflicts of interest. Three important areas in which songwriters' and publishers'
interests are not always the same are controlled compositions, buyouts, and audits.

Controlled Compositions

"Controlled compositions." Perhaps the most feared words in the songwriter's galaxy.
Under the Copyright Act of 1976, the copyright owner has the exclusive right to authorize the first recording of a work; after that original authorization, anyone else can record
it pursuant to certain specific rules. The most relevant rule here is that the new user must
pay to the author or publisher a "minimum statutory rate"—the so-called compulsory
rate. This rate changes periodically, but at the time of the publication of this book it was
$0.08 per copy (or $0.0155 per minute or portion thereof if the song exceeds five minutes in length). In other words, if the Backstreet Boys wish to record your four-minute
song, their record company must either obtain the copyright owner's permission for the
first-ever recording of it or, if the song has already been the subject of an authorized
recording, the record company can automatically record the song upon payment of the
requisite fee. As discussed in Chapter 4, on royalties, the record companies have found
a way to contractually circumvent this rule so they don't pay the full fee. Recording
agreements between artists and record companies invariably include a provision that
results in you—the artist—promising to license to them, customarily at three-fourths of
the statutory rate, all songs you write, all songs you co-write, including the co-writer's
portion, all songs your producer writes or co-writes, and in fact *all* songs you record—
and this holds whether or not you "control" (have ownership of) these songs. Effectively
that means that if you record a song which you neither wrote nor co-wrote, and which
your producer had nothing to do with, if the owner of that song (who is a complete

stranger to you) does not agree to license it at three-fourths of the statutory rate, the excess over three-fourths of the statutory rate will be taken out of your artist royalties!

The amounts involved can be staggering. Three-fourths of the $0.08 rate is $0.06, and the difference, $0.02, is retained by the record company. If you record 10 songs on an album, the difference is $0.20 per album. Sell 1 million albums and you begin to get the idea of what you (and your publisher) are losing ($200,000 in this example). Over a 10-album career, if each album sells 1 million copies, the total is $2 million. If it sells more (Celine Dion had an album, *Falling Into You,* which sold 10 million copies in the United States alone), as they say in the vernacular, forget about it. In addition, record companies invariably limit to 10 the number of titles on any given album on which they will pay even the reduced rate. Thus even if your record contains 12 songs, the maximum mechanical royalty the company will pay is, continuing with the number used above, $0.60. Why do the record companies do this? Why not?

Of course, the major music publishers are controlled by giant media conglomerates, and while the music publishers' biases are in favor of maximum exploitation of copyrights, their bosses' biases are in favor of big bottom-line profits of the entertainment unit which counts the music publisher as a poor cousin to the record or motion picture company affiliate.

What can be done to correct this situation? Presumably there would have to be legislation outlawing this practice in its present form, but the record companies insist that they would merely have to reduce artist royalties accordingly if this profit cow were to be reduced or eliminated. But at least in that case, the artists are responsible for negotiating their own royalties and the writers and publishers are not forced to choose between being straw men or victims. The way it works now, the song side of the creative team is either blamed for the reducing the artist's royalty, or it has to bear the brunt of the royalty reduction. (In most countries of the world, the mechanical rate payable to copyright holders is calculated as a percentage of the selling price of records. Therefore, whether the record contains 10 songs or 20 songs, the mechanical royalty is the same for all.) Antitrust litigation is a possible solution to this state of affairs. However, small, independent music publishers have generally elected not to sue their best customers—the record companies—for fear of destroying what little cordiality there remains in their relationship. In the event that one of their songs is used on a record and it is not written by the artist or producer, and therefore "controlled," the record company might still threaten to remove it unless the publisher agrees to license it at the controlled composition "rate." These small independents would have no negotiating room in this situation were they in the process of suing the hand that was feeding them.

Buyouts

To reproduce a song as part of a motion picture, television show, or television or radio commercial, it is necessary to obtain a synchronization license from the copyright owner. The purpose of this license is to give the user the right to synchronize the song in a timed relationship to what is going on "around" the song—usually visual images. Upon the invention of the home video cassette player (Sony's Betamax and later the Matsushita

Mechanical Royalty Rates Outside of the United States

Foreign record companies, as a rule, pay just as high, and very often higher, royalties to the music publishers and do not seek to reduce artists' royalties to keep their costs down. Outside of the United States and about a dozen other countries where the mechanical rate is set by statute or collective bargaining, an association of mechanical rights societies (Bureau International des Sociétés Gérants les Droits d/Enregistrement et de Reproduction Mécanique, or BIEM) and record industry lobbying organizations, such as the British Phonograph Industry (BPI) in the United Kingdom and the International Federation of the Phonographic Industry (IFPI), periodically negotiates mechanical royalty rates to apply in their territories. While these rates vary somewhat from country to country, they are currently in the range of between 8.5 percent and 9 percent of the published dealer price (PPD) of a record, excluding value-added (VAT) and other taxes (essentially a built-in sales tax). The PPD represents the cost of a record to a record retailer. In the United Kingdom, the rate is currently 8.5 percent of PPD. With a 10 pound sterling PPD for most top-line CDs, this amounts to 85 pence or just over $1.25 per CD. The U.S. equivalent for 10 songs—even absent the special "rate"—is far below the U.K. rate. This mechanical royalty is shared collectively among all of the writers and publishers—usually based on percentages of total music contained on the CD, calculated by time.

version, the VHS video cassette recorder) in the 1970s, the music publishers (who controlled the majority of musical compositions that would comprise the soundtracks to films and other video presentations) considered the per-copy reproduction of the film in the same way as a per-copy reproduction of a phonograph record, but were unsure as to how much to charge for the per-copy use. There might, for example, be as much as two hours of music in a videocassette. There were long uses, short uses, and background orchestral score uses. There could be as many as 50 or more "cues" containing music, all of which would have to be reckoned with. Some films were heavy on the music. Some were not. A videocassette was indeed a copy, like a record, and presumably the songs used on a videocassette for sale to the consumer would be subject to per-copy mechanical reproduction fees, but many music publishers assumed that the formula used to calculate the per-copy fee for a record would not work given these disparate lengths. Nevertheless, some publishers wanted to charge fees on this basis, and others established a fictional "fund" for song royalties of about 5 percent of the wholesale selling price of the cassette, whereby the fund was to be split among the song owners as their interest appeared.

Top Gun: A Top Buyout for Paramount

Top Gun: Paramount Pictures' once maligned investment in a feature film starring a relatively unknown Tom Cruise—a film that had been reworked, reshot, rewritten, and refinanced so many times that its future was not only uncertain, it was most likely nonexistent!

Paramount's music licensing supervisors had put together a marvelous score featuring some of the hottest recording artists of the day and portending the phenomenal musical soundtracks to come over the next two decades which would result in the sale of tens of millions of albums. But they did not want to pay a per-copy mechanical royalty rate upon the sale of video cassettes—if indeed anyone would *ever* be interested in buying copies of this risky film. (This is an example of the brilliant anticipation of the future that the motion picture industry is known for. Here's another. Decades before television was invented, there were provisions in film contracts with screenwriters which prohibited the screenwriters from authorizing a version of the film to be shot and broadcast on "television." It's true!)

Paramount offered a one-time, $2,500 payment to each music publisher who controlled a song in the soundtrack without regard to the ultimate number of videocassettes, videodiscs, etc., that might be sold. The music publishers broke ranks, and most of them agreed to the deal, thinking that at $0.05 a copy—the audio-only copyright rate at the time the film was made—a 50,000-unit sale would not amount to all that much in the long run and $2,500 in hand was better in the short run than a gamble that the film (especially *this* film) would break all previous sales levels, including Jane Fonda's workout video. Had you seen the trailer for the film, you would have jumped on the same bandwagon. Oh, you're wondering how many copies the *Top Gun* video cassette/disc combination sold? 1.2 million copies.

This concept of dividing a specific percentage of the videocassette among the various song owners would be modeled on the European approach, which is based on time.

However, before the family of copyright holders, as a group, could figure out how to charge for the use of songs in such devices which would now be finding their way into homes via videocassettes, and later videodiscs and DVDs, Paramount Pictures (which coincidentally owns one of the premier music publishing companies in the world, Famous Music) came up with the concept of the buyout: if the copyright owner allowed its song to be included in the film—in return for which it would be paid many thousands of dollars as a synchronization fee plus additional performance royalties generated upon the presentation of the film in motion picture theaters outside of the United States and on television in the United States—it would have to agree to forego a per-copy royalty upon the sale of the device.

Music publishers and writers in the United States customarily grant to their affiliates or subpublishers outside of the United States the exclusive rights *in their respective territories* to exercise most rights under copyright. Included among these are mechanical reproduction rights. But each subpublisher, as well as the United States publisher, is also usually authorized to issue *worldwide* synchronization licenses only on a *nonexclusive* basis, for music embodied in motion picture soundtracks. In this way, the film company, wherever it is, can rest easy in the knowledge that it can distribute its film worldwide, without regard to where the film has been shot, without having to seek licenses in each other territory of the world in which the film might be presented.

However, when it came to determining whether a worldwide synchronization license for a *film* also covered the videocassette or videodisc embodying the film, problems arose. Was the reproduction of music on a videocassette a mechanical reproduction or just an extension of the synchronization right? If the right to *mechanically* reproduce musical compositions was *exclusively* granted to the various publishing affiliates or subpublishers around the world *for their territories only,* the value of the synchronization license would be defeated for uses outside of the traditional film medium. What's more, in many countries the manufacture and sale of individual videocassettes and discs would generate a per-copy obligation to pay royalties to the copyright holders, much like a mechanical royalty on the sale of records.

With respect to films made in the United States, since the worldwide synchronization license was entered into in the United States, the powerful film companies decided that the provisions of the synchronization contract—with its worldwide effect—prevailed, superseding foreign countries' laws and society rules. Basically, the companies were saying to the publishers who had granted exclusive mechanical reproduction rights around the world to their affiliates or subpublishers: "Work out your contractual breaches with your subpublishers; we don't care to hear about your view that you have already given away the rights we are demanding. We insist on a worldwide buyout of *all videogram reproduction rights* even if you have previously given away the rights to grant us these and you no longer own them. Either work it out, or we will not include your song in our film." ("Videogram" covers all physical audio-video devices, including videocassettes, videodiscs, and DVDs.)

The buyout concept prevailed and continues to this day. Do you think that Sony/ATV Music Publishing Company (Columbia/Sony Pictures) or Famous Music Publishing Company (Paramount Pictures) or Warner/Chappell Music (Warner Bros. and New Line Cinema) or Universal Music Publishing Company (Universal and DreamWorks Pictures) will fight this take-it-or-leave-it approach? No way. Sorry, writers. (Maybe BMG, which has no affiliated motion picture company, will come to the rescue and litigate the issue.)

Audits

While I have dealt with the audit process in some detail in Chapter 12, it is appropriate to expand on the discussion here because some aspects of the music publishing business require a more in-depth review of this subject.

As noted earlier, when a songwriter licenses the right to mechanically reproduce his or her song on a record, a mechanical royalty is payable pursuant to a license agreement with the record company. This license agreement ordinarily contains an audit right, allowing the songwriter to examine the books and records of the record company to the extent reasonably necessary to verify that he or she is being paid properly.

Songwriters who utilize the services of the Harry Fox Agency, Inc., or other mechanical rights licensing agencies, have the benefit of their agents' auditing the record companies on their behalf. Indeed, the Harry Fox Agency audits the major record companies regularly not only on behalf of those independent songwriters and publishers who are their principals, but also on behalf of some of the major publishers who are owned by the major record companies. While this appears to avoid any potential conflict of interest between the major music publishers and their affiliated record companies, it also is a mechanism through which the major music publishers can pass off their responsibilities to a third party. However, when it comes to their sister record companies, the major music publishers choose to license them directly, thereby—not coincidentally—bypassing the Harry Fox audit juggernaut.

Independent songwriters who control their own publishing rights and license record companies directly also have the opportunity to audit the record companies, threaten lawsuits, and participate in settlement discussions. This may be an advantage for them because, if they utilize the massive audit capabilities of the Harry Fox Agency where an enormous number of songs are the subject of an annual or other periodic audit of a record company, while the audit costs are certainly reduced pro rata, the opportunity for the record companies to make broad settlements increases, and the probability of obtaining a satisfactory settlement for individual works, or groups of works, decreases. And, while the major music publishers have an incentive, as do all copyright holders, to maximize their receipts and profits, it is unlikely that they will go to the wall against their own record company affiliates.

FOREIGN AUDITS

As might be expected, the major music publishers' record company affiliates in other countries are not used to being audited or being the initiator of an audit. For example, since Warner/Chappell (U.S.) does not audit the Warner Records Groups in the United States, Warner/Chappell (France) is not likely to audit Warner, Atlantic, or Elektra Records in France. On the contrary, it will leave this responsibility to the mechanical rights society in France, SDRM, and let the settlements be made in the customary manner in that territory. This is not the right scenario for inquiring aggressively to insure that (1) the songs that should have been registered at the foreign mechanical (and performing) rights societies were indeed registered; (2) the money that should have been collected has in fact been collected; and (3) the division of this money is in accordance with the songwriter's agreement with the publisher. Nevertheless, SDRM is independent of the U.S. parent publishing companies and at least *some* audit is conducted.

Family Ties (Too Close to Sue)

A hot recording artist was signed to a major record company, and of course the major record company's publishing affiliate was the first to hear about it. So the music publishing affiliate offered to enter into a long-term copublishing agreement with the artist (read: "they would control the administration rights in the compositions *forever*"). They offered the artist lots of money, calling it an advance. (This advance would later be recouped against the artist's song earnings, and therefore, except for the short-term risk on the part of the music publisher of losing the investment, the artist would have paid his or her own advance!) Well, when the recording was done, lo and behold the CD contained 20 songs, not 10, and so had to be released as a double CD, though the recording agreement provided for only a 10 times three-fourths statutory rate rather than 20 times three-fourths.

What's more, there were outside songs on the album, and the publishers of those songs were unwilling to reduce their royalty to less than three-fourths of the statutory (which is exactly what happens when the 10 times formula is applied to 20 songs!). So who ate the difference? The artist. What did the artist's publishing company do? It punted.

Although the publishing company had a financial interest in fighting this deal, it had no stomach for it, especially since the record company affiliate's CEO was, ultimately, the boss of the publishing company president. So a double CD which contained 20 songs was licensed to the record company for three-fourths of the statutory rate for a CD containing 10 songs.

There are arguments on both sides here. The fact that the double CD cost twice as much to manufacture, and the retail selling price was less than twice that of a single-album CD was certainly an argument in the record company's favor. Then again, the packaging cost was *not* twice that of a single CD. Yes, the union pension and welfare percentage which is applied against the retail selling price of the CD was now increased, since the double CD would be sold at a higher price than a single CD, but the cost of promoting the double CD would, of course, be the same as it would have been for a single CD. In the end, the record company prevailed.

Could an independent publisher have gotten a better result? Probably not, since if the record company had to pay more for the mechanical royalties than it had contracted for, it would simply take the excess out of the artist's royalties. But at least an independent publisher would raise hell over it and maybe get *something* in return.

In early 2002, Warner/Chappell's foreign affiliates were directed to report not to the head of Warner/Chappell in Los Angeles, but to the record company heads in their own territories. The result is more potential conflict of interest insofar as musical composition rights are concerned.

THE ADMINISTRATING FUNCTION

The previous section discussed audits—the process by which financial records are verified. But it is important to note that unless the administrative responsibilities toward a song are properly discharged, there may be no financial records to verify! The importance of the administrating role of the music publisher cannot be overstated. And, without the proper information from the songwriter, the administrator's performance capabilities are extremely limited.

What happens when a writer's or recording artist's music publishing rights are controlled by a music publisher that is so overloaded with administrative responsibilities that it fails to do some of the things it needs to do to fulfill its administrative responsibilities? Simple. Everyone loses. The writer loses his or her share of the income that has not been collected. The publisher of course also loses its share of the income, but if it has given cash advances to the writer and has the right to keep the writer's share of income until those cash advances are paid back, its losses are doubled. So it is in both the writer's and the publisher's self-interest to accomplish effectively the first two administrative tasks: registration and collection. For at least in these two areas, their interests coincide exactly. A song properly registered results in a dollar collected, which in one way or another works to the benefit of both the songwriter and the publisher.

I used the word "fails" above, rather than "neglects," because too often the errors of administrators are due solely to the fact that they are so big and have so many copyrights to administer that they are bound to slip up sometimes. And sometimes an administrative "failure" is actually caused by the songwriter and the songwriter's representatives, not the publisher at all.

Here's an example which illuminates this point.

One of my clients, the principal songwriter of a popular rock band, assigned responsibility for administering his worldwide publishing rights to a major music publisher, which at the time was administering several hundred thousand copyrights. The administrating publisher paid the songwriter lots of money in return for a percentage of whatever it collected over a period of years as a result of the worldwide exploitation of the songwriter's musical compositions. What the songwriter failed to do was to advise the administrating publisher adequately as to what he was writing and what he was recording. It was as if once the deal was in place, such details would magically find their way into the administrating publisher's computer.

Subsequently, the band had a hugely successful worldwide hit which sold more than a million singles and millions of albums. Everyone was happy. Except one thing went wrong. The B side of the single was an instrumental song which, although it did not appear on the album, received a lot of radio play because it was the theme of a major world sporting event—the Olympics. The publishing administrator had never heard of the song. In the course of a full-scale examination of the status of the songwriter's songs around the world, lo and behold, this song's title appeared. All concerned were surprised to find that no one had communicated the necessary information to the administrating publisher and therefore the song had never been licensed, never registered in Washington, and never registered with any performing or mechanical rights society anywhere in the world. The lesson? Songwriters must treat their copyrights as any other precious offspring. Like children, they must be nurtured, cared for, and paid attention to. And just as no one but the parents can be expected to be responsible for developing a child to his or her full potential, no one other than the person who created a song should be responsible for developing a copyright to its full potential.

FOREIGN TAXES

Although the issue of foreign taxes is too complex to be covered in depth in this book, one observation should be made in the context of audits.

Many countries tax money paid by their music companies to writers or artists, whether or not located outside of their countries. For example, when a dollar is payable by a Japanese subpublisher to an American songwriter or publisher, Japanese tax law dictates that only $0.90 will be transferred. The other $0.10 is paid by the Japanese subpublisher to the Japanese tax authorities, and the original publisher in the United States will never see it. This 10 percent takeout represents a not-insignificant loss of income. Suppose the publisher is a "doing business as" of a songwriter and is in a 30 percent tax bracket. If the entire dollar were transferred as income, the taxes paid would be $0.30, leaving the publisher with $0.70 for every dollar collected. But if only $0.90 is transferred and taxed at the 30 percent rate (for a $0.27 tax bite), the publisher is left with only $0.63—7 cents less—for every dollar collected in Japan.

A similar situation exists in Australia and Mexico and many other countries.

The United States has special tax treaties with some countries (e.g., the United Kingdom, France, and Germany), which provide that instead of a tax being withheld by the foreign government, it will be reinstated and paid to the American publisher once a special tax form is filed, in a timely manner, with the inland revenue of the foreign country (their IRS). (This works something like a VAT that a United States traveler can be reimbursed for at the airport upon leaving the country that affixed the tax to the purchase in the first place.) Under these treaties, the publisher pays taxes in the United States on the entire amount of the monies collected, but it collects 100 percent, not 90 percent, of the royalties due. They usually require that the American publisher be in good standing with the American tax authorities, having filed a federal and state tax return for the prior year.

This process can be handled very smoothly, or it can be a nightmare. And if the appropriate forms are not filed correctly, or are filed late, the withheld money can drift around such that it may take months and even years to recapture it—if indeed it is ever recaptured. It is essential that your accountant or business manager and your lawyer coordinate these filings to avoid the loss of the tax benefit they afford. Have you ever thought of asking who is responsible for filing your RF3EU form in France? I'm sure not. You might want to start thinking about it now.

AT-SOURCE VS. RECEIPTS DEALS

When a publisher says it will pay a writer and the writer's solely owned company a given percentage of the earnings of the songs worldwide, can the writer take that statement at face value? Of course not. In a typical copublishing situation—where the U.S. copublisher administers the songs worldwide and supposedly retains only 25 percent of the earnings, the following issues present themselves:

- What happens when the copublisher makes an arrangement with an overseas subpublisher whereby the subpublisher gives the copublisher substantial advances in return for a percentage of the earnings?
- Does the copublisher own its own companies overseas or have such a close affiliation with them that they might as well be part of the same company?
- Does the copublisher pay on the basis of at-source earnings or receipts earnings?

By way of illustration, let's say a writer's songs are copublished in the United States by a respectable administrating publisher. (Hereafter I will refer to the writer as the "original publisher.") For every dollar earned in the United States, the original publisher receives 50 cents as a writer and 25 cents as one of the copublishers. To collect monies earned in France, the copublisher retained by the original publisher must obtain the services of a French subpublisher or administrator. That subpublisher keeps, let's say, 25 percent as its share. (After all, it has paid substantial advances to the American publisher and has provided substantial services registering the songs, promoting them, liaising with the local record company, exploiting them for television and commercial uses, etc.) That means that for every dollar earned in France, the U.S. copublisher will receive only $0.75. If the copublisher's deal with the original publisher is a receipts deal, the copublisher will take 25 percent of the 75 cents and pay the balance—56.25 cents—to the original publisher.

Now, if the administrating copublisher is, say, EMI Music or Peermusic (to use two of many possible examples), and does the same thing, there is something wrong with the picture. Sure, the subpublishers have the same job to do, but the parent company in the United States is now receiving either directly or indirectly much more than the 25 percent the original publisher thought had been bargained for. When an administrating copublisher such as these ignores the introduction into the mix of a subpublisher which *it* owns or controls and pays the original publisher as if the administrating copublisher had collected the money directly, it is known as an *at-source distribution*. For every $1.00 earned in France, the administrating copublisher will retain 25 cents (either through its subsidiary—or close affiliate—in France or through some combination of sharing with that subsidiary or affiliate) and it will pay the original publisher 75 cents. This is an at-source deal. And it is a lot better result than the 56.25 cents the original publisher would have received under a receipts deal.

You may say that this is a fine result for the original publisher, which is obtaining the services not only of the United States copublisher, but of its foreign affiliates as well, for the same price. Or you may also say that this is not fair to the U.S. administrating copublisher because, in financial terms, it will essentially have become a domestic copublisher only, and all of the earnings outside of the United States will either go to foreign affiliates or have to be shared with them; its ability to recoup its advances will be hindered and the efforts to "break" the song or the record that embodies it in the home country of the writer, which is where the rest of the world is looking before it pays attention to the song or the record, will not be rewarded—so why try?

Not surprisingly, the various interests have tried to come up with some kind of compromise which serves the needs of the original publisher on the one hand and the administrating copublisher on the other. There has been a tendency in recent years to establish a receipts deal at the beginning of a relationship and to convert it into an at-source deal later. Whatever is the result of your negotiations as an original publisher, you must keep in mind that there is a significant difference between the receipts deal and the at-source deal.

THE BLACK BOX REVISITED

As stated previously, money collected in many countries outside of the United States that is not attributable to any particular song or writer finds its way into what is known as the Black Box. You will recall that monies budgeted for expenses which are not used get dropped into the Black Box, as do monies reimbursed to member publishers as rebates of collection society commissions and, in some countries, additional monies with respect to newly introduced types of earnings that are not separately allocated and attributed to specific musical compositions. However, there are two major categories of Black Box monies that an administering publisher's subpublisher can directly affect through its administration services:

- Monies that that have accumulated as a result of the failure to communicate— on the part of the original publisher or administrating publisher—the necessary information on song titles and writers
- Monies that have accumulated as a result of the misregistration or misallocation of funds

One way for the original publisher, or administering copublisher, to insure that access to Black Box income is attained is for an attorney or accountant to examine, on a regular basis, both the registration lists of foreign collection societies and the actual accountings that are issued by those societies to each foreign subpublisher or to each foreign affiliate of a U.S.-based multinational publisher. Unfortunately, this is more easily said than done, as those who have tried to unravel the mystique of foreign accountings have discovered. But with the increased globalization of the music business, it is inevitable that a more open sharing of such information will be achieved in the future. The world's societies are even now talking among themselves to deal with such global issues as how and to whom to allocate performance and mechanical income emanating to copyright owners via the digital download and streaming of sound recordings, and, by extension, the musical compositions embodied on such sound recordings. The same will apply, no doubt, to digital downloads of sheet music as well. They are also in the process of establishing central databases that, for the first time, may allow accurate identification of song titles and their writers and publishing interests on a global basis, thereby reducing the possibility of error in allocating income. (Of course, once global tracking of songs is instituted, an error made at the initial registration will only be exacerbated as it is replicated throughout the world's data systems. That is all the more reason to have someone looking "over the shoulder" of the publishing administrator of the writer, the artist/writer, or his or her own music publishing company to check and double-check that the registration process is being handled with absolute precision.)

COPYRIGHT REVERSIONS

Music publishers are in the business of acquiring copyrights. Or at least that is what one would think. They make substantial investments over incredibly long periods of time in writers, show writers, recording artist/writers, etc., and they lose a lot of money in the process. When everything hits, one would think they would want to finally own what they have risked capital on and in many cases nurtured so significantly that the songs might never have been written in the first place—or been successful—but for their creative input and financial support.

Yet many music publishers today agree to allow the songs they acquire pursuant to various forms of songwriter-publisher agreements to revert in their entirety to the writers 5, 10, or 15 years later. Why? Perhaps it is due to increased or more sophisticated competition from other publishers—especially those who do not identify with the conservative values of the old-time publishers who are used to owning, not renting, copyrights. Some believe that the major reason for this phenomenon is that the multinationals would rather make hay while the sun shines and let someone else harvest the crop in future. That is, they are willing to trade long-term prospects (future income generated from control of copyrights) for short-term bottom-line profits (the market share resulting from the work of a few hot writers whose first wave of income is usually the largest).

There is another reason the music publishers may be less avaricious than in earlier days. As we have seen, under the Copyright Act of 1976, for any works created in 1978 or later, even if a writer transfers to another entity the copyright on those works, the rights can be recaptured by the writer at any time during a period of five years beginning at the end of 35 years after the date of execution of the grant. If the authors are going to get their copyrights back anyway, why shouldn't publishers entice writers to place the works with their companies by offering an even earlier reversion. (Note that the work-for-hire exceptions to this right to reversion do not, in general, apply to musical compositions written in traditional ways by traditional songwriters, which are *not* works for hire.)

Reversions come in many varieties: reversion of copyright after *x* number of years; reversion of administrative control, but not copyright; reversion of copyrights in songs not "covered" or otherwise exploited during *x* number of years; reversion of one or more portions of the above. Most of these variations depend on whether or not the writer's account with the publisher has been recouped. Once the account is recouped, reversion may occur five to ten years later. If it is not, then reversion will not occur until years after recoupment, if at all, until the 35-year recapture provision takes effect.

Sometimes a publisher will allow reversion when the writer's account remains unrecouped, provided the writer pays back to the publisher 110 or 115 percent of the unrecouped balance. This option may be very appealing to a writer. For example, if the writer's copyrights have attained an asset value of from 5 to 10 times earnings, taking control of the copyrights in return for a small fee represents a sound investment. And besides, I have rarely met a writer who does not think that he or she can more diligently exploit copyrights than the publisher can (though I have not often met a writer who *can*). These options are all intricately worked through in the course of negotiations. Let us not forget, after all, that no publisher really wants to lose the asset (the copyright) if it can be avoided.

14 THE PROS AND CONS OF BEING YOUR OWN MUSIC PUBLISHING COMPANY

And therfore, at the kinges court, my brother
Ech man for him-self, ther is non other
— Geoffrey Chaucer

Songwriters who have succeeded in retaining their copyrights have established for themselves an annuity that in innumerable examples has allowed them options they would never have had were they to have placed their copyrights in the hands of traditional music publishers. Yet most of those songwriters have not had the resources available to them to come close to matching the value that can come from a relationship with a major music publishing company. For example, songwriters who are not also recording artists really *need* the help of music publishers to obtain cuts on their songs. Songwriter–recording artists, on the other hand, obtain their own cuts. Some songwriters relinquish their copyrights because they need the money that large publishing companies will often pay them to acquire ownership or co-ownership, and administration rights, to their songs. Even those who can afford to do so may not want to forego the benefits that come from an association with a fully staffed music publisher. Circumstances will necessarily be different for each songwriter, and it is a worthwhile exercise for all songwriters to sit down with their representatives and analyze whether, to what extent, and when it would serve their immediate and long-term goals to self-publish or whether it would be better to align themselves with a large music publishing company.

SELF-PUBLISHING

If you are a songwriter who wants to self-publish, you must take the steps outlined below. If you don't have the time or inclination to take them yourself, you should ask for help from an attorney experienced in copyright law or one of a multitude of small publishing administration companies. The Association of Independent Music Publishers (www.aimp.org) is a great resource. Most managers and business managers don't have the interest or experience to discharge the tasks required in the administration of copyrights.

Registration

The first step is to obtain PA forms from the United States Copyright Office in Washington, D.C. or online. The current cost to register claims to copyright (effective through June 2002) is $30 per registration. The Copyright Office will accept claims for multiple songs if the forms are accompanied by a tape or CD containing all the songs. This will save a lot of money. Although some copyright lawyers will argue that there is some question as to whether a compulsory license fee can be maintained on a per-song basis if a group of songs has been combined on one registration (it is possible, if unlikely, that only one mechanical license fee would be collectible for songs registered as a group), the cost advantages of multiple registrations outweigh the risks.

The Mechanical Variance

Once registered, if your work is recorded for release, you will have to issue a license to the record company. As stated previously, the preferred form of this document is not drafted as a license at all. It is designed as a *variance* of the copyright law. The reason for this is if a license is breached, the entity granting the license can take *only* a breach of contract action against someone who fails to honor its terms. In contrast, breaching a mechanical variance opens the door to a suit on the basis of federal copyright infringement, offering far greater remedies.

The document is couched in terms whereby the company recording a song is advised that it may do so pursuant to the provisions of the compulsory license provision of Section 115 of the Copyright Act. The language also provides relief from some requirements—which would otherwise be extremely burdensome—*as long as the user of the copyright follows the rules set forth in the variance.* These are:

- Rules concerning the timing of the request
- Extremely detailed formal requirements of the notice of intention to use the musical composition
- The calculation of royalties on the basis of every record made and distributed, rather than made and sold
- Various accounting and payment requirements, such as those requiring accounting and payments on or before the twentieth day of each month (under oath, no less!) and additional accounting requirements promulgated by the Register of Copyrights such as the obligation to produce annual detailed cumulative annual statements of account, certified by a CPA

And that's just a sample. The actual language formalizes these already burdensome requirements to an almost farcical degree. It is no wonder that the "variance" has been a welcome relief to record companies. What the variance accomplishes is to put these formalities on hold: they do not go into effect unless the user does not honor the "varied" provisions set forth in the variance. In particular, if the record company does not pay royalties due accurately and on time (usually every three months), the company will have itself waived its benefits and will be an infringer—not a contract breacher.

In contrast, although a traditional license agreement provides for the same royalties to be paid at the same times and intervals, the record company's failure to pay, or to pay on time, pursuant to a traditional license agreement, will generate damages only in the amount of the royalties the songwriter should have been paid plus perhaps interest and a few costs. But this is NOTHING compared to the remedies available against infringers under the Copyright Act, which include such things as the right to sue in a federal court, secure injunctions, claim statutory damages ranging up to $100,000, and recover costs and attorneys' fees. Now that is SOMETHING. None of these remedies would be available to a prevailing party suing a record company for failure to pay royalties under a traditional license agreement.

Performance Society Registration

Once you have determined that the song may be performed (most importantly, if it is going to be played on the radio), the musical composition should be registered with the performing rights society with which you are affiliated. In the United States, there are three such organizations: the American Society of Composers, Authors, and Publishers (ASCAP), which is a membership organization whose members are comprised of writers and publishers only; Broadcast Music, Inc. (BMI), which is a corporation owned by broadcasters (although it is very sympathetic to the concerns of writers and publishers and actually has more writer and publisher affiliates than ASCAP has members); and the Society of European Stage Authors & Composers, Inc. (SESAC), which is a privately held corporation. Once you secure a record release of a song you write, or expect a performance to be broadcast on radio or television, or secure a synchronization use in a motion picture, one of these societies will be happy to allow you to join—as an affiliate in the case of BMI or SESAC or as a member in the case of ASCAP.

Foreign Collection Agreements

You must also ensure that if your recording is made available for sale in countries outside of the United States (with the exception of Canada), someone is appointed as your representative to register the recording with the performing and mechanical rights societies in those countries.

Customarily, Canadian rights are handled by issuing licenses from the United States directly to Canadian record companies. Although the performing rights will be collected sooner or later through your U.S. performing rights society, there are several advantages to appointing a Canadian publisher to assist in administering copyrights in that country.

- Performing rights income will be paid at least a year earlier than would otherwise be the case.
- There will be someone "on the spot" to keep an eye on the uses of your songs.
- The Canadian publisher can hire a local auditor to verify your song's activity.
- You may even be able to get an advance against earnings.
- The Canadian publisher may be able to obtain cover recordings of your songs.

Outside of Canada, a local publisher is all but essential. Without one, the odds of losing income due to inaccurate identification of performance and mechanical uses increase to a level which is simply unacceptable if you care at all about the income your songs generate.

As noted previously, a foreign publisher that represents the interests of a U.S. publisher (or songwriter/self-publisher) is known as a subpublisher. Subpublishers may be selected on a per-country basis or on the basis of a larger regional division of the world. The value of per-country deals is that you can select each representative personally, and each advance paid by a representative selected on that basis stands alone—that is, it is not subject to recoupment against earnings from other countries for the simple reason that neither the various subpublishers nor the deals themselves are related to each other. On the other hand, processing one or two dozen agreements for purposes of representing one song or a small catalogue can be very time-consuming and expensive. In some circumstances it may be appropriate to make separate agreements with subpublishers that are capable of exploiting a song or catalogue, and are motivated to do so because the song may be a big earner, or because in this way they can prove their competence and perhaps convince you to let them handle your entire catalog. But more often than not, it makes financial sense to make an "ex-North America" deal with one publishing company whose various affiliates or subsidiaries will provide the same services and actually coordinate with each other to help promote the song or catalogue, or the artist's recording embodying the copyrights which are the subject of the subpublishing agreement. Nevertheless, high-earning catalogues often warrant country-by-country deals for several reasons, including the absence of cross-recoupment, which is always a feature of deals covering more than one territory.

THE BLACK BOX, ONE MORE TIME

Since Black Box monies can amount to many millions of dollars annually, anything that a United States–based writer or publisher can do to gain access to some of this money is likely to be well worth the effort.

One often-used means to gain access is to establish companies in the countries themselves rather than enter into traditional subpublishing agreements. Sony did it. BMG did it. Even Bug Music, a highly regarded publishing administrator, did it. For example, once a U.S. publisher has established a company in Germany, that company can become a member of GEMA and have access not only to information but to a proportionate share of the Black Box income as well. The fact that many companies established for this purpose are shell companies, whose sole reason for being is to obtain information and increase income, does nothing to negate their legitimacy. Of course, some U.S. publishers have set up such companies for more questionable purposes, such as hiding the money thousands of miles away from the offices of capable auditors whose principals cannot afford to send them around the world to verify accountings.

The Subpublisher as Liaison

I would like to make an observation about an anomaly in most subpublishing agreements. There must be tens of thousands of traditional subpublishing agreements in effect throughout the world today. All of them provide for the administration of the copyrights which are the subject of the agreements. All of them provide for the collection of earnings and the periodic payment to the copyright owner or publisher of the compositions. Rarely, however, do they actually state the underlying hopes, wishes, and expectations of the original copyright owner or publisher, which, simply stated, is that the subpublisher will make a reasonable effort to exploit the copyrights covered by the subpublishing agreement within the subpublisher's territory.

If the songwriter is an artist, there is all the more reason to include such language. It is anathema for a publisher to state in so many words what it will do to exploit the song, the writer, or the artist. (The same is true for record companies. In fact, most recording artist agreements specifically state that the record company is under no obligation to promote the artist's recordings, to sell records, or to meet any particular expectation of the artist in entering into the contract in the first place. This is how the companies avoid lawsuits claiming they did not do enough to "break" the artist, or his record.)

Yet it is not unreasonable for the artist-songwriter to request that the subpublisher be the artist-songwriter's liaison with his or her record company's affiliates in the territory of the subpublisher and that the subpublisher act as the artist's "eyes and ears" in the territory in order to keep the artist and the artist's representatives informed of what is happening (or not happening) in the territory with the artist's record. It is also not unreasonable to want the subpublisher to go beyond the basic collection function, for example, to participate in selecting the single the subpublisher might think would best appeal to the consumers in the territory, and to communicate this to the local record company. In essence, it is not unreasonable to ask the subpublisher to maximize not only the commercial exploitation and promotion of the musical compositions, but the artist-songwriter as well. Below is a sample provision that serves this function. No doubt most subpublishers will not accept the language as it appears here, but *any* written provisions are negotiable and something is better than nothing, especially when the subject of what one expects of one's subpublisher is otherwise usually not even raised.

> *Owner hereby appoints Subpublisher its non-exclusive representative for the Licensed Territory for the purpose of promoting Owner's publishing interests and the recording and performing artist [name of artist] (hereafter referred to as the Artist). To this end, Subpublisher shall use its best efforts to maximize the commercial exploitation and promotion of the Compositions in the Licensed Territory, and the sale in the Licensed Territory of phonograph records embodying Compositions. In*

connection with the foregoing, Subpublisher shall:

1. *Generally liaise with personnel of record companies based in the Licensed Territory to maximize the exploitation and earnings of the Compositions*

2. *Use its best efforts to liaise with the professional representatives of Artist including, without limitation, Artist's manager, business manager, and attorney, to maximize the commercial exploitation and promotion of the Compositions in the Licensed Territory, the sale in the Licensed Territory of phonograph records embodying Artist's performances of Compositions and the commercial success of Artist's personal performance tours in the Licensed Territory*

If Owner shall notify Subpublisher of any corrections or changes in any Compositions including, without limitation, the author(s), title, lyrics, copyright, etc., Publisher shall notify the applicable performing rights, mechanical rights and other collection societies in the Licensed Territory thereof and use its best efforts to ensure that such corrections or changes are made by such societies in an accurate and timely manner.

Print Rights in the Digital Age

In the last chapter I discussed the subject of print rights in the digital age. For a self-publisher, as for any publisher, print rights are beginning to have more value than they used to. More and more small publishing companies are recognizing that they can license digital downloads of their sheet music to the few companies that are specializing in this new world of music exploitation. The sheet music "button" can be placed on the artist's website and the consumer can benefit from instantly being able to access visual notations comprising his or her favorite music.

Of course, no publisher should count out traditional print rights, which can also be licensed individually on a per-song basis or collectively by catalogue. There are a number of outstanding print companies in the United States. If you can't find one, try to find a store that sells print music and look at the names and addresses of the companies that provide this product to get an idea as to which one fits your particular needs. Your attorney will also be able to guide you in this area.

WHY BOTHER DOING IT YOURSELF?

There are basically two options songwriters have for exploiting the rights to their compositions: self-publishing, which usually involves asking their agents or attorneys to provide those services, or even hiring someone to do so, and entering into an administration agreement with an established publisher. Clearly the least expensive way to go—provided the artist-songwriter feels sufficiently organized to accomplish efficient administration of his or her songs, or trusts his or her agent, attorney, or staff person to do the job—is the self-publishing route. The costs of hiring such a person could be substantially less than the percentage of income traditionally charged by an established publisher, but there are disadvantages: there will be no cash advances to operate with (although many business managers consider cash advances as a form of loan that must eventually be paid back and therefore are suspect); there will be no introductions to co-writers; there will be no effort to introduce your songs to motion picture music supervisors, and the like. There may also be lost opportunities that you might not ever be able to identify because the large publishing companies are connected to just about everything that is going on in the music business—particularly now that those companies have been absorbed into huge global entertainment conglomerates. The companies that are most efficient in exploiting global synergies are more likely to be able to create opportunities for you that you would never be able to create yourself.

The option you choose will ultimately depend on the kind of catalogue involved. For a self-generating band which is recording its own material and which does not reasonably anticipate that third parties would be interested in recording their songs, self-publishing is a real option. A "stand-alone" songwriter will not always be as comfortable following this route, although Diane Warren found a way to do it while finding the time to line up her Academy and Grammy awards on the mantel.

THE COST OF ACQUIRING COPYRIGHTS

In past decades, songwriters gave 100 percent of their publishing share, including the copyright and worldwide administration rights, to their publishers. The deal was, essentially, for all time—or at least as long as the various world copyright laws would permit (all rights end at some point). When the original publisher would license subpublishing rights overseas, even for a limited period of years, it would at the same time agree that if the subpublisher were to obtain a cover recording by a local artist, the subpublisher could retain control over the particular composition for the entire remaining term of copyright in that country.

Those days are gone forever. Currently, the term during which rights are allowed to be retained overseas is usually two to three years. And, more significantly, publishers today do not customarily acquire 100 percent of the copyrights in the songs they administer; more often they acquire 50 percent of the copyrights, although they continue to control (administer) 100 percent of them. What does this mean? What does it mean to "acquire" a copyright?

What does a publisher pay for the portion of the copyright that it does own? It might surprise you to know that they often pay nothing. For in the music publishing business, as in the recording business, the companies do not actually purchase the assets they acquire. Yes, the record companies advance the cost of recording, etc. But uniquely in the record business, as we have seen, the artist winds up paying back the cost of recording out of what would otherwise be due in royalties. In the music publishing business, the writer may receive advances against royalties for the assignment of his or her copyrights (or 50 percent of the copyrights) and the worldwide administration rights. But once those advances are recouped *out of the writer's share,* the portion of the copyrights that the publisher "acquired" normally belongs to the publisher for the entire term of copyright, which in most countries of the world today means for a term extending 70 years after the death of the last of the co-writers. In other words, the publisher owns an asset for which it has paid only advances. Of course, there is always the risk that exploitation of the copyright will yield nothing, in which case the publisher will not get the advance back (no earnings, no reimbursement), but with a little bit of luck, the advances will be returned to the publisher out of the writer's share of royalties.

REVERSION OF COPYRIGHTS

Being your own publisher sometimes requires a fairly sophisticated knowledge of the technical requirements that the copyright law establishes to protect third parties from being taken advantage of. The law provides that if a copyright is originally registered in one party's name (e.g., the established publishing company) and the copyright is later assigned to another party (e.g., another publishing company, or, in the case I am about to discuss, to the original writer), if the change in assignment is not registered in the Copyright Office in Washington, a third party (e.g., yet another publishing company), who in good faith checks the Copyright Office records to make sure the party selling the copyright that is being purchased actually has the rights, will have no idea that the reassignment has occurred. Thus, the third party will think that it has acquired something from a publisher that in fact no longer owns the rights. In the world of million-song catalogues, these situations occur more frequently than you can imagine. For all intents and purposes, a reversion—which, quite simply, is an assignment *back* to the writer, should be registered as should any other assignment. There is no official concept of "reversion" in the Copyright Law. But the rules and legal decisions affecting assignment have consistently been applied to the situation in which copyrights revert from an established publisher to a songwriter in the manner described earlier. Not only is there the danger of a third party acquiring copyrights that have reverted, or might at some future date revert, to the songwriter; there is the added complication that if technicalities are not followed carefully, other sources of income (such as performing rights societies) will similarly be misled into thinking that the original publisher remains in charge of the copyrights. Let's see how this potentially dangerous situation can be avoided.

As discussed in Chapter 13 (page 202), permitting reversion in deals in which the writer has some leverage results in a shortening of the period during which the publisher retains rights to the writer's copyrights. As is becoming the custom, control and/or ownership will revert to the writer after a number of years: 5, 7, 10, 12, whatever. The circumstances under which the period can be shortened are customarily tied to the success of the music. If the songs and the records embodying them are failures, the publisher can keep them. If the advances are never recouped, the publisher can keep them. If, however, the songs and the records are successful, even with the often invaluable assistance of the publisher, the publisher will lose them. The publisher will wake up one day after a good run with a catalogue and it will have lost the catalogue permanently. Strange, but true.

Once it appears that the songs may revert to the songwriter, he or she should refocus from being a royalty recipient to being a self-publisher, who will need to take all the steps—and more—that would have been necessary had the songwriter decided to self-publish in the first place. Beyond the basic steps such as registering claims with a performing rights society, there are some additional technical requirements that can become a virtual nightmare. Most particularly, for example, the reversion of the rights that had been held for a time by the publishing company should be registered with the Copyright Office in the same manner as if they had been assigned. But what happens if there is no document signed by the publishing company that effects the reversion? I have already pointed out the dangers in failing to register an assignment. If there is no actual document representing the assignment, what can the writer send to Washington?

- Should the writer register the entire original publishing agreement that contains the reversion clause?
- Should the writer have added to the original publishing agreement for later use an affidavit saying that the conditions set forth in the clause have been met and that therefore the copyrights have "reverted" to him or her?
- Should the writer have required the music publishing company to execute (sign) for later use an assignment of copyright for filing in Washington should the conditions of reversion occur?

The latter procedure may be the most efficient. The assignment can be held in escrow by one of the parties' attorneys together with a precise set of instructions as to when the attorneys can release the document to the songwriter for filing in the U.S. Copyright Office. In this way, when the songwriter's relationship with the music publisher is long over, and the copyrights have "reverted," the songwriter does not have to go back to the music publisher, hat in hand, and ask that the formal assignment document be signed— something to be avoided if at all possible. If you are going to be a self-publisher and you are depending on rights reverting to you from your established publisher, after a period of years, you had better be very careful to follow the formalities of the Copyright Law or you may find that an otherwise innocent third party can walk off with your copyrights and your only recourse may be to sue your original publishing company, which, by then, may have disappeared from the face of the earth. Unfortunately, unless the conditions of reversion are fairly specific, and not conditional, it is not likely that the writer will be able to accomplish this most efficient procedure.

THE VALUE OF THE COPYRIGHT

How can the value of copyrights be measured? Let us say that a recording artist writes 10 songs per album and records 5 albums over 5 years—one each year—all of which sell 500,000 copies (gold in the United States). Although, as we have seen, there is a difference between "sold" records and "royalty-bearing net sales," let us assume that each one of these records is a royalty-bearing record. Let us also assume that each song's length is under 5 minutes in duration so that we do not have to deal with the "long" copyright rate. Finally, let us assume that the artist's agreement with his record company requires that each song be licensed for three-fourths of the statutory rate with a maximum per album cost of 10 times three-fourths of the statutory rate. The mechanical royalty income per record sold will be calculated as follows:

Current rate ($0.08 per song) x 10 X 75 percent = $0.60

For each album selling 500,000 copies, the record company will have paid $300,000. For the five albums—with a sales figure of 2.5 million units—the total is $1.5 million.

The writer and publisher share this $1.5 million on a 50:50 basis; both get $750,000. In a typical situation, 50 percent of the publisher's share (or 25 percent of the total), amounting to $375,000, is paid to the writer's own publishing company and the remaining 50 percent of the publisher's share (25 percent of the total), also $375,000, is retained by the third-party administrating publisher. So, absent any advances which the outside publisher may be able to recoup from the writer's or the writer's publishing company's shares, this works out to $750,000 for the writer, $375,000 for the writer's publishing company, and $375,000 for the administrating publisher.

Returning to the sales of one of the five albums, we have a writer's share of $150,000, an original publisher's share of $75,000, and an administrating publisher's share of $75,000. A rule of thumb in catalogue acquisition is that a buyer will pay anywhere from 5 to 10 times the net publisher's share of earnings of a group of musical compositions. If the writer wishes to sell his or her 50 percent publisher's share, on the basis of a 5 times earnings calculation, that means that he or she can sell it for $375,000 (i.e., 5 times $75,000). On the basis of 10 times earnings, the amount is $750,000. The administrating publishing company has it even better because it, and not the writer's company, actually controls the administration rights and companies purchasing other companies' copyrights will pay a premium to the company that can assign to them the control of the copyrights (along with right to collect the writer's and copublisher's share) rather than just a passive interest in earnings. Different copyrights generate different kinds of income, and buyers who think that these copyrights may have a better financial life in their hands than in the original copublisher's hands may choose to pay more—as much as 15 times earnings. So, for an investment that was really nothing more than a short-term loan (which, in this example, will certainly have been paid back), the copublisher has acquired from the songwriter an asset which is worth anywhere from $375,000 to $1,125,000—after one album!.

Note that to keep it simple, I have intentionally excluded from these calculation other forms of copyright-generated income, such as performance income, which can be substantial; income from licensing synchronization rights, which can also be substantial— particularly if the songs are used in films or in commercials; income from print licensing; income from cover recordings; etc. The net publisher's share of all of these other forms of income would similarly be multiplied by from 5 to 15 times earnings. And don't forget, if a buyer becomes the administrating publisher, the buyer will have the right to use (read: "invest") the writers' share and the writer's own publishing company's copublisher share until it has to account for and pay these shares to the writer and copublisher.

Of course, the writer's own publishing company's 50 percent copublisher share is also worth approximately the same as the administrating copublisher's share, with two important caveats. First, the writer may be contractually obligated not to sell that share to anyone except to the copublisher. Second, the writer's own publishing company's share would be, to a buyer, of considerably less value than the administrating publisher's 50 percent copublisher share since it does not come unencumbered; it is still administered by the original copublisher, and the buyer would have to have faith that the administrating copublisher could be trusted to do a good job and to account regularly and honestly—a leap of faith that a buyer would not necessarily want to make.

THE IMPACT OF ADMINISTRATING COSTS ON TRUE EARNINGS

When a publisher acquires administrative control over the copyrights it represents, it is free to enter into foreign agreements for representation (which it will have to do in order to responsibly collect mechanical and performance royalties earned in foreign countries) in return for which it may be able to obtain advances. However, it will not have to share these with the writer whose songs are being parlayed into these foreign deals.

When an administrating publisher enters into such agreements, it will establish a fixed percentage for its subpublishers to retain—a percentage which customarily exceeds 15 percent and is often as much as 25 percent. Often, these subpublishers are affiliates or divisions of the administrating publisher itself. Conversely, a songwriter who retains control of administration of his or her own copyrights is likely not to have to give away as much as a large administrating publisher would give away in return for the services it requires of the foreign publishers. For example, an important writer/self-publisher who has not entered into an agreement with an administrating publisher, but who nonetheless needs collection agents (subpublishers) in different countries, can give these subpublishers the right (and obligation) to collect income attributable to the compositions in return for anywhere from 90 to 95 to 100 percent of what they collect. Letting them retain 10 percent is tacit recognition that subpublishers have a job to do which takes time, staff, expertise, and experience; where the songwriter is also the recording artist, letting subpublishers retain 5 percent gives them a small "taste" of the earnings which have been generated not by their efforts, but by those of the artist and the artist's record company; zero gives them nothing but the right to use the money they collect for a short time and the "prestige" of saying they represent the important writer's catalogue.

Another argument in favor of self-publishing is that when a writer places his or her copyrights in the hands of an outside publisher—not necessarily one of the majors, but, for example, the publishing company of his or her producer or manager—any advances that the outside publisher may be able to garner from subpublishers or other users of copyrights will ordinarily not be shared with the writer's own publishing company. Thus the artist will have lost an opportunity to fund his or her career, and will have to remain dependent on the goodwill of others, including the outside publishing company, for support.

THE COST OF GIVING AWAY A PIECE OF THE PUBLISHING

We saw in Chapter 8 what giving away a "couple of points" can do by way of crushing an artist's income possibilities. Similarly, giving to others one's songs, administration rights, or copyrights can have severely deleterious effects on the income of the person who gives them away, and to do so without establishing carefully thought out conditions can devastate a career and the financial security that a successful career can provide. Nowhere is this more true than with the songwriter who is also a recording artist. It is worth mentioning here—once again—that a recording artist's record royalties for a given body of songs may be quite minimal. Remember, the artist has to pay, out of what would otherwise be received as record royalties, recording costs, video production costs, tour support, equipment loans, and at least one-half of the costs of independent promotion; the possibility that *all* recording royalties will be totally absorbed by recoupment of these costs is unfortunately quite real, particularly when one considers that the recording costs, etc., for the follow-up album will undoubtedly be debited to the artist's account before any royalty from the prior album becomes payable. Thus in many cases, the song income is likely to be the largest percentage of a songwriter-artist's earnings.

Most people have one career. I do. But a person who is not only a songwriter, but an artist and a performer as well, has three careers and such a person should not mortgage one for another if he or she can help it. At a minimum, the recording artist–writer–performer should be fully aware of the consequences. As we have seen, there are ways to give, while keeping.

In conclusion, there are a host of reasons why one would want to retain one's copyrights and, in particular, administrating control over them. Irving Berlin was perhaps the first writer who saw the value in doing so. Even though he lost almost all of his savings in the 1929 stock market crash, his continuous earnings from the copyrights he retained kept him and his family solvent and permitted him the peace of mind to continue to be a productive songwriter. While self-publishing is not brain surgery, it has its pitfalls and if you are seriously considering taking on the challenge, you should most definitely make sure that your attorney is equipped to meet the challenges. Self-publishing is not for everyone, but for some, it can be a life-saver.

15 WHEN RODGERS MEETS HAMMERSTEIN: Determining Songwriter Credits

When asked, "Which comes first, the words or the music?" Ira Gershwin responded: "The Contract!"

The songwriter who works alone is rare. Irving Berlin did it. So did Cole Porter. Diane Warren does it. George Gershwin did not; neither did Jerome Kern or Leonard Bernstein; nor do most of the pop songwriters of our day. In fact, sharing authorship is increasingly the norm nowadays as the structure of songs has changed from pure "music and lyrics" to "track, lyrics, melody, and rap." Different people bring different talents to the mix; so does the studio owner, who may create tracks to songs he or she never imagined would be written over them.

CO-WRITING AGREEMENTS

Normally, the arrangement among co-writing songwriters is that of equal partners. A lyricist and a composer write a song together, each counseling the other. They go to a third person who owns a studio and who introduces an arrangement and perhaps a word or two and a riff or two to the song. It has become increasingly fashionable for all three writers to agree to share the authorship, and the copyright, three ways.

Once they agree to do this, they often sign a scrap of paper, register the song in Washington in their three names, and forget about it. (They also contribute in equal parts for the cost of the demo—the hired musicians, singer, etc.—but not the studio, since that is one of the contributions of the third "songwriter.")

But what governs the rights of the three co-writers? Not surprisingly, copyright law. And what are these rights? Very simple. All the co-writers are entitled to equal control over their shared copyright. The copyright in a musical work is like owning a piece of land as a "tenant in common"—the legal jargon for a situation in which, even though, by way of example, three people each own only one-third of the land, each of them can nevertheless walk over the entire property without restriction. No one owns a particular, definable, one-third.

This sounds very fair and balanced. But what this also means is that each co-writer has the right to:

- Issue the highly prized (and protected) first mechanical license—whether to an artist chosen by all three co-writers or to whomever they please.
- Authorize changes in lyrics, title, etc., without the permission of the other co-writers.
- Authorize the use of the song, at whatever price he or she wants, in a commercial or film. Even if one co-writer has rejected, say, a use by Coca-Cola or feels the song should be isolated from commercial identification for a time, or should command a higher fee, another co-writer can circumvent that person's wishes without even telling him or her.

This kind of free-for-all can be avoided by having the co-writers sign a joint songwriter's agreement which deals with all of these contingencies. In other words, the co-writers will modify the general rules of the copyright law which essentially treat all co-writers as tenants in common, sharing identical nonexclusive rights. Upon signing a proper songwriter's agreement, all co-writers will understand precisely what is expected of them and what they may and may not do. For example, it will provide that money received by one writer which is attributable to the song in general will be shared properly by all co-writers and that the money attributable to other co-writers will be held "in trust" by the first co-writer, thereby placing a fiduciary burden on him or her to do the right thing.

Don't think that a verbal understanding among songwriters—or people who believe themselves to be contributing songwriters—is enforceable. The fact is that in most states, a contractual agreement must be in writing to be enforced. Furthermore, under the U.S. Copyright Act, a "transfer" of copyright must be in writing as well. Finally, you should be aware of the fact that a court will not automatically take your word for it that you are or were intended to be deemed a "co-author" or "co-owner" of a song.

Recently, a number of court cases have established that when a song is originally written, in order for a person to claim co-authorship, with all of its attendant privileges, there must have been an intention to do just that—that is, an intention to share in the earnings of the song; an intention to be referred to as a co-writer; and an intention to share artistic control—in short, to be a co-copyright owner.

How is an "intention" most effectively expressed? In writing.

When a song has already been written, the intentionality must be even more pronounced. The writer of the musical *Rent* was sued by his "dramaturge," a person who apparently made considerable, lasting, and perhaps even fundamental additions and changes to the musical play—and to its songs, but *after* the fact—that is, after the work was first written and thus after the copyright vested in the original author. The trial court in the ensuing case held that unless the dramaturge could show—in writing—an absolute intention by the original writer to share authorship, and therefore copyright ownership, with her, her case would be dismissed.

She couldn't and it was.

During the appeals process, the parties settled, so we will never know how this case would have eventually evolved, but the "writing" was on the wall. Without a piece of paper that documents the intention of the parties, the participants in creating a song will not be certain as to their rights and will be susceptible to claims and cross-claims once the song succeeds—which is of course the only time that it matters anyway.

CO-WRITERS WHO ARE BAND MEMBERS

What if two or more co-writers are band members? Now we have a much more complicated situation, where nothing is standard. Often bands have a principal writer or two, and the remainder of the band contributes very little in the way of authorship or assistance during the recording process which ultimately results in a recording of the song.

How do bands compensate the co-writers? And how much should the principal writer or two give up in order to keep peace among the band members? After all, it is not particularly healthy in a community of four or five band members for one to receive signifi-cantly more than the rest of the members. Jealousies are exacerbated and financial inequality makes for even more problems—not just among the band members, but among their spouses as well, who always seem to get involved on behalf of their husbands or wives. Now *that's* trouble! Decisions as to how the band should structure the song owner-ship and authorship are made at the beginning of the band's relationship, when not all of the data about the band, its future, the dynamic of the band members, etc., are in; yet, most often, all of them must live with the decision for better or for worse—and for all time. How have different bands dealt with this issue? In a word, differently.

HOW TO SPLIT THE SPLITS

One band—predominantly an instrumental group—decided that although two of the six members wrote all of the songs, the remaining four should share equally in the publish-er's share, to the extent they were able to retain it (and they were able to retain all of it in this case). Therefore, while a song's authorship might list two names, the publisher's share would be split six ways. The justification? The band members, and specifically the two writers, felt that the other four contributed, if only in the studio, to the sound and arrangement of the songs sufficiently to deserve credit for having established the song's identity for all time. I am not saying that they were thought to have "created" or "authored" the song. In fact, they were explicitly excluded from the writer's credits and the writer's share of royalties. But it would be acknowledged that although the two prin-cipal writers had created the "essence" of the song, on one level it was the result of the combined efforts of all six.

Another band followed the above pattern, but added the following twist. Since so much work had been done arranging the songs in the studio during the recording process, the band as a whole was considered to have contributed authorship to some extent. Therefore, a song by this group would have perhaps three writers: the two princi-pal writers, who might share 80 percent of the writer's share, and a third (fictional) writer who would be entitled to the remaining 20 percent. This latter portion would be shared by all six writers, whose "name" would be a contraction of the band's name. Thus one of the two main writer's share would be 43.33 percent (one-half of 80 percent plus one-sixth of 20 percent) while the share of one of the writers who was *not* a main writer would be 3.33 percent (one-sixth of 20 percent). The songs would be registered with the per-forming rights societies with this authorship breakdown, and all income would be divided accordingly by the band's publishing company and its licensees.

Here are three more possibilities:

- A band has one main writer who shares his retained publishing interest equally with another member of the band who is instrumental in taking care of just about every-thing and who has been with the band since the beginning (unlike all of the other members). But the *writer's share* is his own and is not shared with anyone.
- A band has one main writer who shares her copyright and (possibly) her entire writer's share with one other band member on one or two songs per album to

acknowledge the other band member's musical contribution to arranging all of the songs on the album and for being with her in the studio 100 percent of the time, as opposed to other band members who recorded their tracks and went to the beach.

- Each band member receives his or her appropriate writer's share, but the publisher's share is dealt with as follows: Any band member who does not write a particular song (or any song for that matter) receives 10 percent of the net publisher's or co-publisher's share (i.e., 5 percent of the whole song's earnings) as long as he or she is a member of the band through to the end of a given accounting period. If he or she writes or co-writes a song, he or she receives his or her pro-rata share of the publisher's or co-publisher's share left after the various 10-percenters are paid. Thus, if two members co-write a song equally, they share 50/50 in the writer's share of each dollar earned. And, if there are, say, two other members of the band who did not write that song, they each get 10 percent of the publisher's or co-publisher's share, leaving 80 percent of the publisher's or copublisher's share to split equally between the two main writers.

- The band members all agree in advance that the authorship and the publishing share will be split equally among them. Even if one writer only sets up the loop which "inspires" the rest of the song and the other writer goes home and finishes the song, or one band member writes all the lyrics and the rest contribute the music, everyone is treated the same.

Are there other variations? Sure. A multitude of them. The important thing is that the issues be discussed openly—preferably with the band's manager, business manager, and lawyer—and a consensus arrived at. For as in any partnership (and what is a band if not a partnership?), consensus is the way to go. If the situation ever arises in which a majority outvotes the minority, trouble is not far behind.

Problems can set in when the splits become weird. A client of mine authored one-third of a song and therefore the writer's share was split one-third, one-third, and one-third. The publisher's share was dealt with differently, however: First of all, she split *her* publisher's share with a company whose job it was to obtain a recording of the song (and who succeeded in doing so), so her publisher's share went from one-third to one-sixth. But then, for some reason, she agreed to split her remaining publisher's share even further—but not equally—with another of the co-writers. Somehow or another, she ended up with a one-third writer's share, but 11.89 percent of the publisher's share. That was more or less what she wanted to accomplish, and she stood by her deal with her co-writer.

Subsequently, however, she faced an unanticipated problem.

The performing rights societies in the United States will most likely honor an instruction to pay to a copublisher an odd sum like 11.89 percent. But the performing rights societies outside of the United States do not operate on percentages, but rather on divisions of twelfths: Six-twelfths of the song is deemed to be the author's share and six-twelfths of the song to be the publisher's share.

In this case, the author wrote one-third of the song. The writers as a group were entitled to six-twelfths of the song, so each one, including my client, was entitled to two-twelfths of the writer's share of song earnings.

So far so good. The problem arose with the publisher's share. How could the performing rights societies outside of the United States handle a co-publisher whose interest was 11.89 percent of six-twelfths? Question: How many twelfths does 11.89 percent of 100 percent of the publisher's share equal? Something between one-twelfth and two-twelfths. See what I mean? In fact, this writer had created a nightmare for the performing rights societies around the world. Even if she managed to correctly and successfully register her claim with every performing rights society in the world and convince them to pay her publisher's share correctly, who knows what the other co-writers or their publishers might have done? The publisher's share of six-twelfths (100 percent of the publisher's share) was broken down so that one co-publisher retained 11.89 percent and the remaining co-publishers shared 88.11 percent.

Co-writers should be aware of the fact that the performing rights societies around the world conceive of writer's and publisher's shares of songs in twelfths and designate their respective shares accordingly.

Oh, to add confusion to an already complex issue, the mechanical rights societies around the world do *not* work in terms of twelfths, but in terms of percentages, just as the U.S. mechanical rights societies do. Believe me, the societies around the world will not have the patience to register and pay royalties according to the whims of co-authors in the United States—not least, perhaps, because the United States is currently one of the few territories in which songs are more routinely written via co-writes.

16 COPYRIGHT ISSUES: A Sampler

> To see itself
> through, music
> must have an
> idea or magic.
> The best has
> both. Music with
> neither dies
> young, though
> sometimes rich.
>
> —Ned Rorem

COPYRIGHT INFRINGEMENT

A word about infringing other's songs. Don't. A copyright owner wronged ranks right up there with the proverbial scorned woman as among the most feared adversaries that one can ever have to face. And do not think that your little incursion into other people's private property will not be noticed. It will. The copyright owner will find you out if your song is a hit only in Timbuktu. And the copyright owner will use every tool in the book—national laws, international treaties, even lawyers—to seek recompense for your dastardly act.

Under the copyright act, anyone who violates any of the exclusive rights of the copyright owner or author is an infringer of the copyright or right of the author, as the case may be. Period. The remedies (if you are interested) of a successful copyright owner, or author, are impressive: injunction; minimum damages (in cases in which the author or copyright owner cannot prove the actual financial extent of the damage) of from $750 to $150,000; in many cases costs and attorneys' fees; impoundment and "disposition" of the "infringing articles"; and in some cases, seizure, forfeiture, and imprisonment. Not a pretty picture.

There are two basic types of infringement: plagiarism (i.e., copying another's creation and representing it as one's own) and more traditional violations of copyright such as recording another's song without permission (whether or not with the intention to call it one's own creation), performing another's song on the radio or in a club without the broadcast station or club having obtained permission, or printing and selling copies of another's song without permission. (The Internet has provided new and imaginative ways to accomplish this kind of infringement.) True, many infringements are unintentional, but that does not matter. Nor does it matter if the infringements are unconscious. All that matters is that the two works being compared are *strikingly similar* and that the defendant had *access* to the work of the plaintiff. And let me state right here that the broadly held belief that copying a maximum of eight notes does not constitute infringement is a myth. Nowhere is there any statute or case law that supports this contention.

Access and Substantial Similarity

Access to others' recordings and musical compositions is the key to copyright infringement lawsuits. And, believe me, the intellectual property community—from Disney to Mattel, from music lawyers to Elektra Records—understands this full well.

As you can imagine, millions of tapes and CDs—mostly demos—are mailed or messengered into music companies' offices every year. Most sophisticated companies—record and music publishing companies, law firms, and management firms—take steps

Changing Copyright's Image

Despite the fact that most people would agree that creators of original works should have the right to earn income through the sale of those works, or through fees paid for the use of those works, copyright interests have received a bad rap over the last few decades. For example:

- In 1967, United Artists tried to stop a Community Antenna Television Company (CATV), Fortnightly, from delivering television signals over a mountain to people who could not otherwise receive the station's programs.
- In 1983 and 1984, Universal City Studios tried to keep the Betamax VCR off the shelves.
- In 1999, ASCAP was perceived as trying to stop Girl Scout camps from performing copyrighted music around their campfires.
- In 2000, A&M was the lead plaintiff in the recording industry's successful effort to stop Napster in its tracks, a move that many, especially teenagers, perceived as an undeserved victory by the establishment over our basic rights to listen to music via the Internet.

What can copyright interests do to improve their image? One answer is to educate young people so that along with learning about music, and how to create enduring music, they also learn how important it is that the music be protected. The Copyright Society of the United States of America (www.CSUAS.org) has set up, as part of its FACE (Friends of Active Copyright Education) program, a new section of its website called Copyright Kids (www.law.duke.edu/copyright). The basic message is that the copyright laws of the United States and of other countries are necessary and, basically, fair: they protect creators' (including the kids') works; they protect the music and literature that the kids love; and they encourage creation.

Copyright Kids is aimed at junior high school-aged children and older. It teaches copyright basics and registration procedures. It provides sample permission letters for school kids to request authorization to reprint, say, lyrics, in a yearbook, or to use recorded music in a video yearbook. Schools welcome this education aid, and some teachers use the tools offered by these sites to assist their students, individually or as a group, to create a work and to register it.

to insure that they cannot successfully be sued for copyright infringement when a product is released that may (or may not) bear some resemblance to the unsolicited material. These companies routinely choose to not open—and in fact, immediately return to sender—the material they receive which has the appearance of including an unsolicited tape or CD, or which comes from a person or company with whom they are not familiar. Recent court cases have bolstered these companies' confidence in that they have held that unsolicited materials received by these companies do not constitute such "constructive corporate receipt" as to render them liable if it turns out that something they are subsequently involved with "sounds like" the product that was sent to them without their acquiescence. (We shall have to wait to see whether unsolicited MP3 files sent via e-mail to these same companies will be regarded in the same way by the courts.)

It is, of course, quite within the range of possibility that a musical work substantially similar to or even identical to another work can be the result of independent creation. A finding of "access" is a damaging, although not necessarily fatal, blow to the defendant in a situation like this just as a finding of lack of access may not deal a fatal blow to the plaintiff. Substantial similarity in and of itself might give rise to an inference that there was access to the plaintiff's work. But, in the lingo of the Federal District Courts, the courts now require "significant, affirmative, and probative evidence" of access and it no longer appears that the mere sending of a demo to the defendant's record company will fulfill this test.

Yet, whenever one gets into a courtroom—and ends up staying a while—anything is possible. The Isley Brothers' claim against Michael Bolton and his song "Love Is A Wonderful Thing" regarding the claimed infringement of their song of the same title survived the District Court and Appellate Court and was, in effect, upheld by the U.S. Supreme Court when it declined to consider the case on appeal—even though there was no proof whatsoever that Mr. Bolton ever heard the plaintiff's song and even though the songs of the two litigants were not really so similar after all.

Five million dollars in judgments and lots of legal fees later and you can begin to appreciate the paranoia that is rampant among music business companies when it comes to opening that envelope that looks so enticing. OK, it is not so enticing to those of us who receive loads of them, but sometimes the package gets through (perhaps a temporary secretary is opening the mail, or there is a particularly inviting cover).

An earlier Michael Bolton case involving "How Am I Supposed To Live Without You?" had a more favorable result for Bolton. Even though the plaintiff said that he had recorded a demo of his musical work featuring the very artist that Atlantic Records used to make the song a worldwide hit, Laura Branigan, the court held that the lack of substantial similarity in itself was enough to negate the plaintiff's claim. But the proof of access in that case must have taken the breath away from Mr. Bolton's litigator.

Then there was the claim against Ric Ocasek of The Cars in which the plaintiff had sent his "substantially similar" song in demo form to the very A&R person who acted on behalf of The Cars for its record company, Elektra Records, a full year before The Cars' version was released and became a hit. Curious timing, one would think. But this particular plaintiff's argument had a problem—one that was fatal to his case. The Cars and their principal writer were able to prove that their song was actually written *and* recorded two years *before* the plaintiff's song was sent to The Cars' record company! Luckily they had saved the tape and it was computer-dated! The plaintiffs slinked away from this one.

Fair Use

Be very skeptical concerning what you hear about "fair use"—use of copyrighted material that is not considered infringement. The rules covering fair use are contained in Section 107 of the Copyright Act of 1976, which states:

> The fair use of a copyright work. . . for purposes such as criticism, comment, news reporting, teaching . . . , scholarship, or research, is not an infringement of copyright. In determining whether the use made of a work in any particular case is a fair use the factors to be considered shall include:
>
> - The purpose and character of the use, including whether such use is of a commercial nature or is for nonprofit educational purposes;
> - The nature of the copyrighted work;
> - The amount and substantiality of the portion used in relation to the copyrighted work as a whole; and
> - The effect of the use upon the potential market for or value of the copyrighted work.

The fair use provisions in the Copyright Act merely create a framework for identifying when and under what conditions copying will be allowed. It does not excuse infringements which fall outside of the guidelines.

In considering your rights under the statutory provision regarding fair use, you should note several things: First, as you can imagine, the phrase "shall include" invites a great deal of interpretation in each particular case. Second, even the most highly respected copyright law experts cannot tell you in any particular case what a court might conclude in applying the provisions of Section 107 to that case. Third, as a rule of thumb, if you are thinking of using a copyrighted work for what you think is a good cause and according to what you think should be permitted under this section, if there is any commercial gain whatsoever to you or to the people to whom you are thinking of offering your services, the odds are that the use will be prohibited and all of the hefty infringement remedies of the Copyright Act will come bearing down. And, as I noted previously, there is nothing that says it is OK to "borrow" a limited number of notes or bars from a musical composition.

Similarly, recent cases have suggested that unless your creation "transforms" the one you are "borrowing" from, it will not constitute fair use. What is transformation? Legal pundits call it a Humpty Dumpty word. It means what a judge says it means. Basically, it means changing the original, borrowed, work into a new mode of being. This kind of change is not likely in a song context unless the new work is a parody—that is, a lampoon or a spoof.

Finally, if you are thinking of copying someone else's work and are prepared to argue a defense of fair use, do not think that setting up a corporation will protect you. Under the Copyright Act, the officers of a corporation that commits the infringement cannot hide behind the corporate protection of limited liability. The officers of the corporation are as culpable as the corporation itself.

SAMPLING

Sampling—deliberately inserting some of the notes or bars from an existing recording into a new recording—is subject to the same infringement criteria as any kind of borrowing. When technological advances put sampling within the reach of even novice record producers, many thought that this kind of copying was of no particular significance—that using a loop from an old song was even a compliment to the original songwriter or songwriter-recording artist. Then one day, a Federal District Court judge in New York was asked to look into a situation of "sampling" from the point of view of the person whose song was "borrowed." Was it fair use? Was it *de minimus* (i.e., really of no particular significance)? In the first sampling case, which was decided in 1991, Judge Kevin Duffy, a highly regarded federal judge whose understanding and perceptions of the copyright law are legendary, needed only five words to answer that question for all time: "Looks like stealing to me." And that was that. Sampling is *not* fair use. It is theft.

Sampling is not limited to sound recordings, or to audio alone. An example of both is the sampling of a portion of a motion picture: not only are the motion picture company's rights being compromised, but those of the actors as well. Sampling a moment, or a phrase, from *Casablanca* can pit the sampler against not only Warner Bros. Pictures, but against the estates of Humphrey Bogart and Ingrid Bergman as well. Let alone Sydney Greenstreet, Claude Rains, or Peter Lorre. If you think the George Clintons, the Average White Bands, and other musicians whose music is frequently sampled are insistent, wait until you meet the heirs of Paul Henreid and Conrad Veidt!

Infringement Insurance

I do not know of a successful artist who has avoided a claim of copyright infringement being instituted against him. From George Harrison to Paul Simon, it is just one more risk of being in the music business—and a costly one at that. But writers can obtain insurance against infringement. That's right. There is a certain logic to this in view of the fact that unintentional and unconscious acts are as actionable as intentional and conscious ones. (So-called "willful" acts—usually infringements after warnings are communicated to the eventual defendant—will usually incur higher damages however. But willful acts are not usually the result of plagiarism but of the other kind of infringements noted at the beginning of this chapter—recording or performing another's song without permission.) This insurance (known as errors and omissions, or "E&O," policies) covers "honest" mistakes. It is fairly expensive, but definitely worth considering. Sometimes the administrating publisher will agree to share in the cost or add the writer to its own E&O policy (another reason to engage a publisher). Most of the standard E&O policies are issued by insurance companies in the ordinary course of business to protect against an occasional lapse in the due diligence process in producing television programs or motion pictures, and do not really fit the need here. I advise my clients as a matter of course to obtain plagiarism insurance, which has come in handy more often than you can imagine. Instead of simply signing off on a standard form of E&O policy, however, the artist-songwriter's lawyer and business manager should read the document, consider the wording carefully, and, if necessary, rewrite it where appropriate to fit the need it is supposed to serve.

Specifically, the "covered acts" are not defined specifically enough to meet the needs of the songwriter or artist-songwriter, so the traditional E&O language is obsolete when it comes to the kind of coverage songwriters need. Exposure to liability is couched in terms of "products" instead of songs and some policies actually *exclude* intellectual property such as copyrights. In that case, all the money spent on premiums has been spent on insuring against the wrong kind of injuries. Coverage should extend not just to recorded songs, but to all creations that are musical compositions, or parts of musical compositions, to which the creator can establish the existence of as of a certain date and time. This can be accomplished via computer-dated demo recordings or copyright registrations or even by mailing tapes to oneself by registered mail, return receipt requested, with the title(s) of the work(s) on the front of the envelope. Rather than mount a full-bodied assault on the contract language, which will be strenuously resisted by the insurance agent and company, it is better to modify a standard E&O policy binder by simply expanding the definition of covered products.

REALPOLITIK: THE IMPACT OF THE INTERNET ON RECORDING AND PUBLISHING AGREEMENTS

Technical solutions to distributing music via the Internet have been found. Pressplay and Musicnet, for example, as well as numerous other portals offering authorized recorded music, are currently in operation. Now it is in the hands of the music rights owners to find a way to put them to effective e-commerce use. One of the reasons Napster and its progeny were so popular is that there is obviously a great demand for one-source and one-stop shopping. Now all that has to be figured out is how to supply that demand in a cost-effective and efficient way. What else is new?

There are numerous implications of the total absence of a standard with respect to how and to what extent the digital download is dealt with in recording and music publishing agreements: We have already discussed royalty escalations in Chapter 4. In addition, there is considerable indecision with respect to this most important consideration: the location of the download. Depending on where the act of use takes place, different rules and laws may apply and different parties will claim an interest in licensing (or refusing to license) the use and collecting the money generated by the use.

Digital downloads occur *somewhere*. We are not always sure where, but the location of the content provider seems to be the location of choice. Of course private agreement may not survive legislation in the many parts of the world that are beginning to discover that they are themselves "players" in the international entertainment complex. (For example, if the United States or other countries eventually tax downloads, why not place one's server in Guyana, where the tax may be less or nonexistent?) The European Community is already recommending a sales tax on all online purchases. The United States is resisting it.

Some lawyers have thrown up their hands in the course of negotiating recording and publishing agreements precisely due to the fact that there are no standards—let alone global standards—established for determining where a digital transfer to a user occurs. Ordinarily, when negotiators either compromise on a point, or decide it is not worth arguing, they understand the implications of what they are doing. In this case, however, no one can even imagine the consequences of failing to get it right; and no one even knows what getting it right means.

Where indecision abounds, rather than try to solve the issue with the record company's lawyers, the artist's lawyer or manager, in understandable frustration, will often view all things that are not negotiable, or not immediately capable of solution, in terms of money. Increase the advance and we'll drop the subject, they will say. But in the end, the artist will indeed pay for the lack of precision in the negotiation and for the lack of clarity in achieving an understanding as to where a digital download occurs. Writers and publishers will also suffer as a result of this lack of precision.

There are innumerable issues inspired by the fast-paced technological changes occurring in the digital world: 1's and 0's have never been so complicated. Here are a few of those that must be considered in attempting to wedge new ideas into traditional structures:

- Are digital phonorecord deliveries (DPDs) to be treated the same as direct mail with its attendant lower royalty rate? Are Internet transfers to be dealt with differently if they constitute digital downloads or simple Internet e-commerce sales via Amazon.com or CDNow.com? Is one in the nature of direct mail and the other not? Even if the price is the same as retail prices in record stores, should there be a increase in the royalty rate since there is no packaging as such?
- A digital download is different from a hard copy because transfer via the Internet does not involve the manufacturing and distribution process, as the sale of a hard copy does. Does a record company satisfy its release commitment obligation by offering DPDs?
- Where royalties are reduced until such time as a change of policy occurs at the record label, is the royalty rate change to be retroactive? Is the new rate to apply to United States sales only or worldwide?
- Are coupling restrictions a thing of the past? What do you do where they still exist?
- If single tracks are offered via digital download (as seems to be a preferred product of today's Internet consumers), what happens to the A-side protection of the producer when the A track will surely be coupled with a track that he or she has not produced?
- Is every digital download a DPD?
- Is a DPD an ephemeral copy, or is it a real copy, worthy of generating a mechanical royalty?

The Internet Right Model

In view of the difficulties being experienced by companies that wish to clear music rights for their websites, and for other exploitations, and that are at the same time expected to comply with a myriad of laws, several concerned industry lawyers and executives (as well as—uh-oh—members of Congress) have recommended that there be established an *Internet right*—essentially combining (or neutralizing) the various rights that are being exercised when a piece of music is dancing around in cyberspace.

This right would combine the transmission, distribution, and performance rights; it would supersede the synchronization right, the mechanical reproduction right, and the performance right solely for the Internet use. There is naturally a lot of resistance to this idea because, among other things, the various entities that might own the separate rights would have to determine who owns, controls, and administers the combined right. In addition, the wording of the original rights grants by the writers to the publishers is not likely to have addressed the issue of the Internet right. There are two possibilities with regard to an Internet right. One is that courts would have to "discover" it among the "bundle" of rights within copyright. If such a new right were "discovered," publishers and record companies would require new assignments from writers, artists, or their heirs—a virtual nightmare. The other is that the Internet right would have to be established solely by legislative means; that is, it would be a statutory right. This most likely would take the form of a compulsory license—something that is disliked intensely by virtually all copyright owners, who feel they are in a better position to put a value on a specific use and charge appropriately for it in each specific circumstance, rather than be told that all uses and all content are essentially equal and should either be licensed for the same fee, or licensed according to a limited selection of predetermined fees.

Currently, ease of distribution and access to music via the Internet is virtually impossible to achieve. For example: let us say you want to webcast a live event and to preserve the event for other forms of exploitation in the future. At a minimum, you will have to clear the following 10 rights (for each song and for each master—that's already 20, and it's just a beginning) *before* the webcast takes place:

- Webcast itself—both performance and mechanical rights
- Pay per view simultaneous with the webcast
- Pay per view after the webcast
- Television special derived from the webcast
- Edited television specials of indeterminate number for different countries (for example, Europe; North America; Asia; South America)
- CD release of the soundtrack of the webcast
- Videocassette/videodisc/DVD of the webcast
- Videocassette/videodisc/DVD of the various television specials
- In-store displays via looped minutes of the webcast—worldwide
- Actual television commercials using footage from the webcast

The above list is not comprehensive, but includes the most important uses. Did I forget to mention that most songs nowadays are written by more than one person and that each person has his or her own publishing company? And that each of these publishing companies commonly shares responsibilities and income with another? And that even the master rights are often controlled by more than one party? So, the 20 clearances—per song/master—can easily multiply to 40 or more transactions.

COMPULSORY OR NEGOTIATED LICENSES

The original compulsory license—the mechanical reproduction license discussed at some length in Chapter 13—has taken on new significance because record companies have taken the position that digital phonorecord deliveries via the Internet are no different from standard mechanical reproductions on traditional audio formats such as LPs, audio cassettes, and CDs. Music publishers, of course, feel that these uses are not within the authority of the Copyright Office or within the definition of the traditional compulsory mechanical license. Meanwhile, Congress is quite impatient and wants to create what may be a long-lasting "interim" safe harbor via a new form of statutory license designed precisely for the new digital media services which desire to use music. Naturally, copyright interests are quite apprehensive about this possibility.

THE FAIRNESS IN MUSIC LICENSING ACT

For as long as people and companies have had to pay for the right to publicly perform music for profit, there have been attempts by the users to chip away at both the amount of the cost and the obligation to pay. The latest attempt resulted in the passage by Congress of an amendment to Section 110 of the Copyright Act. This provision, the Fairness in Music Licensing Act of 1998, exempts an enormous number of users of music, including restaurant owners, from the obligation of having to obtain licenses to perform (play) music. The name of the act belies its intentions. Writers and publishers see nothing fair in this new law, nor do our trading partners around the world, most of whom are signatories to international treaties which provide for the payment of license fees for the very uses exempted by the U.S. act.

The ostensible purpose of this act was to protect Mom and Pop stores from having to dig deep into their pockets to pay for the use of music in their restaurants. Of course, the copyright interests' position is that people pay for electricity, heat, interior decorators, and decoration, all of which create ambience for restaurant owners, and that music provides a similar "bottom-line" value. Indeed, if it has no value, why fight so hard to use it? It became apparent to everyone that the self-righteousness expressed by the proponents of "Fairness in Music Licensing" was a smokescreen for the simple desire to save money, and some of the exemptions the original drafters of the legislation wanted to include did not find their way into the act as passed.

Passage of the Fairness in Music Licensing Act has already had serious financial consequences for writers, publishers, record companies, and artists in the United States. Given the fact that over 50 percent of the world's music performance and mechanical fees income is from U.S. creations, a phenomenal amount of income that would have otherwise flowed into the United States has been, and will continue to be, lost because countries whose laws are diametrically opposed to the U.S. "fairness" statute will not apply those laws to U.S. authors' works.

THE COPYRIGHT TERM EXTENSION ACT IN JEOPARDY

As part of a quid pro quo in the world of Congressional compromise and intrigue, many procopyright interests (particularly those representing music catalogues that were fast racing toward expiration of copyright protection—such as the big-time Broadway writers and their heirs, the Gershwins, Rodgers and Hammerstein, Cole Porter, Irving Berlin, and Leonard Bernstein—as well as the Walt Disney Company, which was concerned that early Mickey Mouse drawings would become part of the public domain) looked the other way when the Fairness in Music Licensing Act (FMLA) was passed so that the Copyright Term Extension Act of 1998 (widely known as the Sonny Bono Copyright Term Extension Act), would also make it through Congress. The Sonny Bono extension was duly passed, extending the term of copyright protection from 50 years after the death of the last artist or author of a work to 70 years. Most observers of this trade-off thought the FMLA would eventually be voided, but the copyright extension would stand.

The opposite has happened. In fact, anticopyright interests are aggregating their bullets and hoarding them for the next receptive Congress, hoping to restore some of the initiatives that did not find their way into the FMLA as enacted. And in February 2002 the Supreme Court agreed to review earlier federal court decisions which upheld the 20-year extension and which at the same time rejected the contention that the extra 20 years of protection afforded by the Term Extension Act violate the intent of the original copyright clause in the U.S. Constitution. That intent, the argument went, was to balance two needs: the need to promote "science and the useful arts" by protecting the works of creators from unauthorized use and the right of the public to have free access to those works by issuing copyrights for "limited times" *only.* Significantly, another argument presented by the antiextension plaintiffs was that Internet entrepreneurs are hamstrung by the necessity of having to identify, locate, and pay for rights that they feel should be freely available to all. Now the Supreme Court will take another look at those arguments.

Sonny Bono would not be pleased.

MP3: HOW TWO LETTERS AND A NUMERAL TERRORIZED AN ENTIRE INDUSTRY

As most people living in our society know by now, a number of companies have figured out how to compress musical sounds (i.e., entire recordings) and to transmit them over a relatively narrow bandwidth to consumers who acquire them via the Internet, transpose them back into sound, and go their merry way enjoying the music they have downloaded. As most people also know, the ease by which this methodology works has caught the fascination of millions of people across the globe. You have read enough, in this book and elsewhere, to understand the enormous threat that such processes present to the recording industry, which, one must not forget, includes the artists and songwriters whose art is virtually exclusively expressed in the audio tracks themselves.

MP3.com, Inc. is a publicly held company which operates a commercial Internet site at www.mp3.com. MP3 is a free technology protocol, developed by the Moving Picture Expert Group, that enables a user to convert the large ".WAV" files contained on ordinary music CDs into files that are 10 to 12 times smaller than the original .WAV files. Since MP3 files consume considerably less computer storage space than .WAV files, they can be transferred much faster and have accordingly become the preferred modality for moving audio files through the Internet and among computers (the latter being the catalyst for Napster-type exchanges among users). Utilizing its compression technology, MP3.com launched its "My.MP3.com" service, which is advertised as permitting subscribers to store, customize, and listen to the recordings contained on their CDs from any place where they have an Internet connection.

MP3 has not been greedy. Unlike Sony and its Betamax, or Apple and its Macintosh, MP3 has generously allowed its conversion software to be made available for free in order for consumers to create MP3 files, with Microsoft, RealNetworks, and others providing the conduit for such availability.

It should also be noted that MP3.com did not simply offer to the public at large an enormous supply of free musical recordings. Through its Instant Listening Service and Beam-it programs (affectionately referred to at MP3.com's home office as "Da Bomb"), it allows a music consumer to listen to songs found on CDs, with the proviso that it will release its digital versions of music tracks *only* to those users who themselves have purchased, or *who are in possession of,* the applicable CD and who can confirm that they have done so, *or are in such possession.* In the main MP3 infringement case, *RIAA v. MP3.com,* attorneys for MP3.com, Inc., argued that the company's original copying of the music did not constitute copyright infringement; rather, the consumers who did *not* meet the "in possession of" criteria were the guilty parties. In the end, the district court did not buy that argument, and ruled that MP3.com, Inc. willfully infringed the plaintiffs' copyrights by unauthorized copying for commercial purposes.

NAPSTER: A SEVEN-LETTER WORD FOR REVOLUTION

What is Napster? This is the well-publicized software created by a then 19-year-old which permits multiple (read: upwards of 80 million) Internet users to access each others' collections of MP3 files for free. As is clear by now, most of these MP3 files have not been licensed and accordingly the users have been shown the way to wholesale infringement. No one gets paid: neither the record companies, nor the artists, nor the union pension and welfare and health funds, nor the record producers, nor the mixers, nor the songwriters, nor the music publishers.

Napster's defenders feel that a system which permits users to trade songs does not in itself constitute piracy. In the sort of elegant fashion of lawyer-speak, the Napster defendants refer to the stealing as "the use of peer-to-peer technology." In an interview with *Wired* magazine, David Boies, the attorney for former Vice President Al Gore in his Florida vote challenge days, and also for Napster in the defense of the lawsuit brought by the recording industry, stated: "Here you have a new technology—in terms of peer-to-peer sharing of information—and if that technology is going to work, you must allow people to provide central indexes of the data. Somebody's got to maintain those indexes. I mean, it's just like a newspaper that publishes classified ads. You've got to have a place where people can go who want to participate in that kind of activity. And if you, in effect, impose on the directory-service provider liability to investigate, monitor, and control what the users are doing, it is very difficult to see how that kind of technology is ever going to work."

One of the arguments mounted by Napster's attorneys was that Napster was entitled to protection under the Digital Millennium Copyright Act (DMCA), which sought to protect Internet Service Providers (ISPs) from liability for the illegal acts of its users by creating "safe harbors" to the effect that the ISPs would not be liable themselves for failing to control the environment they establish for their users. There are two legal concepts that the DMCA sought to mute by the safe harbor provisions §512 (c) and (d): *vicarious liability* and *contributory liability.* Under the doctrine of vicarious liability, if a person or company has the right and ability to control infringing activity and receives a direct financial benefit from it, such party may be held liable as if he had performed the infringing act directly. The doctrine of contributory infringement also imposes liability on parties that have knowledge of, and induce, cause, or materially contribute to an infringement. Although the courts decided that Napster was *not* entitled to DMCA protection, many copyright attorneys feel that Napster is indeed an ISP and, furthermore, that what consumers do when they copy music provided via Napster is the same as copying using home cassette recorders and CD burners.

The plaintiffs (A&M Records et al., plus Mike Stoller Music and Frank Music Corp.) argued that Napster was not so innocent because its sole reason for being results in the taking of others' property and, as the court held, the Napster system necessarily harms the copyright holders' attempts to charge for "the download market." The court agreed. (The Napster principals also said they did not have the technology to "block" the sharing of copyrighted musical works, which, only when they were about to be shut down, they later acknowledged that they indeed did have all along.)

AFTER NAPSTER: EXIT THE CENTRAL SERVER

In the fall of 2001, the big guns of the recording industry, having at least temporarily stopped Napster, were trained on the U.S.A.'s Music City Networks' Morpheus and Grokster Ltd., a West Indies–based firm. Both base their music sites on KaZaa, a program developed by the Amsterdam company FastTrack, which does not rely on computers operating through a central clearinghouse, as Napster does. They are file-sharing networks which allow users to search the network of users for those with the most powerful computers, or those with fast modems such as DSL or cable modems. The large, worldwide network of other computers, for the time they are being captured, become a search hub, or "supernode," that other users can utilize in order to search the rest of the network—and do multiple transfers, one at a time, from other users. In effect, Morpheus users are "borrowing" the power of others' computers to complete their own private tasks. Sounds like something extraworldly (and maybe it is).

Ironically, the architecture of these programs means that the companies that offer them might not even have to argue that they qualify for DMCA protection insulating them from claims of vicarious or contributory liability because unlike Napster, they have absolutely no means to suspend users and therefore cannot possibly be expected to control those users. If they cannot control users, they cannot be held liable even if they have notice of their infringing activities.

A larger social policy issue here involves the conflict between making commercial products available to all at reasonable prices and at the same time respecting the creative and financial investment of those individuals who bring the property to fruition in the first place. For example, it costs just pennies to manufacture numerous brand-name drugs sold by major pharmaceutical companies, but the R&D investment required to both create the first of the pills and put them through development and testing, as well as go though the Food and Drug Administration approval processes in each country, can cost hundreds of millions of dollars. How do you suppose the pharmaceutical industry would respond to the idea that peer-to-peer sharing is a citizen's right?

Currently, the copyright interests, in association with or at least in the same ballpark as, the technology industry, are trying to develop a business model for the MP3 delivery via a Napster-style software that will permit peer-to-peer sharing but at the same time protect the artists and copyright owners.

What of the future? New and powerful partnerships are developing that will force copyright issues onto the public stage for courts, legislatures, and, ultimately, the people themselves to resolve. There is an ebb and flow of political sensibilities toward, on one side, copyright protection, and, on the other, the right of the public to have free and easy access to public domain material. As this book goes to press, the tide of opinion seems to have swung toward anticopyright interests, with the clearest evidence of this being the survival of the Fairness in Music Licensing Act and the Supreme Court's astonishing decision to review the Sonny Bono Term Extension Act.

Yet the winter of 2002 saw an extraordinary conference in Washington sponsored by The Future of Music Coalition. The Future of Music Coalition identifies itself as a not-for-profit collaboration among members of the music, technology, public policy, and intellectual property law communities which "seeks to educate the media, policymakers, and the public about music/technology issues, while also bringing together diverse voices in an effort to come up with creative solutions to some of the challenges in this space. The FMC also aims to identify and promote innovative business models that will help musicians and citizens to benefit from new technologies."

Though the FMC can be labeled as a largely anti–record industry lobbying organization, it is at the same time a visible sign of a future during which copyright interests will find themselves under a barrage of unprecedented attacks.

17

COMPLIANCE WITH COPYRIGHT LAWS IN THE WORLD OF CYBERSPACE: Hints for the Corporate Counsel

Internet companies cannot commit treason, nor be outlawed, nor be excommunicated, for they have no souls. But they can be sued for copyright infringement.

—Me, after Edward Coke

Most corporations, their management, and their corporate counsels, have never been obliged to comprehend or to process music rights. Certainly some companies, both large and small, have crossed paths with performing rights societies when they have utilized music on their telephone "hold" buttons, or when they have used music in a fairly sophisticated manner at store openings, holiday parties, etc. But few of these companies had any idea what they would be getting into when they took their trademarks and products into cyberspace.

Some of what I am about to discuss has been mentioned before in other chapters. However, for those who may selectively choose chapters to read, and in particular, for those who counsel corporations (whether as in-house counsel or as outside counsel) and may not be as interested in some of the other portions of this book, a brief review of the legal underpinnings of music copyright is in order, highlighting what facts must be reckoned with and what myths need to be debunked.

INTANGIBLE RIGHTS AND THE INTERNET

Music rights do not exist in tangible form. You can't touch them; you can't put them on a table; you can't pour anything into them. Music rights are an idea—a concept. Most of the manmade items that the world has valued since time immemorial are the tangible assets created by the hard work of people: everything from buildings to automobiles, from farm products to steak, from electronics to furniture.

Actually, as we have seen, a copyright is an accumulation of intangible rights. The bundle of rights that makes up a copyright consists of an indeterminate number of rights—long-established ones (e.g., print rights, recording rights, performing rights, and synchronization rights [the recording of sound together with visual images]), and the "new" rights that seemingly emerge with each passing decade. Of course, many of the manifestations of intangible rights are real: sheet music, scores, CDs, etc. But the rights that allowed these manifestations to be created are nevertheless intangible. Got it?

It is the first decade of the twenty-first century and we are faced with an entirely new mother lode of rights: Some we are just learning about, such as digital download rights, webcast rights and streaming (sometimes called Internet radio) rights. As discussed in the previous chapter, maybe there is even an "Internet right" that will be discovered to exist within the protective coating that copyright provides for the expression of ideas!

The federal copyright law (Title 17, United States Code), does not entirely distinguish among many of these rights; nor does it make much of an effort to catalogue them. It prefers the bundle to be flexible—evolving. The problem this presents to those who own music and those who use music is that they are forced to squeeze newly discovered rights into old definitions. Thus a webcast is a performance (and, to some, a mechanical reproduction as well); a download is a mechanical reproduction (and, to some, a performance as well); streaming is . . . maybe both a performance and a mechanical reproduction? Are those webcasts, downloads, or streams which are accompanied by visual images synchronizations? When confronted with such questions, rights owners have universally concluded that the answer is always "yes." That the rights owners are unsure as to exactly why they answer in the affirmative does not weaken their resolve that, yes, webcasts, downloads, and streaming each require at least the permission of the song copyright owner and probably the sound recording copyright owner as well.

This period of expansion and accompanying uncertainty is not the first time rights owners and users of music have had to face anomalies such as these. When the video-cassette was first introduced in the late 1970s and early 1980s, it was unclear whether the reproduction of a song on the videocassette was a mechanical reproduction (for which copyright law provides certain privileges and responsibilities) or a synchronization (for which copyright law provides mostly responsibilities). The question has really never been answered—except by virtue of the fact that the entertainment industry (film and music divisions in particular) has decided to consider these reproductions to be synchronizations so that the original license fee for the use of a song in a movie, for example, covers all subsequent reproductions on videocassettes, discs, and DVDs (together called *videograms*).

So we have law achieved by consensus. Is the same type of law-without-legislation taking place now in the world of the Internet? It seems so. Digital downloads, webcasts, and streaming uncover rights that the copyright owners *decide* exist. Perhaps this is payback time for what the rights users did to the rights owners in the videogram area. Of course, until these issues are litigated, legislated, or arbitrated, the question as to what rights exist and who owns or controls them will not be resolved definitively.

LICENSING FROM MUSIC PUBLISHERS
AND SOUND RECORDING OWNERS

Nothing in the law establishes a legal definition of music publisher. This is totally a creation of the music industry and it has served it well over the years. Authors' rights are dealt with in the writers' contract with the publisher. Of course, since this relationship is not legislated, room for bargaining exists, so each writer's relationship with his or her publisher is unique.

The administration of songs can be quite complex, and large publishing companies have developed over the years to take the administration responsibilities out of the hands of the smaller publishers and writers. Therefore it is most often these music publishers with whom rights users have to deal in order to obtain permission for the use of musical compositions. Insofar as performing rights are concerned, music publishers have bundled their rights and placed the responsibility to license such rights into the hands of monopolies, the two largest of which are ASCAP and BMI. These two entities, together with SESAC, control the performing rights to almost all of the musical compositions in the world. Their own "catalogues" are comprised of U.S. authors' songs and they share the representation of the remainder of the world's music. For all practical purposes, these organizations are obliged to give licenses to anyone who requests them. The rates, however, are different for each organization, since their negotiating strengths differ, in part because of the difference in number and quality of their music catalogues.

Since the performing rights societies in the United States are not permitted to control their rights exclusively, they differ significantly from their affiliates in other countries in that those who seek performing rights can go directly to the source in the United States because the original copyright owners retain the right to license performing rights directly. Notwithstanding the hybrid nature of the American societies (that is, while they act as monopolies, the rights they have acquired from the music publishers are nonexclusive), they are still considered by the U.S. government dangerous aggregators of the performing rights in essentially 100 percent of the world's music. In particular, ASCAP and BMI are controlled quite closely by the Justice Department and operate under consent decrees that are regularly reviewed.

Under certain circumstances, performing rights must be obtained for sound recordings as well. Specifically, rights must be obtained for sound recordings created since 1995 (the year in which the Digital Performance Right in Sound Recordings Act [DPRSRA] was passed), and copying of sound recordings created after 1972 is also subject to a plethora of protections which must be dealt with. The Recording Industry Association of America (RIAA)—through its Sound Exchange Division—has begun to assume the responsibility toward the licensing of the performing rights in sound recordings that ASCAP, BMI, and SESAC have assumed with respect to musical compositions.

Clearance of the mechanical reproduction and synchronization rights to most, but not all, songs (but not with respect to rights to reproduce sound recordings) can be obtained through the Harry Fox Agency, Inc., or through its principals, the music publishers, most of whom are members of the National Music Publishers Association. As with the U.S. performing rights societies, the Harry Fox Agency, Inc., acts, in the United States, on behalf of the mechanical rights societies around the world that control equivalent rights.

With the exception of certain qualifying users of music who can obtain a statutory license automatically from the government to webcast or otherwise provide noninteractive digital audio services, the clearance of the rights to mechanically reproduce sound recordings must be obtained from the sound recording copyright owner. This is usually one of the five major entertainment conglomerates (Universal, BMG, Sony, AOL Time Warner, and EMI), innumerable labels distributed by them, and yet even more "independent" record labels that are nearly impossible to quantify or, in many cases, to identify and locate.

One result of the many mergers that have recently taken place (for example, MCA with Polygram and A&M, forming Universal; Geffen and Interscope with Universal; Virgin and Chrysalis with EMI) has been huge staff cutbacks, so that companies that have doubled and tripled their catalogues have to get by on the administration side with the same size staff that they started with prior to the mergers. (A similar diminution of the combined staffs of Warner Music Publishing Company and Chappell Music Corporation occurred when Warner bought Chappell, forming Warner/Chappell Music Publishing Company.) Clearance procedures that were always a nightmare in the past are now even more difficult to negotiate, particularly within a time frame that is commercially practical.

COPYRIGHT LAW PROVISIONS APPLICABLE TO THE INTERNET

Anyone who utilizes music on the Internet as part of a website must make a "copy" of that music (both song and sound recording) merely to make the music available online. These "copies" are only a means to the end—an end which will generate mechanical and performance royalties to copyright owners. Respecting this fact of physical science, the copyright law now includes a provision (Section 112) which permits *some* people to make these copies without responsibility or liability to copyright owners. The Copyright Act refers to these copies as "ephemeral"—or incidental—recordings. As is typical in Congressional attempts at legislating in the area of the Internet, there is a laundry list of limitations and exceptions in Section 112 which *exempt* persons who utilize music on the Internet from the necessity of seeking permission from copyright owners. These exemptions are analogous to those in Section 114 which exempt certain transmissions and retransmissions of music from claims of copyright infringement by copyright owners. In the one case, however, the law helps users of music and then limits the help and in the other case, the law helps copyright owners and then limits their remedies. Anyone who has to deal with this area should certainly seek out expert counsel. Just to give you an example of how incomprehensible the law can be, here is one sentence from a Congressional "explanation" of Section 114:

> *Among those limitations is an exemption for non-subscription broadcast transmissions, which are defined as those made by terrestrial broadcast stations licensed as such by the FCC. 17 U.S.C. 114(d)(1)(A)(iii) and (j)(2). The ephemeral recording exemption presently privileges certain activities of a transmitting organization when it is entitled to transmit a performance or display under a license or transfer of copyright ownership or under the limitations on exclusive rights in sound recordings specified by section 114(a). . . .*

Who says lawyers don't earn their fees?

David Nimmer, the highly respected copyright law expert, recently wrote an article in the *UCLA Entertainment Law Review*, preparatory to including it in his (and his father's) invaluable treatise "Nimmer on Copyright." It was entitled, "Ignoring the Public, Part I: On the Absurd Complexity of the Digital Audio Transmission Right."

Enough said?

Actually, not. In the world of copyright exploitation, one's truly innocent behavior can have dire consequences. This law can actually have the effect of freezing the development of the Internet. Innocence is no defense. So be careful.

The Government to the Rescue: Statutory Licenses

As noted above, the statutory license available to users of certain sound recordings for certain subscription services is fraught with exceptions and limitations. Actually, there are two statutory licenses established by the DPRSRA. One deals with performances of sound recordings that meet certain programming and other requirements, and the other deals with certain ephemeral (or incidental) reproductions of sound recordings, usually an interim step taken to store the music in the hard drives of computers known as "servers" prior to an authorized use such as a webcast. (The term *webcast* is generally used to refer to audio streaming on the Internet, or "Internet radio.") Under the ephemeral recordings exemption, for example, a radio station can record a set of songs and broadcast from the new recording rather than from the original CDs, which would otherwise have to be changed rapidly during the course of a broadcast.

Just to give you some idea of the complexity of the law, let me cite some of the exceptions and limitations to obtaining a statutory license to stream sound recordings that are subject to copyright protection. (Note that one-artist-only webcasts and channels that perform the recordings of one artist continuously are not permitted to obtain a statutory license.)

- If a "phonorecord" is used for transmissions made under other than a statutory license, the statutory license does not apply. (Huh?)
- The statutory license authorizing the making of an ephemeral recording is conditioned in part on the transmitting organization being entitled to transmit to the public the performance of the musical composition under a license or transfer of copyright.
- If a subscription service makes *prior* announcements, in text or audio, it is not permitted to obtain a statutory license. For example, such services may not publish advance program schedules or make advance announcements of the titles of specific sound recordings or the featured artists to be performed on the service. Such services may not provide to a third party the list of songs or artists to be performed by the transmitting entity for publication or announcement by the third party.
- Services may announce, up to three times per hour, the names of two artists whose sound recordings will be performed by the service within an unspecified future time period. Anything more will deny the Internet service the right to a statutory license.
- Transmissions that are part of archived programs that are less than five hours long are ineligible for a statutory license.
- Transmissions that are part of archived programs more than five hours long are eligible for a statutory license only if the archived program is available on the webcaster's site or related site for two weeks or less.
- Eligibility for a statutory license is limited to transmissions that are not part of a continuous program of less than three hours' duration.
- Eligibility for a statutory license is limited to transmissions that are not part of a program, other than an archived or continuous program, that is transmitted at a scheduled time more than three additional times in a two-week period.
- A transmitting entity may not avail itself of a statutory license if it knowingly performs

a sound recording in a manner that is likely to cause a listener to believe that there is an affiliation or association between the sound recording copyright owner or featured artist and a particular product or service advertised by the transmitting entity. This would cover, for example, transmitting an advertisement for a particular product or service every time a particular sound recording or artist is transmitted.

The list goes on.

So, as you can see, determining whether a statutory license is available for a particular use is no piece of cake. Yet, without a statutory license, a website utilizing music will have enormous, and probably overwhelming, difficulties in attempting to comply with the law. Seeking specific permission from sound recording owners is expensive, time-consuming and, ultimately, prohibitive in every way. [A recent attempt to clear Internet rights with the largest company in the world, Universal Music Group, was met with the following (paraphrased) response: "We don't do that; we don't know why, but we don't. How about an 'up to' 30-second license? We can do that!" What kind of "Internet radio station" can exist without the recordings of the largest company in the world?]

The fine print in the law that governs whether or not a statutory license is obtainable is very fine indeed. And provisions change frequently as the law's impact becomes more understood and modifications are sought and obtained. Consider yourself warned.

Blanket Performance and Synchronization License Agreements

The underlying principle behind all of the current standard agreements from each of the "blanket licensing" organizations (ASCAP, BMI, SESAC, the Harry Fox Agency, Inc., and the RIAA) is to charge fees based on revenue—with a minimum fee per year. The revenue-based model itself is susceptible of variations. For example, as with the all-industry-negotiated rate in the traditional broadcast media, ASCAP and BMI could charge webcasters a percentage based solely on revenues less some agreed-upon percentage of operating expenses, or they could charge a percentage based solely on revenue derived from digital sales, but not hard goods sold via an Internet interface. But the websites that engage in webcasting are balking at this method. They argue that much of what is available on their websites does not include music and only a percentage of those portions that do include music are devoted to streaming, or the active performance of it. Variations on the theme abound and it will not be clear for years how the societies will deal with this issue. Blanket license agreements for a variety of music uses can be viewed or actually downloaded from the following websites:

- Performing rights—www.ascap.com (www.weblicense@ascap.com), www.bmi.com (www.weblicensing@bmi.com), and www.sesac.com
- Mechanical and synchronization rights—www.nmpa.org.

Some of the sites are under construction and the agreements are still being drafted; but an attempt to comply, and regular communication with these organizations, will be useful in defending a claim from either the organizations or their members in case of a problem. SESAC has a particularly user-friendly site whereby one can download the license agreement relevant to a user's particular needs.

Some people have recommended that the societies create a "hobbyist" license for $25 to $50 a year. The Digital Millennium Copyright Act expanded the so-called "ephemeral" exemption of Section 112 (see above, under "Copyright Law Provisions Applicable to the Internet") to include recordings that are made to facilitate the digital transmission of a sound recording where the transmission is made under the DPRSRA's exemption for digital broadcasts or statutory license. Unfortunately, as the DMCA now reads, a hobbyist would not qualify for the DMCA exemption because a hobbyist would not be able to meet the sound-recording criteria of the law. Said hobbyist would have to seek and obtain permission from an array of writers, publishers, record companies, and performing and mechanical rights societies every time he or she wanted to make an "ephemeral" copy via which legal, authorized rights could be exercised. This seems too bad, as the hobbyist license approach would afford a marvelous opportunity to "sign up" millions of young Internet users while educating them in the niceties of copyright compliance at the same time.

TERM OF COPYRIGHT

The copyright in a song written in the United States in the 1990s now extends for the author's life plus 70 years. (See Chapter 16, page 229, for a discussion of anticopyright interests' attempts to reduce the term of copyright to the author's life plus 50 years.) A copyright secured by a company as an employer who has contracted for a work for hire extends for 95 years. Works for which copyright was secured under the 1909 Copyright Act (the one preceding the current act) also enjoy a copyright term extending 95 years, provided certain formalities—no longer necessary—were followed when they were supposed to be, pre-1993. Throughout the rest of the world, the copyright term is essentially the same as exists in the United States, although most other countries do not have the work-for-hire option: everyone who creates is an author. In addition, the copyright terms in countries outside of the United States were not subject to the renewal formalities provided under the 1909 Act and therefore the determination of whether a U.S. work is in or out of copyright outside of the United States is much easier to calculate.

SAMPLING, BORROWING, AND STEALING

As Chapter 16 discusses in some detail, "borrowing" copyrighted material is not permitted. Using any copyrighted work without permission, for just about any purpose—especially one with a commercial aspect—constitutes an intentional act of copyright infringement. While the copyright law permits some uses as noninfringing under its fair-use provisions, most "borrowing"—including sampling—does not meet fair-use criteria. The idea that using a de minimus portion of a song is entitled to a fair-use defense is just plain wrong. (This defense is not to be confused by the defense of de minimus non curat lex, which is a general defense, not specific to the intellectual property field, available to all when a claim is of such little consequence as not to be worth the court's time.) The fiction perpetuated by those who are unfamiliar with copyright law that borrowing up to eight measures—or four measures—of music is permitted by law should be abandoned once and for all.

As part of its FACE initiative (Friends of Copyright Education) aiming at copyright education, the Copyright Society of the United States has established a website for teenagers which cites several examples of when a fair-use defense can be asserted and when it cannot. These are useful not only for teenagers but for corporate counsels as well, and the information can be found at www.law.duke.edu/copyright.

RIGHTS MANAGEMENT

There are a myriad of laws, case interpretations, and customs affecting the use (commercial or otherwise) of photographs, models, film clips, etc. Corporations that face these issues must establish a management plan that invites the easy and broad sharing of information. Ironically, much of this can be exchanged through the mechanism of the Internet itself; many companies (including law firms) have established "internal" websites through which information and decision making can be opened up to the widest possible audience.

The task of managing intellectual property and complying with copyright and associated laws consists not just of identifying the problem; it includes determining how to control how the intellectual property rights are used and how they can be cleared in a reasonable fashion under the particular circumstances of the use. That is why it is necessary to establish guidelines for identifying whether the proposed use or language regarding the use requires special counseling in the event the use is ultimately made. In particular, companies whose legal counsel are dispersed and decentralized throughout the world should establish an intellectual property network so that lawyers and managers who are involved can keep each other informed, possibly by selecting a central "rights management" person as well as one person in each division designated as the "contact" person for corporate compliance.

Another valuable means by which a company can manage its risks is to issue educational pamphlets on copyright, rights of privacy, and other intellectual property issues. Some of these can be "timeless" so that they can become a permanent part of the company's office manual. Other pamphlets, newsletters, etc., can be issued as the circumstances, such as changes in the law and the changing needs of the company, warrant. This is a particularly useful procedure because as new managers are hired, the total level of intellectual property education of a company's managers is necessarily diluted. The "rights management" attorney can be charged with this responsibility.

In order to accomplish the information-exchange goals alluded to above, attorneys throughout the spectrum of the company's deal making should be informed of the availability of the rights-management attorney and the function of that office. In this way, language that appears in any contract that has intellectual property aspects can be scrutinized by an expert.

DANGEROUS LANGUAGE ALERT

A contract dealing with webcast distribution may include the following language, embedded well toward the back of the document, in the middle of other standard boilerplate language:

- Customer holds all rights *throughout the world* material to its obligations under this agreement and to the licenses granted hereunder [including the rights of] . . . transmission distribution, performance, display and broadcast of the event and materials . . . and all copying . . . necessary to effectuate these activities . . . . [italics added]
- Webcaster's exercise of any . . . rights granted . . . herein, will not violate or infringe any right of privacy, personality or publicity, any Intellectual Property Right, or any other right of any party.
- . . . Customer has the worldwide right to license to webcaster the right . . . to publicly distribute, transmit, and perform the event . . . via streaming video protocols . . . and to use reproduce and display . . . the materials contained in the event . . . and to maintain the archive of the event . . . for on-demand access and distribution, transmission and performance.

Pretty inclusive language. Pretty dangerous language. Does the person negotiating the overall agreement have enough familiarity with the DMCA and the DPRSRA to sign off on language such as this? Does that person understand technically what the company is actually seeking to accomplish or to present to the public to be able to counsel the company on this language?

Would it not be a lot more efficient and risk-free to seek the input of someone who lives and breathes this area of the law every day? It is unwise for a corporation to parcel out its contract-negotiating responsibilities among a variety of lawyers who are not acting as mutual resources for each other. It is far better to consult outside counsel who specialize in Internet and copyright law, to create the position of rights management person, as suggested above, or to expand the job description of one inside counsel to assume this responsibility.

The infringement issues raised above do not present insoluble problems. On the contrary, they merely require a different kind of attention and decision making. Copyright infringement consequences can be significant, but if a company is diligently trying to do the right thing, the damages anyone will be able to recover can be significantly reduced. For example, the statutory damages for *copyright infringement* (which, by definition is intentional, even if "innocent") are dramatically lower than those for *willful copyright infringement* (which, while also intentional, is subject to much higher damage penalties).

Of course, the issues explored here are exacerbated when a company has many divisions and—even more so—when those divisions exist in different states and countries. The need for corporations to establish rights use and clearance guidelines is as compelling as it is to have general corporate policy and other legal guidelines that have become routine over the past decades. There is no other responsible way to manage the risks of infringement of copyright or other intellectual property rights. Among these risks in the copyright area are the attendant costs, including not only the legal fees of the company (the defendant), but also, potentially, the legal fees of the prevailing party (the plaintiff) for which the U.S. Copyright Law includes specific provision, to be assessed at the discretion of the court.

MUSIC CLEARANCE: THE MUSIC INDUSTRY'S REVENGE

People who want quick solutions have no idea how complicated it is to clear music rights. First of all, there are multiple rights involved. As noted in the previous chapter, in a live-performance webcast of any sort, one must deal with the mechanical and performance rights emanating from the webcast; in-store uses of footage from the webcast (e.g., a CD or a videogram, that is, cassette or DVD); and perhaps a TV special, perhaps more than one (one for the United States and one for Europe, one for South America, and one for Asia). And don't forget pay per view. Oh yes. One more thing to add to the "don't forget" list: the moral rights of authors and their heirs outside of the United States. This is a wild card courtesy of foreign intellectual property laws that will allow the heirs of *their* John Philip Sousas (whose music in this country is in the public domain) to stop cold any use of their ancestor's music which *they* believe is inimical to the ancestor's moral heritage. The concern is particularly relevant in the area of commercial advertising. Thus a Mercedes Benz commercial using a French song long out of copyright protection might offend the heirs of the writer of the song, while a Citroën commercial using the same song might not.

For a company whose principal function has nothing to do with music, it is virtually impossible to understand how difficult it is to clear the necessary rights for something as seemingly straightforward as a webcast—or even the simple use of a song on a website. What's more, the rights have to be cleared both for the song and the master. And if the song is a particularly current "edgy" one, the likelihood is that there are multiple writers and copublishers on the music publishing side who will have to be dealt with. For a five-song webcast, there are upwards of 50 to 200 rights that have to be cleared. For example, if three writers and unaffiliated publishing companies are involved together with one master rights owner, 7 rights would have to be cleared for one work; but if all three writers and their publishing companies were in partnership with third-party music publishers (like EMI or Warner/Chappell), then there would actually be six publishing companies to deal with—for a new total of 10 rights. Multiply this by 5 songs and you get 50 different rights to clear. Obtaining these rights can be so expensive as to be practically prohibitive for the average marketing budget.

INTERNATIONAL ISSUES: ONE-STOP SHOPPING

One-stop shopping is impossible in the current global environment. Even the collection societies have not figured out what to do.

Slow responses are the norm. *No* response is, unfortunately, not rare. Yet decisions must customarily be made on very short notice. And even where the responses are quick and satisfying, the process of drafting and negotiating the formal licenses is enormously burdensome. Every music company would prefer to use its own form, none of which really fit the imaginative uses that the licensee comes up with (at least *someone* is being creative!). The staffs of the music companies are simply too small to deal with the avalanche of paperwork generated by the multiple uses and clearances involved; neither the music companies nor their prospective licensees have a clue as to what to charge; and both legal fees and clearance company fees multiply to unconscionable levels.

One of the problems of course is that the Internet is global, and it is very difficult to effectively limit the exploitation of music to individual territories. For example, ASCAP's rate structure, while one that does not require time-consuming negotiations, is limited to U.S. territory. So anyone who wants to webcast or use a song as part of a conventional website beyond U.S. borders is going to be back into the negotiation mode, like it or not.

The music publishing and record industries have always been designed along territorial constructs. Rights licensing has necessarily found its solutions in territorial determination. Subpublishers and record company affiliates are institutionalized throughout the world, and the processes of international licensing have, traditionally, followed a certain model, a model that is *not* global.

WHAT IS TO BE DONE?

The performing and mechanical rights societies of the world met in November 2000 in Santiago, Chile, under the auspices of the Confédération Internationale des Sociétés d'Auteurs et Compositeurs (CISAC), determined to find a partial solution to the music publishing portion of the problem—to figure out how to offer world licenses via reciprocal agreements among themselves. While the temporary solution they agreed upon still requires users to enter into licenses for their territory, multiple negotiated licenses may have seen their last light, at least in the non–sound recording arena. Of course, many, if not most, eventual users wish to use the songs *with* the masters. Nevertheless, some progress toward establishing a global licensing structure has been made. This is how it works.

- The prospective licensee contacts the content provider (usually the music publisher).
- The content provider is represented by a society in the country in which the content provider is located.
- The society licenses the rights worldwide, but on a nonexclusive basis only and on a nondiscriminatory basis as well (to avoid territory-shopping).
- Prompt distribution of the license fee is arranged.
- Any taxes that are payable are charged in the country of use (i.e., the download), if that country in fact taxes the transaction.

This procedure produces not only ease of licensing, and a sort of one-stop buying; it also provides legal certainty for the licensee. This is appealing not only to the licensee, but to the licensee's attorneys as well, who are being asked, if only by implication, to "certify" that the licensee won't be sued for copyright infringement.

Following the Santiago meeting, a number of the world's most important societies—including BMI, BUMA (The Netherlands), PRS (the United Kingdom), SGAI (Spain), SIAE (Italy), and GEMA (Germany)—established a "fast track" licensing procedure designed to optimize business cooperation and ease of licensing. At this conference, a majority of the world's active international repertoire representatives entered into agreements that authorize each other to grant licenses for online music use on a worldwide basis. This is a remarkable achievement, although long overdue.

The official statement issued by the parties signing these Bilateral Internet Licensing Agreements states:

The parties recognise that one transmission of music over the Internet may result in performances in multiple countries. It is clear that online music users do not want to enter into license agreements with each performing right organisation in the various countries where their musical works may be performed online. We realise that the extensive use of copyrighted music is not limited to territorial boundaries in the online world. We hope that others will agree that this is a necessary step to assure the legal performance of music online, and that many other societies will enter into such agreements.

The agreements cover webcasting, streaming, online music on demand, as well as music included in video (TV, motion pictures, etc.) transmitted online. They provide for a mechanism to assure proper distribution of license fees to authors, composers, and music publishers on a worldwide basis. The agreements were effective as of the issuance of the document, but extended only through December 31, 2001. Presumably new insights will prevail in 2002.

In March, 2001, the Executive Bureau of CISAC persuaded ASCAP and SACD (a French rights society) to transfer to CISAC two database subsystems—the Musical Works Information Database (WID) and the International Documentation on Audiovisual works (IDA). They also managed to establish some general guidelines for fixing an applicable price scale for system access. As a result of this international cooperation, the interoperability of the world's licensing organizations has been greatly enhanced.

This new information system is CIS (Common Information System), a series of tools that establish a global digital copyright administration standard. It will streamline the exchange of information among member societies. According to the CISAC information releases, it is the foremost international cooperative development effort being pursued in the field of online collective administration of intellectual property rights. There are two major components of CIS: (1) international standard numbers for the identification of works and relevant parties to the creative process, where there are two main works identifiers, ISWC for musical works and ISAN for audiovisual works, and (2) a support network of more than 10 global databases that serve as the repository of authoritative copyright information. The CIS comprises "a set of legal, financial and technical rules that aim to define the visibility, security and accountability required from the management of CIS, including data integrity and control"; it is a "non-profit endeavor whose services will be developed and operated at cost," its primary purpose being "to enable CISAC societies to improve their information exchanges and realize collective operational savings." The ultimate goal is not merely "to improve documentation, but to provide better distributions for rights holders." Although CIS is still evolving, the hope is that soon it will able to make music rights clearance more effective and efficient—and certainly cheaper—than it is now. Certainly it represents real progress toward establishing a verifiable global system that will, in time, facilitate global licensing not just of music, but of all other forms of intellectual property that can be transferred via the Internet.

So it seems that the music industry is awakening after too long a sleep. Much of what currently passes for international cooperation consists merely of an interlinking of national sites. But there is a better solution on the drawing boards now—one that really is as global as it should be. The Confédération Internationale des Sociétés d'Auteurs et Compositeurs, BIEM (a group of 41 European mechanical rights collection societies), the RIAA (the United States' recording industry trade arm), and the IFPI (International Federation of the Phonographic Industry, the world recording industry trade arm) are discussing the establishment of an integrated music industry identification standard through which information about songs and recordings will be collected, tagged, and stored in a database—whether WID, or IDA, or some new system—that can be integrated with existing management systems.

Once competent and accurate song and recording identification is established on a global scale, it will be relatively easy to facilitate the licensing of rights wherever they may be requested, and to whatever extent their use may be sought.

I never thought I would see the day when global cooperation and collaboration would be so close to achievement, but here we are. The Internet is forcing copyright interests throughout the world to address and reconcile—quickly—issues such as these. (See Chapter 16, page 226, for a discussion of one approach—the Internet right.) It will be interesting to see if the disparate groups (record companies, artists' representatives, unions, producers, songwriters, and publishers) can get it together before consumer (and corporate) complaints get too loud and the world's government(s) decide to step in and fix the "problem" themselves.

18

INTERNET ENTREPRENEURSHIP:
Doing It Yourself

"So, the lunatics
have taken over
the asylum?"

—Attributed to
Richard A. Rowland,
President of Metro
Pictures

Clearly the Internet is transforming the manner in which music is promoted and sold. How now can it be used to assist fledgling recording artists to come to the attention of a public eager for the creative wares bursting forth all over the world—a public which is willing to part with money thereby making the effort worthwhile financially?

Enter the ethereal world of Internet commerce. Never have technology and music, money, and art, been so intertwined as they are in the world of the Web. For several years now, those composers and performers who desire to communicate with eventual fans have for several years now had a variety of means open to them via the Internet: their own websites, links to others' sites, fulfillment sites through which one's CDs, sheet music, and merchandise may be sold in hardcopy form; sites that highlight and even review new music; webzines; and the ubiquitous sites through which one's music may be uploaded, downloaded, streamed, and otherwise transmitted to and among computers and computer-compatible devices. From Diamond's Rio and other playback machines adapted to the various formats of compressed music files such as MP3 files: the distribution mechanisms are beginning to reach a critical mass.

One truth has evolved from the recent period during which the myth of "opportunity for all" has had a certain amount of currency: it's not easy to reach a large enough audience to make the initial investment of time and money worthwhile—an audience that, depending on the size of the investment, can range from 1,000 people to a million or more: Traditional resources must still be assembled and utilized. And here is the dilemma: do you want to make a living, or do you want to try to compete with the majors?

You will note that my point of view in this chapter jumps back and forth between advocating the do-it-yourself approach and warning that many artists would be foolish to try to become entrepreneurs. Perhaps this is the result of one of the inherent aspects of the law: lawyers have to see all sides. But I think that it has just as much to do with the inherent difficulties of the Internet, which is still in its infancy. In any case, there is much to think about before embarking on this kind of pursuit and I will explore some of the issues you will have to consider before doing so.

COMPETING WITH THE BIG BOYS

At whatever level you decide to compete, you will need money, facilities to write, rehearse, and record, good songs, touring, equipment, appropriate clothes, a techie, maybe a van, co-writers, producers, engineers, videos, and all of the paraphernalia embodying promotion, marketing, advertising, and sales forces customarily provided by a record company.

If this is not daunting enough, remember, you will also need to obtain the services of the same types of professionals any working artist (whether individual, group, or band) will traditionally require: personal managers, accountants, and lawyers—and not just any old lawyers, lawyers of various disciplines: music business lawyers, trademark lawyers, possibly immigration lawyers, and, where minors are involved, lawyers knowledgeable in the area of minority contracts. Maybe even corporate and tax lawyers. These professionals will be necessary to help you budget your recording; organize your expenditures, receipts, check stubs, etc., for the purpose of preparing and eventually defending tax returns; to negotiate your partnership and internal band agreements; to negotiate agreements with co-writers, with studios providing services for promises of future payment, with investors providing money for promises of future payment, with trademark services (including clearance of band names for the Internet, the unions, and the various states and countries of the world in which there may already be a conflicting name existent), with photographers regarding ownership and use of photographs for promotion, advertising, merchandise, and artwork on CDs and digital downloads, and with unions. You will need to develop databases; print and distribute flyers, mailings, posters, and other merchandise. You will need assistance in mixing, mastering, and manufacturing or otherwise distributing your musical output. You will have to deal with encryption technology and requirements both for your own protection and that of your Internet distributors. You will have to seek reviews and mention in the press. You will have to identify, negotiate with, and service foreign companies with whom you hope to ally yourself for the exploitation of your products outside the United States. You will have to either deal with the venues yourself or find people who will do this for you—both agents and managers.

You think all this sounds a lot like a record company? You're right. Sure, the Internet is a wonderful new outlet for the discovery and dissemination of new music, but it is a whole lot easier to be on the receiving end than on the selling and distributing end. It always is.

ARTIST, SONGWRITER, PERFORMER— AND E-COMMERCE EXPERT?

Artist, songwriter, and performer. Enough professions to keep three people busy. Yet many of our music industry creators are all three. But if you are going to exploit your music via the Internet, you will have to add a new profession: Internet expert. And much of what you will have to know is mysteriously similar to what you used to depend on your record company and publishing company to handle for you.

Lots of people will be more than happy, for a fee—or even for free—to give you an abundance of advice as to what your site should look like, and what pages you will need to create and flesh out (let alone keep current!). Even if you do not seek to distribute your music via the Internet, you will no doubt want to develop an exciting and effective website to promote yourself and your products.

However you cut it, you used to have one item on your plate: your music. Now you have two: your music and your website. Both have to be marketed and promoted, and the expertise and services required to succeed in one is actually quite different from what is required to succeed in the other. Search engines (some of which charge per "hit"), newsgroups, other bands' sites, banner ads, reciprocal links, common interest sites, affiliated sites—all are destinations that you will want to feature your product.

And, if you want your website to distribute your music as well, you should be aware that outside of the United States, the sale and exploitation of product can range from expensive to prohibitive. Licensing the manufacture and sale of hard goods overseas is very complex. Royalties, accountings, taxes, idiosyncrasies of foreign societies—the whole infrastructure of delivering music to the consumer has been in place for decades and old systems do not dissolve overnight. Selling music products overseas via the Internet can be even more complex.

Insofar as digital downloads are concerned, while the politicians have been struggling with this issue for some time, no taxes are yet chargeable in the United States. However, it will likely come to pass one day that taxes or some kind of tariff will have to be charged as the Internet begins to interfere substantially with bricks-and-mortar stores—or even catalogue sales. The European Union has been struggling with the tax issue for a while, and, although it is not yet resolved, one must remain alert to the fact that there are governmental institutions around the world which are intruding on the free and unrestricted distribution of music via the Internet. It is only a question of how intrusive they will choose to be, how alike or different the intrusion will be from country to country, and how much it will cost the distributor and/or the consumer to access music for digital download via the Internet.

MAKING A LIVING

What's wrong with just making a living? There is a level of success in the music business which may not be up to the multiplatinum level demanded by the multinationals or the venture capitalists in the mainstream music world but which for many is nonetheless worth pursuing. In fact, while you may not sell enough records to make a dent in the Billboard Hot 100, you can still make an awful lot of money if you do it right—in fact, a whole lot more money than most artists will ever see as a result of contracts with major labels.

A client of mine refers to artists with such modest goals as the middle class of the music business. Think of Ani DiFranco; think of Prince, after he discarded his career-long dependence on a major record company. To the argument that you have enough to do as an artist, my client answers that you no longer will have to spend time wondering (or trying to fix) what others are doing on your behalf. That saving alone buys you a lot of time.

What we are really talking about is a good, old-fashioned, mail-order strategy with a contemporary twist: the use of the Internet as a means of advertising, funneling traffic, and utilizing digital technology to transmit music via downloads and other means.

You may be thinking, "But I can't reach the people this way!" Do you mean the people you want to reach or millions of people? If you mean millions of people, then you are right: you can't reach the platinum people. But if you mean the people you *need* to reach, then you *can* do it. There are ways to target the very audience which will find your artistry appealing—people who appreciate what you do and what you have to say.

Remember, as an entrepreneur you have total artistic control and you need not make any compromises to fit the agenda of a record label. You *are* the record label.

Now you may be thinking, "How can I compete with 100 years of collective experience represented by many of the major labels?" The answer, of course, is, "How many times does a major label screw up?" Whenever a company is in the volume business, there is the likelihood—in fact, the guarantee—that it will mess up along the way in discharging its responsibilities. A label with 50 or 100 acts—hoping one or two will succeed—is in the volume business. You are not.

When you are an artist, as a perusal of Chapter 4 of this book will attest, you are at the bottom of the food chain. You are the last to be paid. Some artists compare their royalties to the last little morsels of a cookie. If you do not have the stomach or the patience for the major label paradigm, then don't complain. Do it yourself.

STEALING AND PROTECTING AGAINST IT

The Napster phenomenon has received almost as much attention and publicity as an elected official's extramarital affairs. Those who will *never* set foot in the music business are nonetheless aware of the fact that Internet companies have been making music available for "sharing"—or, as copyright interests put it, "stealing." One of those consequences has been the heightening of sensitivity of the world's populations regarding the validity of copyright in the works that are being "shared." When you make your music available on the Internet, the boundless opportunities to reach consumers is matched only by the boundless opportunities for those consumers to appropriate your product without compensation. This is the lesson—good and bad—that the Napster and associated litigations have taught us.

Thus we come to the only protection copyright owners can depend on: encryption. Encoding is the *sine qua non* ("without which nothing") of digital distribution. Imprecise, inefficient, careless encoding—or even the total absence of encoding which, believe it or not, is still fashionable among many artists (but not their record companies)—will provide uncountable numbers of web surfers the opportunity to copy the product which was created only after the infusion of an enormous and incredibly complex and costly investment of time and money.

I cannot say enough about the necessity of encryption. Such sites as MP3, Liquid Audio, and Digitalpressure, as well as the major record company sites that have finally made their presence known, are fairly well encrypted, although the imagination of the hacker has not had much opportunity to be fully tested. (This is another reason to trust the institutional sites rather than the fly-by-night sites with your music—no matter how appealing these newer sites may be and no matter how much you might identify with their philosophies or demographics.)

Transmitting your music over the Internet, whether via Liquid's hosting services, via high-resolution file transfer protocols, or via music archives such as the Internet Underground Music Archive (IUMA)—whatever the formats—involves a certain amount of risk. You can manage this risk by doing what you have always done: go with a brand you trust and which others have trusted for a long period. This may not coincide with your philosophy of helping an underdog or a maverick, but if you are not prepared to accept the consequences of such decisions, you would be well advised to play it safe.

DO'S AND DON'TS OF INTERNET ENTREPRENEURSHIP

Don't be surprised if your search for success through an effort to do it yourself results in exactly the opposite: an inability to fund that effort, a lot of disappointed fans, and even an accumulating debt resulting from the expenditure of money necessitated first, by seeking customers and, second, by trying to satisfy them. There is a reason most of the executives in the record industry have business school backgrounds. The ultimate irony of pursuing Internet entrepreneurship in the manner described in this chapter is that, as a musician, you live in the world of the idea. The abstract. The dream. Doing it yourself on the Internet is another world entirely. Use new methodologies when you can, but do not try to be what you are not: a record company. Columbia and RCA Records have almost 200 years of experience between them. Can you really expect the well-meaning efforts of one individual to duplicate this experience?

Perhaps I have (almost?) dissuaded you from accepting the daunting challenge of becoming an Internet entrepreneur. That was not my intention, and to prove it, I offer a few pointers in case you want to take the chance of offering your creations to the vagaries of cyberspace. Here is my top 10 list of do's and don'ts (actually eight do's and two don'ts):

1. Don't make any exclusive arrangements with anyone. The Internet is still too fluid a system to give up the flexibility of trying alternative means to achieve your goals.
2. Do try to find a distribution method or methods which can aggregate your music in such a way as to focus it sufficiently in a specific genre, for example, so as to target a specific demographic that you must reach in order to have success.
3. Do make certain that the sites with which you establish links and/or affiliations are trustworthy, both as to the manner in which they make and fulfill promises and as to the manner in which they protect your music.
4. Do try to use the facilities through which you distribute your music so as to develop databases of persons, Internet addresses, or other sites which inquire about your music so that you can use this extremely valuable information when offering other products and when touring.
5. Do focus yourself first before trying to target what audience you are going to try to reach. Know who you are, what you stand for, what you are trying to communicate, and who you are trying to reach (their age, their location, their nonmusical characteristics, and tastes).
6. Do view other bands' websites, including those that are not in the same genre as your music. You will be able to quickly distinguish between those websites that are effective and those websites that are not.
7. Do be careful when you design your website. If it does not effectively articulate your image and does not have the technical means to achieve the sales and interest in your music that is your goal, it will fail. And so will you.

8. Don't expect a lot of sales (for a new artist, anything more than 10 CDs a year would exceed the average, believe it or not), but use your site as an information-gathering resource. Through links to, and with, other, similarly styled musical acts, you can begin to collect data you can use to target and reach new audiences when you are touring. Eventually, you should attract the attention of radio programmers—perhaps find a friend at a station who would program a track or two. This data, at its most basic, will also help you develop a mailing list for gigs and flyers for your tours and for sales of records. Ironically, MP3's very success almost guarantees its failure as a means for any given artist to achieve his or her goal of a specific number of unit sales beyond a nominal number. In the year 2000, more than 250,000 songs from more than 50,000 artists were accessible via MyMP3.com. This makes South by Southwest (also known as SXSW, the annual music convention held each March in Austin, Texas, where as many as 300 bands perform in three days) seem like a chamber music festival.

9. Do constantly update your website. Nothing turns off a fan more than a rusting and dust-gathering image.

10. Do be flexible in how you utilize the Internet. There are a variety of means by which you can do this in addition to the traditional goals of promotion and distribution. (The *Blair Witch* phenomenon is a case in point: the film was introduced via the Internet, but then distributed and promoted via traditional means.) You can learn from the example of an inspired record company, which will try to find a way to coordinate with artists to utilize the Internet in new and creative ways that not only can reach hard-to-contact consumers but can achieve a certain level of "cool" as well.

MANUFACTURING AND DISTRIBUTION

The manufacturing and distributing function requires a different mind-set entirely from the one you need to use the Internet effectively, either as a way to reach potential listeners and as an information-gathering tool. It requires time! Time away from writing; time away from rehearsing; time away from thinking about who you are and what the purpose of your art is; time away from performing. Consider the time it will take merely to set up your home studio at the level necessary to produce recordings at the level consumers expect. Thus, at all levels of the recording process—writing, rehearsing, recording, mixing, mastering, manufacturing, promoting, and, finally, distributing your CD—time is a commodity that must be husbanded carefully.

And it requires money! Money for designing the website and keeping it current; money for encoders (software to convert your newly recorded CD so that it can be disseminated via the Internet without risk of having it stolen); money to raise the level of such encryption to CD level, which is not as easy as you think; money for manufacturing and packaging CDs; money for mailings; money for production of the music; money for instrumental rental; money for registering copyrights in both the songs and sound recordings; money for registering trademarks and service marks; money for tape; money for market research; money for club distributions; money for shipping the CDs; money for lawyers, accountants, and managers to negotiate with studios and investors, money for co-writers, professional engineers, and producers; money for negotiating contracts with foreign distributors and representatives; money to manufacture merchandise and then ship it; money for being featured at the top of search engines' lists; money for designing banner ads. And don't forget the cost of *getting* the money for all of the above.

An instructive story. In 1919, Charles Chaplin, Mary Pickford, Douglas Fairbanks, William S. Hart, and D. W. Griffith—all frustrated in their efforts to control their own business and artistic lives—established their own motion picture company, United Artists Studios. Apt name. It was not long before they learned that they could not do what they did for a living and run a picture company at the same time. Although Mary Pickford did not leave the studio until 1951, it had been clear for a long time that United Artists would eventually morph into a First National/Republic/Paramount/Columbia/Warner/MGM-type motion picture company—and that was that. Actually, today, United Artists and MGM are one and operate under the same management. So it goes.

WHICH PEOPLE *SHOULD* DO IT THEMSELVES?

There are three kinds of artists who, I think, have the best chance to become successful do-it-yourselfers in the world of e-commerce: hip-hop artists, classical artists, and formerly successful pop and rock artists. The ways in which hip-hop artists and classical artists can benefit from the Internet are covered in Chapters 19 and 20, respectively. Following is a brief discussion of how formerly successful artists might go about doing it themselves.

An artist who has had a great deal of success almost invariably still has hundreds of thousands, if not millions, of fans who recall their feelings years earlier when they were first introduced to the artist's music. Assuming that an artist from the 1970s or 1980s (or earlier) has something left to say, that artist can record a CD fairly inexpensively (don't mention this to my good friends at the Hit Factory) and make it available via the Internet—either as a hard-copy CD or via download technology—for $10 or so and sell a few hundred thousand copies.* Not bad for a minor investment. The mainstream record companies—those with significant clout in finding their way into the featured record bins in record stores, on websites featuring music, and on radio playlists as well—will rarely look twice at the "formerly" successful artist. Record companies that tried to specialize in such artists have failed. Former successes have only a slight chance at a comeback via the traditional record industry and the record companies could care less. Tori Amos, Foreigner—there are a large number of artists whose appeal is broad, but apparently not broad enough to warrant the majors granting them an exclusive recording relationship.

It is not out of the question to create a workable studio with 36-track recording capabilities for a cost of under $40,000. Further, the usually outlandish costs of mixing and mastering can be achieved via the Internet. A record recorded in Los Angeles can be sent via FTP to New York or London for mixing, and sent back again via FTP, all in a day's time. Customs delays, air courier charges, shipping time, and lost time are all absent in this fast-moving—and cheap—electronic world. There are, of course, huge security issues, but by the time you have learned the tricks of this particular trade, hopefully you will have learned methods of encryption that will protect your music.

The appeal of Internet distribution will resonate with these artists especially.

Consistent with this point of view, certain identifiable websites whose appeal is directed to the audience of older artists are beginning to develop. The ability of these websites to focus on this kind of artist and to develop branded identities specializing in them (as well as other categories of artists to whose appeal traditional record companies may be resistant) may signal the future of a new layer of access for consumers to the music of their choice.

A WORD OF WARNING—AND ENCOURAGEMENT

The owners and distributors of "content" (read: the traditional record companies) are finding ever new ways to diminish, or at least keep under (their) control, the percentage of income they wish to share with the creators. So I suggest that you and your representatives review royalty provisions ever more carefully to ensure that they cover new and untested forms of exploitation. It used to be that hard sales, performances—and maybe licenses—were the entire universe of exploitation. Today, although that universe is expanding rapidly, companies are trying to squeeze into old paradigms traditional models of royalty computation. For example, most traditional record companies maintain that the digital download of a recorded song should bear the same royalty as if the sale were made over the counter at a record store.

As we saw in Chapter 4, a $16.98 "record" royalty base in the United States is customarily subject to a 10 percent breakage deduction, a 25 percent new technology deduction, a 25 percent packaging deduction, another 10 to 15 percent to make up for so-called "free goods," and maybe even an additional 10 to 15 percent reduction just for the hell of it. A $16.98 download is viewed in precisely the same way, although there is no wholesale dealer and no retailer—let alone a product that can break! Instead of sharing in the traditional 50:50 split of income from what are essentially licenses (via Pressplay or Musicnet, for example), record companies have figured out how to glom as much as 92+ percent of receipts from subscription services.

The record companies argue that their investment risks are the same whether the music is on a CD or downloaded. The costs for production, promotion, radio promotion, advertising, touring, video exploitation, etc., are justification enough to the record companies to exact precisely the same royalty reductions as they do for actual hard-copy sales. While there is certainly some truth behind this rationale, there are equally strong arguments for a more equitable sharing of the income.

Which brings us back to doing it yourself. If you can find a way to reach your audience—even a substantially diminished audience compared to what a traditional record company can reach—you can profit enormously. Precisely because you do not have to reach megalevels of buyers, you can present your art in an economically feasible way without having to learn all of the tricks of the trade discussed in earlier chapters of this book.

The Music Business is a cruel and shallow money trench
A long plastic hallway where thieves and pimps run free
And good men die like dogs
There's also a negative side

—**Attributed to Hunter S. Thompson**

Beating on a beat box—making a snare and a kick drum—that people can rap to. What else do you want? What else do you need? On street corners—starting as DJs—promoting others' music and then making their own. Rhythm is the beginning and rhythm is the end. Provided it's *new.* And has never been heard before! Can you believe that DMX went platinum (1 million sold) *bootleg* before it hit the music stores. Why? Because it was so different from everything that came before. This is the currency of hip-hop! Make them hungry. Establish the buzz. The fans are no slouches. They know what they want; they know what they hear; and they know what they see!

ROOTS

First, a little history. In 1984 Harry Belafonte produced a small film, *Beat Street,* which featured urban ghetto kids break-dancing, painting graffiti on walls, rapping, and generally developing a musical style that was light-years from what had gone before. Fast cuts by the camera, head spins, windmills, even some pop lockin'. What was this music? Surely, its origins and references (rhythm and blues) were well established and even mainstream by the time this seminal film was released. And maybe that was the reason for the explosion into a new dimension. But hip-hop really started much earlier.

A wonderful website, B-Boys.com, traces the evolution of hip-hop from Kool Herc, in 1973, so-called father of hip-hop. Born in Jamaica in 1955, he introduced to New York the raw rhythms and structures that we know today as Hip-Hop and laid the foundation for the Break-Boys. After Kool Herc came Grandmaster Flash and the Furious Five in 1979; and Kurtis Blow, Afrika Bambaata, George Clinton (and his funky contribution), Ice T, and Michael Jackson's legendary moonwalk during the early 1980s. Salt 'n' Pepa and Run-D.M.C., N.W.A.'s gangsta' rap, and Tribe Called Quest bring us up to the 1990s, followed by Dr. Dre, Tupac Shakur, Notorious B.I.G., Missy Elliot, Lauryn Hill (taking time off from being a student at Columbia University), Suge Knight and an array of more and more adventurous and talented groundbreaking artists who catapulted this genre of music into the world's consciousness.

Hip-hop is music; but it is also a culture than defines urban life as much as urban life defines it.

THE MILIEU

At first glance, the world of hip-hop seems to be very different and to operate by different rules than the pop music world. Seemingly, one would need a cultural historian, a psychiatrist, and a translator to make sense of it. But the essential characteristics of the music business—minus a few idiosyncrasies—are no less applicable to the world of hip-hop than to other kinds of music. The same concerns facing the pop artist and songwriter—the same copyright laws; the same laws of contract; the same federal and state income taxes; and the same international treaties—are faced by hip-hop artists, although often these artists do not know it. (Reportedly, Cheryl James of Salt 'n' Pepa was surprised at the consequences of contracts that she and her partner signed. "We never even thought of a lawyer," she stated when testifying against her record company.)

That said, it must also be acknowledged that the musical vocabulary of hip-hop—and R&B and rap—is different from that of traditional pop songwriting. Whereas the rest of the popular music world divides songs into music and lyrics, and customarily collaborators will be credited as having written "words and music," in the hip-hop world, songs are divided into three parts: the track, the melody, and the words. And, true to the traditions of Tin Pan Alley in the 1950s, everyone involved in producing a hip-hop song tries to get his or her name into the authorship list—whether they are true contributors or not. This is not only because there is a lot of money in music publishing and writers automatically own part of the copyrights of their creations. Being one of the writers has something to do with pride of authorship as well; the entire team of people who participate in creating a musical work in the hip-hop area see themselves as co-contributors and being named as an author is merely a manifestation of this phenomenon. Even the musician who creates an incidental keyboard part over the background track will claim to be an author. In truth, in the world of hip-hop, in contrast to the rest of the musical scene, the keyboard contribution alone can make or break the song; it can be the single, defining contribution that justifies the creator's rise to the level of author. Thus, with a hip-hop song, it is likely that from 5 to 10 names will find their way into the authorship list, often including writers whose works were recorded and released years earlier, but whose music has been sampled.

This is a world of emergency lawyers; late night calls; tinkering and manipulating with sounds that can date a song as being old-fashioned or mark it as the latest thing simply on the basis of a "sample." Hip-hop represents the nanosecond when a member of a disadvantaged community explodes into the mainstream society at large. And, as with any immigration or emigration from one economic or social community to another, this migration carries with it all of the attendant dangers that such moves engender.

The music of hip-hop, because of its very reason for being, is on the cutting edge of the culture. It is a fast-moving art form that changes almost daily. If a record is not catching on in the clubs or at the radio stations within two weeks, many record companies will simply kill the record and release something new, no matter what the financial consequences.

The artists bringing you this music change almost as rapidly. From Tupac Shakur and the Notorious B.I.G. (both of whom were killed—possibly by their compatriots), to Lil' Kim and Busta Rhymes, who, mere weeks after their stars had begun to climb, were referred to as the "rap elders" as St. Louis's Nelly's debut album passed theirs by in an extremely brief period. The speed by which these transfers of status occur is mind boggling.

Beyond their charismatic live appearances—on as well as off stage—hip-hop musicians are very well schooled in the rhythms, riffs, and songs of the fifties, sixties, and so on. The phenomenon is mostly black, but, as we saw with Elvis, the Beatles, and the Rolling Stones, music that originates in the black community does not stay there for long. At this writing, Eminem is the breakthrough white artist who has emerged to express the hip-hop ethos.

URBAN MUSIC: THE PRODUCER'S COSMOS

The current trend toward producer-driven music makes the producers of this music as important as, or even more important than, the artist. This oddity creates a lot of different priorities, methods of payment, and abuses.

On the positive side, the team effort of the production company, writers, producer, sidemen, and artist constitutes a real creative effort. The contribution of the production company is much more visible here than in the pop world. The logistics alone of creating tracks and adding melody, raps, and instrumentation, often seeking the input of musicians, producers, or rappers with a reputation, is mind-boggling.

On the negative side, particularly in the touring area, there has emerged quite a lot of violence and a not-so-new phenomenon in the live performing world—the unscrupulous promoter. With a few exceptions noted below, hip-hop touring has been a bust, with the unfortunate result that new, young hip-hop artists do not have access to the traditional avenues to long-term success.

The urban music market is so huge that the record companies have begun to invest massive amounts of money to claim their fair share of the charts in this area. The producers, alone or through surrogates, create tracks by the dozen, called "beats." They often incorporate samples. The artist essentially goes into the studio and shops for a beat that he or she likes and adds his or her own rap to it. This is an electronic world and very little music is produced acoustically. The artist is the only real, live, contributor to the sound.

DIFFERENT STROKES FOR HIP-HOP FOLKS
Street Teams

Urban music is often marketed by what are known as *street teams.* The record companies or producers hire lots of kids to sticker as much of the city as they can afford to. They will paper the side of a van and drive around; they will go into the clubs at night and hand out flyers; they will "snipe" any blank space available on the side of a construction site. You have all seen them. The artist's representative builds this kind of promotion into the recording and distribution agreements. Who should be in charge of the process of establishing street teams? The artist, producer, or manager—certainly not the record company. Why not? It is not that the record company is not capable of doing so, although mainstream record companies are not likely to be as effective as someone who is part of the community. It is, rather, the resistance of eventual record buyers to the image of corporate America doing the promotion. In addition, some of the things street teams are asked to do are illegal, but the underage kinds who are paid a few dollars to snipe the city are not as likely to be arrested. And these kids are the ones who congregate in the areas where the promotions will be most useful. Many artists in this area of music have established their popularity and credibility via street-team marketing: Lil' Kim, Undeas, and Junior M.A.F.I.A. for example. Their production companies are celebrated for their guerilla marketing achievements.

The Rap

If anything distinguishes hip-hop, it is the rap, the sometimes mesmerizing poetic, lyrical monologue we have all heard. There are many varieties of rap. For example, in freestyle rap, the artist raps spontaneously, without prepared lyrics. Freestyle rap, which is common on the streets, is also an exciting characteristic of the MC battles between and among rappers. People always want to know if a rapper can freestyle. Not all rappers can. Freestyle lyrics are not listened to and absorbed in the same way that the traditional hip-hop lyric is. The message of the traditional hip-hop lyric is more important than the beat, and the rapper that communicates best is the rapper that will succeed in the commercial world.

In all hip-hop, the power of artist's rap—the words and the rhymes—will determine whether the artist succeeds or fails. Artists in the R&B genre do not have the rap to fall back on, and their music, more than hip-hop music, tends to achieve immediacy and relevance via image and style. Of course, looks and style are an essential element of hip-hop as well, but the power of the rap can transcend a less-than-powerful image.

Ironically, the more successful the rapper, the more likely he or she is to slip into the mainstream—the artist's "issues" shift from concerns arising within the ghetto to issues of money and success. Such a shift in focus, no less than overexposure, can hurt a rapper more than a pop artist. Rappers who become celebrities risk being branded as sellouts. Obviously there are exceptions: currently Jay Z, for example.

Production Costs

One of the major practical differences between hip-hop music and other forms is the cost of recording. Budgets for one hip-hop track can exceed $100,000; the cost of an album-length CD can run over $1 million. Included among these costs are the costs associated with sampling. In fact, sampling costs are where recording budgets often go off the track. It is difficult to estimate what those costs will ultimately turn out to be, and the contract is usually signed after the samples are already in place, when it is too late to make a change in the track. Since the records are producer-driven, the producers/production companies can retain as much as one-half of the gross royalties paid by the record company plus a flat fee per track of as much as $100,000.

Royalty Points

Royalty points in hip-hop contracts are also higher than those in hard-fought, highly publicized rock and roll deals. Further, the control over the points and the artist is often in the hands of the producer. The record company neither speaks the language of the artist, nor is it particularly trusted by the artist. Indeed, the artist often does not even meet record company personnel: the producer or manager or independent label assumes total negotiating responsibility and forms the only connection between the hip-hop artist or group and the record company. This one-step-removed line of communication, in which the artist or group is not a part, makes the connection between the artist and the record company, already tenuous at best in the pop field, even further detached. It completes the alienation that naturally results when people do not physically relate to one other. Ironically, this alienation parallels the detachment that motivated the artist in the first place to express him- or herself through the hip-hop genre.

Sound and Lyrics

Hip-hop producers, like rock producers, often establish a distinctive "sound." Since the beginning of rock and roll (or at least since Phil Spector and his "wall of sound"), producers have had their own sound. To capture and to replicate this is the key to continuity and continued success. If Jermaine Dupri's sound guarantees sales and attention, why not stay with it?

Much of the hip-hop lyrical focus is shocking. Many who hear hip-hop lyrics for the first time (e.g., Tipper Gore) feel that the *only* purpose of the words is to shock, and that therefore they are not art. For those who think that a work that shocks is not art, I submit a story about Igor Stravinsky (1881–1971). Stravinsky, an innovative Russian/international composer, was asked what he thought of a work by the American composer John Cage (1912–1992), which contained six minutes of silence. (Cage's work was at the time considered avant-garde). Stravinsky said that he looked forward to Cage's next work, which he hoped would be even longer!

Rap as Protest

Rap as protest—protest against violence, unemployment, lack of opportunity—is alive and well even as it blends into other styles featuring more melodic lines, etc. (e.g., Nelly and his sing-songy tunes). It is also often "anti-"—antiwoman, antiestablishment, antitradition, and sometimes anti-Semitic. The advocacy represented by the rapper's points of view is repeated over and over again in different ways and finds an ear not only in the black population, but in the white, suburban, well-to-do population as well. The ultimate consequences of this commingling of cultures cannot be all that bad. The protesters of the '60s, while never fully realizing their dreams, made their point and the consciousness of our entire society has changed as a result. What societal changes are in store for us in view of the protests of the new century are obviously speculative, but changes there will be, and some of them will certainly be the result of the consciousness-raising effected by the widespread communication of the hip-hop generation's messages to the world at large. One rapper, when asked why there was so much violence at hip-hop shows, referred to the fact that the things that make the youths in the audience angry at their situation in society are the very things that are pounded at them by the rappers. Since hip-hop constitutes an expression of what the audience itself is living, and since the subject matter is not saccharine material like that of the pop (read: bubble-gum) world, the audience is naturally engaged and, sometimes, aroused to the point at which violence regrettably can and often does erupt.

Bootlegs

Bootlegs. The anathema of the music (and film) business. But wait. Can bootlegs help build a artist's career (and the attendant profits of the artist's record company)? Sure. Some record-keepers note that hip-hop sales are higher in white America than in black America. But what they fail to note is the fact that in black America—particularly in the communities of New York, Los Angeles, and Florida—there is a preponderance of bootlegs over ordinary commercial copies of records. The Midwest has no bootlegs, so the only way to acquire this music is to buy it. So the Soundscan numbers that show that the majority of buyers of rap music in Wisconsin are white are misleading. The truth is that blacks in Wisconsin are as, or more, likely to possess hip-hop records than the white population. They just acquire them differently. Rapper "Cheech" reports: "They say White America is picking up our rap? It's not true. *Everyone's* picking up our rap."

White Label

What is a "white label" recording? Just another means of promotion. Preferably, the recording is a lousy copy, with no artwork; but it's fresh, and it's hot! A producer of white label recordings is happy to sell a few hundred copies and go home. Maybe he'll give them to the club or radio DJs, who then bootleg them if they're half good. White label recordings contain more than one track. They are akin to compilation records, but the songs tend to blend into each other. Something new is actually being created and dupli-cated in a wholesale way without anyone's authority or any documentation establishing ownership. Illegal? Sure. But so what.

The Importance of the Mix

The mix can make a huge difference in hip-hop. Mixers do not get paid royalties always, but a simple remix of a commercial release, for radio purposes only, can make such a difference that enormous amounts of money are at stake here. Do you like a particular pop song? Change one chord and you have a hip-hop song and a killing. The music "bed" is different. Then a rapper "raps" on it, thereby transforming it into a cutting-edge track. With the addition of some musical elements, such as strings, you have hip-hop. (Sometimes I think of the joke about ravioli as a metaphor for hip-hop. Two square noo-dles and a piece of cheese constitute no more than just that; twist three corners and you have two square noodles and a piece of cheese with three ends twisted. But twist the fourth corner, and voilà! Ravioli!)

Career Ceilings

With a few notable exceptions, career development hardly exists in the hip-hop world. The audience is very fickle. Its fondness for a particular artist or "look" or "sound" can dissolve as fast as it starts. Similarly, as noted above, tour success has in the past elud-ed most rap/hip-hop artists. Again, there are exceptions, and the phenomenal touring success of hip-hoppers starting with 1999's Hard Knock Life Tour and the Up in Smoke Tour of 2000 promises venues and outlets not only for known acts, but for up-and-com-ers as well. It is, after all, show business, and the more that the proponents of the genre get the chance to communicate their art to others, the more it will be fine-tuned to fit the needs of the population and the more it will reflect the population's own needs, wishes, desires, and fears—a nice return to the point in the circle from which it began.

HIP-HOP AND POP CULTURE

Hip-hop musicians are idols and role models not just to black kids, but to white suburban rich kids as well. Identifying with hip-hop raps is the ultimate rebellion for white kids.

Hip-hop romanticizes killing, drugs, misogyny, and bravado, in many cases using language of jarring crudeness. Yet hip-hop, as an expression of rebellion and the conflict between generations, is no different from a lot of popular music from the 1950s or 1960s or just about any other decade before or since. The manner of expression has changed, and the force from which the expression gains its energy certainly has different origins, but the melding of music, yearning, anger, and politics reflecting cultures, trends, and styles spins a common web. Certainly the birthplace of hip-hop and rap was the ghettos and projects of urban centers in America. But the characteristic rawness of this genre is not unique to the inner cities.

Almost 20 years ago, the (white) country singer David Allan Coe recorded two underground albums of songs that are considered to be among the most racist, misogynist, homophobic, and obscene songs ever recorded. Ironically, at the beginning of the new century, the white rapper, Kid Rock, has invited Coe to open his acts for him. Coe's music has taken on a new life through the Internet and through the welcome that the new "interpreters of the culture" have given it.

Currently, in the truest tradition of the music business, hip-hop artists *and* their audiences are embracing all sexes and all cultures. Women artists, for example, are fomenting a rebellion against the misogynist elements of hip-hop. It is no coincidence that Destiny's Child, a female group, was *VIBE*'s Artist of the Year in 2000 or that Beverly D'Angelo has risen in profile to present the women's response to the "booty shaking" that is rampant in male hip-hop.

A Word from the Mainstream

A statement made by Michael Green, president of the National Academy of Recording Arts and Sciences (NARAS), during the 43rd airing of the Grammy awards, directly addressed public concerns about this provocative and controversial form of music:

> *This has certainly been a dynamic year for music—all you have to do is look at the diversity represented on this stage tonight to witness the walls of division crumble under the weight of a connected world. Of late, the controversy over extreme lyrics has been a heat-seeking missile and it is important to remember that the Academy is not here to defend or vilify, commercialize or censor, art. We are here to recognize those recordings that are notable, noticeable, and oft time, controversial.*
>
> *People are mad, and people are talking. And that is a good thing because it is through dialogue and debate that social discovery can occur.*

Listen, music has always been the voice of rebellion—it is a mirror of our culture, sometimes reflecting a dark and disturbing underbelly obscured from the view of most people of privilege, a militarized zone which is chronicled by the CNN of the inner city—rap and hip-hop music. We cannot edit out the art that makes us uncomfortable. Remember, that is what our parents tried to do to Elvis, the Stones, and the Beatles.

The white teenagers from the suburbs buy a majority of the music in question. They live out their rebellion and delineate their rite of passage vicariously through this music, and most of the adults who pass judgment have never listened to—or more to the point, have never even engaged their kids about—the object of the contempt. This is not to say that there is not much to fear in this violence-drenched society of ours; we should genuinely be concerned about the younger kids, the latch-key kids who are not experienced and don't have a relevant parental connection to help them understand what's real and what's shock theater. Accept the fact that musicians, movie stars, and athletes are not perfect, they make mistakes and can't always be counted on to be role models. Art incites, it entices, it awes, and it angers; it takes all of its various incarnations to maintain the balance, vitality and authenticity of the artistic process. Let us not forget that sometimes it takes tolerance to teach tolerance.

BUSINESS MANAGEMENT AND THE MANAGEMENT OF BUSINESS

Lawyers who specialize in this world tell me that rappers and hip-hop artists in general hardly ever listen to their business managers. This creates an environment where it is simply a matter of time before taxes and debts will overwhelm the artist. There is little that a business manager can do to help the artist avoid judgment day; the bankruptcy laws are around, but maybe not for long with present protections. Further, there are consequences to bankruptcy. If an artist can convince the bankruptcy court to allow him or her to walk away from all debts (except back taxes), the consequences will last for many years to come—certainly for the remainder of the artist's "youth." And hip-hop artists who play in the financial world must wake up to the fact that the game has rules and it is a tragedy when they do not take steps to protect their earnings from the day when those earnings, just like the earnings of almost all other creative people in the music world, dry up.

One money-earning solution for many rappers, MCs, and hip-hop artists who have signed exclusive agreements to provide services either to a record company or to a particular project is to do side projects without the knowledge of their record company (or the business manager or the lawyer for that matter). The financial equivalent of sneaking a smoke or hiding from Mom may or may not catch up with them; but there are a lot of more traditional, and safer, ways to accumulate capital and maximize earnings.

Whether you are a Wall Street wunderkind, a young classical pianist, or a band of underage rockers—or rappers—-you need advice from trustworthy representatives—lawyer, business manager, personal manager, whoever. It is these (mostly state-licensed) professionals who are qualified to provide guidance and to protect you from grasping fans, producers, record companies, and, yes, even family members. Hip-hop artists and rappers are no different, yet it takes a special professional to understand these young people and care about what they have to say. Fortunately, there are a growing number of lawyers and business managers who practice in this field and who believe that to represent hip-hop artists is no less a privilege than to represent any young creative person.

THE CHANGING IMAGE
Across the spectrum of hip-hop artists, managers, and producers a number of individuals have achieved considerable financial success, an ascendancy which automatically makes them once removed from the world of the streets. Others have deliberately turned away from the violent, antisocial, "thug" image cultivated by some of the genre's most visible icons. Destiny's Child is actively involved in raising awareness and funds for the National Alliance of Breast Cancer Organizations and the National Breast Cancer Coalition. Common, a Chicago-based hip-hop musician, has set up a foundation, the Common Ground Foundation, which raises money to be spent on such things as instruments, travel, computers, and post-high school tuition for low-income youths. Talib Kweli rejects the hustler/thug image out of hand. He uses the medium—which he calls "alternative music"—to entertain, yes, but he also uses it to "bring information and to promote literacy and multicultural education in Brooklyn."

CONTRACTUAL ISSUES FROM THE HIP-HOP WORLD
Hip-hop artists, and their representatives, must be cognizant of specific contract issues that exist only in the hip-hop field. For example, while most rock groups are self-contained and are largely, if not totally, responsible for writing the songs they perform and record, in the hip-hop world, it is equally customary for most, if not all, of the songs to be written and controlled by others, in whole or in part. In the urban world, therefore, one needs what is known as "outside protection"—that is, protection from the contributors of the songs so that they will (1) license the first use of the songs in the first place; and (2) license them at a rate and according to the provisions of the artist's controlled compositions clause in the artist's agreement with his or her production company or record company.

Interludes and Controlled Compositions Clauses
Most hip-hop albums are full of what are known as *interludes* (usually described as musical elements 1 1/2 minutes in length or less), and record companies simply will not pay for them. If a record contains 5 or 10 of these brief moments of music, the costs of obtaining the rights from third parties will play havoc with the artist's royalties and could even absorb all or a major part of them. Even if it is the producer and not the artist who is responsible for these kinds of additions, however excellent the artist feels the choices may be, the artist will ultimately pay for them. If the contract with the distributing record company *is* the production company, of course, the producer and the producer's company will also be ham-

strung by the costs that will be charged against royalties. The only two ways to protect against this debacle is to either raise the mechanical cap or limit the interludes. As noted in Chapter 4, it is not only mechanical royalties due with respect to the manufacture and sale of records that are affected by the controlled compositions paragraph. This contractual area is chock full of danger and must be given special attention.

THE RAP COALITION: SELF-HELP EXEMPLIFIED

Go to the website www.rapcoalition.org. Finally someone (in this case Wendy Day and her associates) is providing something that rockers and blues artists of the past were never offered: the information necessary to control their own fate! This not-for-profit organization provides help to fledgling artists (and those not-so-fledgling artists who did not do it right the first time) in the form of management guidance and legal services. Here is an extraordinary example of how the Internet is helping not only to disseminate useful information, but also to break the walls of secrecy that have for so long and so effectively kept doors from opening for young artists. And, although Dr. Dre and Eminem have publicly questioned the value and impact of the Internet, they too are benefiting from Internet exposure.

It should be noted that rapcoalition.org, as well as others that exist to help artists maximize their chances of success, have a bit of a bias against record companies. However, as I have pointed out more than once, record companies serve a genuine and often underappreciated purpose in developing the careers and selling the records of artists and so, as with any resource, one must weigh the information carefully in order to make an informed decision.

For example, one of the sites, which does some calculations on the bottom-line "mathematics" of the record business, concludes that even an artist whose records may have sold hundreds of thousands of copies is working for about $12 per hour. Even if this is not an accurate figure, it is undeniable that, given the long hours performing musicians put in, the average per-hour return is quite low. However, it is my hope that artists and their managers and other representatives will be able to use this information to enhance their negotiating capabilities rather than to give up entirely on an industry that, like it or not, has enormous global strengths and value.

In any event, owning one's own record company or Internet distribution service is not going to be everyone's cup of tea. The wheel has been invented before, and probably better than most of us can reinvent it today. Each artist is different, and each artist has a distinct milieu and environment, so no one formula for whether to leave the traditional system or embrace it will work for everyone. Nevertheless, the information and advice provided by The Rap Coalition is well worth considering. This organization has established a division—Visionary Management—whose sole purpose is to act as a school for managers. In Chapter 5, on management, I noted that managers, unlike other professionals such as accountants and lawyers, are not trained by means of any consistent, approved, and universally respected school or method. The Rap Coalition may prove to be an exception. Let's hope so. As they say on their website: "Let us take care of the we, and the art will take care of itself." This is a truly out-of-the-ordinary organization whose sole purpose is to help hip-hop artists to control their own fate.

HIP-HOP RULES

Never, at least since Ira Gershwin, have words in song meant so much. Rap, after all, is talk. Ja Rule, a well-known rapper, says, "What else can you rap about [than] sex, violence and materialism." Lyrics have taken on a much more vital level of meaning. Ira would be envious.

But hip-hop is not really the sea change from rock and roll that it appears at first glance. Rebellion, Women, the Good Life, the Hard Knock Life—these are still the staples of the music. Only the environment is new.

Given all of the Congressional criticism of hip-hop, and the willingness of the major record companies to kowtow to this criticism, it is actually quite remarkable that so much of what is expressed actually gets disseminated—whether through broadcast, through traditional record sales, or through downloads, which remain largely unlicensed and uncontrolled. While there remains a tendency for the majors to go with the sure thing, change is possible and indeed change occurs on a continuum that would perhaps shock our founding fathers. Mos Def, commenting on the corporate music industry's practice of promoting the same overexposed, clichéd product, said: "If all you make available is acorns, people will eat the f****n' acorns." Yet whenever the art of hip-hop—which after all is a reflection of our culture—is able to offer alternatives to the corporate-sponsored musical pabulum that dominates the charts, everyone wins.

20 CLASSICAL MUSIC

Classical music is the kind we keep thinking will turn into a tune.
—Kim Hubbard

The difference between a violin and a viola is that a viola burns longer.
—Victor Borge

What is classical music? Of course music composed during the so-called classical period, from the mid-seventeenth to the early eighteenth century, especially the classical symphony and concerto, qualifies. But are there any characteristics that apply only to classical music—*all* of it—and not to the so-called "popular" genres, including pop, rock, and rap? One possibility is structure—formal structure that goes beyond melody and beat, incorporating complex orchestration, exposition of theme, development, and recapitulation. Perhaps the best way to define it is explain what it is not. It is not mainstream; it is not something that spontaneously touches a large percentage of all listening populations. It is for specialty, though eminently varied, tastes; it appeals to knowledgeable buyers and listeners who want to have a profound experience of the kind that they do not find in what we call popular music; it is remarkably resilient and takes on different meaning in the hands of different interpreters (which of course also fits jazz; so be it).

Whatever it is—and I submit that we know it when we hear it—it is in trouble.

A LITTLE HISTORY

The classical record business was wildly profitable from 1980 onward for many years. Profitability on sales pushed the 30 percent level. On $100 million in sales at one company, the pretax profit was $27 million. Yet by the 1990s, under management that chose to apply popular music standards to classical music divisions, things went south fast. The few record companies that continued to invest in new classical artists and young composers had precious few outlets to bring these artists and composers' works to the attention of potential record buyers. *The Ed Sullivan Show,* which made household names of Renata Tebaldi, Robert Merrill, Itzhak Perlman, Anna Moffo, and Mario Lanza during the fifties and sixties, was long gone, and nothing had replaced it.

Senior executives who knew nothing about classical music, its heritage, or its extraordinary worldwide market potential decided that this genre could not possibly earn enough by way of sales to recoup their companies' investment. The numbers crunchers put a stop to what they perceived to be the excesses of prior generations, and the major labels made a fundamental decision to look at themselves not as libraries (catalogues) or nurturers of great artists, but as large-scale bookstores. Once they began to demand that Beethoven sell the way James Patterson or *Tuesdays with Morrie* sell, and that their recordings be judged on a finite number of sales units, they found that they could never meet their goals. So the companies gave up. BMG Classics, successor to RCA Red Seal, one of the diamonds of the lot, had essentially dismantled itself by the late nineties.

DEMISE OR REJUVENATION?

Much has been written about the demise of the classical music industry. Companies are shutting down; artists are being dropped in huge numbers from every classical record label, and sales that were so promising upon the introduction of the CD have plummeted. Even though the proposed AOL/Time-Warner/EMI and BMG/EMI mergers never took place, the fears of the classical music community were nevertheless realized in 2001 when Warner closed down two of its three classical record labels, Erato and Teldec, and EMI essentially shut down its U.S. classical division, Angel Records. While some new labels which record and release classical records have appeared in recent years, these records are not offered to the public in significant quantities. A recent analysis of one particular label's sales history on Soundscan disclosed that 13 copies out of their entire label's 25 or so releases were sold in the U.S. in the first 7 months of 2000. (They shipped 400 worldwide just to fill the distribution pipeline, but no one was buying. No one.)

We have seen the end of the exclusive recording agreements for each and every one of the world's greatest orchestras, including one of the last holdouts, the renowned Berlin Philharmonic. Nowadays it is recording occasionally for EMI! So it goes.

Music ensembles (from trios to quartets, quintets, and chamber and symphony orchestras) are going to have to make their own recordings if they want to preserve their legacies and enjoy the recorded fruits of their labors. They can no longer rely on the record companies to provide these archives. Even the New York Philharmonic is selling archival records that they have long kept in the vaults (for example, the Bernstein and the Mahler collections), as are the great London orchestras. Indeed, the London Symphony Orchestra has even filled the void by initiating its own recordings—and guess what? Its first, *Les Troyens*, won several 2002 Grammy awards, including Best Classical Album and Best Opera Recording.

Artists of worldwide stature have gone begging, not just for an exclusive record company relationship—but even for a single record! Even if they or their patrons find the money to pay for the cost of the orchestra, the recording venue, the engineer, the conductor, and the producer, they still have to find a record company that has the budget to pay for the artwork and the manufacture and release of the record. In most cases, finding such a company is impossible, so they must reluctantly decline the kind offer of backing.

At the same time that the majors have all but abandoned the classical music genre as a viable commercial proposition, the number of staff members who specialized in classical music, particularly those who were the bearers of the "institutional memories," has declined drastically. Some have died; others have retired, not to be replaced; still others have been laid off. What this does to a record company's intangible assets is incalculable. The abandonment of classical music programs by the major record labels comes, ironically, at a time when more creative marketing—via reissues or compilations and use of the Internet—can generate substantial income while at the same time incurring no additional production expenses and resulting in records bearing minuscule royalty obligations, compared to the standards of today. Yet those who know the catalogues best have, one by one, left the companies whose legacies they are best able to exploit.

Currently, the major retail outlets, such as Tower Records' Lincoln Center store in

New York City, are putting additional nails in the classical music coffin. Instead of paying for shipments of records on a customary 30- to 60-day basis, they tried, in 2002, to require record companies to give them 360 days before they have to either pay or return the records for credit. Small record companies and their distributors cannot possibly survive these credit terms, and according to one report, Tower Records has notified its buyers not to purchase any more records from three companies which together are responsible for distributing as many as 55 separate labels, including the renowned Dorian, Nimbus, Harmonia Mundi, Bis, Hungaroton, and Supraphon labels. In 2001 *Musical America,* the "bible" of the classical music business, said that Tower's actions were having a "chilling" effect on the "rugged pioneers in a field that so desperately needs rugged pioneers." And we're not just talking about Tower's Lincoln Center store, its classical flagship, but all 113 of its U.S. stores (it has 183 worldwide). Of course, the majors (Universal, Sony, EMI, and BMG, but not Warner/Elektra/Asylum) were happy to agree to the 360-day terms because it meant that Tower would buy more product from them. And now Best Buy, which stocks 35,000 (mostly popular) titles, has decided to do the same.

Yet, there are exceptions. We have record labels such as Sony Classical whose menu is substantially fueled by soundtrack recordings such as *Titanic* and *Star Wars,* the phenomenal success of which so enriched the label's budget that it could invest in the development of a Tan Dun (who, in addition to his impressive symphonic and choral works, made a mark in *his* soundtrack for the film *Crouching Tiger, Hidden Dragon)* and the extremely successful Daniel Bell's *West Side Story*—with a home video, no less. And Peter Gelb, the head of Sony Classical, has invested a considerable amount in commissioning new works by composers such as Tan Dun and John Corigliano.

The Star Factor

Another reason why classical record sales have plummeted in recent years may be that there are so few overpowering musical personalities such as Vladimir Horowitz, Leonard Bernstein, and Maria Callas. There are very few classical artists whose records consumers "must have." Yet there *is* an audience out there. Look what happened with the Three Tenors' records. Pavoratti, Domingo, Yo-Yo Ma, now the violinist Mark O'Connor, maybe Reneé Fleming—there is still a great deal of big-time talent out there. But try to name a couple of instrumentalists today who have a similar hold on the public's imagination—or a conductor who is making magic with his orchestra. Maybe violinists Joshua Bell or Sarah Chang, pianist Eugeny Kissin, or Simon Rattle, new conductor of the pre-eminent Berlin Philharmonic. But names of "stars" do not come easily to mind these days.

The Relevancy Factor

One often-asked question is why there is a need for any of the world's great (let alone near-great or mediocre) artists to record one more time the world's classics, all of which have been recorded *ad nauseum.* Who would want to pay today's $15.99 price (which inevitably must be charged) for an unknown pianist interpreting Chopin's *Nocturnes* when you can get Artur Rubinstein's renowned recordings for far less. (As we shall see, some unknown pianists' recordings—of almost the entire classical repertoire—are now widely available on budget labels for $6.99.)

Why bother, then, to examine the secrets of an industry that has become all but irrelevant? Simple. It *needn't be* irrelevant. Consider the following:

- In 2001, about 4000 newly recorded (not reissued) classical CDs were released. (This number will decline fast if the Tower Records policy noted above is enforced and replicated by other retail outlets that have up to now dedicated a fair amount of shelf space to classical recordings). Many of these are retailing at $9.98.
- Millions of classical music enthusiasts from all over the world visit the shrines of music annually to pay homage to its interpreters: from Carnegie Hall to Lincoln Center; from Tanglewood and Chicago's Ravinia Festival to concerts in Central Park; from Summermusic, in Waterford, Connecticut, to Wolftrap, in Virginia. I have seen statistics that indicate that more people attend opera in New York City each year than baseball games.
- Bon Jovi's keyboard player is actually conservatory-trained, at Julliard. Believe it or not, this is not unusual. Two of The Cars (Greg Hawkes and Elliot Easton) attended Boston's Berklee School of Music, which, while primarily a jazz and pop conservatory, has respected programs in the classical field as well.
- It is not unusual to step into a hotel elevator in Los Angeles that is playing Mozart on its sound system.
- A surprisingly large percentage of digital print distribution (some estimates are as high as 50 percent) consists of classical music.
- More than 40 million Americans study a classical instrument each year. There are 3,500,000 keyboards sold each year in the United States.
- The American Symphony Orchestra League (ASOL) has announced that its subscription audiences for classical music are getting younger—and larger.
- In 2000, public attendance in the United States for orchestra concerts was over 31 million, up 30 percent from 1990.

Go figure!

Is someone missing something? Should your kids keep practicing Mozart minuets? Are there reasons why "classical" music has remained classic? How can young artists and their managers build on the lessons learned?

AN ESSENTIAL FOR SUCCESS: SPIRITUALITY

There is a long-perceived need in human beings for a connection to things spiritual. In most societies, this connection is achieved, in part, through music. We are in an age in which spirituality and an effort to come to grips with the nonmaterial aspects of our civilization are important aspects of our daily life, and entire populations are searching for ways to manifest this vision and to experience this way of looking at the world. They are finding it in literature, religion, film, the outdoors, and of course in music. However, for some reason (and this time I cannot easily tell you "what they'll never tell you"), the "nourishment" people are searching for, at least in the world of music, is not so easily found. Whether they do not know where to look for it, or do not find it in records or live performances, or simply do not have the ability to decompress from the pressures of twenty-first century society is not clear.

This failure is not the fault of Brahms.

In the concert area, most live performances are merely a reiteration of what has been done previously. The creative spark that recasts a work for a new generation is too often missing. You often come out of a concert wondering why you have gone.

When the hundred and fifty or so leaders of the members of the United Nations gathered in New York for the U.N.'s 50th Anniversary a few years ago, the New York Philharmonic "entertained" them with Beethoven's *Ninth (Choral) Symphony*. It was a concert remembered only for Mayor Guiliani's asking Yassir Arafat to leave the concert because of his aggressive past history in the Middle East. Everyone was checking their watches; the concert was not televised. Happily, it ended and everyone forgot it. Why? Because it had no meaning other than one more iteration of a familiar work.

Sponsoring a big deal event? Dig out the Ninth!

It doesn't have to be that way. Rarely was this great symphony's resplendent spirituality ever evinced more effectively than when Leonard Bernstein conducted it at the recently dismantled wall in Berlin in 1989. Televised, newsworthy, an absolutely memorable event—not just for the million or so Germans who were there, but also for those additional millions around the world who did and will for all time experience it on video and on CD.

We do not have to go back to the nineteenth century to find music that in its ineffable way can touch the soul. Nonesuch Records' mid-1990s release of Henryk Gürecki's 1963 *Symphony No. 3* (in its third recording—not even its premier release) sold more than a million copies. This is a Polish symphony about a very sad and troubling subject—World War II—with a soprano performance in the Polish language and a symphony orchestra and conductor not among the most famous or sought-after in the marketplace. Yet it had an extraordinary appeal. A memorable performance by the great soprano Dawn Upshaw didn't hurt. Was it a fluke? Certainly records do not sell themselves. In the Gürecki case, the hook was the use of a portion of the score in the famous crash scene from the motion picture *Fearless*. Word of mouth boosted U.S. sales; once people were connected to this symphony's wordless message, sales took off worldwide.

The first Three Tenors' album—recorded at the Baths of Caracalla in Italy on the occasion of the World Cup Soccer finals—sold 3 million units in the United States. And let's not forget Andrea Bocelli, who, after a 1997 PBS Special, grabbed the imagination of U.S. consumers just as he had won over the hearts and souls of Europeans over the prior two years. Let's also not forget that companies fought each other in almost embarrassing ways to grab the follow-up records of the Three Tenors, but the second didn't do as well as the first, nor did the third do as well as the second. There is also the lesson of *Chant,* the bizarre recording of Spanish monks which sold several million copies, beginning in Europe in the early 1990s and spreading to the United States. The lucky record company (EMI—again) began spending its windfall profits on other artists and other projects, as though the success which was experienced with the *Chant* recording was going to replicate itself over and over again. This "brilliant" reasoning almost bankrupted EMI's

U.S. classical division, Angel Records.

A fluke is only a fish. No way is it a harbinger of the future. Fortunately, the nonfluke examples of classical recordings that have made it big—almost always helped along by artists like the Three Tenors, the Irish Tenors, and Kiri Te Kanawa who have found ways to distinguish themselves from the ordinary—are numerous. No, the classical music industry has not drowned. It is still swimming, if in fairly deep water.

NEW LIFE FOR AN OLD GENRE

It is important for anyone reading this chapter to understand that much of what has been written before in this book about royalties, music publishing, audits, management, investments, etc., is applicable to classical music, and classical musicians and composers, as well. Indeed, a clear understanding of those issues previously discussed may be essential to the survival of the classical music industry. All of the elements of the classical music industry—from the artists to the record companies, from the lawyers and the managers to the agents—must find a way to comprehend how the successful and financially sound portion of the popular music business works so that they can find a way to apply this knowledge to their own world.

Here is a telling example from my experience. I represented a classical music ensemble that performed mostly public domain material—you know, Bach, Telemann, Vivaldi. Yet all of their arrangements of public domain works were copyrightable. This particular group understood this on some level and registered their arrangements in the Copyright Office and with their performing rights society. But what they did not know (until I told them) is that the performance of their recordings outside of the United States and Canada generated significant performing rights income (collected automatically by the performing rights societies around the world) for which publishing companies would be willing to pay substantial advances, while at the same time administering their copyrights around the world and making sure that they were properly registered with foreign performing rights societies. As discussed in Chapter 13, proper registration of a work is absolutely essential in order to collect both performance and mechanical income. In this case, the music publisher administrator also insured that the mechanical royalties generated by the sale of this particular group's recordings overseas were properly credited, paid, and collected. Not only was the money accurately collected, but it was collected years earlier and at considerably less cost than it could have been had the group tried to take on this collection and administration function itself.

Arrangements like this are made every day in the popular music business; but those in the classical world have either no idea or very little understanding of the cash-generating options staring them in the face. A lot of money is involved. Maybe that is what scares them, since money is something that classical musicians and their representatives rarely expect to see from the exploitation of their careers outside of live performing. I have never encountered so many low self-images in any group of like-minded people in my life. Maybe it is because the piano teacher's ruler was wielded too often; maybe it is because, like all artists, they are dreamers, not strategizers; maybe it is because there are so many of them competing for the same work that the circumstances of their lives reduce their confidence and keep their spirits low. Whatever the reason, it is time to get over this resistance and to start using the tools and resources available to them.

The CD Arrives, But the Bad Days Follow

In the early 1980s, classical record companies finally got what they wanted and needed: a new technology. Not only did CD recordings sound fabulous; they were virtually inde-structible as well, at least compared with the LP. The companies were able to mine their catalogues, reconfigure all of the recordings they had long ago forgotten they owned, and resell them all over again. How incredibly lucky they were!

But as with many good things, this one came with a curse.

Once the (perceived as) limited classical music market absorbed all of these new releases, the consumers stopped buying! They had been given everything they could ever want. And they did not want anything else.

The Rise of the Budget Label

The budget labels have done fantastic things for a slew of new artists—most of whom are quite accomplished musicians. The revolution in the pricing and structures of classi-cal recordings in recent years has had a tremendous impact on the availability and the reach of new recordings.

In order to induce sales, record companies have always priced long-released recordings or "lesser" artists' recordings lower than so-called "top line" recordings, but they considered those records "low end" products. Then a brilliant German entrepreneur, Klaus Heymann, decided to glamorize so-called "budget records" by offering recording opportunities to heretofore unknown artists—from violinists to pianists, flutists to singers. His record company, NAXOS, is based in Hong Kong, and Mr. Heymann's extraordinary sensibility toward classical music and the effect it traditionally has on populations all over the world has combined with a sound sense of marketing and distribution in a way that changed the classical music business forever.

NAXOS, whose CDs retail for about $7, does not customarily pay royalties to the artists, but the artists get to record what they want, their records fill the record store bins with all the new recordings the stores could possibly desire, and everyone wins. It is A&R without the A—almost totally repertoire-based. The choice of music is a more salient marketing point than the name of the artist. If, at the same time, the artist can build on the record catalogue to enhance his or her celebrity, performing career, and finances, all the more power to the artist. (NAXOS, notoriously, neither signs major artists nor does a great deal to promote the artists it does sign.)

But, like the CD phenomenon, the budget juggernaut came with a curse. As it turns out, the budget-record scenario has also lowered the perceived value of classical records and has inadvertently damaged, perhaps forever, the willingness of consumers to pay a sufficiently high price to allow record companies and artists to produce truly memorable, even legendary, recordings. A standard cost for an orchestral recording of a world-class orchestra, such as the Philadelphia Orchestra or the Chicago Symphony, ranges from $150,000 to close to a quarter of a million dollars. Sad to say, symphonies of this caliber rarely record anything anymore.

This consequence of setting prices so low that the public perceives that the records are not worth very much may turn out to be the ultimate legacy of the budget label. In the popular music field, try to buy a Rolling Stones or a Pink Floyd record for less than full retail. Sure, there are sales, but the going price for these records, some of which are over 30 years old, at the Lincoln Center Tower Records store is $18.98—three times *more* than they cost when they were originally released! But select a Eugene Ormandy, Philadelphia Orchestra recording, and you'll pay between $7.98 and $12.98.

THE INTERNET: IS IT THE ANSWER?
Supply and Demand

It did not help record companies (or artists) when a late 1990s change in the tax law made it impossible to deduct the cost of retaining huge inventory stocks. The record companies can no longer keep the large back orders of inventory they used to maintain, and accordingly, they do not. The customer who wants to back-order a work heard on the radio can forget about receiving it any time soon. But, as with so many clouds, there is a silver lining to this one as well.

There are fewer applications of the Internet more important than the ability to make available huge choices of music 24/7. The technology needed to provide for real-time downloading has already been invented. Many of the new classical music artists that are utilizing the Internet are paralleling what pop artists are doing—making available their music via downloads *and* hard copy delivery. MP3 files are just as applicable to classical music as to popular music, and the energy level and innovations of the classical music Internet enthusiasts are no less sophisticated than those one can see in the popular field. Further, one of the things that makes classical music exploitation on the Internet more feasible than exploitation of popular music is that, in many instances, the music per-formed is out of copyright. The time and cost of clearing rights is totally absent, making the process a whole lot more efficient.

Once the Internet and the record industry have figured out how to work together, music sites can make available all of the world's classical music (and I mean *all*) for instant download without the necessity of maintaining expensive inventory.

However, the digital distribution of classical recordings is an area which will not set-tle down until encryption methods are unassailable. Can you imagine the entire classical repertoire being un-encrypted? Sure, there will be new interpretations to compete against old ones. But, whereas popular music has tens of thousands of new artists enter-ing the marketplace each year performing new music, it is the opposite in classical music. Whereas in popular music, it is the "new" that has the greatest appeal, in classical music it is the "old." The existing catalogues are simply invaluable, and the record com-panies will be very reticent to make them available via all of the wonderful means offered by the Internet until they can be sure their rights can be preserved.

Reaching the Surfers

Theoretically, the Internet is a place where independent artists and labels can have the same direct access to consumers as the big companies. Nevertheless, the lesser-known names all face an up-hill battle to prove their bona fides. Known trademarks are still more valuable than unknown trademarks; an authorized Van Cliburn recording of the Tchaikovsky *First Piano Concerto* will usually have more resonance than one by an unknown performer.

Classical Music Websites

The almost absurd number of competent instrumentalists and singers who play and sing classical music in the world today makes it incumbent on all of them to find new and effective ways to reach an audience. The Internet affords this opportunity for the classical artist almost more than it does for the popular artist. Why? Because there are hardly any other outlets for the classical artist. Numerous music sites have sprung up featuring young artists, and it is only a matter of time before these artists figure out how to exploit these opportunities to create a kind of branding that will begin to exploit their names and talents.

There are also a large number of classical "sheet music" sites on the Web. Downloading this music is usually accomplished via PDF files—in other words, files that are like photographs. The downloading and printing of PDF files is fairly cumbersome and time-consuming, and not at all interactive, but the music is visible and readable nevertheless. Other sites, whose main target is the popular music buyer, have far more sophisticated options and some are interactive in that they will play back via your computer's sound card all or portions of a work and will change keys, repeat measures, etc. A client of mine, Musicnotes.com, is the industry leader.

The generic sites that are currently affording classical artists visibility are mostly sites whose financial models have not done well over the years, and it would be a shame for these sites to disappear just when they have begun to become "branded" (translate: "trusted"). You know what you get and you get what you ask for. We have to cross our fingers and hope that these few compatible sites remain available to surfers.

Promotion via the Internet

One new option available to record companies in the digital world is the Internet "radio station." By utilizing radio stations to do what they have done since time immemorial, record companies can now extend their reach globally in an effort to promote artists. Coincidentally, this new opportunity can be used to introduce a broader population to new music, new artists, and new composers much more efficiently than ever before. Instant access (for a price) to these new works will make these artists and composers ever more valued in the marketplace, benefiting both the record company and the artists, who will experience an enhanced demand for their live performances. And soon, via webcasts, these live performances—which many feel present the ultimate musical experience—will be available via the Internet.

The Internet permits a multiplicity of performances on demand. It will not be long before every musical venue is wired for instant download, or streaming. There are already dozens of performances currently available on a number of websites. These are not "cooked" performances, presented through the filter of an editorial process; that's why they are called "virtual." The Vienna Philharmonic customarily presents a concert on Saturday nights; yet its concert hall can seat only 2,400 people. How wonderful if those concerts could be experienced virtually live in one's home—with video. The popular music industry has DigitalClubNetwork.com, which presents mostly unsigned bands performing live in the wide network of music clubs throughout the United States and around the world. Why not a similar approach to classical venues?

THE ROLE OF RECORD COMPANIES

Whatever one's ideas about promoting artists, it is incontrovertible that unless they are brought to the attention of eventual consumers, there is little likelihood of success. With (most) television opportunities a thing of the past, and motion picture biographies of instrumentalists and singers unlikely, the best way to do this for classical artists is through recording. Besides, even if the artist is able to generate a semblance of a live performing career without records, the impermanence of a live concert itself dictates that only through recording can these works and these new artists be made to last.

Having a record deal has another crucial function—one that is understood by classical managers. Being with a major label is simply irreplaceable as a "calling card." Classical managers will take an artist associated with a major label more seriously. Purchasers of talent will take the artist more seriously. Being signed to a major label really *can* contribute a lot to one's status and prestige and economic viability. If a major record label says "This artist is important," then he or she *is* important. It becomes a self-fulfilling prophesy.

How should classical artists entice record companies to record them?

Although there is nothing wrong with the concept, it is really not necessary to record CDs entitled *Mozart for Cats* or *Songs Your Russian Grandfather Sang While Hoeing the Steppes.* The marketplace is more flexible than that.

The disparity between the appeal of the known and the appeal of the unknown, which is endemic in all fields of entertainment, will require artists to find creative ways to generate interest in their work. The conductor Gilbert Levine, a Knight Commander of the Papal Order of St. Gregory for his work in using music to further interfaith relations (the last musician so honored was Wolfgang himself), recently presented Haydn's *Creation* with the Philharmonia Orchestra of London in several of the great cathedrals of the world, including Baltimore's Basilica and the Vatican's St. Peter's (for the eightieth birthday of Pope John Paul II). This inspired presentation of a work with a somewhat tired past gave the work a new vitality, which did not go unnoticed by the media. Many of the concerts were televised (by, among others, PBS in the United States). Again, the Internet would seem to be a perfect venue for these magnificent concerts, whether presented live or via recordings.

Suppose a pianist discovers a previously unknown work by a great composer. Or suppose a pianist identifies a work that has been underperformed because its cadenza is poorly conceived and the pianist writes a new cadenza, lifting the work to the level that it aspired to but fell just short of. Or the pianist finds works—or composers (remember Mozart's "nemesis," Salieri, in the play and film *Amadeus?)*—that have been largely forgotten or abandoned by the mainstream, but deserve to be revisited, or visited for the first time in a technological world that can do them justice.

Once a recording exists, its value is limited only by the imagination of the artist, the artist's representatives, and the artist's record company.

The High Price of Low Pricing

When retailers made the transition from the LP to the CD in the early 1980s, they were concerned with the response of customers to a new price structure. Compact discs were expensive to produce, and were not, in fact, manufactured by all of the record labels when the format was introduced because they did not have the facilities to do so. The extra cost to the retailers was considerable, and CDs were not in great supply. During the first roll-out, competition and demand were very high, so retailers decided to use the CD as a loss leader to get rid of LPs, expecting that they would eventually be able to raise prices to a more appropriate margin of profit. They have never recovered from that decision. Even when the cost of making CDs dropped considerably, the record companies *still* charged the same price to dealers and the retailers felt they could not reverse their earlier actions and raise prices, leaving them with the same small profit margin. The only way retailers could figure out how to make up the difference was by literally selling the store. As competition became fierce in the classical music industry, as the retailers had to discount even more drastically, and as budget records began to fill up space in record stores, the record stores actually began to construct a complex system of selling advertising within their stores themselves. This system is now extremely sophisticated. Every inch of a store is available for sale. Some methods are obvious, such as window dressing and listening stations; some are surprising, such as stickering headphones at listening stations and pasting advertisements on light boxes. The record company has to pay for all of this—and it will, but only if it is committed to this model of promotion.

Budget labels for classical music do not have the money to buy in-store advertising. They must rely on rock-bottom prices, made possible because their production costs are low and there are no royalties due to the artists. Just as today's kids fiddling around with MP3 files and other Internet transmissions over their computer "sound systems" seem to be satisfied with degraded sound quality, classical music buyers have shown that they are quite happy buying a Beethoven symphony performed by the Bulgarian Opera Orchestra for $4.98 rather than performed by the Berlin Philharmonic Orchestra conducted by Herbert Von Karajan for $10.98, or the latest recording by the London Symphony Orchestra conducted by Joe Blow for $17.98. One sad side effect of this practice is that the consumer, while presumably enjoying the recording, will not have had the magical opportunity to experience the ultimate greatness that made the artists, or the conductors and their orchestras, almost as legendary as the masterpieces which they recorded. Without this experience, it is not at all certain that the consumers who purchase budget priced records will ever be totally captured by the possibilities of classical music.

Promotion Methods for Classical Records

Record promotion in the classical business can be considerably more potent than in the popular music business if handled carefully. And it *must* be handled carefully, as there is so little money to spend on promotion. How much can a classical record company expend on promotion when it expects its new release to sell 10,000 units? A rule of thumb is around $3.00 a record, or, in this example, $30,000. How the allotment is spent is interesting. Artists, and their inexperienced managers, will have a million ideas about how to draw the consumer to its product: quarter-page ads in the *New York Times,* for example, radio spots, some of those highly visible "in-store" displays. But $30,000 doesn't go all that far. Only experienced artists' managers, or record company product managers, are likely to know how to get the most bang from the buck. And believe, me, they *need* that knowledge. Remember, if the records don't sell, the artist can move on to another label, try to make a go of it via Internet distribution, or make a living performing. The record company will be left to collect "returns."

While the proliferation of independent record companies in the classical field mirrors, in part, the development of independent popular record companies, the smaller labels cannot compete with the big companies. The small label, even more than the big label, must rely on savvy promotion. A small label which does not have the *Titanic* soundtrack millions to dip into may have only one shot to "break" an artist. So savvy record companies and wise managers commit their limited resources to press and publicity. You will more quickly buy a record recommended by a reviewer or a radio station than by the record company telling you why you should own it. However, if its one-shot promo campaign does not succeed, that may be the end of promotion for that particular record and perhaps also for that particular artist. A major label does not face these constraints (Some of the major classical record labels have begun to establish focus groups in order to determine whether a record has a chance of catching on. Stokowski would not be amused.)

While the promotion effort is being mounted by the record label, the distributors are simultaneously supposed to be picking up the baton and continuing the push toward the retail account. This used to be called selling. But nowadays, it is more common for the distribution companies to respond to the accounts rather than vice versa in order to sell them on a particular project. They take orders and collect money. There is no "sell"—hard or soft—in the classical record business.

No wonder the artists are depressed.

Interestingly, retailers, whose stake is in the artist's ultimate celebrity, notoriety, and record-selling prowess, have never, to my knowledge, actually made their own commitment to develop artists and careers. While this is not particularly surprising, it seems shortsighted, since promotion at the retail level would seem a perfect way to create demand for a product.

Balancing Supply, Demand, and Optimism

One thing the record company must avoid: responding too quickly to a surge in interest. As noted in an earlier chapter, records are shipped on a 100 percent return guarantee; this means that if records do not sell at retail, or if middle-level distributors (such as rack jobbers) do not receive orders from retailers to match what they have purchased from the ultraenthusiastic sales staff of the record label, those records which the rack jobbers and the retailers were unable to sell can, and will, be returned to the record label for credit. On the other hand, the record company will have only a brief window within which to respond to a surge of interest. This is a very delicate balancing act when dealing with classical records, which, on average sell 1,500 copies, but which in extraordinary circumstances can sell 1 million copies.

In a perfect world (the popular music business?) a record released in one month can have a slow build-up over many months until it is selling a few thousand copies a week, then five thousand, and so on until it begins to chart and build sales based on its radio play. Soundscan counts, the build-up due to touring—all of these things construct a steady growth of demand, and the supply of records is increased to meet it. When there is no such trend, the record companies have a problem. And trends like this are rarely observable in the classical music world. Without records in the racks, no matter what the demand, there will be no sales. How many records of a particular title are required to fill all of the slots in the distribution chain? About 60,000. (In the popular music world, this number is much larger—probably as many as 200,000.) The cost of manufacturing this much product is enormous, and I think it is evident that it is simply not feasible for a company—particularly a small company—to fill this supply line, except in very rare instances.

THE COMPOSER-ARTIST: SPECIAL CONSIDERATIONS

Unlike the situation with most popular music recording artists, those music recording artists who have a classical bent (for example, Michael Bolton and Billy Joel) and those who are more traditionally schooled in the classical arts often have aspirations to compose more extensive works than short lyric or art songs. These composer-artists often find themselves in a conflict with their record companies, which want them not only to record exclusively for them, but to record the works they write exclusively for them—preferably radio-ready-length songs.

This kind of restriction can cause quite a dilemma for the composer-artist—especially for an instrumentalist. For example, a violinist is likely to compose works for the violin. Unlike works written for the popular music audience—which are created spontaneously by the artist—classical works are often commissioned by organizations that not only seek to present the world premiere of the work that they have commissioned, but also to have the composer present the work at that event. And of course, the commissioning party may wish to record the work as part of its archive or even as a commercial recording to enhance the funding of its not-for-profit institution.

Many times these works are no more than 10 or 12 minutes in length, and yet when the commissioning institution is restricted from including the work among those in a recording of the evening's performance, the commissioning institution is harmed. Indeed, the threat of such a restriction may even keep the institution from commissioning the work in the first place. Given that the work would never have been written but for the hard-fought-for funds and artistic imagination of the creative personnel in the organization, this seems hardly equitable for the institution, the composer, or the community at large, which would presumably benefit from the availability and celebrity of the work for decades to come.

Another argument in favor of some flexibility toward this kind of composer-artist is that the work that person composes may have nothing to do with the nature of the works to be scheduled or likely to be programmed for recording by the artist for the record company. Even if the artist's record company desires to promote the artist via the nineteenth-century-repertoire format, what harm would it do the company to allow the composer-author-artist to record a twentieth-century work on an album of twentieth- and twenty-first-century material? It would seem reasonable not to impede the artist from pursuing a composing career, even if that entails allowing the artist to step out of his or her exclusivity obligations—as long as this does not unreasonably interfere with the artist's recording responsibilities to the record company.

It should also be noted that many classical composer-artists write for instruments other than their own primary instrument, for ensembles (full orchestra or chamber-size ensembles), or even for duos, trios, quartets, and quintets. Frequently these composer-artists could not perform such works even if they wanted to, yet they may be asked to appear at the premiere as a guest, or they may have a role in these works, for example, as featured instrumentalist. And they may want to participate in the recording of them—perhaps as one of several instrumentalists or even as conductor.

While just about all recording artist agreements require the exclusive services of the artist for a period of years or a number of albums, the situation described here is relevant only to classical artists. It is rarely the case that an exclusive recording artist for one label writes such a significant work that his or her services are requested, or even appropriate, for a competitive label. The only time that an exclusive artist's musical services (either as signer or instrumentalist) are typically sought by another artist's label is when the exclusive artist is requested to appear as a sideman on the other label; and the right to do so is subject to yet even more verbiage in the traditional recording artist agreement, covering such things as how the artist's name can be used on the packaging and in advertising and promotion (usually in a size and placement no different from that of other musicians appearing on the recording), whether the artist's photograph can be used (usually not), and whether the track on which the artist is appearing can be released as a single. This is not the case in the world of motion picture soundtrack composers-artists and in classical music, in general.

Whoever is responsible for negotiating the artist's recording agreement must understand the choices the artist may desire to have in his or her musical career and must seek relief from the rigid exclusivity rules customarily imposed on artists by their record companies. Many negotiators view any contract as if it were a custom-made document and are reluctant to negotiate its terms; they are paralyzed by the appearance of finality that these 50- to 100-page behemoths suggest. That is a major mistake. Most provisions in most documents are negotiable, and if the artist's representatives do not attempt to craft their artist's contracts specifically to their particular artist's needs and desires, almost certainly provisions will be included that will negatively affect the artist's career.

CLASSICAL MANAGEMENT

At one time, classical management was really mostly about booking. With the voluminous increase in talented and accomplished singers and the numerous alternatives available today to disseminate information about young artists, classical management companies today must do much more than arrange bookings. They must use public relations (worldwide), publicity (radio, TV, magazines, newspapers), records, videos, creative types of demos, and a large number of other tools—in particular the Internet—to assist an artist in building a career. They do, however, still act as booking agencies, which is why they must be licensed by their states as employment agents. (By the way, just as in the popular music business, not only are many managers who seek and obtain employment for their artists not properly licensed, but if you were to ask them if they were licensed, they would not even know what you were talking about.) For this two-pronged service, a classical manager customarily charges a 20 percent gross commission rather than the 10 percent that a traditional booking agent charges. This standard is not followed in the area of the classical music business specializing in vocalists, where multiple performances are the norm, and the gross income is naturally higher than for a single recital or performance with orchestra. In these situations, the management commission is usually 10 percent.

The Big Agencies

The world of classical management is hard to penetrate; most people do not know how, or to what extent, managers are successful—or unsuccessful for that matter. As with personal managers in the popular music field, one of the great strengths of classical managers is their relationships with the buyers of talent; but as with managers in the popular music field, this is also one of their great weaknesses. Yes, you want them to have access to the opera companies and orchestral managers as well as to the record companies. Yet you do not want to think about whose interest they may have at heart when you learn that they are spending winter and summer holidays with the very same people. You begin to wonder whether there might be a conflict of interest present here— albeit not an official, actionable one.

Classical managers represent conductors of great orchestras; presumably, then, they have unlimited access to those conductors, to whom they can offer their instrumentalists. Do they? Of course they do. Will they? Should they? You figure it out.

One of the problems that I alluded to earlier (see Chapter 5, page 55) is that often an artist does not know whether a big agency is using its clout for him or her, or for other artists. Certainly large agencies are involved in more "action" than smaller ones. They deal with more people more often because of their volume of clients and the multiple attendant deals. But there is an intriguing flip side. The large agencies are so big that some of them actually break themselves down into divisions, even within disciplines. Ostensibly, these divisions are set up to create "boutique-like" units within the larger institution, but many feel that as a matter of practicality, it does not work. In many cases, each division continues to grow until it is so large itself that any benefits that were sought are lost, if not totally forgotten. Even if the divisions remain relatively small, they rarely communicate among themselves—often distrusting one another—making it impossible to generate the very synergy that attracted the artist to the big agency in the first place. In fact, such synergy turns out to be a myth; there is no more spirit of cooperation within the agency than there is between Warner Bros Records and Warner/Chappell Music—notwithstanding their fervent claims to the contrary.

These divisions distrust each other, and, where the disciplines are different, they do not understand each other. Having no taste for embarrassing themselves by admitting their own limitations of knowledge and experience, they decide not to talk to each other. Part of this results from natural competition; part from poor management at the top. Some of it is just plain neurotic. But the consequences for the individual artist are unfortunate. The artist is unable to see how he or she fits into the agency's operations, and is unaware and uninformed as to the available opportunities—which indeed, for reasons which will never be disclosed, may never have been presented to the artist at all, but declined out of hand by the agency.

Is Smaller Better?

In the classical music world, as in the popular music world, many new small management "boutiques" have begun to spring up. In both instances, it is extremely difficult for any young artist to find a professional that will put the resources of the management office behind the artist for free. That is, if there is no income, there is no commission. Under these circumstances, a small management company, even more than a large management company—notwithstanding its ambition and the fact that its heart is in the right place—will not be able to pay its bills. But unlike the popular music business, where artists can self-book at the important start-up venues, if there is no classical manager to book dates, there will be no dates on which the artist can build a career and reputation. (This is where a recording contract can make a valuable contribution. Once a classical artist has been signed by a record company, competent management will be more open to the possibility of working with the artist. At the same time, of course, record companies know who the effective managers are and can recommend them.)

The music world has changed a great deal in the last forty years. The huge agencies are disappearing—or I should say that some of them are. The big management agencies, like any institutions that try to do too much for too many, are perceived by many as being waterlogged. Of course, they probably always have been, yet several of them are still here whereas most of the artists who complained are long gone. Still, many feel that these institutions have lost their ability to take care of the needs of artists—in particular new artists—many of whom are being drawn to small boutique agencies headed in large part by refugees from the big agencies. Smaller agencies often gain their credibility by beginning as small service agencies in the public relations/press/publicity area. They are assigned work by the larger agencies, and may eventually inherit the larger company's artists when the artists see what life might be like with someone who is paying attention. And maybe the boutique manager even loves the music the artist is creating. The large agencies, in fact, have a reputation of not even understanding the music, the heritage, the difference between good and bad, on-pitch or flat. What they do understand is power and influence, and they usually have the instincts to spot a remarkable talent in the bud.

Will the boutique agencies get too big one day? Probably. But in the meantime, there is an acknowledgment by many artists that smaller is better and it is their own talent and hard work rather than the contacts and power of their manager that will determine the success or failure of their careers.

Assessing Classical Management

At their best, classical managers, like personal managers in the pop world, open doors and facilitate and develop relationships. They create possibilities for the artist—recording, performing, etc. They take charge of the business of music, thereby allowing the artists to do what they do best. But—and I have seen this time and time again with artists from every genre of music, and classical musicians are no exception—too many artists abdicate responsibilities they should shoulder themselves. Yet classical artists, like all artists, are ultimately responsible for the decisions affecting their careers. If an artist chooses the wrong representatives, they should be replaced. An artist who does not question the advice he or she is given is responsible for any negative consequences.

The reason this is of particular relevance to the classical music business—and why I am emphasizing it here—is that the classical music industry is so small that a dent in a classical music career is communicated with the speed of light to all of the people who can harm an artist. A poor performance or a poor review gets telegraphed throughout this relatively small business, which is fraught with jealousies and envy. Generosity and sympathy for artists who have had an off day are not sentiments that one finds in the classical music industry. ("Yes, the orchestra is good, when Mr. X is not conducting." "Did you notice that she won't sing the high C in the aria at the end of Act 1 of *La Bohème?*") Performing in a poorly directed or conducted program—or even simply being miscast—can ruin a classical singer's career. The "high society" of Monday Night Opera–goers is only a cracked note away from throwing rotten tomatoes and eggs at the culprit. The same holds true for instrumentalists—some of whom do not know when to stop performing certain repertoire and do much to destroy their reputations in a fraction of the time that it took to build them. Decisions have more immediate impact than in the popular music business and alternatives are far fewer in the event an error or stupid mistake is made. No wonder classical artists tend to leave all of their decision making to the managers. They do not really want to know. If they did, however, maybe they would have fewer complaints because they would understand the lengths to which their representatives have to go to set the table for them.

So, it is not easy being a manager either.

PRESENTING THE SINGER

Many of you are familiar with the Grateful Dead and Phish, the touring acts that actually encourage(d) their fans to tape-record their performances. Well, in the classical music field, this kind of taping is so prevalent today that many concert halls around the world have simply given up and people arrive not just with hidden DAT recorders in their vests, substituting a microphone for a lapel flower, but with actual camcorders which they place on their shoulders as the concert begins and do not put down until the battery starts to beep. Some say that on any given night at the Metropolitan Opera House in New York, at least five first-class DAT tapings are going on.

Now DAT taping of concerts is against copyright law (and most likely a violation of the terms of the performer's and the ticket buyer's contract with the venue as well), but it does provide a neat answer to a pervasive problem in the classical music world. Given the large number of competent singers and instrumentalists in the world today, how does one present an artist to a record company, manager, or buyer of talent? One obvious answer is, tape the artist's recitals and concerts. Once you have a DAT tape of the artist's recital or other performance, you can then burn a CD containing a selection of these performances and off you go with a convincing package. While this action is obviously not one that an attorney can endorse, it is certainly an attractive alternative to sitting and waiting for the phone to ring.

As in the popular music business, another route would be to make a demo recording of the artist—you know, an aria with piano background or something similar. But this kind of product simply cannot compare with a DAT recording of your artist singing with the renowned Metropolitan Opera Orchestra!

There is another possibility, however, which is entirely legal: recording with a great world-class orchestra for little more than the cost of a good demo. How is this achievable? Well, given today's extraordinary technology, one can record an orchestral program without the singer. Then the tapes can be brought to a high-end sound studio, where technicians can actually reconstruct the sound texture of the original recording environment. Add the singer's voice, and voilà! A fantastic recording that would never be available to an up-and-coming artist.

Then there is Music Minus One (www.musicminusone.com), a company that sells recordings of a selection performed by orchestra, jazz group, or chamber ensemble, minus the solo part—either instrument or voice—which the user, with their permission, then adds. This alternative does not run afoul of copyright or other laws, and the background orchestral tapes can be used over and over again by more and more artists, as long as Mozart's, Verdi's, Puccini's, and Rossini's tunes have resonance. As their website announces: "Your Orchestra Awaits."

MUSIC EDUCATION

What can or should be done to "hook" today's youth on classical music? Educators will talk in terms of the educational matrix: the system. Make music part of the curriculum, they say. Others say this is not enough, that love for music is more effectively nurtured if it is introduced in a way more central to the students' "lives and feelings." Presumably, that means private instruction.

In my opinion, a three-pronged approach is best—emphasis on music in the home, private instruction, and expanded programs of music education in schools. The reality is, however, that as more and more parents defer to the schools for all kinds of learning and introduction to new things, emphasizing music in the schools is probably the most practical way to inculcate a love of music—especially classical music—in young people. But once schools accept that this is *their* obligation, we need to consider what the overall goal should be. Knowledge? Inspiration? A level of performance ability so that the child can function in an ensemble such as a high school band or orchestra? Or a dance band or trio? Or, simply, pleasure?

Whatever the goal, a preoccupation with making sure that all students have a common level of achievement in the arts is no more practical or wise than insisting that all students develop scientific skills. It is not always appropriate for all children to be strongly pointed toward one field or another. Nevertheless, it is the careful and effective introduction of the subject that is key to students' future passive *or* active appreciation of what the arts can bring to their lives.

Music education, like a pill or nourishment, must be served up on a regular basis. The best music programs begin in kindergarten and develop in an age-appropriate manner with the students being invited to experience new and broader challenges as they grow older. By fourth grade, instruments are traditionally introduced and the beginnings of dramatic/musical performances are presented. The most financially sound schools can follow this pattern to the letter; most schools cannot.

There is an assumption that well-to-do suburban and ex-urban communities offer what is not available in the inner cities. Except in very few situations, this is not true. Seldom do these school systems have the money or the trained personnel to provide the resources necessary to achieve a high level of teaching. But there are other resources.

In New York City, for example, where I live, the Department of Cultural Affairs has a program which helps schools present live performances in schools. As many adult music lovers will attest, their motivation to pursue music as a avocation or a career was first fueled by hearing a particular live musical performance—whether in school or at a concert hall or watching one of the *Live at Lincoln Center* performances on PBS.

We have heard a lot in recent years about the incredible work of faith-based institutions in lending support to local, state, and federal governmental efforts to help people in need. Among their services, in some instances, is the introduction to young people, at the grassroots level, to the richness that music can bring to their lives. As one example, in 1995 the United Jewish Appeal Federation of New York established the Music for Youth Foundation to support and advance music education programs in the New York City metropolitan area. It has since expanded, through a partnership with the National Foundation for Advancement of the Arts, and now provides annual cash scholarships and educational opportunities for young people—both individuals and groups—nationwide.

Included within the New York State Council on the Arts mission statement is the following: "The Council believes in the rights of all New Yorkers to access and experience the power of the arts and culture." Among other things, this philosophy is what drives the Council's grant-making decisions. One of their grant recipients, the New York Festival of Song, which is dedicated to the reinvention of the art song recital, has a significant educational outreach program. It is worth repeating their philosophy:

> Exposure to music as a creative endeavor is an integral part of a student's education, requiring specific thinking skills, an active imagination, a fresh look at history, and an appreciation of cultural differences. We have the greatest impact when we go beyond simple music appre-

ciation, and actively engage students in applying their new understanding to the creation of their own music and poetry.

Is there still room in our lives for classical music? My answer is a resounding "yes!"

For the same reason that Kenneth Branaugh's *Henry IV* and Ralph Fiennes' (or Mel Gibson's) *Hamlet* resonate with twenty-first century audiences, new recordings of Bach, Beethoven, and Brahms can be exciting and commercially successful. Just as we have Lawrence Olivier and John Gielgud—all the great Shakespearian actors in the last 50 to 75 years on film in one format or another—we also have multiple versions of all the classical masterpieces. Obviously, there is a perceived need to replicate these performances again and again. Why? Because each generation needs to make these masterpieces work for them.

And in a fundamental way they do. This is why they are called masterpieces.

An instrumentalist, a vocalist, or a conductor identifying him- or herself with prestigious, if obscure, music, or mounting a performance which will have publicity value (as one Hungarian pianist did by playing all of Beethoven's piano sonatas in the course of two concerts), is one way to develop a career. Some of these projects are sponsored, and some receive terrific press and publicity. The artist's reputation—and career—builds over time. Everyone in the small and insular world of classical music reads the same things—the same reviews, the same articles, the same news stories. The more they read about a particular artist, especially when the news is positive, the better the artist's chance to establish a long-lasting reputation.

Which brings me to another rationale for record companies to record classical artists regularly. I am not talking about artists whose appeal is tentative and fleeting, as is true of so many artists in the world of popular music. An artist who stays in the classical ring and is willing to pay his or her dues for 10, 12, or 15 years, and records regularly, will accumulate 15 to 20 records over that span of time. (Sarah Chang, the great violinist, started recording at the age of 9. At 20, she had already recorded two dozen CDs!)

This scenario has numerous benefits for both artist and record company. Not only will the records show the maturation of the artist during the period of recording, but they will also constitute a sort of "mini" catalogue. The record company can highlight the artist by showcasing the artist at record stores via personal appearances. And the record *company* will have innumerable options with which it can market an *artist,* and not just a *record.* For once, volume counts.